Informalization

Theory, Culture & Society

Theory, Culture & Society caters for the resurgence of interest in culture within contemporary social science and the humanities. Building on the heritage of classical social theory, the book series examines ways in which this tradition has been reshaped by a new generation of theorists. It also publishes theoretically informed analyses of everyday life, popular culture, and new intellectual movements.

EDITOR: Mike Featherstone, *Nottingham Trent University*

SERIES EDITORIAL BOARD
Roy Boyne, *University of Durham*
Mike Hepworth, *University of Aberdeen*
Scott Lash, *Goldsmiths College, University of London*
Roland Robertson, *University of Aberdeen*
Bryan S. Turner, *University of Singapore*

THE TCS CENTRE
The Theory, Culture & Society book series, the journals *Theory, Culture & Society* and *Body & Society*, and related conference, seminar and postgraduate programmes operate from the TCS Centre at Nottingham Trent University. For further details of the TCS Centre's activities please contact:

Centre Administrator
The TCS Centre, Room 175
Faculty of Humanities
Nottingham Trent University
Clifton Lane, Nottingham, NG11 8NS, UK
e-mail: tcs@ntu.ac.uk
web: http://tcs.ntu.ac.uk

Recent volumes include:

Consumer Culture and Postmodernism
Mike Featherstone

The Culture of Speed: The Coming of Immediacy
John Tomlinson

The Dressed Society: Clothing, the Body and Some Meanings of the World
Peter Corrigan

Advertising in Modern and Postmodern Times
Pamela Odih

Informalization

Manners and Emotions Since 1890

Cas Wouters

SAGE Publications
Los Angeles • London • New Delhi • Singapore

First published 2007

 SAGE Publications Ltd
1 Oliver's Yard
55 City Road
London EC1Y 1SP

SAGE Publications Inc.
2455 Teller Road
Thousand Oaks, California 91320

SAGE Publications India Pvt Ltd
B 1/I 1 Mohan Cooperative Industrial Area
Mathura Road
New Delhi 110 044

SAGE Publications Asia-Pacific Pte Ltd
33 Pekin Street #02-01
Far East Square
Singapore 048763

Library of Congress Control Number: 2006940063

British Library Cataloguing in Publication data

A catalogue record for this book is available from the British Library

ISBN 978–1–4129–3575–3
ISBN 978–1–4129–4718–3 (pbk)

Typeset by Newgen Imaging Systems (P) Ltd, Chennai, India
Printed in India at Replika Press Pvt. Ltd
Printed on paper from sustainable resources

For my grandchildren
Sam Voerman
Julia Voerman
Oskar Frakking

Contents

Preface   x

1 Introduction   1

2 Manners: Theory and History   11
   2.1   Changing Regimes of Manners and Emotions   11
   2.2   Manners and the Modelling Function of Good Societies   14
   2.3   The History of Manners and Emotion Regulation   19
   2.3.1 The period of courts and courtesy   19
   2.3.2 From courtesy to etiquette   23
   2.3.3 The expansion of good society   27
   2.4   Long-Term Processes of Formalization and Conscience
          Formation: Second Nature   30

3 Social Mixing and Status Anxieties   35
   3.1   Social Mixing, Status Anxieties, and Violence in
          Face-to-Face Class Conflicts   35
   3.2   Status Anxieties and Avoidance Behaviour   38
   3.3   Fear of Social and Psychic Contamination   42
   3.4   From Rules of Precedence to Rules for All   46
   3.5   Status Anxieties: Fear of Falling and Fear of Rising   48
   3.6   The Internalization of Avoidance Behaviour: Avoiding
          Expressions of Superiority   50

4 Decreasing Social and Psychic Distance – Increasing
   Social Integration and Identification   55
   4.1   General Trends and National Differences in Class
          Distinctions, National Integration, and
          Informalization   55
   4.2   Romanticization: The Lower Classes as 'Our
          Own Noble Savages'   63
   4.3   Claiming the Right to Privacy as a Way of Maintaining
          a Distance   64
   4.4   Diminishing Aversion to Familiarity: Increasing
          Social and Psychic Proximity   69
   4.4.1 General warnings against familiarity   70
   4.4.2 Christian names and the informal pronoun   72
   4.4.3 Social kissing   80
   4.4.4 Instant intimacy and instant enmity   84

4.5	Language Usage	85
4.6	The Constraint To Be Unconstrained, At Ease, Authentic, and Natural	90
4.7	Levels of National Integration and Mutual Identification Compared	93

5 Introductions and Friendships, Forms of Address, and Other Differences in National Habitus Formation — **101**

5.1	General Outline of National Developments	101
5.2	The German Habitus in Comparison with the American Habitus: Public and Private	104
5.3	German Forms of Address: Titles and Occupational Denominations	106
5.4	Friendship in Germany and England	108
5.5	The Informal Pronoun: Duzen	117
5.6	Introductions in Germany	120
5.7	The Formality–Informality Span: FKK and Camping as German 'Social Escape'	121
5.8	Introductions in England	124
5.9	To Greet or Not to Greet: The Right of Recognition is the Right to 'Cut'	128
5.10	The English Habitus	130
5.11	A Note on Royalty and the Season	136
5.12	The Formality–Informality Span: Gatecrashing, Watering Places, and Cruise Ships	137
5.13	Introductions in the Netherlands	139
5.14	The Dutch Habitus	141
5.15	Class and Good Society in the USA	149
5.16	American Status Insecurity as a Function of Both Class and Nationality	152
5.17	American Introductions, Snubbing, and Ways of Addressing Readers	154
5.18	The American Habitus	159
5.18.1	Superlatives and popularity	160
5.18.2	'Service' as profitable and pacifying	162
5.18.3	Stalled social integration	164
5.19	Concluding Remarks	165

6 The Spiral Process of Informalization: Phases of Informalization and Reformalization — **167**

6.1	The Fin de Siècle	167
6.2	The Roaring Twenties	169
6.3	From the 1930s to the 1960s	171
6.4	Periodization Matters: The Two World Wars	173
6.5	The Expressive Revolution	174

6.6	The 1980s and 1990s: Reformalization	176
6.7	A Spiral Process of Informalization	181
6.8	Spiral Processes of Informalization and Social Integration: Two Phases	184
6.9	Social and Psychic Changes in Spiral Processes	187
6.10	The Spiral Movement of the We–I Balance: Individualization	191
7	**Connecting Social and Psychic Processes: Third Nature**	**197**
7.1	Three Regimes in Change	197
7.2	Connecting Social and Psychic Processes	200
7.2.1	Formalization and the balance between external social controls and the internal control of conscience: the rise of an authoritarian superego-dominated personality	204
7.2.2	Informalization and the 'superego–ego' balance: the sociogenesis of a we-less superego-dominated personality	208
7.2.3	Informalization and the 'superego–ego' balance: towards a more ego-dominated self-regulation – a 'third nature'	212
7.3	Towards a Controlled Decontrolling of Superiority and Inferiority Feelings?	217
Appendix 1: Informalization of Manners and of Labour Relations		**221**
Appendix 2: On Norbert Elias and Informalization Theory		**226**
Notes		**238**
References		**243**
Manners Books		251
Name Index		**257**
Subject Index		**262**

Preface

My mother, like most mothers, tried to teach me good manners. And like most children, I hated it. In our conflicts, she used expressions like 'etiquette demands that you...', thus reaching out for a higher authority than herself to confront me with. By using the more abstract concept of etiquette, she referred to the wider society in which, she threatened me, I certainly would become a failure without the good manners that make for pleasant relations. Today, many people still distinguish the concepts of etiquette and manners in this way. For them, the concept of etiquette refers more directly to the good manners of a good society – a term referring to the social groups that possess the strength of a social establishment, and it is therefore often understood as being both superior and essential (as my mother did), or as being both pretentious and hollow (as I did). The American Laetitia Baldridge, for example, wrote in her 1990 manners book that

> there really isn't any room in the nineties for 'just an etiquette book.' There's a need for something else – a manners book to teach us how to train our children or somebody else's on this subject, so that we will have a strong nation and a healthy society in the future. Etiquette is protocol...Manners embrace socially acceptable behaviour. (1990: 4)

All this is obvious ideology. As there is no need to become entangled in these evaluative connotations, I will be pragmatic and non-ideological by using both words, etiquette and manners. Yet, I do prefer the terms manners and manners books because it is easier to speak of manners in a descriptive and non-evaluative way, and also because the word 'mannerless' can never be taken literally: human beings cannot *not* behave (nor *not* feel). Moreover, the word manners can also be used in an anthropological sense, whereas the term etiquette cannot.

This book results from a larger comparative study of changes in American, Dutch, English, and German etiquette or manners books from 1890 to 2000. I started this project in the early 1990s, after having decided to expand my interest in Dutch manners and make it into an international comparative study. I commenced by making myself acquainted with the manners books of the three other countries and also with the body of literature on manners books. An overview of the literature was gained with the help of existing bibliographies, bringing them up-to-date where necessary.

With regard to England, I have profited from a bibliography and a number of excerpts from nineteenth- and twentieth-century etiquette books compiled by Stephen Mennell, who very kindly supplied me with copies. The studies of etiquette books by Davidoff (1973), Curtin (1985, 1987), and Porter (1972) served as an introduction to the earliest part of the period I investigated. As a means of finding my way into the world of German manners books, the study by Horst-Volker Krumrey (1984) was of great help. It reports changes in German etiquette books between 1870 and 1970. When my research took me to Berlin, I also benefited from discussions with him. An introduction to the history of American manners was found in a book on this subject by Arthur M. Schlesinger Sr (1946). On American etiquette books of the twentieth century, Deborah Robertson Hodges published an annotated bibliography (1989). Both that book and conversations with its author have been helpful in studying the American sources. The same goes for an interview with Judith Martin, better known as Miss Manners. Stephen Mennell has recently finished his book on *The American Civilising Process* (2007). Our books complement each other.

My research project and I owe a lot to Michael Schröter, Berlin, Jonathan Fletcher and Lisa Driver-Davidson, Cambridge, and Irwin and Verda Deutscher, Washington. Not only as hosts but also as partners in discussing problems and data, they have all – and most especially Michael Schröter – been most helpful.

In the 1990s, reading several other studies of manners and manners books helped me to become familiar with the history of manners, studies such as those by Anderson (1996), Aresty (1970), Caldwell (1999), Carsons (1966), Cavan (1970), Finkelstein (1989), Halttunen (1982), Hemphill (1996, 1999), Kasson (1990), Martin (1985), Martin and Stent (1990), Mason (1935), Nicolson (1955), St George (1993), Visser (1991), and Winter-Uedelhoven (1991). But most important, of course, was gathering and studying a large selection of etiquette books in several libraries, a major criterion being whether a book had gained wider recognition – that is, whether and how many times it was reprinted. From these and other books – for instance, large numbers of manners books for sale in the major bookshops in Berlin, London, and Washington at the time of my visits – I made excerpts of whatever seemed interesting from the perspective of the general research questions.

In this book, the manners books that have served as primary sources of empirical evidence are presented in a separate list, entitled Manners Books. In many cases I have used successive editions of the same book to show how codes changed over time; in the text, I indicate from which edition I am quoting.

Earlier reports of my research project, on which I have drawn in writing this book are Wouters (1987, 1990a, 1995a, 1995b, 1998a, 2001, 2002, 2004a, 2004b).

In various stages of the writing process, I have received comments on parts of this book from Eric Dunning, Jon Fletcher, Joop Goudsblom, Tom Inglis, Richard Kilminster, Stephen Mennell, Michael Schröter, and Bram van

Stolk. I feel grateful for their support and valuable comments. The English of this book has been corrected by Stephen Mennell and Eric Dunning. Many thanks Eric! Many thanks Stephen! At a later stage Barbara Evers has corrected changes in the text. Many thanks Barbara!

Of course, my work owes a great deal to the support of my intimates and friends, among whom I should like to mention Truus, Julia, Roos, Joost, Sam and Julia, Luuk and his Elly, Angela and her Eric. And it pleases me enormously to dedicate this book to my grandchildren Sam Voerman, Julia Voerman and Oskar Frakking.

1

Introduction

Interest in the history of manners is fairly new and has grown together with interest in the history of emotions, mentalities, and everyday life, all of which became serious topics of research only from the 1960s onwards. Among the studies that prepared the way was the work of the Dutch historian Johan Huizinga, particularly his *The Waning of the Middle Ages*, originally published in 1919. This book had an unusual focus on manners, emotions, mentalities, and everyday life in the fifteenth century; it presented a lively sketch of the wide range of behaviour, the intensities of joy and sorrow, and the public nature of life. This work was exceptional, however, and remained marginal until the 1930s when the historians Lucien Febvre, Marc Bloch, and others, associated with the French *Annales* school, again took up an interest in mentalities, lifestyles, and daily life.

When it appeared in German in 1939, Norbert Elias's *The Civilizing Process* was the first systematic study of the history of manners and emotion regulation. Pivotal to this work was an analysis of the extensive European literature on manners from the fifteenth to the nineteenth centuries. Elias focused particularly on manners regarding basic human functions such as eating, drinking, sleeping, defecating, and blowing one's nose, as well as on those regulating sexual and aggressive impulses. Because such manners are universal – in the sense that humans cannot avoid these activities or their regulation, no matter what society or age they live in – they are highly suitable for historical and international comparison. The book provided an empirical basis for integrating historical sociology and historical psychology. Elias presented a large number of excerpts from manners books in chronological order, thus uncovering evidence of long-term changes in these codes as well as in people's habitus or psychic make-up, and revealing an overall directional trend in codes of behaviour and feeling.

As a serious object of study, the history of manners and emotion regulation has faced a major obstacle in the strong social pressures of status competition and status fears. No matter what social definition of 'good manners' may prevail, if these 'good manners' do not come 'naturally', that is, more or less automatically, the effect is ruined. Only manners springing from the inner sensitivity of a deeply rooted 'second nature' will convey the impression of being 'natural'. Otherwise, the taints of status aspiration and status-related anxiety attach to an individual, provoking embarrassment and repulsion in others. For this reason, status competition and inherent status anxieties have exerted pressure to associate the entire topic of manners with lower classes and with 'lower instincts'. That is, as good manners themselves came to be taken for granted, the subject of manners became limited to spheres in which good ones were taken to be absent.

Throughout the period from the 1920s to the 1960s, manners were discussed mainly in the context of the 'problems' of behaviour among the lower classes, of children having to learn such things as table manners, as well as of social climbers and *nouveau riche* who were usually seen as being too loud and too conspicuous. Status fears have thus functioned as a barrier to developing the level of reflexivity needed for serious interest in the subject. This is why the historian Michael Curtin opens his outstanding dissertation on Victorian English manners by presenting and solving the following paradox in his short, three-page preface. On the one hand, as the first sentence of his preface, he writes: 'Etiquette is a subject which interests only a few.' Whereas on the other hand, on the same first page, the statement is contradicted by the pretty convincing argument that 'etiquette is all around us' and that it is 'important because it is so pervasive'. On the next page he offers the following explanation of the contradiction between interest and importance:

> [I]t is only in the twentieth century, after at least six hundred years of lively and public interest and concern, that the cause of good manners has gone underground. While the Victorians had already dethroned manners from the high position they reached in Georgian times, they lacked the twentieth century's shame and penchant for euphemism, when dealing with matters of etiquette.

It was shame, Curtin argues, that prevented well-mannered persons from admitting that they were following explicit rules, and which made them believe and/or pretend 'to obey some inner light or to express one's individuality or creativity' (1987: i–iii).

This shame consists of status fears, that is, the fear of admitting, even to oneself, that one is oneself orientated to the example of social superiors and is driven by status motives. This orientation and motivation, especially in this combination, have become tabooed on account of their direct connection with feelings and displays of superiority and inferiority, to status triumphs and status defeats. Thus, these shame fears have impeded people from perceiving their own manners as the outcome of social and psychic processes.

More recently, the social ascent and integration of a wide variety of groups – the working classes, women, youth, homosexuals, blacks, and other immigrants – spurred the development of the level of detachment and reflection needed for studies in the social history of manners and mentalities. In the 1960s and 1970s, these groups began to be emancipated and further integrated within nation-states. With, in the background, an avalanche of protest against all relations and manners perceived as authoritarian, they succeeded in coming to be treated with more respect. This implied a decline in the social and psychic distance between people and a widening of their circles of identification. Similarly, in the same period, processes of decolonization saw whole populations emancipated and integrated, however poorly, within a global network of states. As differences in power and rank diminished, the motivation to keep up social and psychic distance lost vigour, resulting in greater interest in the daily lives of 'ordinary' people. With increased mobility and more frequent contact between different kinds of people came the pressure to look at oneself and others with greater detachment, to ask questions about manners that previous generations took for granted: why is this forbidden and that permitted? Moreover, in the 1960s and 1970s, there was increasing 'permissiveness', together with growing leniency in codes of social conduct and feeling, in Western societies. Many modes of conduct that had formerly been forbidden were now allowed, particularly in matters of sexuality, and conduct and emotions became less formally regulated in such spheres of behaviour as the written and spoken language, clothing, music, dancing, and hairstyles. These informalization processes have been the driving force for the growing interest in the study of manners, mentalities, and emotion regulation. My own interest in manners and manners books is a case in point (see Appendix 2). This interest originated in the late 1960s from being impressed both by the enormous changes in manners taking place at that time, and by reading Norbert Elias's *The Civilizing Process* (2000 [1939]).

In studying changes in American, Dutch, English, and German etiquette or manners books from the end of the nineteenth century to the end of the twentieth, I have searched for anything that seemed typical of a country or a time, anything that would reveal something about the relations between people of different rank (or class) and sex, and that would imply a change in the demands being made on emotion regulation or, more generally, on self-regulation. In addition, I systematically compared changes in formal and informal, public and private manners, in such matters as introductions, the use of personal pronouns, social kissing, dancing, dating, visiting hours, and so on. Through all this it was possible to observe general trends, a major one being a long-term process of informalization. This has involved in the code of manners coming to allow for an increasing variety of behavioural and emotional alternatives; manners becoming more lenient, more differentiated and varied for a wider and more differentiated public. One exception was significant: displays of superiority and inferiority becoming tabooed.

The changes widely associated with the concepts of a 'permissive society' and an 'expressive revolution' (Parsons, 1978: 300–24) are characteristic of processes of informalization. These concepts refer to the growing latitude, relative to earlier centuries, given to the display of a variety of behaviour and emotions. Many forms of expression, which by the end of the nineteenth century had come to be blocked, restricted, or strictly forbidden, came to be allowed in the course of the twentieth. People have become more frank and more at ease in expressing and discussing their feelings. However, all these words – permissive, expressive, frank, at ease, allowed, loosening – have connotations that are strongly on the side of liberation and are therefore inadequate for capturing the whole process of informalization. They are one-sided because, as the spectrum of accepted emotional and behavioural alternatives expanded, an acceptable and respectable usage of these alternatives implied a continued increase of the demands that were being made on self-regulation. In the first place, there was no 'liberation' of displays of superiority and inferiority – quite the contrary; and in the second place, the ways in which individuals fashioned their selection of alternatives became increasingly important as a criterion for status attribution. Furthermore, this status criterion also came to include the demand that any selection of alternatives should at least look 'natural': a constraint to be unconstrained, at ease, and authentic. Informalization also involved rising external social constraints towards such self-restraints as being reflexive, showing presence of mind, considerateness, role-taking, and the ability to tolerate and control conflicts, to compromise.

Directly connected to this informalization of manners are other general trends such as growing interdependence and social integration, declining power differences and a diminishing social and psychic distance between people, expanding mutual identification, and an 'emancipation of emotions' – their representation in the centre of personality, a shift from conscience to consciousness. All this will be explained in this book. Of course, in all four countries under study, these general trends and overall processes coexist with many differences regarding pace and place. My historical and international comparison focuses on these differences as well as on general trends.

My research project has resulted in two books – the present book and another entitled *Sex and Manners: Female Emancipation in the West, 1890–2000* (2004). It reports my findings about the changing codes governing the relations between the sexes. The present book has four leading research questions.

- To what extent can the overall twentieth-century process of informalization be specified for the relations between the classes in the four countries under consideration? This question directs attention to connections between changes in ranking and formality, and changes in emotion regulation, particularly with regard to feelings and gestures of superiority and inferiority.

- A second leading question concerns characteristic differences between the four countries involved, which leads to direct international comparisons aimed at finding any striking (and therefore illuminating) contrasts, and placing them in the context of a wider framework of changes in national class structure, national integration, and national habitus – *habitus* being a shorthand expression for the mentality, the whole distinctive emotional make-up of the people who are thus bonded together.

- A third leading general question in this study concerns the relation between the overall direction of these changes and shorter-term sequences and movements, currents and undercurrents, accelerations, decelerations, or deviations.

- The fourth research question concerns connections between social and psychic processes, that is, between directional changes in the regimes of manners and in the regimes of emotions. In sum, in this book, I focus on changes in the manners that regulate relations between social superiors and social inferiors. I compare national developments in integration and habitus formation, and I highlight accelerations in the process of informalization and the periods of reformalization that followed them. In the final chapter of this book, I conclude and sketch the occurrence of an overall trend towards the development of a particular kind of habitus and personality structure.

The overall research question – how to describe, interpret, and explain these twentieth-century changes in regimes of manners and self-regulation – is basically the same as the one Norbert Elias raised in *The Civilizing Process*. His investigation dealt with these changes in Western Europe mainly between the fifteenth and the nineteenth centuries. Elias drew connections between changes in personality structure and changes in social structure in France and other European societies, and offered explanations for why this happened. According to his theory, the main driving force of the directional process is the dynamic of social relations, that is, changes in the ways in which people are and feel themselves to be bonded to each other. Under the pressures of social competition and the increasing division of functions – better known in its economic aspects as the 'division of labour' – increasing numbers of people tended to become integrated together within expanding and increasingly dense networks of interdependence. Elias showed these changes to be connected with changes in sources of power and identity, in competition for status and a meaningful life, and also with changes in how the manners of people of different class, sex, or age showed a demand for respect or fear of the loss of it. In one of his formulations:

> The main line of this movement . . . , the successive rises of larger and larger groups, is the same in all Western countries, and incipiently so in increasingly large areas elsewhere. And similar, too, is the structural regularity underlying it, the increasing division of functions under the pressure of competition, the tendency to more equal dependence of all on all, which in the long run allows no group greater social power than others and nullifies hereditary privileges. (2000: 433)

This process of changing power and dependence relations was seen by Elias as the motor of changes in experience, ideals, ways of behaving and relating to others, self-regulation, and emotion regulation. In this book, I will extend Elias's investigation through to the beginning of the twenty-first century. With Elias, I understand the study of changes in codes of manners and feeling as a means of illuminating changes in relations *between* individuals and groups (social classes, sexes, and generations – *sociogenesis*) as well as the psychic processes that occur *within* people – that is, in how individuals manage their emotions and 'relate to themselves' (*psychogenesis*). In other words, changing manners also provide evidence for changes in the prevailing patterns of self-regulation, habitus, and personality structures. Of course, many studies of manners books already focus extensively on changes in social class and status, but the question of what these changes mean in terms of self-regulation, habitus, and personality structure has received much less attention. Only in the work of Norbert Elias is the relation between social structure and personality structure, or, with a slightly different emphasis, between social status and identity, a dominant theme.

Following Elias, my study of late-nineteenth- and twentieth-century manners books focuses on changes in social hierarchy and emotion regulation or self-regulation. It will be shown that, during the period covered by my research, direct references to large differences in power and respect fade from these books. Discussing social hierarchy, particularly the connected feelings of superiority and inferiority, did become increasingly embarrassing and difficult. This trend can be traced back into earlier periods. It was continued in the twentieth century. By the end of the nineteenth century, social classes within the four countries on which my study focuses were already interdependent to the extent that expressing social and psychic distance, whether pertaining to people of different social class, age, or gender, had to be done in relatively cautious and concealed ways. Increasingly, information on differences in rank was disguised or concealed.

Yet, while the trend towards restricting the expression of feelings of superiority and inferiority continued in the same direction, in other respects, the trajectory of change in codes of behaviour and feeling was unique to the twentieth century. The period of research covered by Elias's study shows a long-term process of formalization in which the regimes of manners and emotions expanded and became increasingly strict and detailed while a particular type of self-regulation, a type of habitus and personality with a particular conscience-formation developed, spread, and became dominant. This process continued in the nineteenth century, allowing one to interpret the period preceding the one covered by my research as involving a long-term process towards the formalization of manners and the disciplining of people. In the twentieth century, however, analysis of these codes points to a process of informalization. This obviously leads to questions about the overall direction of social and psychic processes, and also to more theoretical queries. In this book, these will lead to a description and interpretation of a twentieth-century spiral process of informalization, and to the development of a theory of formalization and informalization as phases in processes of social and psychic integration.

A quite simple illustration of the ongoing process of social integration consists of the fact that, in the course of the twentieth century, the public who read manners books expanded. Authors in the four societies under study came increasingly to direct themselves to wider middle-class and 'respectable' working class circles, and thus manners books came to represent growing numbers of people from more and more layers of society. This expansion reflected the ongoing partial social emancipation of these people, and also, of course, the growth and spread of wealth over broader social layers. The same movement also characterized other advice literature: 'the articles in the early decades [of the twentieth century] are aimed at a much more affluent group of women than in later decades, and we would expect the subculture of these affluent women to be less traditional than that of average women' (Cancian and Gordon, 1988: 329). The widening of the circles of readers of manners books reflected a widening of the circles who were directing themselves in terms of the dominant code, which, there-fore, in the course of the century increasingly became the *national* code. These integration processes were carried by the successive ascent of larger and larger groups. As their status and power relative to other groups increased and they came to be represented in the centres of power and their good society, that is, the circles of social acquaintance among people of families who belong to the centres of power, their members increasingly came to adopt the same code of manners and feeling, and they came to experience others as belonging to their own group or nation.

The next chapter, Chapter 2, 'Manners: Theory and History', starts out with discussions of manners (books) as a source of evidence, the functions of manners, and the modelling function of a good society. It also contains 'the story thus far', a reminder of what preceded the period of the research conducted here – that is, an overview of the history of manners in Europe and the USA as a long-term process of formalizing manners and disciplining people. At the end of Chapter 2, these formalizing processes are connected to demands on self-regulation and to the rise of a conscience-formation, characterized as typical of a 'second-nature' type of personality.

Chapter 3, 'Social Mixing and Status Anxieties', deals with the early period under study. I present and discuss several examples of changes in the regime of manners and emotions that grew out of increasingly strong and successful pressures on good societies or 'old-money' establishments to open themselves up and to allow more social mixing. Thus, the process of social mixing is perceived as diminishing the social and psychic distance between groups of people who had previously avoided each other. On the basis of examples, I draw special attention to status anxieties by sketching motives for avoidance behaviour such as the fear of social and psychic contamination, and by pointing to the social and psychic implications of increased social mixing such as having to overcome the fear of social falling and the fear of social rising. As rules for avoiding specific groups of people could no longer be explicitly set out, they were transformed in rules for avoiding specific groups of feelings, thus turning tensions between people into tensions within themselves.

In Chapter 4, 'Decreasing Social and Psychic Distance – Increasing Social Integration and Identification', I first provide an introduction to national differences in the codes regarding relations between social inferiors and superiors, starting with the observation that both English class sensibilities and the American ideology of a classless society fostered the spread of claims to privacy and to more subdued references to class differences relatively earlier than in Dutch and German manners books. Subsequent sections contain series of examples of what was written on the 'dangers' of social mixing, on familiarity, privacy, reserve, social kissing, the use of more evocative and informal language, and the use of Christian names and the informal or familiar pronoun (in Germany and the Netherlands). Most examples and changes in this chapter are grouped according to nationality, thus showing national differences and similarities. The chapter ends with a brief comparison of the processes and the levels of social integration and mutual identification in the four countries under study, a sketch that stands out in relief against a concluding overview of the broad general developments that have accompanied informalization processes.

In Chapter 5, 'Introductions and Friendships, Forms of Address, and Other Differences in National Habitus Formation', the comparison of national similarities and differences of the four countries under study is continued and specified by focusing on national differences and peculiarities. The comparison serves to draw a sketch of the main differences in national habitus formation, and these in turn are understood and explained largely from the specific class structures of the different countries and the specific ways in which the classes in these countries have mingled and amalgamated. After a general outline of differences in national developments, habitus formation in each country is connected via a variety of comparisons to the formation of centres of power and their good societies and to processes of social integration. Some comparisons pertain to the ways in which the authors of manners books address their readers, how they draw social dividing lines such as between public and private, formal and informal, and what they have written on social introductions and forms of address. In addition to the use of these differences as a basis for comparing national habitus formations, attention is given to topics in manners books that stand out as specifically German, English, Dutch, or American, among them friendship, the right to 'cut', camping, cruise ships, popularity, and the use of superlatives. In each country, the particular course of the process of social integration provides a major key to the understanding of processes of national habitus formation.

In Chapter 6, 'The Spiral Process of Informalization: Phases of Informalization and Reformalization', I present and discuss the changes observed by authors of manners books (and a few authors *on* manners books) since the 1880s. These authors usually agree about the direction of change; their observations clearly underpin the trend towards diminishing formality and rigidity in the regimes of manners and emotions, and towards increasing behavioural and emotional alternatives: informalization. The authors of manners books (and, again, a few authors *on* manners books) all seemed to agree upon these directional trends. Their main differences concern interpretation and evaluation. However, it was only in the 1920s that these differences became more marked, since before that decade, all authors tended to welcome the relaxations which were taking place.

From the end of the nineteenth century until the 1920s, expressions of relief were dominant. Early in the twentieth century, however, a question was raised that would continue to be asked right up to the present day: is it possible that we are straying in the wrong direction?

The observations acknowledge that the directional trend of informalization became dominant at the end of the nineteenth century (in what is called the 'Fin de Siècle', 'La Belle Époque', or 'the Gilded Age'), accelerated in the 'Roaring Twenties' and then again in the 1960s and 1970s – the 'Expressive Revolution'. In each round of acceleration, more people from an increasingly broad range of social strata came to be involved. The whole trend proceeded as a spiral process in alternating short-term phases of informalization and formalization, the latter consisting mainly of formalization of previous informalization, in one word: reformalization. The most recent phase of informalization ended in the late 1970s and was followed by another phase of reformalization. In the last three paragraphs of Chapter 6 these short-term phases in the long-term informalization process are placed in a larger explanatory framework by connecting them to other phases, more specifically to phases in the processes of social emancipation and integration. What was involved was a spiral process towards social integration.

Chapter 7, 'Connecting Social and Psychic Processes: Third Nature', starts off with the example of changes in ideals and practices of raising children, being an example of a wide range of social experiments towards the 'controlled decontrolling of emotional controls'. It serves as a context for sketching long-term developments in the regimes of state, family, and personality. The sketch provides a view of significant connections between social integration and psychic integration, demonstrating more generally the interconnectedness of changes in social structure and personality structure. The social and psychic processes studied and discussed in this book are illuminated by introducing the concept of a *third-nature personality*. The rise of this type of personality has run in tandem with the 'emancipation of emotions', but this emancipation did not include feelings of superiority and inferiority. During the period covered by this research, displays of superiority and inferiority became increasingly tabooed, and correspondingly, the feelings of superiority and inferiority became (and remained) more strongly repressed and denied than other emotions. In this context, racism, sexism, ageism, nationalism, ethnocentrism, and so on, are brought under the new conceptual umbrella of '*superiorism*'. The book ends with a reflection on the chances that the third-nature type of personality will spread and that, in its wake, the various forms of superiorism will be brought under firmer social and psychic control.

The book has two appendixes. Appendix 1 starts from the use of the concept of informalization with regard to the labour markets in cheap-labour countries, and it compares this meaning to the informalization of manners as described in this book. This appendix points to what happens if informalization takes off before formalization has reached a critical level. Appendix 2 describes the genesis of the concept of informalization as used in this book. It includes some of the personal correspondence that Norbert Elias and I had about this very concept, which was introduced as a significant modification regarding the interpretation of 'permissiveness' and also regarding Elias's answer to the question on how these changes would fit into his theory. In his view, the increasingly lenient and loose codes of behaviour and feeling seemed to place fewer demands on self-control, thus representing a temporary reversal of the trend he had observed in his study, whereas I was inclined to think the opposite: less formally regulated manners placing greater demands on self-regulation. This was conceptualized as informalization (Wouters, 1976).

This book contains many quotations from manners books. The authentic sound and the eloquence of these various voices in the choir of history functions as empirical evidence. I have tried to orchestrate them according to issues or themes, nationality, and historical sequence. As this sequence is not always indicated before each quotation, the reader is advised to keep an eye on the publication date in the reference following it.

2

Manners: Theory and History

2.1 Changing Regimes of Manners and Emotions

Erasmus, the Dutch humanist, advised his readers in the sixteenth century not to spit on, or over, the table but underneath it. After that, spitting became ever more restricted until it was banned altogether. In the 1960s, most British buses still had 'No Spitting' signs but in the West, generally, even the very urge to spit has disappeared.

Medieval people blew their noses with their fingers. In 1885, the author of a German manners book warned his readers: 'Beware not to clean your nose with anything but a handkerchief.' Evidently this had not yet become a general habit – fingers and sleeves or shirt also served the purpose, for he acknowledged 'Indeed, courage and mastery over oneself is required in order to be able to control oneself so constantly and persistently, but only in this way does one accustom oneself to an uninterruptedly decent demeanour' (Höflinger, 1885: 12).

These examples show some of the changes that have come about in Western manners – changes in behaviour as well as in the sensibilities and norms regulating what range of behaviour was allowed, what was prescribed, and what forbidden. Some changes in this range became formalized as good manners, others as laws. The code of manners and the judicial code supplement and reinforce each other; both provide motives and criteria for punishment and reward. They provide important criteria for social ranking. Manners therefore function as power resources in the competition for social status and meaning.

Every single individual is born in a rather undifferentiated and pliable emotional condition. They are all different individuals but, at birth, the range of these differences is limited, and it seems most likely that for many millennia the *spectrum* of inborn differences has remained basically unchanged. Therefore, its explanatory power is limited: the range of differences in newly born individuals cannot possibly explain changes in spitting and nose blowing, nor other changes on the social level such as from feudalism to capitalism or from formalization to informalization.

Any code of manners functions as a regime – that is, as a form of social control demanding the exercise of self-control. It functions as a regime of manners and emotions. The examples on spitting and use of a handkerchief already suggest that any particular regime of manners and emotions corresponds to a certain range of socially accepted behavioural and emotional alternatives, as well as to a particular level of mutually expected self-controls.

Because individuals cannot escape the social pressures to attune themselves to the social codes, laws, manners, and morals of their place and time, they accordingly develop particular patterns of manners, self-regulation, and emotion regulation. These include particular types of habitus and conscience, as well as particular ways of consciously directing themselves. But regardless of the specific way and direction of their development, people always remain emotional as well as rational beings. In regulating their emotions, they articulate their individual selves, but they can never be *not* emotional. Nor is it possible for them *not* to behave. What varies is the intensity and complexity of emotions as well as the degree and pattern of control over them. The latter is displayed in their manners. Therefore, the study of any regime of manners can reveal a corresponding regime of emotion regulation or self-regulation.

Any regime of manners and emotions symbolizes and reinforces social dividing lines. In the nineteenth and twentieth centuries, as a rule, authors of manners books pretended to present the codes of behaviour and emotion regulation of established classes and their good society; these appear to have functioned as an example or model for other social groups and classes. Also as a rule, the dominant code of manners served (and continues to serve) to maintain the prevalent social dividing lines, particularly a social distance between the established classes and those trying to enter their circles. Indeed, manners function as instruments of exclusion or rejection *and* of inclusion and group charisma: individuals and groups with the necessary qualifications are let in while the 'rude' – that is, all others lower down the social ladder – are kept out. The dual function of manners is evident in a comment such as 'They are not nice people': manners are a weapon of attack as well as a weapon of defence. Any code of manners contains a standard of sensibility and composure, functioning to preserve and stress the sense of purity, integrity, and identity of the established classes and sex.

From the Renaissance onwards, European societies tended to become somewhat more open and socially more competitive. In this process, the sensibilities and manners cherished by people in the expanding established groups functioned as a model for growing numbers of people from other social groups who were aspiring to respectability and social ascent. As the latter groups gained access to the centres of established power, the history of manners reflects the social ascent of increasingly wider social groups in these societies. This process of social integration involved some form of mixing of the codes and ideals of the groups that have risen with those of the previously superior groups. The sediments of this mixing process can be traced in manners books: major directional trends in the manners and ideals presented reflect changes in the *balance of power* between all social groups – classes, sexes, and generations. They also reflect changes in the patterns of self-regulation of increasingly wider social groups, and the formation of a particular social or national *habitus*. Trends in manners are therefore indicative of trends in power relations or class structures as well as in social or national habitus. An important aspect of the latter can be specified as trends in the prevalent *balance of controls*: the balance between the external social controls on behaviour and the internal social controls over impulses and emotions.

In addition to these two interconnected part-processes within overall processes of social integration, two others can be discerned. A third one is that trends in manners are also indicative of changes in the *balance of involvement and detachment*, that is, in the – social and psychic – proximity and distance between those concerned. As manners became less hierarchical and less formal and rigid, they also tended to indicate emotionally closer and more concerned or intimate relations as well as greater caution, circumspection, and sensitivity.[1] Fourth and finally, trends in manners are also indicative of changes in the *We–I balance* of the people involved, that is, in the balance between the emotive force of their we-identities (the groups people refer to as 'we') and the emotive force of the I-identity of individuals (Elias, 1991). Expanding group-feeling or widening we-identification to the level of nations somewhat weakened the identification with we-groups such as classes, ethnicities, sex and gender, age, and religion – in the process of social interweaving, the boundaries between the latter faded somewhat as they became the constituting parts of a larger whole. As individuals became less strongly and less directly subordinated to their we-groups, their I-identities could take on a stronger emotive charge. The change of the We–I balance in the direction of a national We ran in tandem with a growing basis for individualization – a change in the We–I balance of individuals in the direction of the I. Apparently, the process of social interweaving provided a basis for individualization, as well as triggering a widening we-identification and nation formation.

Some changes in manners, however, are symptomatic of changing power balances *between* nation-states. As France became the dominant power in Europe, French courtly manners increasingly took over the modelling function previously fulfilled by the manners of the Italian courts. In the nineteenth century, with the rising power of England, the manners of English good society came to serve as a major example in many other countries. At the beginning of the period of my research, around the turn of the nineteenth to the twentieth century, according to many German and Dutch etiquette books, English manners had become the main model all over Europe. In 1890, a German author wrote that nothing could be worse than to be taken for a barbarian by an Englishman (Franken, 1890, quoted in Wander, 1976: 8–9). And in another German book, a translation of which was also published in the Netherlands, one reads: 'At present, one gives preference more often to the English customs; these are also adopted by the French themselves' (Bruck-Auffenberg, 1897: 3).

After World War II, when the United States became a superpower, American manners served more easily as a model. Before that war, the USA had already been rising in this regard, in particular because of the relatively early development of a youth culture in that country, and of an appealing entertainment industry closely connected with it, summarized and symbolized in the name of Hollywood.

2.2 Manners and the Modelling Function of Good Societies

The codes expressed in manners books tend to reveal a mixture of actual and ideal behaviour, but it is important to realise that these ideals are *real* in the sense of not having been constructed by social scientists. Such books provide evidence of changes in the way all kinds of relations are ideally fashioned among the established who form the good society of every society. The concept of a good society is used in nineteenth-century manners books and it was introduced into sociology by Norbert Elias:

> 'Good societies' are a specific type of social formation. They form everywhere as correlates of establishments which are capable of maintaining their monopoly position longer than a single generation, as circles of social acquaintance among people of families who belong to these establishments. ... In Britain there is a 'high society' with a long tradition, where, until recently, the court was the pinnacle of the hierarchy and at the same time the centrepiece which integrated it ... When the integration of a country is incomplete or belated, as was the case in Germany, many local 'good societies' develop; none, however, gains undisputed precedence over all the others and becomes the authoritative source for the behavioural code or the criteria of membership for all the others. Whereas in Britain and France, the 'good society' of the capital city quite definitely took precedence over all local ones, and Washington 'society' is possibly just beginning to draw such functions to itself in the United States, in the short period of the united *Kaiserreich*, the court society in Berlin succeeded only partially in playing this centralising and integrating role. (Elias, 1996: 49)

Since the authors of manners books take their cue from good society and the manners that prevail there, their books reflect changes in the manners and ideals of the 'minority of the best' (Elias and Scotson, 1994). Good societies have a modelling function. It is here, in the centres of power and their good societies, that the dominant social definition of proper ways to establish and maintain relations is constructed and/or confirmed. But not in isolation. At any time, the manners prevalent in good society will reflect the balance of power and dependence between established groups and outsider groups in the society as a whole. These manners will also come to reflect the subsequent emancipation of lower strata and their integration into society, including, for some of their members, into good society.

Authors of manners books try to capture the sensibilities and practices that reflect the dominant codes, and to sell this knowledge to insecure social climbers. These authors are not backed up by any profession, in academia or anywhere else, and they neither possess nor produce any expert knowledge other than that based upon participant observation in good society. This knowledge can only become profitably exploited (published and sold) if they know how to address people who aspire to acceptance in higher social circles but are insecure about how to achieve this. Every author of a manners book has to deal somehow with the difficulty of presenting the manners that include to the excluded, the higher-class manners to lower-class people, without ever making this (too) explicit. For these books to be sold, the readers had to be lifted up, not put down.[2]

In the period of the *ancien régime*, the modelling function of courts as a good society was taken for granted, to the extent that observers noticed the function mostly in passing. For example, in the introduction to the Dutch translation of Freiherr von Knigge's famous courtesy book (1788), one reads:

> The courts, as they are the centre to which everything flows, are also the centre or general source from which the mentality and way of life of nations is steadily springing and receiving its alterations. This goes in particular for the more civilized circuits; not only in the monarchical countries, although it is from there that everything spreads to nation after nation, at least in Europe ... even those far away in the barren North have tuned in. (Swildens, 1789: lxxxix, quoted in Spierenburg, 1981: 28)

In the nineteenth century, an interesting formulation of the modelling function for manners of power centres and their good societies was provided by de Tocqueville. In the second volume of his *Democracy in America* (1840), he distinguished between the copying of manners in aristocracies and in a democracy (America). In a democracy, he wrote, 'manners are constantly characterized by a number of lesser diversities, but not by any great differences. They are never perfectly alike because they do not copy from the same pattern; they are never very unlike because their social condition is the same' (1945, II: 229).

The first extensive study of the modelling function of good society was by the French sociologist Gabriel Tarde. In his *Laws of Imitation*, published in 1890, Tarde encapsulated his view of the modelling function through the metaphor of a water-tower: 'Invention can start from the lower ranks of the people, but its extension depends upon the existence of some lofty social elevation, a kind of social water-tower, whence a continuous waterfall of imitation may descend' (Tarde, 1903: 221; see also Sorokin, 1964: 549–640).[3]

In his study of American manners books, the historian Arthur M. Schlesinger Sr took this modelling function more or less for granted, together with its result – a levelling or a declining of contrasts in the codes of behaviour and feeling. An example is provided in the following observation:

> The rules of etiquette were calculated, as an astronomer would say, for the meridian of the city, and ever there it was good Society that paid principal heed. Nevertheless the little candle threw its beams afar and as time toned down the differences between urban social classes and between country and town as well, something like a nationwide consensus of manners came about. (Schlesinger, 1946: 65–6)

This is a strange image, because time was presented as an actor in the process of social levelling, and also because good society was presented as paying principal heed to the rules: as if the little candle could have existed before and independently of good society. Of course, these rules developed in relations, and they are expressions of this development and of these relations. Personifying time as an actor, and reifying – that is, giving independent existence to – rules, norms, and ideas are modes of thought both of which result in concealing relations, inequalities, and interdependences. To reify the social code is to place that code outside individuals and their relations, and to allow for the dream that it is principally up to individuals whether or not to pay heed. This emphasis on individual freedom of choice may explain the popularity of this kind of approach, particularly in the USA where it also supports the ideology of the 'American Dream'.

The modelling function of good society operates only partly through the medium of rational individual choice because differences in manners and rank become ingrained in the personality of individuals – their habitus – as they grow up. In whatever stratum or social class an individual is born,

> [t]he collective identity, and as part of it the collective pride and the group charismatic claims, help to fashion his individual identity in his own as well as in other people's experience. No individual grows up without this anchorage of his personal identity in the identification with a group or groups even though it may remain tenuous and may be forgotten in later life, and without some knowledge of the terms of praise and abuse, of the praise gossip and blame gossip, of the group superiority and group inferiority which go with it. (Elias and Scotson, 1994: 105)

Identification with established groups is in most cases almost automatic, particularly at times when their superior position is hardly contested or not contested at all. As there can be no I-identity without a we-identity, the identification with the established is a we-identification that develops as part of any developing We–I balance of individuals. It includes the more or less automatic adoption of their definitions of 'a good life', and of what it takes to pass for 'a man of the world' or 'a woman of the world'.

Authors of manners books have shown themselves to be well aware of the modelling function of good societies, although, in the course of time, in increasingly less explicit ways. For instance, Emily Post, author of America's most famous twentieth-century etiquette book, first published in 1922, described and explained the process by relating it to growing prosperity: 'What was once considered the tradition of gracious living of the few has in these times of plenty rightly become the heritage of us all' (1960: xxvii). Authors also stated repeatedly that prosperity may be a *necessary* condition, but that it is not *sufficient* in itself. As another American author put it:

> Riches are desirable, but many a one who has had money at his command has been entirely unable to find ingress to good society.

The basis of etiquette does not rest upon money, neither will money buy good manners. Yet the rich seek the culture and the courtesy of good society, because of the finish and the éclat thus given to their wealth and their homes. (Houghton, 1882: 16)

In nineteenth-century England, it was aristocratic rather than middle-class manners that were taught in etiquette books: 'Aristocratic manners did not appear to contradict economic success but rather to crown it with a diadem of high culture' (Curtin, 1985: 413). The spread of 'gracious living' and the 'toning down of differences' in a trend towards 'a nationwide consensus of manners' are undisputed developments, but their explanation in terms of a 'social water-tower', 'imitation', 'growing prosperity', and a search for 'éclat' and for the 'diadem of high culture' will have to be augmented.

Apparently, the prestige or status motives indicated by such terms as 'finish', 'éclat', and the 'diadem of high culture' were overwhelmingly important as reasons for participating in good societies. In the twentieth-century, however, these motives came increasingly to be hidden, repressed, and denied. In the countries under study, they were widely debated as matters of *taste* and *style*, but debates about them usually turn sour when the related *status* aspects are touched upon directly: 'What the world needs now is a manual for artistic codes in theatre, concert halls and museums. First lesson: conceal such a need completely, for the right stuff and the right tone come naturally, don't they?' (Swaan, 1985: 32–3). In this context, Norbert Elias described important connections between the formation of good societies, status motives, and the transformation of constraints by others into self-restraints:

A compulsive desire for social prestige is to be found as the primary motive of action only among members of classes whose income under normal circumstances is substantial and perhaps even growing, and at any rate is appreciably over the hunger threshold. In such classes the impulse to engage in economic activity is no longer the simple necessity of satisfying hunger, but a desire to preserve a certain high, socially expected standard of living and prestige. This explains why, in such elevated classes, affect-control and self-constraint are generally more highly developed than in the lower classes: fear of loss or reduction of social prestige is one of the most powerful motive forces in the transformation of constraints by others into self-restraints. (Elias, 2000: 395–6)

Once these external social constraints have been transformed into habitual, second-nature self-restraints, the social constraints from which they originated and that keep backing them up are no longer experienced or perceived as such, and the same goes for the status motives that have been a most powerful motive force in the transformation.

Good manners are usually seen as trickling down the social ladder, and if seen only from the perspective of individual social ascent they do indeed trickle down. At times of large-scale social mobility, however, as one or more entire social groups ascend by getting represented in the established centres of power, some of their manners will rise up the social ladder with them. There is also identification downwards in such periods. On the whole, indeed, the social mixing of people tends to coincide with some mixing of their codes and ideals. In contrast to *individual* social ascent, the ascent of an entire social group involves a change in the whole shape and volume of the social water-tower, to use Tarde's metaphor. It involves some form of mixing of people and their manners. The particular ways in which the codes and ideals of the ascendant group mix and blend with those of the previously superior groups helps one to understand, if not explain, particular changes in emotions and emotion regulation, and the formation of a particular national habitus (Elias, 1996: 459–60).

The sediments of such mixing processes can be seen in longer-term changes in etiquette books: the patterns of self-regulation of increasingly wider social groups come to be reflected in the codes of manners. In turn, major directional trends in these codes and ideals are indicative of changes in power relations between all social groups – classes, sexes, and generations – and changes in the level of integration in any particular society. This is why trends in manners are indicative of trends in power relations or class structures as well as in national habitus.

These trends are indicative of changes in social composition and in the representation of the centres of power and their good societies. For example, the former Dutch Queen, Juliana, had already compared her function as a queen to that of a social worker, but her daughter, Queen Beatrix, clearly presents herself, and is to a large extent perceived, as a woman with a job. Moreover, she strongly claims her right to have a private life. Both, a job and a private life, were unthinkable in court societies, and they are clearly examples of an upward movement – 'trickle up' – along class lines, for work used to be an attribute of the lower classes. The example of Queen Beatrix also serves to illustrate a related trend in the modelling function of good societies. By presenting herself as a woman with a job, the queen also came to represent all women with a job.

> As long as the power at the disposal of the social positions of kings and queens was large by comparison with that of the mass of the people, the need to represent in their persons the people's ideals was smaller. The steady shift in the distribution of power conceptualised here as 'democratisation' made the holders of the royal position more dependent on the mass of subjects. From being rulers of the state they became symbols of the nation. The moral demands made on royalty in Britain are thus an example – one of many – showing the processes of democratisation and nationalisation of sentiments, conscience and ideals at work as strands of one and the same overall transformation of society. (Elias, 1996: 166)

In a similar way, the social code of good societies came to represent increasing layers of society as these layers became emancipated and more socially integrated. In order to avoid social conflict and maintain their elevated position, the people in the centres of power and good society had to increasingly take rising groups into account. As part of this, the former had to show more respect for the ideals, sentiments, morals, and manners of the latter. Thus the dominant code of good manners, modelled after the example of good society, reflects *and* represents the power balance between all those groups and strata that are integrated in society at large.

Finally, the modelling function of good societies also helps one to understand and explain why the nineteenth century witnessed an 'aristocratization of the bourgeoisie' alongside an 'embourgeoisement of nobility', to be partly succeeded and partly supplemented in the twentieth century by an 'embourgeoisement of the working classes' and a 'proletarianization of the bourgeoisie': informalization.

2.3   The History of Manners and Emotion Regulation

In this section I will present 'the story thus far', that is, an introductory sketch of overall changes in Western regimes of manners and emotions from the Renaissance to the end of the nineteenth century, from where my study departs. The sketch owes a debt to Norbert Elias's *The Civilizing Process* in two ways. First, it uses his theoretical perspective on manners; second, to illustrate changes up to the nineteenth century, it relies on empirical data extracted from his research, and on their presentation by Stephen Mennell (1989 [1998]). In addition to the nineteenth-century manners books that I have studied, this introductory sketch draws on many other studies of manners books, among them the studies of English manners books by Michael Curtin (1987), Leonore Davidoff (1973), and Cecile Porter (1972); the studies of American ones by John Kasson (1990), Karen Halttunen (1982), and Dallett Hemphill (1996, 1999); and the study of German manners books by Horst-Volker Krumrey (1984).

2.3.1   *The period of courts and courtesy*

The manners books studied by Elias included prominent ones that were translated into foreign languages, imitated, and reprinted again and again. These books were directed primarily at the secular upper classes, particularly people living in courtly circles around great lords. Early modern terms for good manners such as 'courtesy' derive from the word 'court'. With few exceptions, these books address adults and present adult standards. They deal openly with many questions that later became embarrassing and even repugnant, such as when and how to fart, burp, or spit. These changes in feelings of shame and delicacy are made vividly apparent in the chronological sequence of excerpts presented by Elias. The series on table manners, for example, shows that people at feudal courts ate with their fingers, using their own general-purpose knife or dagger to cut up food. The main restriction on using the knife was not to point it at others nor at oneself: one should not clean one's teeth with it. Everyone ate from a common dish, using a common spoon to transfer the food onto a slice of bread. Readers were advised to refrain from falling on the dish like pigs, from dipping already bitten or nibbled food items into the communal sauce, and from presenting a tasty morsel from their own to a companion's mouth. Diners were not to snort while eating, nor blow their noses on the tablecloth (for this was used for wiping greasy fingers) or into their fingers.

This kind of advice was repeated throughout the Middle Ages. Then, from around the sixteenth century, the regimes of manners and emotions entered a period of continuous flux. Codes became more differentiated and more demanding. In the sixteenth century, the fork was introduced as a proper item of cutlery, although only for lifting food from the common dish. Likewise handkerchiefs and napkins began to appear, albeit at first only as optional items of tableware: if you had one, you were to use it rather than your fingers. Only by the mid-eighteenth century had plates, knives, forks, spoons, and napkins for each guest, and also handkerchiefs, become more or less indispensable utensils for the courtly class. In this and other respects, the code of these upper classes was then beginning to resemble the more general usage of later centuries.

Erasmus wrote in 1530 that it was impolite to speak to someone who was urinating or defecating; he discussed these acts quite openly. In his conduct manual, *Il Galateo ovvero De' Costumi* (1558), Giovanni della Casa wrote that 'it is not a refined habit, when coming across something disgusting in the street, as sometimes happens, to turn at once to one's companion and point it out to him' (Elias 2000: 111). This warning is in line with other evidence from early manners books, which indicate that urinating and defecating were not yet punctiliously restricted to their socially designated, proper places. Quite often, needs were satisfied when and where they happened to be felt. Over time, these bodily functions increasingly came to be invested with feelings of shame and repugnance, until eventually they could only be performed in strict privacy and not spoken of without embarrassment. Likewise, certain parts of the body became increasingly 'private parts' or, as most European languages phrase it, 'shameful parts' ('pudenda', deriving from the Latin word meaning to be ashamed).

The same trend is apparent in relation to behaviour in the bedroom. It was quite normal to receive visitors in rooms with beds, just as it was very common to spend the night with many in one room. Sleeping was not yet set apart from the rest of social life. Usually, people slept naked. Special nightclothes slowly came into use at about the same time as the fork and the handkerchief. Manners books specified how to behave when sharing a bed with a person of the same sex. For instance, a manners book from 1729, quoted by Elias, warns that 'it is not proper to lie so near him that you disturb or even touch him; and it is still less decent to put your legs between those of the other'. From the 1774 edition of the same book, an advance in the thresholds of shame and repugnance can be deduced, for this pointed instruction was removed and the tone of advice became more indirect and more moral: 'you should maintain a strict and vigilant modesty'. The new edition also noted that to be forced to share a bed 'seldom happens' (Elias, 2000: 137). Gradually, to share a bed with strangers, with people outside the family, became embarrassing. As with other bodily functions, sleeping slowly became more intimate and private, until it was performed only behind the scenes of social life.

In directing these changes in manners, considerations of health and hygiene were not important. They were used mainly to back up – sometimes also to cover up – motivations of status and respect. In all cases, restraints on manners appeared first, and only later were reasons of health given as justifications. Nor did changes in poverty or wealth influence the development of manners prior to the mid-nineteenth century, after which their importance did increase.

In general, as Elias's examples showed, what was first allowed later became restricted or forbidden. Heightened sensitivity with regard to several activities, especially those related to the 'animalic' or 'first nature' of human beings, coincided with increasing segregation of these activities from the rest of social life: they became private. Again and again, what was once seen as good manners later became perceived as rude or, at the other extreme, so ingrained in behaviour as to be taken completely for granted. Social superiors made subordinates feel inferior if they did not meet their standard of manners. Increasingly, fear of social superiors and, more generally, the fear of transgression of social prohibitions took on the character of an inner fear, shame.

All new prescriptions and prohibitions were used as means of social distinction until they lost their distinguishing potential. Gradually, ever-broader social strata became willing and anxious to adopt the models developed above them, compelling those above to develop new means of distinction. For instance, it became a breach of good manners to appear naked or incompletely dressed or to perform natural functions in the presence of people of higher or equal rank; doing so before inferiors could be taken as a sign of benevolence. Later, nakedness and excretion not conducted in private became general offences invested with shame and embarrassment. Gradually, the social commands controlling these actions came to operate with regard to everyone and were imprinted as such in children. Thus all references to social control, including shame, became embedded as assumptions and as such receded from consciousness. Adults came to experience social prohibitions as 'natural', emanating from their own inner selves rather than from the outer realm of 'good manners'. As these social constraints took on the form of more or less total and automatically functioning self-restraints, this standard behaviour became 'second nature'. Accordingly, manners books no longer dealt with these matters or did so far less extensively.

Social constraints pressed towards stronger and more automatic self-supervision, the subordination of short-term impulses to the commandment of a habitual longer-term perspective, and the cultivation of a more stable, constant, and differentiated self-regulation. This is, as Elias called it, a 'civilizing' process.

In his explanation, Elias emphasized the importance of processes of state formation, in which taxation and the use of physical violence and its instruments were progressively centralized and monopolized. Medieval societies lacked any central power strong enough to compel people to restrain their impulses to use violence. Over the course of the sixteenth century, families of the old warrior nobility and some families of bourgeois origin were transformed into a new upper class of courtiers: impulsive warlords became tamed nobles with more muted affective drives. In this way, the territories of great lords were increasingly pacified, and at their courts, encouraged especially by the presence of ladies, more peaceful forms of conduct became obligatory. Such conduct was a basic part of the regime of courtly manners, and its development, including ways of speaking, dressing, and holding and moving the body, went hand in hand with the rise of courtly regimes.

Within the pacified territories of strong lords, the permanent danger and fear of violent attack diminished. This relative physical safety facilitated the growth of towns, burgher groups, commerce, wealth, and, as a result, taxation. Taxes financed larger armies and administrative bodies, thus helping the central rulers of the court societies to expand their power and their territory at the expense of others. The dynamic of the competition for land and money went in the direction of expanding the webs of interdependence, bonding together the people of different territories. Political integration and economic integration intertwined and reinforced each other, culminating in the absolute monarchies of the later seventeenth and the eighteenth centuries.

The inhabitants of these states were increasingly constrained to settle conflicts in non-violent ways, thus pressuring each other to tame their impulses toward aggressiveness and cruelty. Moreover, families of bourgeois origin had risen in power, enough to compete with the nobility and forcefully to demand more respect. Their former social superiors were obliged to develop the habit of permanently restraining their more extreme expressions of superiority, particularly violent ones. Such displays were successfully branded as degrading. As they came to provoke shame and repulsion, impulses in that direction and the corresponding feelings of superiority (and inferiority) came to be more or less automatically repressed and rejected. Thus, in a widening circle of mutual respect and identification, the more extreme displays of superiority and inferiority were excluded from the prevailing regime of manners and emotions.

In the early modern period, the general level of mutual identification was such that, for example, displays of physical punishment and executions were common public spectacles. Moreover, these were still considered necessary to bolster central authority and to seal the transfer of vengeance from private persons to the central ruler. From the early seventeenth century onward, the more extreme, mutilating punishments were mitigated or abolished. During the nineteenth century most corporal punishments were abandoned or, like executions, removed to within prison walls. And in the twentieth century, in most western European countries executions were abolished altogether. The taming of aggressiveness coincided with an increase in sensibility to suffering, that is, in the scope of mutual identification. Growing sensitivity to violence, suffering, and blood can be deduced also from changes in manners such as increasing restrictions on the use of the knife as an instrument and symbol of danger. For instance, it was frowned upon to eat fish or cut potatoes with a knife, or to bring the knife to one's mouth. In a related trend, the slaughtering of animals and carving of their meat were removed from the public scene into slaughterhouses. The carving of large cuts of meat was also increasingly removed from the dinner table to the kitchen.

2.3.2   *From courtesy to etiquette*

In the absolute monarchies all groups, estates, or classes, despite their differences, became more dependent upon each other, thus also increasing the dependence of each of the major interest groups on the central coordinating monopoly power. Administration and control over the state, its centralized and monopolized resources, first expanded and spread into the hands of growing numbers of individuals. Then, with the rise of bourgeois groups who were no longer dependent on privileges derived from the crown, royal or 'private' state monopolies were gradually transformed into societal or 'public' ones. This shift from private to public occurred relatively early in the Netherlands, where monopoly administration had been taken over by merchant patricians in the late sixteenth century, and the transition was most dramatic in France, in the late eighteenth century. This process accelerated in the nineteenth century, with the rising power and status of wealthy middle classes and the declining importance of courts, the former centres of aristocratic power.

The transition from the eighteenth-century 'courtesy genre' of manners books to the nineteenth-century 'etiquette genre' reflects this change. The new genre presented a blend of aristocratic and bourgeois manners. The aristocratic tradition persisted, for example, in the continuing importance of being self-confident and at ease. Even the slightest suggestion of effort or forethought was itself regarded as bad manners. Whereas courtesy books typically advocated ideals of character, temperament, accomplishments, habits, morals, and manners for aristocratic life, etiquette books focused more narrowly on the sociability of particular social situations – dinners, balls, receptions, presentations at court, calls, introductions, salutations. Etiquette books were directed at sociability in the centres of power and their good society. Here, the dominant social definition of proper ways to establish and maintain relations was constructed. Particularly in England, etiquette books specified how to maintain public and private boundaries, how to practise reserve and avoid intruding on another's privacy (Curtin, 1987). The manners of good society were decisive in making acquaintances and friends, and for gaining influence and recognition. They also functioned as a means of winning a desirable spouse. In comparison with court circles, the circles of good society were larger, and sociability in them was more 'private'. In many of those circles the private sphere was more sharply distinguished from the public and occupational sphere.

Elias observes that 'in every social stratum that area of conduct which is functionally of most vital importance to its members is the most carefully and intensively moulded'. Manners books will reflect these areas. In court society, he specifies,

> the exactitude with which each movement of the hands while eating, each piece of etiquette and even the manner of speech is fashioned, corresponds to the importance which all these functions have for court people both as a means of distinction from below, and as instruments in the competition for royal favour.

For courtiers, these skills and manners are described as 'preconditions for the respect of others', for here this kind of social success plays the same role as professional success in bourgeois society:

> In the nineteenth century, with the gradual ascendancy of economic-commercial and industrial bourgeois-strata and their increasing pressure for access to the highest power positions in the state, all these skills cease to hold the central place in the social existence of people; they cease to be of primary significance for success or failure in their status and power struggles. Other skills take their place as primary skills on which success or failure in life depends – capacities such as occupational skills, adeptness in the competitive struggle for economic chances, in the acquisition or control of capital wealth, or the highly specialised skill needed for political advancement in the fierce though regulated party struggles characteristic of an age of increasing functional democratisation. (Elias, 2000: 425)

In writing these passages, Elias emphasizes discontinuity and thus he creates the impression of a rather complete break. This tends towards underestimating the continuity in the functions of good societies. The rank and reputation of each individual member of the economic and political bourgeoisie was not dependent on occupational and political capacities alone. These reputations continued to be socially constructed in the circles of good society. In other words, professional success in bourgeois society continued to depend heavily upon the social success of a position in good society. It was no longer as 'vital' as social success had been for courtiers, but professional success and success in good society remained strongly interdependent.

The novelties of occupational work and the division into professional and private spheres did not change the modelling function of good societies nor the fact that entrance into them offered important power chances. What was affected, though, was the visibility of their functioning. The relegation of most forms of sociability to the sphere of private life made the modelling function almost invisible, and this may help to explain why its importance was (and is) easily underestimated and hardly or not researched. As occupational and political businesses depend on building trust, that is, on making friends and acquaintances in the field, all involved practised the custom of inviting each other to dinner and to other sociable occasions, such as parties organized in private drawing rooms. Thus they continued to seek the protection and reinforcement of their occupational and political interests in the formation and functioning of a good society (or a functional equivalent further down the social ladder or in the country or provinces).

The life and career of the bourgeois classes both in business and the professions depended heavily on keeping promises and on the rather punctual and minute regulation of social traffic and behaviour. Accordingly, nineteenth-century manners books placed great emphasis on acquiring the self-discipline necessary for living a 'rational life'; they emphasized time-keeping and ordering activities routinely in a fixed sequence and at a set pace. Thomas Haskell has pointed to the 'disciplinary force of the market' in connection to the norm of promise keeping and the ascendancy of conscience. This 'force of the market provided the intricate blend of ceaseless change, on the one hand, and predictability, on the other, in which a preoccupation with remote consequences paid off most handsomely' (Haskell, 1985: 561). An overall change in sensibility occurred via the expansion of the market, the intensification of market discipline, and the penetration of that discipline into spheres of life previously untouched by it. The expectation that everyone would live up to promises – as comprised in contracts made on 'the market' – became a mutually expected self-restraint, which became taken for granted to the extent that it came to function as part of people's conscience. This type of conscience-formation presupposes state formation in the sense that the monopolization of the use of violence by the state and ensuing pacification of larger territories provided a necessary condition for the expectation of promise keeping and living up to contracts to become taken for granted and engrained in the personality as conscience (Elias, 2000). Taking the development of these conditions into consideration helps us to understand why

> it was not until the eighteenth century, in Western Europe, England, and North America, that societies first appeared whose economic systems depended on the expectation that most people, most of the time, were sufficiently conscience-ridden (and certain of retribution) that they could be trusted to keep their promises. In other words, only then did promise keeping become so widespread that it could be elevated into a general social norm. (Haskell, 1985: 353)

This argument adds to the one put forward by Durkheim in writing about the order behind the contract: 'For everything in the contract is not contractual' (Durkheim, 1964 [1893]: 211). Durkheim's polemic with people like Rousseau, Hobbes, Spencer and Locke, who all presupposed some sort of absolute primal contract, may have made him write in rather absolute terms himself, emphasizing the 'regulation which is the work of society and not that of individuals', but what he means is

> that people do not trade and barter at random but follow a pattern that is normative. For men to make a contract and live up to it, they must have a prior commitment to the meaning of the contract in its own right. Such prior collective commitment, that is, such a non-contractual element of contracts, constitutes the framework of normative control. No trade or barter can take place without social regulation and some system of positive and negative sanctions. (Coser, 1971: 136)

This system mainly consists of the monopolization of the use of violence and ensuing pacification – that is, rising levels of mutually expected protection of people and their property. In sum, the order behind the contract, 'in current parlance, is designated by the name, state' (Durkheim, 1964 [1893]: 219).

The entrepreneurial bourgeoisie largely took the state, the order behind the contract, for granted. It was their point of departure. Their whole social existence heavily depended upon contracts, contracts regulating the conditions of such activities as buying, producing, transporting, and selling. In turn, the making of these contracts as well as the conditions stipulated in them depended upon an individual's reputation for being financially solvent and morally solid. To a large extent this reputation was formed in the gossip channels of good society (or its functional equivalent among other social strata). In developing the level of trust and respect in a relation necessary for signing a contract, an invitation into the world of sociability was (and is) an appreciated strategy. Men could demonstrate and prove their respectability and trustworthiness in general, including outside the boundaries of business life, for example, in their relations with friends and acquaintances, with women in general and with their own wife in particular. They could show this to a potential client by inviting him into their home and into the rest of their secluded good society world. To be introduced, accepted, and entertained in the drawing rooms and parlours of the respectable or, in other words, to be successful in good society, was an important and sometimes even a necessary condition for success in business.

A reputation for moral solidity referred to the self-discipline of orderliness, thrift, and responsibility, qualities needed for a firm grip on the proceedings of business transactions. Moral solidity also pertained to the social and sexual sphere: without demonstrable control over their wives and families, working bourgeois men would fail to create a solid impression of reliability and ability to live up to the terms of their contracts. Therefore, bourgeois means of controlling potentially dangerous social and sexual competition depended to a substantial degree on the support of a wife for her husband. Her support and social charm could make a crucial difference, as is implied in the opinion that 'nothing makes a man look more ridiculous in the eyes of the world than a socially helpless wife' (Klickman, 1902: 25).

At the same time, these pressures offered specific opportunities to women. Whereas men dominated the courtesy genre of manners books, in the etiquette genre, women gained a prominent position, both as authors and as readers (Curtin, 1987). As the social weight of the bourgeoisie increased, middle-class women enjoyed a widening sphere of opportunities. Although confined to the domain of their home and good society, in the nineteenth century, upper- and middle-class women came more or less to run and organize the social sphere of good society. The workings of this social formation took place in large parts in women's private drawing rooms. To some extent, women came to function as the gatekeepers of good society. Leonore Davidoff has also pointed to the connection between the rising middle classes, the rising importance of social circulation in good society, and rising opportunities for women:

> Society in the nineteenth century, especially in England, did become formalised. One way of formalising a social institution is to use specialised personnel to carry out its functions. In nineteenth-century England upper- and middle-class women were used to maintain the fabric of Society, as semi-official leaders but also as arbiters of social acceptance or rejection. (Davidoff, 1973: 16; see Wouters, 2004)

2.3.3   The expansion of good society

Compared with courts, the circles of the new good society were larger, more open, and more competitive, and as they expanded the people in them developed increasingly detailed and formal manners regarding social circulation. Particularly in Britain but also in other countries, a highly elaborate and increasingly formalized regime of manners emerged consisting of a complicated system of introductions, invitations, calls, leaving calling cards, 'at homes' (specified times when guests were received), receptions, dinners, and so on. Entrance into good society was impossible without an introduction, and any introduction required the previous permission of both parties. This regime of manners did not only regulate sociability, but also functioned as a relatively refined system of inclusion and exclusion, as an instrument to screen newcomers seeking entry into social circles, ensuring that the newly introduced would assimilate to the prevailing regime of manners and self-regulation, and to identify and exclude undesirables. Sometimes, this was made quite explicit, as in *Etiquette for Ladies* of 1863: 'Etiquette is the form or law of society enacted and upheld by the more refined classes as a protection and a shield against the intrusion of the vulgar and impertinent' (quoted in Curtin, 1987: 130). A basic rule of manners among those acknowledged as belonging to the circle was to treat each other on the basis of equality. Quite often this was expressed in what became known as the Golden Rule of manners: do unto others as you would have them do unto you. Some were treated with relative intimacy. Others were treated with reserve and thus kept at a social distance. In short, members treated everyone either as an equal or as a stranger; in this way more extreme displays of superiority and inferiority were avoided.

After an introduction, a variety of relations could develop, from merely a 'bowing acquaintanceship' to one with the 'right of recognition', as the English called it: 'If you meet a rich *parvenue*, whose consequence you wish to reprove, you may salute him in a very patronising manner; or else, in acknowledging his bow, look somewhat surprised and say, "Mister-eh-eh?"' (Millar, 1897: 37–8). As a rule, these differentiations in social distance among those included in good society ran parallel with differentiations in social status. Thus, even within the ranks of good society the practice of reserve functioned to keep people considered not equal enough at a social distance and thus to prevent other displays of superiority and inferiority. Procedures of precedence, salutation, carriage of the body, facial expression, and so on, all functioned according to rank, age, and gender to regulate and cover status competition within the ranks of good society.

As large middle-class groups became socially strong enough to compete in the struggle for power and status, they also demanded to be treated according to the Golden Rule. As good society expanded in the nineteenth century, circles of identification widened and spread, becoming increasingly multilayered. As ever-wider groups ascended into these ranks, status competition intensified, pressurizing all towards greater awareness and sharper observation of each other and of themselves. Sensitivities were heightened, particularly to expressions of status difference. As standards of sensibility and delicacy rose, the manners of getting acquainted and keeping a distance became more important as well as more detailed.

To keep one's distance from strangers was a matter of great concern. Especially in cities, the prototypical stranger was someone who might have the manners of the respectable but not the morals. Strangers personified bad company that would endanger the self-control of the respectable, prompting loss of composure in response to repulsive behaviour or, worse, the succumbing to temptation. In the nineteenth century, authors of manners books came to describe the fall of innocent young men as lessons in moral virtue and vigilance. Their repeated warnings against strangers expressed a strong moral appeal, revealing a fear of the slippery slope towards giving in to immoral pleasures. The author of a study of a number of such American stories relates that:

> [T]hese anecdotal dramas encompass many pitfalls – from seemingly harmless pleasures like dancing to the mortal dangers posed by alcohol – for conduct writers see young men's mistakes not just as individual dangers, but as part of a web of dangerous activity: one slip inevitably leads to the next. (Newton, 1994: 58)

These warnings were directed at young men in particular. Playing a single game of cards with strangers, for example, would 'always end in trouble, often in despair, and sometimes in suicide', an early-nineteenth-century advice book warned. By its nature, any careless indulgence in pleasure would lead to 'a lethal fall' (Tilburg, 1998: 66–7). In a similar study, Stuart Blumin also reports on a whole genre of

> purportedly true stories of individual drunkards, nearly all of whom were identified as wealthy, educated, or respectable, or by specific non-manual occupations before they took to drink. Moderate drinking invariably led to heavy drinking and drunkenness, and drunkenness to financial ruin and the destruction of family life. Often it led to the death of the drinker, his impoverished wife (the drunkard in these tales was almost always male), or his children. The loss of respectability, of the ability to pursue a respectable occupation, of wealth, and of family life in a well-appointed home (the forced sale of furniture is a common motif) was crucial to these tales, and spoke clearly and powerfully to the major preoccupations of the upper and middle classes. (1989: 200)

Newton concludes:

> Self-control, self-government, self-denial, self-restraint, and discipline of the will are all terms used repeatedly in the conduct book lexicon to reinforce the social construction of masculinity. The true man, then, is he who can discipline himself into qualities of character that lead to material and personal success. This discipline also extends to controlling and subjugating the passions as well. Control of anger, of sexual appetite, of impatience, even of emotion are instilled in the American male psyche as essential to the manly character. Thus the young man is set in competition with himself in the great battle of life. (1994: 58–9)

This strong moral advice was intended to teach young men the responsibilities needed not only for a successful career but also, as marriages were no longer arranged by parents, for choosing a marriage partner. Advice betrayed the fear that such choices would be determined mainly by sexual attraction.

Social censorship verged on psychic censorship: warnings expanded to the 'treacherous effects' of fantasy. This kind of high-pitched moral pressure stimulated the development of rather rigid ways of avoiding anything defined as dangerous or unacceptable via the formation of a rigorous conscience. The pressures of growing interdependencies stimulated the rise of conflict-avoiding persons, obsessed with self-discipline, punctuality, orderliness, and the importance of living a rational life. For them, the view of emotions came to be associated predominantly with dangers and weaknesses. Giving in to emotions and impulses would either lead to the dangers of physical and/or sexual violence or to the weaknesses of devastating addictions and afflictions. Thus the successive ascent of large middle-class groups and their increasing status and power relative to other groups were reflected in the regimes of manners and emotions, in a particular type of self-regulation.

2.4   Long-Term Processes of Formalization and Conscience Formation: Second Nature

Developments from the Renaissance to the end of the nineteenth century can be described as a long-term process of formalizing manners and disciplining people: more and more aspects of behaviour were subjected to increasingly strict and detailed regulations that were partly formalized as laws and partly as manners. In this long-term process of formalization, expression or display of emotions that could provoke violence were increasingly curbed and tabooed. This regime of manners and emotions also expanded to include restrictions on behaviour defined as arrogant and humiliating, as wild, violent, dirty, indecent, or lecherous. As these kinds of unacceptable behaviour became sanctioned by increasingly vigorous practices of social shaming, emotions or impulses leading to such behaviour came to be avoided and repressed via the counter-impulses of individual shame. This explains why, in the psychic make-up of individuals, the emotions and impulses that increasingly came to be branded as 'dangerous' are closely connected with feelings of superiority and inferiority and also with feelings of shame. Norbert Elias hinted at these interconnections by describing shame as

> a form of displeasure or fear which arises characteristically on those occasions when a person who fears lapsing into inferiority can avert this danger neither by direct physical means nor by any other form of attack. This defencelessness against the superiority of others ... results from the fact that the people whose superiority one fears are in accord with one's super-ego, with the agency of self-constraint implanted in the individual by others on whom he was dependent, who possessed power and superiority over him ... It is a conflict within his personality; he himself recognises himself as inferior. He fears the loss of the love or respect of others, to which he attaches or has attached value. (Elias, 2000: 415)

Apparently, both the chances of physical attack and those of (further) conscience formation depend upon the length and density of networks of interdependencies, as perceived in terms of inferiority and superiority. In these processes, not only transgressions such as outbursts of physical – and sexual – violence, but also other ways of inflicting humiliation increasingly came to be seen as intolerable displays of arrogance or self-aggrandizement, and sanctioned accordingly with stronger individual shame and collective repugnance and moral indignation. Any admission of these 'dangerous' emotions and impulses was likely to provoke compelling feelings of shame and anxiety. They came to be increasingly avoided, repressed, and denied, while the activity of avoiding and repressing was done more and more automatically and habitually: impulses triggering counter-impulses. Thus, via an expanding regime of manners, a widening range of behaviour and feelings was banned, and disappeared from the social scene and the conscious minds of individuals.

In the nineteenth century, among upper- and middle-class people these processes of formalizing manners and disciplining people resulted in increasingly compelling regimes of manners and self-regulation. They also resulted in the formation of a type of personality characterized by an 'inner compass' of reflexes and rather fixed habits (Riesman, 1950). Impulses and emotions came to be controlled increasingly via the more or less automatically functioning counter-impulses of an authoritative conscience, with a strong penchant for order and regularity, cleanliness, and neatness. Negligence in these matters indicated an inclination towards dissoluteness. Such inclinations were to be nipped in the bud, particularly in children. Without rigorous control, 'first nature' might run wild. This old conviction expresses a fear that is typical of rather authoritarian relations and social controls as well as a relatively authoritative conscience.

The long-term trend of formalization reached its peak in the Victorian era, from the mid-nineteenth century to its last decade; the metaphor of the stiff upper lip indicated ritualistic manners and a kind of ritualistic self-control, heavily based on an authoritative conscience and functioning more or less automatically as a 'second nature'.

Just as Durkheim 'discovered' an 'order behind the contract' at a time when this order had become largely taken for granted, Freud 'discovered' an unconscious at the time when it had reached a peak. And both are connected with the development of the second-nature type of personality that Riesman called inner directed:

> The inner-directed man tends to think of work in terms of non-human objects, including an objectified social organisation, while the other-directed man tends to think of work in terms of people – people seen as something more than the sum of their workmanlike skills and qualities. ... Human relations in industry, as well as relations among industries and between industry and society as a whole, seem to the inner-directed man to be managed by the anonymous cooperation brought about through the 'invisible hand' – Adam Smith's wonderful phrase for economic planning through the free market. (Riesman, 1950: 111)

Particularly in the last decades of the nineteenth century, the 'domestication of nature', including one's own (first) nature, increasingly came to trigger both the experience of an 'alienation from nature' and a new romanticized longing for nature. The more nature was exploited and controlled, the more the image of an unexploited nature was valued. In an enquiry into the roots of present-day middle-class culture as it developed between about 1880 and 1910 in Sweden, Frykman and Löfgren point to the new interest in mountains and seaside scenery, which, they argue, satisfied many of the new emotional longings: 'The absolute stillness, the dying of the day, the open landscape, all gave a feeling of total belonging, of a quiet ecstasy...It was like a ritual return to a mystical past and a real life' (1987: 55). The connection with the rise of a second-nature type of personality seems obvious, for the 'new interest in mountaineering and wilderness treks mirrors a masculine cult of asceticism, achievement and individuality. The man who endures hardship and deprivations to conquer a mountain single-handed...masters both an inner and an outer nature' (1987: 52), an interpretation documented by the words of an alpine enthusiast. Most other sports, too, will have been sought for bringing this feeling of total belonging and control, which helps explain the rising popularity of sports (Elias and Dunning, 1986). The same feeling was also projected into the romanticized past of an old harmonious peasant society, where each person knew his or her station in life. Frykman and Löfgren describe a comparable development regarding 'our animal friends': when middle-class people 'had mastered the animal within' and had developed a moral superiority to 'the more bestial lower classes', they felt a growing intimacy with animals and at the same time distanced themselves from them. They developed 'an abhorrence for "natural ways" together with a longing and fascination for "the natural way of life"' (1987: 85–6). The struggle against the cruel treatment of animals, as championed by a vanguard of humanitarian idealists of which there was a large variety in the decades at the turn of the century, was at the same time a struggle against the lust and drives of the 'animalic' (first) nature of people, their violent and indecent inclinations. In these respects too, people were 'set in competition with themselves in the great battle of life' (Newton, 1994: 59).

As the processes of social differentiation and integration continued and social and psychic bonds expanded and intensified, the social and psychic tensions generated in conjunction with these bonds also increased and with them the intensity of the longing to defy these tensions in spontaneous, authentic, relaxed, and informal conduct. This coincided with the informalizing processes that are studied in this book. Throughout the twentieth century, however, that typical second-nature domestication of 'first nature' survived, although increasingly losing adherents and vitality, particularly since the 1960s. Here is an example from an early-twentieth-century manners book demonstrating a fear of the slippery slope that seems typical of a second-nature type of personality:

> Each lie breeds new lies; there is no end to it. Let no one begin to lie to members of the household or to cheat with customers, for no escape is possible: one has to continue! Each deceitful deed, each untruth, must be either frankly admitted – only few have the courage to do so – or propped up, overcome by new untruths again. ... your

whole life will be one chain of lies that, like the links in a chain mail, will cover you all over; it will be an entangled ball, from which neither beginning nor end can be found any longer. Disentangling it has become impossible, it can only be cut. . . .

Therefore, beware of beginning.

Do not take that first step.

And if you have already turned into the wrong path, possibly have walked it a long way already – then turn around at once, avert yourself . . . It is better to die than to be false! (Oort, 1904: 10–11, 14)

A similar rigidity in dividing the world into black and white, right and wrong, is captured in the lyrics of a popular (US) song of the 1940s: 'you've got to accentuate the positive, eliminate the negative, . . . don't mess with Mister In-Between'. Mister In-Between is the personification of the slippery slope, of course. His presence would jeopardize all beauty and virtue, but 'virginal purity' in particular. The following words, quoted from a book published in the first half of the 1910s, are fairly typical of the ways of addressing young girls from 'good families':

She must never forget that she is a woman, and never lose touch with that value. And what is that treasure a woman should guard ceaselessly? It is encapsulated deep in her heart, without her being conscious of its high value. Only when her virginal feeling is affected, in her awakens a force, which brings blood to her cheeks, makes her eyes flicker, and gives her the appearance of a supernatural being. This feeling of virginal purity is the highest good for every girl. As soon as it is offended, in her awakens the voice of virtue, and happy is the woman who listens to it. It is the noblest and purest gift of heaven to her, the most precious thing she can possess, because it is so closely connected to honour and virtue that these will be lacking forever if one loses it. Therefore, one may often observe that a woman who has taken that first step on the wrong path, cannot return and continues to sink deeper, until she is the most miserable creature possibly existing on earth. . . . The girl takes care not to allow the least of liberties for which she must feel ashamed later. From the very moment on, at which both no longer dare to look freely and frankly into each other's eyes, love has been poisoned and swiftly vanishes. How many, for whom the gates to happiness had opened already, have thus denied themselves access for ever. (Seidler, c.1911–15: 9, 11)

In these words, the authoritarian conscience of a second-nature type of personality comes vividly alive: 'It' is called 'a force' [in her] and 'the voice of virtue' [in her], and if not obeyed, it poisons love and makes life miserable. The first step on this path of vice is the point of no return: the slippery slope is an omnipresent bogey of the second-nature type of personality. Even to mention what exactly it is that the voice of virtue warns against is considered too dangerous and delicate for words. And it would have sounded way too physical, of course. Therefore, the dangerous 'it' can only be suggested, hinted at. On the one hand, 'it' is a treasure that can be given only when she finds someone who is prepared to give his all, all his life. 'It' is dressed up beautifully with feelings of honour, virtue, happiness, and even with the feeling of virginal purity. But on the other hand, 'it' is scarcely dressed at all, merely wrapped in the rags of misery. 'It' has two sides, divided by rigid social and psychic dividing lines, just like Jekyll and Hyde.

3

Social Mixing and Status Anxieties

Towards the end of the nineteenth century, large groups with 'new money' were expanding and rising, creating strong pressures on 'old-money' establishments to open themselves up. In the twentieth century, this process was continued in succeeding waves of emancipation. Increasing numbers of people were absorbed and assimilated within larger and increasingly dense networks of interdependence. Power differences between social groups diminished and ever more of them came to be represented in the centres of power and their good societies. In this process of social integration, more and more groups of people came to direct themselves by the same codes, which thus increasingly became national codes. These processes implied a diminishing of institutionalized as well as internalized power differences – that is, in social stratification as well as in individual ranking. People of different social classes became interdependent to the extent that the old avoidance behaviour of keeping a distance was becoming progressively more difficult, until they could no longer avoid immediate contact. In this process of increasing social mixing, the more extreme ways of showing superiority and inferiority were banned. Manners became less hierarchical and less formal and rigid. At the beginning of the period of research, however, whole groups and classes were still outspokenly deemed unacceptable as people with whom to associate. In this chapter, I shall concentrate on a few general connections between increasing social mixing on the one hand and changes in regimes of manners and emotions on the other.

3.1 Social Mixing, Status Anxieties, and Violence in Face-to-Face Class Conflicts

In his classic study of iconographic documents, *Centuries of Childhood*, Philippe Ariès claims that at the seasonal festivals of the sixteenth and at the beginning of the seventeenth century, the social dividing lines between the classes allowed for some social mixing. However, the practice was debated, as can be seen from one of the dialogues in Baldassar Castiglione's classic *The Courtier (Il Libro del Cortegiano)*, first published in 1528, in which the question of whether courtiers should play only with other noblemen was discussed. In his summary, Ariès presents a few interesting quotations:

> 'In our land of Lombardy', says Pallavicino, ... 'there are several noblemen who at festival-time dance all day in the sun with the peasants, and play with them at throwing the bar, wrestling, running and vaulting, and I see no harm in this'. A few of those present protest; they concede at a pinch that a nobleman may play with peasants,

but only if he can 'win the day' with no obvious effort: he must be 'practically sure of winning'. 'If there is anything which is too ugly and shameful for words, it is the sight of a nobleman being defeated by a peasant, especially in wrestling.' (1965: 93)

These words suggest that the social position of the aristocracy at that time was being experienced as somewhat more precarious than before, when it was still sacrosanct. In fact, the viewpoint they express champions a larger social distance from the 'third estate', an avoidance behaviour indicative of a fear and a threat, turning even the thought of possibly losing a wrestling match, and thus being forced 'under' some peasant or other, unbearably repulsive. This restriction on social mixing, as defended by these noblemen, is indicative of their growing dependence on rising social classes.

In later centuries, members of the bourgeoisie reacted in a similar way to the social ascent of 'the masses'. Inherent in the expansion of the bourgeoisie was the growth of social classes of 'subordinates', workers employed in commercial companies. The growing interdependence between the bourgeoisie and working classes coincided with rising tensions between them, and in the eighteenth century, members of the bourgeoisie had become anxious enough to restrict social contacts between themselves and social subordinates to the minimum (Ariès, 1965: 312–14). Alexis de Tocqueville described these restrictions as arising from status anxieties: 'But what perhaps strikes us most in the mentality and behaviour of our eighteenth-century bourgeois is their obvious fear of being assimilated to the mass of the people, from whose control they strained every effort to escape' (1955: 93). He argued that 'the French bourgeoisie, while seemingly a uniform mass, was extremely composite. Thus I find that the notabilities of a quite small town were split up into no less than thirty-six distinct groups'. De Tocqueville showed how this social splintering had arisen out of 'constantly wrangling over questions of precedence' and ongoing 'disputes about questions of prestige' (1955: 94–5). Indeed, eighteenth-century status competition within the bourgeoisie was intense. All were trying to draw the status line directly on the rung below the one to which they themselves had climbed. A basic strategy was exclusion: to avoid contact with anyone of lower status.

At the end of the eighteenth century and throughout the nineteenth century, social dividing lines were losing some of their former rigidity, but they were still strong and obvious enough for social arbiters simply to advise or prescribe restrictions of movement and other avoidance behaviour without further explanation. It was viewed as completely self-evident that the bourgeoisie would avoid the petit bourgeoisie, and that both would avoid lower-class people whenever possible, but when this social distance could not be maintained and contacts nevertheless took place, they advised maintenance of a psychic distance. It was called 'reserve' and 'self-control'. In contacts with domestics, 'self-control' was called 'indispensable, as their manners and expressions can easily spoil our mood'. This Dutch author continued: 'If we wish to maintain our authority over them, then an imperturbable calm, an inexhaustible patience, and a more or less stately affability should constantly create the illusion that we never lose control of ourselves. Anger makes us look ridiculous in their eyes' (A, 1894: 111–12). Indeed, in relation to all lower-class people, reserve and self-control should keep the emotions covered with a degree of solemnity that would prevent any social superior from losing his temper, showing anger, and entering into a conflict. As an American author warned in 1885: 'To get angry with an inferior is degrading; with an equal, dangerous; with a superior, ridiculous', thus implicitly recognizing that, 'while the expression of anger was the prerogative of social superiors, in a heated dispute that superiority might easily be lost' (quoted in Kasson, 1990: 160). Only the anonymous English author of *The Habits of Good Society*, published in 1859, presented an exception to this rule, thus possibly representing an earlier rule. This seems likely because the anonymous author claimed to be very old – to remember the French Revolution, so he may have reflected older attitudes and rules, close to the ones Samuel Johnson lived by: ' "I have beat many a fellow," Johnson remarked . . . in his old age, "but the rest had the wit to hold their tongues" ' (Boswell, 1986 [1791]: 343). As the author of *The Habits* remarks,

> There are men whom nothing but a physical punishment will bring to reason, and with these we shall have to deal at some time of our lives. A lady is insulted or annoyed by an unwieldy bargee, or an importunate and dishonest cabman. One well-dealt blow settles the whole matter. It is true that it is brutal, and certainly should be a last resource; but to last resources we are often driven, and the show of determination brings imprudence to an armistice. I would say, then, know how to use your fists, but never use them as any other argument will prevail, but, when all others fail, have recourse to that natural and certainly most convincing logic. A man, therefore, whether he aspires to be a gentleman or not, should learn to box. It is a knowledge easily gained. There are but few rules for it, and those are suggested by common sense. Strike out, strike straight, strike suddenly; keep one arm to guard, and punish with the other. Two gentlemen never fight; the art of boxing is only brought into use in punishing a stronger and more imprudent man of a class beneath your own. . . . Never assail an offender with words, nor when you strike him, use such expressions as, 'take that' etc. There are cases in society when it is quite incumbent on you to knock an offender down, if you *can*, whether you feel angry or not, so that, if to do so is not precisely good manners, to omit it is sometimes very bad manners; and to box, and that well, is therefore an important accomplishment, particularly for little men. (*Habits*, 1859: 191–3)

Indeed, those who knew how to box could be 'practically sure of winning' when engaging in a conflict with a lower-class person, thus meeting the same condition that Castiglione had formulated for noblemen before they were to engage in wrestling with a peasant at a festival.

In the twentieth century, the topic of boxing disappeared from manners books. A late reference dates from the early 1920s. As can be seen by that time the tone had become quite defensive:

> Of course, a gentleman who knows how to box will never abuse his ability. He simply wants to acquire the art for being able to defend himself if attacked. Someone who has to defend himself and who knows how to box, will not only be able to ward off an attack much better, but also more fair in treating his opponent than anyone who does not master the art. (Viroflay-Montrecourt, c.1920: 75–6)

Here, a reference to fairness was added to Castiglione's condition to be 'practically sure of winning', a supplement that nominally takes the welfare of the attacker into account. That the latter never is another gentleman was taken for granted. And yet the argument is defensive in many ways: in its emphasis on the ability to defend if attacked, in its exclusion of abuse, and in its reference to fairness and the interests of one's 'opponent'. Precisely this defensiveness shows the 'art of boxing' to be on its way out as a means of settling face-to-face class conflicts.

3.2   Status Anxieties and Avoidance Behaviour

This defensiveness, and the whole trend of taking others and their interests more into account, including the interests of lower-class people, runs in tandem with an overall trend towards expanding networks of interdependence in such processes as state-formation, commercialization, industrialization, and urbanization. Particularly in the second half of the nineteenth century, these processes accelerated. As commercial businesses and administrative organizations expanded in an ongoing process of differentiation and integration, groups of social superiors and social inferiors again and again became interdependent to the extent that prohibited social superiors from expressing their feelings of superiority as openly and as extensively as before, whether in avoidance behaviour or in other ways. Social 'superiors' could neither afford any longer to avoid their social 'inferiors' so easily nor punish them so effectively for 'not knowing their place'. Eventually, avoidance behaviour was softened and feelings of superiority and inferiority were kept under stronger control – but not without a struggle. Manners books contained passionate appeals to maintain the social distance. For example, in 1860, a German etiquette writer (translated into Dutch) started out his discussion of manners between social superiors and social inferiors by uniting his readers on the basis of their common aversion to radicals: 'Communism or similar socialist delusions...is an appalling error, and participation in the efforts to introduce it is a crime'. For 'in human society, there are superiors and inferiors, and this distinction must exist and shall never cease to exist; this is as clear as can be'. On the other hand, this author advised being benevolent and kind towards people of inferior social position and education:

> Is it any wonder, then, that people from the lower classes fail to put complete trust in their superiors in position and rank if the latter do not even consider it worthwhile to acquaint themselves with their customs and manners of expression? In general, one should behave towards one's inferiors in a simple and considerate manner, not with formal politeness nor cool graciousness, but with warmth, openness and confidence. (Birch, 1860: 174–6)

A *Handbook of Courtesy* of 1868 gave similar 'double' advice. On the one hand, respect was demanded and emphasized:

> The head of the household or the master is to treat his inferiors with respect... Contempt reduces the self-respect of servants and makes them indolent and negligent in the fulfilment of their duties. ... The man of breeding... realises that servants are human beings just like him, who merely, due to their lesser civilisation, have been placed in a lower station in life. (Handbook, 1868: 86, 118, 139)

On the other hand, this anonymous author also acclaimed avoidance behaviour, for only by living in 'truly civilised circles' can a young person be 'effectively civilised':

> Once young people have become accustomed to these circles, they will feel out of place in uncultured, bad or crude company, and will come to avoid all contact with it. For once they feel that it is detrimental to their development, then associating with less well-bred people will become intolerable to them. The Englishman Sterne made a very apt comment on this point: bad and uncivilised company is like a muddy dog that makes you dirtier the more affectionate it gets. (Handbook, 1868: 142–3)

Apparently, as more people of different social classes became interdependent to the extent that they could no longer keep up the old avoidance behaviour, social superiors in established circles reacted, on the one hand by emphasizing the necessity of friendlier manners, and on the other, by accentuating class borderlines. This 'carrot-and-stick' type of advice, characteristic of a series of changes in the balance of involvement and detachment between the classes, was born out of status anxieties; it represented the hope of making social inferiors content with their station in life while keeping them at the largest possible distance. It shows the dual function of manners as a weapon of attack as well as a weapon of defence. It emphasizes the importance of showing mutual respect, as well as the importance of keeping one's distance.

At the beginning of the period under study, in the last decades of the nineteenth century, social superiors again saw themselves increasingly obliged to maintain some manner of friendly relations with people previously perceived as 'obtrusive folk'. In 1910, it was noticed that 'circles of polished society have constantly widened – wealth and talent now is sufficient for entrance' (*Manners and Rule*, 1910: 4). As increasing numbers of people were drawn into the expanding networks of interdependence, the balance of power and dependence changed to allow emancipation chances for groups of outsiders. As the latter started to realize their chances, bringing emancipation processes to the fore, the members of established groups became involved in the counterpart of emancipation processes, namely accommodation processes, which resulted in a narrowing of the socially accepted ways of obsequious approach and haughty avoidance. Open displays of 'contempt' and other displays of superiority feelings became unacceptable: 'Be *courteous* and *friendly* towards those people whom fortune did not endow with as many temporary privileges as ourselves, and honour the real merit, the genuine value of people, also those of the lower classes' (Eltz, 1908: 59). Avoidance behaviour became a much debated issue, in manners books as well as elsewhere. Many authors repeatedly cautioned against forms of 'insulting avoidance' and 'uncalled-for aloofness'. Writers of manners books advised people to show more mutual respect (more 'carrot'), especially in face-to-face contacts, often by strongly attacking old, traditional expressions of superiority. In 1908, an English author wrote:

> Let us never assert our superiority obnoxiously before those who are not as well dowered by fortune as ourselves; they already know it but too well...Do not let us look down on those who are just one set beneath us in the social scale. So many find it easier to act the Lady Bountiful than to fraternise with those whose income and family connections are but little separated from our own. We must also remember, in dealing with servants, to temper firmness with kindness. (Quoted in Porter, 1972: 72)

To varying degrees, the established classes in all the countries under study had to accommodate to the demands of the newcomers (the newly rich) by introducing some of them into the circles of their good society, while keeping a toned down social distance in relation to all others. Quite early in the century, in 1908, this strategy was attacked by someone who observed: 'It is considered bad taste now to use the terms "upper" and "lower" classes or "superior" and "inferior"; but it is no offence against taste to keep up irreconcilable class separation, and to assume all the superiority that was once frankly claimed' (quoted in Porter, 1972: 72–3).

The policy of being reserved towards strangers was also affected by the rising demands of social mixing. In the nineteenth century, this policy of keeping one's distance was seen as a firm requirement, because, as Curtin comments, 'Strangers might not only be demeaning social inferiors;

their uncertain moral character – perhaps repulsive or, worse, tempting – was a danger to the respectable in a way that associations with social inferiors alone were not' (1987: 150). In the new century, however, especially in the expanding cities, at work and on the streets, in public conveyances, and entertainment facilities such as dance halls, cinemas, and skating rinks, people who once used to avoid each other as strangers were now forced either to try to maintain or to recover social distance under conditions of rising physical, social, and psychic proximity, or to accommodate and become accustomed to more and more social mixing. For example:

> In public conveyances, you are not always confronted with the finest company. Sometimes farmhands, fishwives or other such people come to sit down next to you. Cringing in your seat with a gesture of alarm or looking down at them with an expression of contempt, such behaviour does not exhibit any upbringing at all. You might as well have been born into that class yourself, and although one naturally does not associate *en frère et compagnon* with people like that, they are human beings just as we are and, as such, deserving of our respect. (Stratenus, 1909: 139)

Apparently, it was deemed necessary to state that they were 'human beings just as we are'. This kind of statement was born from the pressures of social mixing and of having to show more consideration (more 'carrot'). In a section on manners towards servants this author wrote:

> Many will be astonished to hear us declare that our degree of civilization can be deduced even from our attitude towards social inferiors. Generally we are not very attentive to the way in which we address a maid or a servant; indeed, at times we are careless enough to humiliate them almost unbearably in the presence of strangers. Thus we principally abuse our higher rank and their dependence... moreover, we create a far from favourable impression on others who can't help but think: didn't any of their parents ever correct them, never told them that everyone will be convinced that the ability to afford servants must be a recent acquisition if one doesn't know how to treat them as *people*? (Stratenus, 1909: 52)

In every wave of democratization and social mixing, it was stated emphatically that certain groups of people are human beings, too. As such, domestics came in early and stayed long, most probably because of their position and its inherent tensions of being physically close while kept at a large social and psychic distance. In the first decade of the new century, social mixing expanded to 'farmhands, fishwives or other such people' and reactions such as 'cringing in your seat with a gesture of alarm' obliged authors of manners books to take responsibility for their role as contemporary social arbiters. Again this implied reassuring readers that social inequality is 'natural' or self-evident, while at the same time demanding greater consideration.

An example from the late 1920s disapproved of reacting 'as if a leper had approached' and showing 'visible horror and even indignation when a lower class person comes to sit next to her' (Zutphen van Dedem, 1928: 163). Emphatic statements that certain groups are also human clearly expressed the strength of one's superiority feelings while at the same time recognizing the sting of humiliation in avoidance behaviour. In the words of Norbert Elias:

> the avoidance of any closer social contact with members of the outsider group has all the emotional characteristics of what one has learned in another context to call 'the fear of pollution'. Established groups with a great power margin at their disposal tend to experience their outsider groups not only as unruly breakers of laws and norms (the laws and norms of the established), but also as not particularly clean. ... In the case of very great power differentials, and correspondingly great oppression, outsider groups are often held to be filthy and hardly human. (Elias and Scotson, 1994: xxiv–xxvii)

Indeed, in addition to coarseness, vulgarity, and anomie, dirtiness ranged high among the arguments put forward to justify avoidance behaviour towards the lower classes. Public debates contained many expressions of status anxiety, of fearing 'social pollution' or 'social contamination'.

3.3 **Fear of Social and Psychic Contamination**

Other motives for avoiding 'uncalled-for' social mixing can be illustrated from a Dutch manners book published in the first decade of the twentieth century. The author started out a chapter entitled *Coteries* by reprimanding the many young girls of that era who would have liked to proclaim differences in rank to be antiquated, and themselves to be the equals of any young countess or baroness. 'Very well', she wrote,

> but do you also consider any working-class girl as equal to yourself? . . . And even though it is possible and even likely that you will answer in the affirmative, you cannot deny that you would not like to become friends with her, not because she would be less sweet or discreet or educated, but only because it would put you in an awkward position in front of her family, her other friends and acquaintances.

This is because the working-class 'pure soul' lives in 'peculiar circles'. The author elaborated this point by presenting the example of an outing at which several people from these circles offended and grated the senses of the young rich girl. She succeeded in putting up with several embarrassing incidents and remarks, until a man told her in a half-friendly, half-surly way, how strange it is to see her preferring this company to that of those 'nasty "grand folks."' At that moment, the author wrote, she felt how strongly her parents, her brothers, sisters, friends, in short all her beloved ones, were hated. Her cheeks flushed red, she filled with indignation, she left (Stratenus, 1909: 94–5). The conclusion was that this poor working-class girl certainly

> is an excellent woman, and perhaps you would have to search a long time among your other acquaintances before finding another such pure soul; but that doesn't change the fact that she belongs to a different class than to which you in Society do, and that you will never ever succeed in removing this borderline without the lever coming down upon yourself, causing some painful injury. (Stratenus, 1909: 95)

The argument why all people should stay in the *coterie* in which they were born was continued through a lively description of the problems facing a young girl from a highly respectable family when she consorted with patricians and nobility. It demands great wisdom and sensibility, she wrote, to be able to bear the frequent displays of disparagement toward her person and her class (1909: 96).

Indeed, teething troubles and painful injuries ranged among the sanctions against 'uncalled-for' social mixing. As a rule, anyone who consorted with social inferiors was eventually shunned or cast out. Around the turn of the nineteenth to the twentieth century, both the individual and his or her group would be blamed for any 'uncalled-for' social mixing, that is, for any step outside the boundaries of the accepted status dividing lines. This helps us to understand why contact with people who had failed to observe the commonly accepted norms led to similarly intense feelings of uneasiness as contact with lower-class people. It provoked a similar threat: loss of identity, personal identity, as well as group- or we-identity. Usually, without being able to capture it in words because it was so self-evident, people generally sensed quite well that their status and reputation, their whole identity – both I- and we-identity – strongly depended upon their relation to more powerful groups. This was not anything peculiar to the *fin de siècle* period. People of lower rank commonly sense that members of groups of social superiors are strongly inclined to unite against them by modelling the whole image and status of their group of social inferiors after the example of the 'minority of the worst' among them. Generally, the harder people try to model this we-identity after the example of the 'minority of the best' in their we-group, the more intensely every single downward 'transgression' of borders between status groups is experienced as an assault on their we-identity, and thus on their personal identity as well. In more extreme cases, it can be experienced as 'betrayal' and punished as such by expulsion. Apparently, this status anxiety or 'fear of social contamination' is a form of the fear of abandonment, the fear of being exposed as inferior and subsequently abandoned by one's own people, of being expelled by the group one feels one belongs to (Elias and Scotson, 1994: xxiv, 7).

Clearly, the fear of social contamination is the fear of being degraded by the corrosion of the status or reputation of one's we-group or by being expelled from it; it is a fear of losing we- and I-identity, of losing social and individual meaning in life. Therefore, fear of *social contamination* as a motive is helpful in understanding and explaining avoidance behaviour. But there is more to it. This behaviour was and continues to be motivated also by the fear of losing self-control, which can be called the danger of *psychic contamination*. Self-control was, and still is, seen as a significant prerequisite for maintaining and improving positions of power and status:

> It is a mark of good breeding to be able to meet all emergencies calmly and without excitement or uncontrolled anger. There is no better test of good breeding than the controlling of temper. Do not confuse this serenity of manner with cowardice... By learning to control the temper one develops that mental attitude of strength which is undeniably one of the greatest assets in the social and business worlds. (Troubridge, 1931: 309)

In this way, self-control came to be connected with control over others, to social control and administration: 'For being able to control others, it is necessary to control oneself' (A, 1894: 108). In order to safeguard both, but especially to safeguard self-control, these people avoided those who would tend to put it to a test: the 'coarse' and 'rude' kind of people. In the quotation on contacts with domestics presented earlier, self-control was called 'indispensable as their manners and expressions can easily spoil our mood'. A more general warning read: 'Don't lose your temper on any provocation whatever' (*Etiquette for Ladies*, 1923: 66). Provocations were plentiful, particularly at times when avoidance behaviour was under attack.

An example is presented in a chapter entitled 'The Art of Avoiding and Excluding' which appeared in a Dutch manners book of 1928. It started out by stating: 'If one belongs to the more sensitive and the more refined in one's finer aesthetic feelings, one must refrain from many things in which a person of coarser sensibilities can indulge without objection' (Zutphen van Dedem, 1928: 150). One was, for example, to avoid mobs or commotions on the streets, especially by refraining from going out on a Sunday and from attending public celebrations. Also mentioned were slums, lower-class pubs, cheap seats at movie theatres, certain public meeting places for men and adolescent boys, and certain local trains and trams at the times of day when factory workers were travelling to or from their work. However, even for those who avoided all these places, certain means of self-protection were still deemed 'indispensable in public intercourse'. The 'more refined persons' had to be able to protect themselves in public social intercourse in two ways. They were to

> avoid even the slightest contact, as far as possible, with the bodies and garments of other people, in the knowledge that, even greater than the hygienic danger of contamination, there is always the danger of contact with the spiritually inferior and the repugnant who at any

moment can appear in our immediate vicinity, especially in the densely populated centres of cities, like germs in an unhealthy body. (Zutphen van Dedem, 1928: 162)

What was one to do if such 'contaminating' contact nevertheless took place, 'if low forces tried to pull one down'? 'Then the person who feels an aversion to harsh words and arguments has the right to defend himself by "freezing." Fire spreads, endangering large areas, but ice doesn't have to hurt anyone who does not reach out a hand for it' (Zutphen van Dedem, 1928: 160–1). These words clearly indicate that, if one loses self-control, one is 'pulled down' and 'degraded'. One 'forgets' oneself, as the expression goes, that is, one gives leeway to anger and indignation, and this is the fire that spreads. Against these dangers of social *and* psychic contamination, firm social dividing lines functioned as a firewall. To a large extent, avoidance behaviour was born from the fear of embarrassing provocations.

In the chapter on 'The Art of Avoiding and Excluding', just such a provocation was described: in a train compartment, a 'gentleman' was accompanied by three boisterous men, one of whom rested a muddy foot on the seat next to him. The gentleman asked him to remove his foot, but the only answer was another muddy foot on the seat. The gentleman then threatened to knock both feet off the seat if they were not removed in thirty seconds. He calmly submitted to their mockery while waiting, and then proceeded to act as promised. In response, the three men vented no more than 'harmless raillery'. 'Had the situation got out of hand,' then, according to this author, 'the gentleman would have proved incapable of controlling the situation in a mental sense' because he lacked 'the necessary self-control and firmness of conduct'. If that were to have happened, the three men, particularly the most impertinent one of them, would have felt themselves to be the victors, which was depicted as something that 'every civilised person must go to any extremes to prevent'. For this reason, the author concluded, no one is to venture into the kind of experiment described in this incident, 'if not compelled by every single pressure, if not every fibre of our feelings says that it is a necessity, if not the absolute master of our emotions, and not completely certain that one will be acting as an "instructor" towards an ill-behaved pupil' (Zutphen van Dedem, 1928: 191).

The novelty, however, is not only that self-control and psychic ascendancy are emphasized so strongly, but also that physical ascendancy is merely hinted at. This author did this by writing that the 'instructor' in her story had been an officer in the army. By thus suggesting that he did have command over the 'art of boxing', she complied with the necessary condition mentioned by Castiglione: to be 'practically sure of winning'.

Later in the century, particularly after World War II, the necessity of mastering some art of self-defence takes the form only of a semi-fantasy. In the 1980s, in the context of a discussion of 'altercations', one reads: 'If the occasion demands a reply, speak clearly and firmly in a calm, dispassionate voice. One diminutive gentleman claims that on such occasions he tries very hard to pretend he is John Wayne being challenged to draw by a "dude" whom he knows he can kill' (Debrett, 1981: 233). This imagination clearly functions to back up psychic ascendancy and self-control rather than physical ascendancy.

This shift from physical towards psychic ascendancy is one of the trends that have accompanied processes of social differentiation and integration. In these processes, the whole structure of the way individuals steer themselves undergoes change. At the end of the nineteenth century and in the first decades of the twentieth, as the old social dividing lines were eroded and the pressure to curtail more outright displays of superiority increased, the fear of social and psychic contamination diminished. Social mixing made it more necessary to achieve greater mastery over the fear of being provoked, pulled down, and degraded. As warnings continued against equating 'dirty' and 'indecent' with the 'lower classes', and many types of 'lofty grandeur' came to be viewed as insulting stiffness, a different pattern of self-control came to be demanded: a stronger and yet more flexible self-regulation in which these feelings of superiority were expected to be kept under control. The change to this new pattern is captured in the following quotation:

> I once heard a lady mention a dirty narrow street where she had to go, and another lady wrinkled her nose and said: 'A lady should rather keep away from an indecent neighbourhood like that', whereupon the first had the nerve to reply: 'Wherever *I* go, it *is* decent.' (ECvdM, 1912: 270)

The claim 'Wherever *I* go, it *is* decent' exemplifies the new pattern of self-control: a more stable, more all-round, more even, and more differentiated self-steering ability. For such a display of self-confidence and buoyancy implies mastery over the fear of being provoked *and* over feelings of superiority. To express this claim might very well have served to boost her feelings of superiority (based upon psychic ascendancy), but to the extent that this very claim referred to a real capacity, it comprised such control over these feelings that the people in the 'indecent' neighbourhood would find no reason to take offence.

3.4   From Rules of Precedence to Rules for All

Around the turn of the century, but especially in the first decades of the twentieth century, the confrontation with new forms of social mixing, at work and on the streets, deprived members of socially superior groups of the precedence to which they had been accustomed and had largely taken for granted. How strongly they experienced their precedence as belonging to the order of things can be gathered from the following advice:

> A woman driving a carriage should not forget what is also a law for gentlemen, that if she gets behind another carriage in which acquaintances or people of a higher age are seated, it is considered to be a gross

impoliteness to overtake that carriage. If one did, one would appear to be expressing: 'your horses are poor dopes compared to mine, I would not like to drive that slowly'. Therefore, in such a situation, restrain your impatience and turn into the first side street, rather than insulting someone by outstripping him. (Stratenus, 1909: 61)

Travelling in carriages, these people were seated in a literally elevated position, high above the rank and file of folk on foot (*voetvolk*) down below, and literally looking down upon them.[4] Moreover, the quotation clearly brings out their experience of being completely among their own kind of people; this was a means of transportation their subordinates could not afford. Seated in their carriages, they experienced the streets as an extension of their drawing rooms; accordingly, the code of social traffic prevailing among them was extended and also counted as the code of road traffic. As a group, their superiority and precedence seemed natural and inviolable.

As both road traffic and social traffic expanded, differentiated, and speeded up, members of the established classes had to accommodate, that is, to take other participants in social and road traffic more into account. Rules of precedence and other privileges were removed from the traffic codes or replaced by rules that would apply to all participants equally. The process required the unlearning of rules of precedence and the learning of universal bureaucratic rules.

Some of the problems involved in the transition are explicated in a study of letters sent to the municipal authorities of Amsterdam at the beginning of the twentieth century. Most of these letters are reported to have been carefully written by 'the middle class, and mostly men, who sought support from the city council – small shopkeepers and tradesmen, small business-men and office employees' (Daalen, 1988: 84). Many of them referred to their precarious social status and expressed anxiety about other people making correct assessments of their status. They wanted the city authorities to protect their precedence and other privileges. Some expressed a fear of social and psychic contamination by requesting the authorities to maintain or create spatial segregation between themselves and social inferiors, a spatial ordering similar to that which Lofland (1973) has described in cities in the USA. When 'fencing-off failed and people were confronted with others whom they preferred to avoid, friction and quarrels arose', as letters of complaint about incidents in tramcars show. Tram compartments were not divided into different classes, making tramcars preeminent places for social mixing. Most letters from passengers addressed to the public tram company reported incidents that, in the eyes of their authors, should not have occurred, and they attached great importance to describing their own behaviour, as well as the behaviour that was deemed desirable, as being calm, cool, collected, and composed. For example:

Since the tram was growing somewhat crowded, as I was sitting against his shoes, I requested him to be so kind as to move his feet. Immediately he let loose a flood of foul language, directed at myself and my wife and told me in no uncertain terms I should go and sit somewhere else if this place didn't suit me. (Daalen, 1988: 93)

The writers of these letters claimed protection against the undesirable behaviour of other passengers such as the use of vulgar language, snubbing, spitting, or bumping. They expected this protection from conductors and drivers, some of whom, to their disgust, took sides with troublesome passengers. Tipping ranged among the problems: 'Some writers describe scenes where conductors refused a tip, considering it to be offensive, while in others passengers became angry because certain conductors expected to be tipped' (Daalen, 1988: 93). The study of these letters reveals a characteristic uncertainty or ambivalence which stemmed from the difficulty these passengers found in understanding that they were complaining about manners and demeanour, which in fact lay beyond the bounds of public transport rules. On the one hand, they continued to expect that the impersonal bureaucratic rules would be used to enforce their code of behaviour and, therefore, give precedence to their delicate sensitivities. Thus, they 'appealed to the city authorities when they failed to distinguish themselves socially from others and to protect their social status'. On the other hand, they attached great significance to these rules because they 'also wanted to promote an impersonal method of problem-solving, a bureaucratic way of functioning' (Daalen, 1988: 95). This ambivalence appears to be characteristic of periods in which new forms of social mixing were becoming unavoidable, requiring greater compliance in exchange for the certainty that everyone will be treated equally.

The expansion and differentiation of traffic regulations tended towards equalizing all traffic participants and towards raising the demands made on their self-regulation and their self-control. Therefore, as this episode depicts a number of typical and related changes such as in the balance of controls and the balance of involvement and detachment, it can be taken as a model for studying and understanding numerous other episodes of social mixing, previous and subsequent.

3.5   Status Anxieties: Fear of Falling and Fear of Rising

With every crumbling of old social dividing lines, all those involved came under pressure again and again to associate with others in a broader spectrum of social positions and to negotiate the terms of their relations, more and more ceasing to use the gruff issuing and the servile obeying of commands. In order to be able to associate and negotiate successfully, social superiors had, in each new wave of emancipation and accommodation, to conquer their 'fear of falling' and social inferiors their 'fear of rising'.

Social inferiors involved in emancipation processes were confronted with the necessity to live up to the responsibilities and demands of their rising social positions. These included and corresponded to higher demands on their capacity for self-regulation, that is, higher degrees of self-knowledge and social knowledge. They also had to adjust their conduct at least to some extent to the manners and sensibilities of their social superiors. This followed from the need to associate and negotiate with them. In order to rise with their group and not to lag behind, social inferiors had to conquer their old attitudes of subordination. If not, they would tend to shun new situations of social mixing, afraid to 'cut a poor figure', or even to 'lose control' and to prove lacking in composure. Thus, the social process of emancipation runs in tandem with the psychic process of overcoming this fear of social 'heights', also known as the 'fear of freedom' (Fromm, 1942).

The people on the other side of crumbling social dividing lines, those involved in accommodation processes, also went through a phase of experiencing a fear of losing traditional sources of power and identity. In order to associate, mingle, and negotiate with people whom they used to avoid formerly, they had to overcome the fear of falling, a fear of social 'depths'. Many remained convinced of the superiority of their own lifestyle, but as successful social mixing required a higher level of identification and solidarity with people from lower-status groups, they came to experience excessively arrogant displays of superiority as awkward and embarrassing. In the past, such displays of superiority had functioned partially to counter and cover their fear of falling, which included fears of social contamination and of losing self-control, of lacking composure. To the extent that, through closer contacts, this fear of falling diminished, these displays lost their function; and without them, the code of manners lost some of its rigidity and stiffness. Thus, the range of acceptable behaviour expanded: a spurt of informalization occurred.

Emancipation and accommodation are also learning processes in which there are differences in tempo and emphasis. On this basis, three different groups can be discerned: there are always trend-followers, radicals, and moderates (Stolk, 1991: 59–60). Over the years, trend-followers do follow, but only slowly; in comparison to moderates and radicals, they stay conservative. On both sides of any crumbling social dividing line, these three different groups can be observed. On both sides, trend-followers usually lag behind in mastering their fears of rising or falling. Their sources of identity, and their whole personality, are still closely intertwined with the old relation between the social classes.

Social inferiors involved in emancipation processes may lag behind in overcoming the fear of not being able to meet the requirements of social rising and emancipation. For usually the habit of subordination is engrained deeply in their personality. Their whole personality can be so closely intertwined with the old relations between social classes that they try to uphold the old social dividing lines as much as they can. These stragglers tend to view the emancipation of their group more as a threat than as a promise. For the moment, they are incapable of utilizing the new opportunities, but when others do just that, this forces them even more strongly into a corner. Yet, the more the members of their we-group successfully utilize chances for social ascent, the more will those who lag behind be confronted with their lagging behind, their relative loss in status. Therefore, increasing numbers of them will also come to want to utilize these opportunities; but for the moment still lack the psychic equipment to do so. Accordingly, their attitude towards situations and relations demanding less submissiveness from them is also ambivalent. In the course of two or three decades, however, many give in to the pressure and the desire to ascend and abandon their old subordinate position and eventually succeed in conquering and mastering their fear of rising. From this perspective, conservatives follow the trend.

Initially, in a period of transition, conservative members of socially declining groups tend to cling to their traditional avoidance behaviour, and try to shun new situations of social mixing. As this implies a restriction of their chances of maintaining their social positions and avoiding a relative decline in social status, these trend-followers cannot escape the social pressure to control the fears which prevent them from more successful social mixing as well as from controlling feelings of superiority. As long as they lag behind in overcoming their fears of falling and, accordingly, in accommodating, they will continue to complain and grumble to themselves and to their friends about the situations in which they have to mingle with these 'ill-bred' people. Thus, they partly hide and partly continue to express their fear of falling, expressing an ambivalent attitude towards the new code of manners.

Before the last wave of democratization and informalization in the 1960s and 1970s, authors of manners books at times did mention or discuss the dangers and problems of social mixing from the perspective of the socially rising, but they described them far more frequently from the perspective of the members of good society. Accordingly, they more often look back with nostalgia than with satisfaction. This explains why it is much easier to find illustrations of the fear of falling than of the fear of rising.

3.6 The Internalization of Avoidance Behaviour: Avoiding Expressions of Superiority

The trend towards the curbing of expressions of superiority is not new to the twentieth century; it can also be observed in earlier periods, for instance: 'Almost all books on manners in colonial America ... contain an emphasis on "superiors" and "inferiors" that would dramatically lessen in the course of the nineteenth and twentieth century ...' (Kasson, 1990: 12). Another earlier example of the increasing pressure to curb expressions of superiority is the change in the meaning of the English word *snob*:

> In the terminology of the 1860s a 'snob' was a businessman trying to become a gentleman ... Within two generations the meaning of 'snob' was completely inverted. A 'snob' was now any social superior who on 'false' basis of wealth *or* breeding rather than achievement or inherent human qualities, held himself to be better than those socially below him. (Davidoff, 1973: 60)

The word *vulgar* has known a similar career. Originally, the word referred to the 'lower' classes, the masses living a low life 'close to the ground'. In nineteenth-century English manners books, the word came to refer to people trying to cross the social barriers, to

> the vulgar and impertinent, who, having neither worth to recommend them nor discernment to discover their deficiencies, would, unless restrained by some barrier, be continually thrusting themselves into the society of those to whom their presence would be not only unwelcome, but, from difference of sentiment, manners, education, and habits, perfectly hateful and intolerable. (*Etiquette for Ladies*, 1863: 5, quoted in Curtin, 1987: 130)

In the twentieth century, the word increasingly came to refer to acts rather than people, and probably the worst form of vulgarity and arrogance was obtrusiveness: 'It is absolutely vulgar to force recognition, and you must be careful not to place yourself out of court by a too evident desire to be seen' (*Etiquette for Ladies*, 1923: 16). Early in that century, the word was used to disallow loud expressions of superiority: 'One occasionally meets vulgar people who seek to impress those around them with their own (supposed) superiority, by decrying all that is going on, or explaining in tones meant for everyone round to hear what infinitely better performances they have heard at other places... very ill-bred indeed' (Klickman, 1902: 68). The 1916 edition of this book contained the same sentence without the word 'vulgar' (1916: 98), an example of the English trend towards avoiding, if possible, contact and direct reference to anything low. To do so would grate on sensibilities, for, together with the expansion of an elaborate system of excluding strangers and screening acquaintances, the expectancy had arisen that one would be able to avoid all that. The nineteenth-century development of a system of complicated rules had created thick enough walls around good society for allowing the ideal of good manners – manners for circulating and relating in each other's good company – to become quite egalitarian:

> Elaborate flourishes of deference were associated with servility, not with decent respect for one's own place and for another's higher rank. Haughty and aggressive superiority lost its prideful magnificent gloss and was instead regarded as uncouth, ridiculous, or damnable, while condescension, once positively compared with haughty superiority, was increasingly resented as patronage. (Curtin, 1987: 84)

Later in the twentieth century, the word vulgar was still used, but mostly to express a similarly direct attack on superiority feelings:

> The possession of good manners forbids rudeness to inferiors... It is only the vulgar person who takes pleasure in hurting the feelings of others. It makes no difference how wealthy or how poor or

ignorant a person is, as a fellow being he is entitled to sympathy and respect. ... The greatest vulgarity – and you will do well to remember this – is to look down upon a person as inferior to oneself, merely because he or she has to earn his or her living by domestic service to others. ... Arrogance is a form of selfish pride. The well-bred man or woman is never arrogant. (Troubridge, 1926–31: 3, 305)

Emphasis on gatekeeping rules also allowed the English to avoid speaking of vulgar people, to restrict use of the word vulgar to acts, and to brand the act by associating it with sheer arrogance. It seems unlikely that this restricted use of the word would have been possible if the good society, addressed and represented by authors of English manners books, had not been the highly segregated world of an establishment surrounded by social dividing lines that were kept sufficiently impenetrable.

In all the countries under study, the pressure to control expressions of superiority continued throughout the century. In the 1930s, some etiquette books, mainly Dutch and German, still contained separate sections on 'good behaviour' towards social superiors and inferiors. Later, these sections disappeared. Ideals of good manners became dissociated from superior and inferior social position or rank. The trend tended towards drawing social dividing lines less on the basis of people's belonging to certain groups – class, race, age, sex, or ethnicity – and more on the basis of individual behaviour. An example of this process is the use of references to 'best Society' or 'best sets', or even 'the very best sets' (*Etiquette for Americans*, 1909: 163) in American manners books. Until the late 1930s, these references had not been exceptional. Emily Post, for one, wrote:

> Best Society abroad is always the oldest aristocracy ... those families and communities who have for the longest period of time known highest cultivation. Our own Best Society is represented by social groups which have had, since this is America, widest rather than longest association with old world cultivation. Cultivation is always the basic attribute of Best Society, much as we hear in this country of an 'Aristocracy of wealth'. (1922: 1)

In the new edition of 1937, however, this statement was deleted. Now the reader was informed: 'In the general picture of this modern day the smart and the near-smart, the distinguished and the merely conspicuous, the real and the sham, and the unknown general public are all mixed up together. The walls that used to enclose the world that was fashionable are all down' (1937: x–xi). In accordance with this observation, Mrs Post had changed the title of her first chapter from 'What is Best Society?' to 'The True Meaning of Etiquette'. Although the term 'Best Society' was largely removed from the chapter and the book, she had not given up the idea altogether, for she continues by writing: 'On the other hand, there are countless private houses whose walls are standing intact and whose shades are pulled down when the indoor lights are lighted.' These people are reported to make their 'individual selection', and then 'define that selection as Society...a selection not by family name but by individual qualification' (1937: xi). By formulating 'The True Meaning of Etiquette' mostly in terms of individual qualification – that is, in terms of personal qualities such as charm, tranquillity, taste, beauty, and so on – Mrs Post had turned the perspective away from the social level to the psychic level. And she even descended further, to the level of biology: 'We've all heard the term "nature's nobleman," meaning a man of innately beautiful character who, never having even heard of the code, follows it by instinct. In other words, the code of a thoroughbred... is the code of instinctive decency, ethical integrity, self-respect and loyalty' (1937: 2).

This is an example of social avoidance internalized: from avoiding lower-class people to avoiding layers of superiority feelings. Display of such feelings would not only humiliate and provoke social inferiors, but also grate on the senses of anyone in good society. Superiority feelings had come to be considered as a lower class of feelings, and to display them as betraying a flaw of the personality. They had to be avoided. Appeasing this avoidance, the feeling of superiority was allowed to take refuge in human biology, as innate natural instinct.

The author of the 1948 edition of *Vogue's Book of Etiquette* took another turn by explicitly rejecting 'Best Society' as a standard and accepting the standard set by the majority of the people instead:

> In the last twenty years, particularly in America, etiquette has become less arbitrary and more democratic, because it has discarded the old source of its authority and taken up a new one. The old sanction of this rule was, 'The inner circle (or the "best" people) behave this way.' Its new standards of behaviour are based on what millions of people have accepted as right or wrong. (Vogue, 1948: 3)

In the same year, an author launched a direct attack on displays of superiority: 'No matter what your position, be careful not to adopt a superior manner; in the first place it is offensive, and in the second place it shows very definitely that you are not superior' (Eichler, 1948: 232).

In England, the change away from 'best people' can be noticed in a retrospect in the introduction to a manners book of the 1950s:

> One casualty of the new spreading wave of middle-class living is the old criterion of all etiquette writers – The Best People...Today, few people would care to go on record defining The Best People....In place of the old hard and fast formulas there is a new, gentler code of manners...less cruel, less exacting, less censorious and much easier to live by. (Edwards and Beyfus, 1956: x)

Here, the swing is not from 'the best' all the way to 'the millions'. The observation of social equalization contains some scepticism: the reference to 'on the record' suggests that it had become politically incorrect to define

'The Best People', but that 'off the record' many people would find no difficulty in this definition.

As subordinate social groups were emancipated, references to 'better' and 'inferior' kinds of people, to hierarchical group differences, were increasingly tabooed. Whereas at one time people of inferior status were avoided, later in the twentieth century behaviour that betrayed feelings of superiority and inferiority came to be avoided: avoidance behaviour was internalized, turning tensions *between* people into tensions *within* people – including the tensions of ambivalences at a higher level of involvement and detachment. In the process, the once automatic equation of superior in power and superior as a human being declined to the point of embarrassment, and the new sensitivity to this difference urged one social arbiter to write:

> In this book, there occasionally crop up the words 'superior' and 'inferior'. These words are not used in the social sense, in any way, but are used merely to indicate difference in rank. Thus, it may be assumed that an older person is 'superior' to a younger person; that a child is 'inferior' to its parents and so on. The words imply no slur on the character of the person concerned, whatsoever. (*Etiquette for Everyone*, 1956)

As social superiors were less automatically taken to be better people, good and bad behaviour was increasingly thought to be found in all classes: 'the words "he's a gentleman" may apply with equal truth to a jobbing gardener or a sovereign' (Penelope, 1982: 10), and 'Bad behaviour is prevalent in all walks of life from the highest to the lowest; it is not confined to one class of person nor to one section of the community' (Bolton, 1961: 8).

4

Decreasing Social and Psychic Distance – Increasing Social Integration and Identification

4.1 General Trends and National Differences in Class Distinctions, National Integration, and Informalization

The examples presented in Chapter 3 are not only indicative of a progressively diminishing social and psychic distance between people but also of an ongoing, more inclusive process of social integration: increasing numbers of people came to direct their feelings and behaviour to the same national standard, the same regime of manners and emotions. During the period covered in my research, manners books in each country under study contained many comments on the ongoing processes of democratization, social integration, and informalization. In this chapter, I will sketch some international trends and national differences in these interconnected processes.

In the first half of the twentieth century, social class, avoidance behaviour, and (other) expressions of superiority and inferiority were dealt with more openly in the Dutch and German etiquette books than in the American and English ones. Throughout the century, most Americans shared an ideology of a classless society in combination with an ideology of social success, which implied that, in American manners books, information on class or status was likely to be censored somehow or only presented in hidden ways. For different reasons, however, the same goes for English manners books. The English preferred not to mention the lower classes, lower parts of the body, and lower impulses and emotions. At the beginning of the research period, this barrier to observation and discussion had extended almost entirely from the lower classes to class altogether, from lower parts of the body to the entire body, and from lower emotions and impulses to anything emotional. The words emotional and impulsive had become almost synonymous with irrational. At that time, *parvenus* or *nouveau riches* were nearly the only representatives of lower classes mentioned in manners books, except of course for servants. In the 1980s, a retrospective account ridiculed this whole habitus, symbolized in the well-known metaphor of the 'stiff upper lip', by defining the latter as 'a condition brought about by an excess of good manners and a genuine attempt not to sneer when talking of the Lower Classes' (Gammond, 1986: 63).

In the 1920s, an **English** author observed that 'the old formidable Class distinctions are fast being broken down. Not so very long ago, one had to be born in the inner circle, before one could be received in Society, and many conventions were only known to the favoured few' (Terry, 1925: 11). About five years later, another author predicted that 'abolition of these class distinctions can only be a matter of time', and tried to help the process by attacking 'that particular type of Englishwoman... who seems to revel in displaying, by the icy frigidity and supercilious condescension of her bearing, her sense of immeasurable distance separating her from those beneath her in the social scale' (Scott, 1930: 16–17). In the last year of the 1930s, an author observed: 'That old institution, the domestic servant, as our grandmothers and mothers knew her in the old days, is as dead as the dodo.' She continued without nostalgia and even attacked the feeling:

> But do you know how to deal with the modern maid? Or are you still resenting her new liberties, and sighing after the old days, when orders were orders, and amusements were for the master and mistress of the house, and no one else?... *Let suggestions take the place of orders.* (Troubridge, 1939: 66–8)

In the mid-1950s, the observation that manners have changed 'from the rigid pomp, circumstance and ceremonial of our ancestors to the comparative freedom of the present times' brought an author to a conclusion that is close to the heart of the process of informalization: 'one might be tempted to think', she wrote, 'that they [manners] no longer matter; but it is just because of this more care-free life which we now enjoy that the whole business of etiquette has become so difficult' (Bolton, 1955: 7). This author perceived the process of social equalization as a 'levelling up':

> Since the last war, due to improved and universal education, higher salaries and greater equality of opportunities, there has been a great 'levelling up', and many of the erstwhile class barriers, once so sharply defined, are gradually being broken down so that probably the only noticeable distinctions left today are in manners, deportment and speech. (Bolton, 1955: 12–13)

According to the authors of another manners book of the same period, these distinctions were also disappearing, for they wrote of women in the office: 'now that class distinctions in speech, dress and behaviour are disappearing... it is much more likely today that she will catch the boss's eye' (Edwards and Beyfus, 1956: 137). Indeed, along with social and psychic proximity came sexual proximity: increased sensitivity to the erotic and sexual aspects of relationships (see Wouters, 2004a).

In 1969, in the revised edition of this 1956 book, the authors reflected upon the social changes that were then occurring in a way that both mirrored and illuminated important aspects of the process of informalization – the acceleration of which had necessitated the book's revision:

> It might be supposed that the immense social changes which have occurred over the last ten years would have made a revised edition of a book on etiquette a very slim volume. The ideal of a classless society,

the growing independence and equality of women, the respect for honesty in speech and social behaviour, the general climate of tolerance to what was earlier taboo, and the emphasis on self-expression in individual behaviour, must surely make nonsense of the concept of etiquette.

On the contrary. We find that the volume is fatter than ever. The surprising fact has emerged that not only do many of the old conventions persist as strongly as ever, but that many of the innovations have produced their own form to meet changed social situations, and that both categories apply in a far wider sphere. The overlapping and intermingling of the old and the new, the acceptance of the unconventional approach alongside the traditional, makes a sure-footed path through the current complexities of social behaviour more hazardous than ever. ...In spite of the general onslaught on formality, traditional codes of behaviour, and the very concept of etiquette and good manners, we find that many of the old values have survived and even won new converts. ... The difference between now and ten years ago is not so much a loosening of formulas as a further softening of censure toward those who do not conform. The 'classless society' has in many of its aims and interests become synonymous with a middle-class society... More, not fewer, people are involved in the world of social good form. (Edwards and Beyfus, 1969: ix–x)

Indeed, more people from different social strata came to orient themselves to the same national codes, while, at the same time, these codes were coming to represent more of their interests and their habitus. This is an aspect of social integration, a process in which old forms of 'keeping a distance', reserve and avoidance behaviour, lost their function and faded, while a rising level of trust in social and psychic proximity allowed for an increase of socially accepted behavioural and emotional alternatives. A rather unexpected illustration of this interconnectedness was presented in the preface to an authoritative English manners book, *Debrett's Etiquette and Modern Manners* (1981: 7). The author noted that, in his youth, he was told that 'the good fairy Do-As-*You*-Would-Be-Done-By should be emulated', but that he later discovered that 'the true spirit to emulate is that of Do-As-*They*-Would-Be-Done-By, whether one agrees with them or not'. This 'discovery' would have been unthinkable at a time when keeping a social and psychic distance was strongly emphasized. Even to think of the possibility to 'Do-As-*They*-Would-Be-Done-By, whether one agrees with them or not' seems to presuppose a society in which social groups or classes are highly integrated. The process of social interweaving necessitated more social mixing and pressured all those involved to overcome some of their mutual suspicions and fears. They experienced constraints to develop a more solid basis of mutual trust and a higher level of mutually expected self-restraints which allowed for 'a further softening of censure', for the social acceptance of a wider variety of behavioural and emotional alternatives – that is, for informalization.

In the USA, from as early as the beginning of the nineteenth century onwards, 'nearly all the works [manners books], whether of foreign or native origin, carefully avoided the old-time references to the etiquette of inferiors toward superiors' (Schlesinger, 1946: 21). It demonstrates the force of the ideology of being a classless society. The same ideology would keep authors of manners books from writing openly about the problems related to increased social mixing. For example, the plea of a 1920s author for 'more discrimination' contained no reference to class: 'In clubs or hotels, at summer resorts, or in the many common meeting-places of American life more discrimination is required. There are unfortunately many persons abroad in the land without proper social credentials, who seek new fields of adventure by the easy American manner of beginning a conversation' (Wade, 1924: 27–8). In comparison with the European countries under study, the degree of social mixing in the USA has always been larger, if only because the circles constituting a good society have remained less united, their ranks far less efficiently closed. Therefore, the level of uncertainty of rank and status has also been permanently higher. And yet references to social class have been avoided. Instead, one finds vague categories such as 'persons without proper social credentials'. Until the 1960s, readers of American manners books could not find out from these sources that the population of the USA consists of a good many classes and ethnic groups, including an indigenous population. This silence and vagueness are conspicuous demonstrations of avoidance behaviour.

Another trace of this particular type of avoidance behaviour can be found in the rule that a host or hostess should 'not introduce two ladies who reside in the same town'. The author who mentioned this rule continued:

> This is many times an awkward and embarrassing restriction, particularly as the other – the English rule – renders it easy enough, that the 'roof is an introduction' and that visitors can converse without further notice. So awkward, however, are Americans about this, that even in very good houses one lady has spoken to another ... and has received no reply 'because she has not been introduced', but this mistaken idea is, fortunately, not very common. Let every lady remember, whether she is from the country or from the most fashionable city house, that no such casual conversation can hurt her. ... They may cease to know each other when they leave the house. (Hanson, 1896: 36)

In 1937, Mrs Post wrote: 'Under all informal circumstances the roof of a friend serves as an introduction' (1937: 10), but in the 1920 edition of a manners book (earlier editions had come out in 1901 and 1915), this rule was still mentioned as an English custom, not generally accepted by Americans, who 'consider it better form for a hostess to introduce her guests' (Holt, 1920: 9).[5] Obviously, this rather severe formality points to the existence of fiercely competing social classes, and to a fashionable circle that 'lives by snubbing' (Hanson, 1896: 39). After World War II, these circles, functional equivalents of a good society, were described by an English student of American manners:

> Whatever the criteria used, there will be found in each community a small group of women whose dominant position is generally conceded, and who represent a court of appeal by whom applicants will be judged and included – or excluded. This competition for social success takes up so much of the time and energy of the more prosperous and distinguished American women that it would be easy to draw the conclusion that American society – at least the top ten per cent – has a hierarchical structure similar to that found in Western Europe. There is a volume called *The New York Social Register* which attempts to list the distinguished of the whole country (applicants for inclusion must present letters from two *women* whose husbands or sons are already included); but although the number included is small, the doyennes of each community will consider some inclusions unjustified, as well as some exclusions. (Gorer, 1948: 193–4)

More recently, the author of a book on manners between 1620 to 1860 has concluded: 'the study of manners shows the crucial role they have played in maintaining a class society among a people who did not (and still do not) want to admit it' (Hemphill, 1999: 9). The same author has said about antebellum conduct writers that:

> While they balked at acknowledging class differences between the middle and upper classes, they did not hesitate in pushing the lower class to the wings of their social world. To the extent that the serving class was expected on the stage, it was as props. ... Most of the newly codified rituals of the era – the 'introductions, recognitions, and salutations' – were gate-keeping devices to serve the cause of social exclusivity. (1999: 130–1)

Under the relentless pressure, continued in the twentieth century, of the ideal of individual freedom and of the ideology of being a classless society, most remarks on changes in social dividing lines in American manners books were made in retrospect, in or after periods of transition. They nearly always cheered the changes: 'The contemporary spirit ... is liberated from much of the burden of what used to be called "keeping up." It is much more honest and simple than it was' (*Vogue*, 1948: 4).

German comments on the fading of social dividing lines are characterized by their large contrasts. Here is a rather harsh voice from the 1920s: 'In all cultured nations there are leading superior strata from which the work of the masses is organised and fertilised. ... Weak, incompetent elements descend from them. Strong, hard spirits work their way up from the masses' (Bodanius, 1924, quoted in Krumrey, 1984: 115). In contrast, a book published early in the Nazi period did not bear any trace of their (the Nazis') dominance:

> Dignity is no longer a social class privilege. Even in the simplest circles, no one can be justified in withdrawing from the international demands of good manners. ... Today, not only have these differences [between aristocracy and bourgeoisie] largely vanished but, in addition, the man of work, the farmer, the business man, and all others, have come to feel equally subject to the same laws of propriety and morality. (Dietrich, 1934: 6)

After World War II, in 1949, an author observed: 'looking down upon lower strata is supposed to be outdated, but in the subconsciousness of many people these prejudices lived on' (Martin, 1949, quoted in Krumrey, 1984: 176). In the early 1960s, comments on the process of social equalization still showed pointed contrasts. One author emphasized insecurity:

> In our present mass society, borderlines between individuals as well as between classes are fading. ... Perhaps new and legitimate customs will develop by the time people again come to realise what their 'role' in the world actually is. ... As long as manners keep insecurely floating as they do today, it will be up to the insightful individual to move about as carefully as possible in a society that quite often will appear to be purely chaotic. (Andrea, 1963, quoted in Krumrey, 1984: 435)

At about the same time, the authors of another book gave a much more positive interpretation of the same changes:

> The dividing lines between classes, still very much present a generation ago, have disappeared...That, of course, requires face-to-face contacts with completely different people from those with whom one restricted oneself before...People of the most simple descent have, by a change in comparative wealth, been enabled to lead a life in which they are also forcefully confronted with more demanding codes of behaviour...In this process, the groups willing to attune to the dominant behavioural codes have spread and are numerically stronger than ever before. (Meissner and Burkhard, 1962: 26)

Later comments all bear traces of the last wave of democratization and informalization. The following remarks appeared in a book first published in 1970 and also in the revised editions of 1988 and 1990: 'Today, good manners no longer distinguish between "the best people" and "other people"; they function to enhance the mutual understanding between all people. Away with all trivialities and platitudes!...Whoever abstains from formal authority, gains personal authority' (*Umgangsformen Heute*, 1988: 18, 48).

In the 1920s, a **Dutch** author commented in a nostalgic tone: 'What one used to call *stand* (class, estate), descent, family: all this has lost its value, and so has wealth. Strong equalizing currents have washed it all away.

But what remains, what cannot be destroyed...is nobility of mind'
(Viroflay-Montrecourt, [c.1920]: 57–8). It is a nostalgia of the established.
In the 1950s, another Dutch author represented a nostalgia of rising groups
of outsiders:

> In 1931 a radio operator married a girl formerly employed in the
> workroom of a fashion house. The young couple rented a flat built for
> the lower-middle classes according to the latest requirements. It
> contained a shower cabin, but the young woman continued to visit
> the public bathhouse every Saturday: she did not dare to admit to her
> mother, sisters, and friends to having a shower at home; they would
> suspect that she was putting on airs, and for the sake of maintaining
> a good mutual understanding, she did not want to appear so 'grand'.
> (Schrijver, 1959: 12)

The drift of the story is that people in the then recent decades had overcome
these silly status-ridden anxieties – in this case a fear of social elevation –
and had become more equal.

In the 1980s, after a survey of a variety of changes in the most recent
decades, including a reference to large groups of immigrants now living in
the country, the authors of a manners book concluded: 'In such a society,
you can no longer really say how things should be done, but only how they
are done – and why. ... Instead of fixed rules of etiquette, we now need
flexible *guidelines* that everyone should be able to interpret depending on
the situation' (Grosfeld, 1983: 6). These authors claimed that, 'in a society
which honours the equality of all human beings', empathy and sensitivity to
a wide variety of situations and relations have become basic requirements
(1984: 10–11). For example, 'whether to use an informal or a formal mode
of address is no longer as much a question of distinctions between people
(man/woman, older/younger, higher/lower) as it is of distinguishing situations (formal/ informal, business/personal, public/private)'. This is called
'a development from altimeter to plane geometry' (1984: 50). What is
needed is 'the capacity, without forcing ourselves, to have understanding for
other people in the most widely divergent situations, based on essential
respect for whoever the other person might be' (Grosfeld, 1983: 347).

In comparison with their American, English, and German counterparts,
Dutch etiquette books dealt more openly and more often with class
distinctions, avoidance behaviour, and other expressions of superiority and
inferiority. As late as the 1950s, avoidance behaviour was rather openly
propagated. In 1957, the author of a Dutch manners book presented advice
of the carrot-and-stick type, displaying both a fear of falling and a fear of
social and psychic contamination (including the fear of being tempted).
On the one hand, she warned that the 'answer to the question "What does
your father do?" should not be a criterion for more or less fellowship or
friendship' (Bruyn, 1957: 50–1). On the other hand, she drew a very sharp
demarcation line between 'modern young girls', obviously middle class,

and the budding (working-class) youth culture that was about to evolve into the distinction between 'mods' and 'rockers' (Dutch equivalents were called *pleiners* en *dijkers*), and into the 'generational conflict' of the 1960s:

> Unfortunately, every town, even every village, has a street that is used less for traffic than to lounge about and dally. Most of the young going there are loafers: boys gazing at girls and girls gazing at boys, searching in porches, halls and cloakrooms of cinemas under the pictures of movie stars for a reflection of their own tenuous featherbrains – foolishly hoping for once to achieve a maximum of success with a minimum of clothes. On her way to school or from school back home again, the modern girl, being the civilised and independent person she is, will possibly avoid these gutters of the silly uncultured, if only on pure aesthetic grounds. For what is more ugly, tasteless, uncivilised than such a gathering...

Subsequently, many negative traits were attributed to the loitering youngsters that came to these 'disgusting' meeting points, and they were called various names, such as woman hunters, rascals, deadbeats, scum, foam, trash, vermin, and street filth. They 'very rightly deserve to be disdained' (Bruyn, 1957: 62–3). This example is rather exceptional in its use of offensive words. The author obviously tried to raise a wall, if not an iron curtain, between 'modern young girls' and the 'street filth of the gutter', thus revealing not only a fear of falling in status but a fear of falling sexually as well: these young lower-class men embodied unadmitted, repressed sexual longings and tensions (see Wouters, 2004a, §6.5 and §8.3a)

Similar tensions are revealed in the following description of a dance hall in the early 1960s by an English author:

> On one side of the room is gathered a group of flashily dressed youths who lounge untidily against the walls, or flop heavily over chairs gazing with undisguised insolence at the collection of young girls sitting opposite them. The girls in their turn sit there giggling self-consciously and making loud, provocative remarks obviously aimed at the unattached young men around them. Eventually one of the boys will summon a little strength from some deep reserve of energy, put away the flick knife with which he has been cleaning his nails, and slump across the room and indicate to the girl of his choice that he desires to dance with her. Not for him the polite 'May I have the pleasure of this next dance?' No, an expressive hunch of the shoulder and a jerk of one eyebrow is the only invitation to the dance that he can muster. If the young lady in question then measures up to his expectations, it is possible that she may be asked to join him in the refreshment room for a cup of coffee or a coke – quite often she may even be expected to pay for her own refreshment. The necessary social preliminaries now having been overcome, it is by tacit consent that he will be

permitted to see her home – provided of course, that she does not live too far off his own normal route – and as a reward for this munificence, will expect to be allowed to spend some few minutes in a shop doorway or other suitable dark recess in amorous dalliance. The fact that neither of these two young people have ever set eyes on each other before, that they have no mutual friend to vouch for the respectability and good intentions of each other does not matter, boy has met girl and at the comparatively cheap cost of a ticket of admission to a dance hall plus the price of a cup of coffee, a good time has been had by all. It is in this casual, slaphappy way, that countless of young men are meeting numbers of young women every day. (Bolton, 1961: 11–12)

The tone of this description is negative enough for the next line to come as a surprise: 'It would be foolish to maintain that this is always harmful and that such friendships based upon such a happy-go-lucky method of introduction must always end in disaster. Many happy and successful marriages have resulted from just such a casual way of meeting...'. The author proceeded by comparing this new way to the old, and concluded: 'But in this, as in every form of good manners, there is the happy medium and a request for formal introduction and the intent to make haste slowly in the progress of love and marriage will bring its own rewards' (Bolton, 1961: 13).

While the drift of these Dutch and English descriptions is the same, there is a considerable difference in the way it is said. In general, both the English and American authors of that era did not turn their backs as easily on the lower classes and lower bodily functions as Dutch (and to a lesser extent also German authors) did. Since the last wave of democratization and informalization, however, that is, from the end of the 1960s onwards, these differences have disappeared: manners books no longer contain such strong examples of the fear of falling or of comparably strong feelings of superiority.

4.2   Romanticization: The Lower Classes as 'Our Own Noble Savages'

In successive waves of emancipation and informalization, the necessity (and the urge) to distinguish oneself from the lower classes (and lower instincts) diminished, and aspects of working-class codes of behaviour and feeling 'trickled up' the social ladder. At the same time, in prevailing manners and attitudes towards the lower classes, there was a gradual shift in the carrot-and-stick balance towards more 'carrot' and less 'stick'. This was a shift towards greater identification with these classes. The English, in particular, became fascinated by the lifestyle of the working classes, and at times romanticized or idealized (parts of) it for its 'naturalness'. This romanticization figures as one side of a coin which has looking down on the working classes as its other side, but as the working classes became emancipated, the involvement–detachment balance or the balance between upgrading and degrading them was tilted in favour of the first. An example is Orwell's description of the 'proles' in his *1984*: 'The proles had stayed human. They had not become hardened inside. They had held on to the primitive emotions which he himself [Winston Smith] had to re-learn by conscious effort' (Orwell, 1954: 135). An earlier example is from 1939, when the fashion of the Lambeth Walk, a dance that came out of a musical, washed over England. It was called after a London working-class neighbourhood 'with a spontaneous talent for dancing and song':

> The point of the show is essentially the contrast between the *natural* behaviour of the Lambethians and the affectation of the upper classes. The upper classes wish to masquerade as Lambethians; sixteenth century lords and ladies played, in pastoral make-believe, as shepherds and shepherdesses. The middle classes wish to be Lambethians because it temporarily lets them off a sticky code of manners which they usually feel bound to keep up. The working classes wish to be Lambethians because Lambethians *are* like themselves, plus a reputation for racy wit and musical talent – partly they represent that part of the working class which knows how to have a good time.
> (Harrison and Madge, 1986 [1939]: 157)

The identification of the Lambethians with their dance is interpreted as stemming from a 'far more spontaneous feeling than they have ever shown for the paradise-drug of the American dance-tune. ... These Lambeth Walkers are happy because they find they are free to express *themselves* without the hypnosis of a jazz-moon or a Führer' (Harrison and Madge, 1986: 183). Words like these give the impression that the English had discovered the 'noble savage' among their own lower classes.

In the 1950s, the sociologists Young and Willmott exhibited a similar sentiment by announcing that they had 'discovered' the wider mum-centred family pattern among the working classes in the middle of London and, therefore, by studying these kinship relationships, entered 'the province of anthropologists' (1957: 12). Yet, at the same time, words like these mark the end of a phase of more rigid social segregation and the breakthrough of a new phase of social integration. They also mark a widening of the circles of identification, although still in the guise of romanticization, a rather unstable, even potentially dangerous form of identification: the carrot-and-stick balance may quite suddenly bend over to the stick.

4.3   Claiming the Right to Privacy as a Way of Maintaining a Distance

Another symptom of rising identification with lower classes is the rising sensitivity to social dividing lines and the related feelings of inferiority and superiority as expressed in a shift from an emphasis on the dangers of social (and psychic) contamination to an emphasis on the right to privacy.

Nominally, claims to the right to privacy function to enable the avoidance of people and to prevent accusations of social discrimination, for justifications of this right need not bear any trace of these functions.

Claiming the right of privacy as a way of avoiding social discrimination was developed first in **English** good society. As early as the nineteenth century, groups of established people succeeded in maintaining their superior position by appealing to privacy: 'Privacy and precedence were types of deference which were relatively formal and explicit' (Curtin, 1987: 83). Privacy included the right to be asked beforehand whether or not to accept an introduction to an inferior, and also the right of recognition, which implied the option not to renew the acquaintanceship at the next meeting. Not being recognized implied being treated as a stranger or being cut, that is, completely ignored. What is known as English reserve consisted of the following two connected and overlapping parts: 'First and most important, it meant the suppression of emotional expression. . . . But the second type of reserve – the careful maintenance of public and private boundaries or, more simply, privacy – was equally common and an indispensable part of good manners' (Curtin, 1987: 128).

Curtin finds in privacy his main reason for distinguishing between the courtesy books of the courtly period and the etiquette books of the later period: 'Courtesy taught one how to act in company; etiquette, how to avoid intruding on another's privacy. . . . etiquette writers liked to dwell on those rules which kept people apart, not those that brought them together' (Curtin, 1987: 130). Indeed, 'etiquette writers paid great attention to the rules that regulated intimacy and the exchange of visits between acquaintances, but the whole thrust of these rules was the protection of privacy, not the encouragement of sociability' (Curtin, 1987: 73). Of course, courts were even more highly protected social spaces, but English good society was a good second to courts. Advice like the following is typically English. It is not found in other countries:

> A lady should not bow to another who, being a stranger to her, has addressed a few remarks to her at an afternoon party, as the fact of meeting at the house of a mutual friend does not constitute an acquaintanceship, and does not authorise a future bowing acquaintance. . . . A bowing acquaintance is a difficult and tiresome one to maintain for any length of time, when opportunities do not arise for increasing it. (*Manners and Rule*, 1910: 207)

Advice like this is remarkable for its detailed distinctions, for its authoritative tone, and for its use of the word 'authorise', which clearly suggests the presence of higher authorities in control of it all. It was only in England that introductions had to be acknowledged; it allowed social superiors the possibility of not 'authorizing' them. This rule, and the whole formalized, hierarchical system of introductions, cards, calls, etc. had the double function of keeping all those one rung down the social ladder at bay, while gaining access to those on the next higher rung (see §§ 5.8, 5.9, and 5.10). This system is typical of a highly secluded good society with an elaborate and strict regime of gatekeeping and rigorous social control. However, this regime had also allowed for a relatively early shift from avoiding people to avoiding certain feelings and certain displays of feeling, producing that highly demanding English blend of easy-going sociability and reserve:

> The salient issue of nineteenth-century good manners was not the attainment of a formalistic control over demeanour but rather a perfected and extended control which realised all the old objectives but with effortless nonchalance. The formalities of manners were by and large readily mastered, but the easy, self-confident, and unself-conscious style turned informality itself into a difficult art. (Curtin, 1987: 18)

Indeed, only the smoothly controlled decontrolling of emotional controls can turn sociability into an art.

In an authoritative English manners book that was published in 1981, the veil around the right to privacy is lifted somewhat. The authors explicitly express some of its important social and psychic functions:

> One of the features of a civilised country is every person's right to privacy, even in public, and for this reason distracting behaviour of any kind – speaking loudly, shouting in the street, excessive gesticulation, whistling, singing, playing radios, or arguing – breaches good manners. Clearly, the people who behave like this, behave poorly; lower class manners are to be avoided, and it is done by referring to the right of privacy. (Debrett, 1981: 233)

Here the explanatory connection between the right to privacy and avoiding people who behave poorly, and therefore demonstrate lower-class manners, is made very directly and clearly. The formulation is careful: the people who 'behave poorly' and lower-class manners are separated by a semicolon. Yet the formulation comes very close to stating that the right to privacy functions to facilitate the avoidance of lower-class people.

According to Kasson in his study of nineteenth-century **American** manners books, the urban middle classes thought highly of privacy, but here the word privacy is restricted to the right to be alone in performing bodily functions: 'they pursued sexuality within a context of moderation, self-control and, above all, privacy. Parents increasingly slept apart from children' (1990: 170). Kasson claims that privacy extended far beyond bodily exposure and sexual intimacy, but none of his examples go beyond the family household. Obviously this kind of privacy is related to but different from the one that functions to facilitate the avoidance of social discrimination and lower-class people. The latter emerged later.

It was not before the 1937 edition of Mrs Post's manners book that the word 'privacy' appeared in the index. The new chapter, 'Modern Exactions of Courtesy', started out with a hymn of praise to the right to privacy:

It is obvious that the first rules of courtesy, which exact consideration for the rights and feelings of others, are as diverse as are the differences in human temperament, taste and point of view. But even so, no exaction of perfect behaviour is more essential to all thoroughbred people than the right to privacy. (Post, 1937: 621)

It is telling that, in the USA, references to Best Society were becoming submerged at about the same time (in the 1930s) as references to the right to privacy were surfacing. The change can be perceived as a shift from the vices of status competition to the virtues of consideration, and also as the individualization of Best Society: a shift in focus from the group to its individual members. This change from keeping a social distance (avoidance behaviour) to maintaining the right to privacy follows the same mechanism as the change from legitimizing the code in 'Best Society' to legitimizing it in 'innate natural instinct', turning the perspective away from the social to the psychic level, and further down to the level of the species. In both cases, the main function is to protect sensibilities by softening and distracting attention from differences in social class and status. It also helps to maintain class privileges.

In the 1950s, Harold Nicolson, a member of British 'high society', was impressed by the relatively low importance attached to privacy in the USA. He portrayed Americans as having a

curious indifference to, or disregard of, what to us is one of the most precious of human possessions, namely personal privacy. To them, ... privacy denotes something exclusive, patronising, 'un-folksy', and therefore meriting suspicion. Thus they leave their curtains undrawn at dusk, have no hedges separating their front gardens, and will converse amicably with strangers about private things. (Nicolson, 1955: 18)

In the **Netherlands**, the concept of privacy appeared in the late 1950s, a decade in which most manners books still contained warnings against familiarity and advice to keep a distance. This is how it was introduced:

The Dutch language has no word that expresses the English concept of 'privacy': the right to be alone. It is not without reason that the English language has such a word and ours has not. It is a difference rooted in national character, and it can also be recognised in other places. We have low fences around almost every garden and yard, for example, but the English like high walls and hedges around their gardens, lest passers-by can look inside.

The author continued to point to similar and related differences, such as the English custom of not washing, grooming, brushing one's teeth, shaving, dressing, and so on 'in the presence of others, not even (or especially not) in the presence of the spouse'. The Dutch have not developed this kind of sensitivity, she continued, but she asked her readers to take English manners as an example, and at least to finish dressing in the bed- and bathroom, that is, not to walk through the house only partly dressed, especially not in the living room (Schrijver, 1959: 17–18).

During the wave of informalization of the 1960s and 1970s, virtually no manners book was published, but in the new manners books published from the early 1980s onwards, the concept of privacy was highly praised. It always appeared in its English form – that is, untranslated. Dutch authors seemed to take delight in the 'discovery' of this benevolent right: 'Loneliness is something very abominable, but perhaps one thing is even worse: the lack of privacy' (Groskamp-ten Have, 1984: 193). About the wish of people to be alone, another author wrote: 'If we possibly can, we should not begrudge anyone their right to privacy and we should make it possible. Parents should also respect their children's right to be alone and, if possible, create the conditions' (Bakker-Engelsman, 1983: 162).

In the early 1980s, the wish to keep a social distance by claiming the right to privacy was said to be rooted in an altogether universal human psychic need, and was legitimized as such: all individuals sometimes need to withdraw from company. Thus a wish that clearly originates from a highly relational and social level was projected onto the level of the species. Both this wish and its rooting in biology can be understood more adequately, I think, as stemming from the rising pressures of status competition experienced by individuals in increasingly dense and extensive networks of interdependence.

Throughout the twentieth century, the authors of **German** manners books continued to advocate the maintenance of a 'healthy distance'. Until the 1990s, the word privacy was virtually non-existent in German. The word *Privat* (private) was known, but refers to the domestic sphere as opposed to the public sphere. The right to privacy conceived of as the right of each individual to be left alone and to maintain a personal space undisturbed by unwanted intrusions, even in the public domain, could only be expressed through a lengthy description. In the late 1980s, an author of a manners book even denied the existence of such a right when answering the question 'Is it really correct for a colleague at the office to take something of alleged importance out of the drawers of someone else's desk?':

One's home is a private domain. The desk at the office, however, is part of a shared place of work. Private objects, not meant to be seen by others, do not belong there. Any object in the chain of business proceedings must be available to others at any time. When the matter is urgent, one cannot come to a stop at the desk of a colleague, just because he or she happens to be absent at that moment. (Zitzewitz, 1986: 104)

In the 1990s, the word privacy, 'Germanified' as *Privatheit*, slowly spread from the world of architects and others involved in erecting big buildings for offices, hospitals, and so forth.[6] The following quotation is from a study of changes in office planning:

> Offices and office buildings are increasingly characterised by the central concepts of *Privatheit* and interaction. The process occurs between extreme poles such as closeness and distance, bustling and serene, or connected and cut off in concentration. ... All individuals claim a private, secure, marked and secluded space, as in the private home. The office is turning into a home of a higher order. ... Appropriation of space by creating the largest possible degree of *Privatheit* is the first step towards a sense of well being at the office. (Kelter, 1991: 103–4)

An editorial article on 'das Kombi-Büro' (the Combi-Office) in the journal *Bauwelt* (Construction World) wrongly located the origins of the word privacy in the USA:

> *Privatheit*, a concept hardly known in Germany, refers to the American fundamental right to 'privacy' and the unrestricted self-fulfilment and inviolable dignity of its people as guaranteed by the Constitution. *Privatheit* research has shown that these budding conditions are one side of a coin that has the hotly debated team spirit on its other side. Team spirit, as has been acknowledged in social psychology, cannot exist without *Privatheit*. (*Bauwelt*, 1991: 228)

4.4 Diminishing Aversion to Familiarity: Increasing Social and Psychic Proximity

Familiarity used to be perceived as an intrusion, a failure to keep a proper distance. As such, it could be perceived as a specific violation of the right to privacy. I shall sketch the line of development in this sphere by focusing, first, on general warnings against familiarity and, subsequently, on the spread of manners that signal increasing acceptance of greater social and psychic proximity: the increasing use of Christian names and the informal pronoun, and the spread of 'social kissing'. In the first set of examples, direct warnings against social mixing and familiarity are given, the tone is still set by established groups attempting to maintain their superior social distance, whereas the other sets of examples show the influence of the newly integrated former outsider groups and their demand for social acceptance and proximity. Therefore, the sequence of these warnings can be interpreted to a large extent as signalling expanding processes of social integration and mutual identification, in which the sensitivities and tensions in relationships between people of different class or rank rose to the level of requiring a more constant balancing-act of involvement and detachment.

4.4.1 General warnings against familiarity

At the turn of the nineteenth century, the concept of familiarity was often used as a warning against failing to keep enough social distance. Here is an American example: 'Discretional civility does not in any way include familiarity. We doubt whether it is not the best of all armour against it. Familiarity is "bad style"' (Hanson, 1896: 70). A book that appeared in Germany and also in the Netherlands warned against familiarity as a danger to friendships:

> It quite often happens that befriended families become enemies after having spent some time together in a summer resort; or, if they succeed in avoiding enmity, that they lose some respect for each other because of having become too intimate. Indeed, 'No man is great in the eyes of his valet.' The Great Wall of China that every sensitive person should raise around himself and also around his house, would be quite appropriate here: a certain reserved distinction that no one dares to touch. (Bruck-Auffenberg, 1897: 226)

An English author warned against familiarity between acquaintances, that is, between people who 'recognize' each other:

> To ordinary acquaintances retain the utmost reserve – never allowing them to read your feelings, nor, on the other hand, attempting to take any liberties with them. Familiarity of manner is the greatest vice of society. ... In former times great philosophers were said to have demons for familiars, – thereby indicating that a familiar man is the very devil. (Millar, 1897: 85)

Twentieth-century English manners books no longer contained direct warnings against familiarity because, by that time, the Great Wall of 'reserve' had become an integral part of the social habitus of the English establishment. For open and direct references to familiarity, one has to look at manners books that appeared a few decades earlier. The following quotation, for example, is from 1861: 'Indiscriminate familiarity either offends your superiors, or else dubs you their dependent. It gives your inferiors just but troublesome and improper claims of equality' (Etiquette for All, 1861: 15, quoted in Curtin, 1987: 125). In nineteenth-century England, it had already become taken for granted that

> [t]he proud ... disdained all kinds of familiarity ... because they interpreted aloofness as a sign of strength, independence, and self-sufficiency ... The well-mannered individual was not 'familiar'; he did not intrude on others; he did not ask personal questions; he did not thrust information about himself onto others; he kept his knowledge of others to himself; he did not talk to strangers; he did not snoop or eavesdrop; and he did not stand closely to his interlocutor, talk loudly, or gesticulate wildly. (Curtin, 1987: 126–7)

While in England reserve was taken for granted to the extent that emphasizing the need for social and psychic distance, even with friends and relatives, would have been embarrassing, warning against the dangers of familiarity remained a major theme in German and Dutch etiquette books until the 1960s. Between 1939 and the 1960s, the author of the most popular Dutch etiquette book, advised: 'Under all conditions, we would do well to keep some distance. Keeping one's distance means avoiding too much familiarity. We all know that this danger exists in dealing with subordinates, but... is there such a thing as excessive familiarity with our friends and relatives? Yes!' (1939: 26). This was legitimized as follows: 'Anyone who gets too close to us sees too much, too much of the petty, too much of the not so nice side of us, and the glimpse that we thus give others into our innermost regions can be a surprisingly unpleasant one that can never ever be eradicated' (Groskamp-ten Have, 1939: 26–7). These words of caution against insufficient (psychic) distance indicate the existence of the fears that people have about themselves. A German manners book of the 1950s contains another example of such 'self-anxiety':

Being alone can be nice, refreshing and relaxing... And it can be dangerous. For it just seems to provoke 'letting oneself go'. No one is there, nobody is watching us and our fingers, our hair, our plate. No one, who by providing an obliging reference to our better, yet at present messy, inner self could call it to order again. Being alone demands more discipline than one thinks. Because all control by others is absent. (Graudenz und Pappritz, 1956, quoted in Krumrey, 1984: 485)

Apparently it was not only familiarity that could endanger the maintenance of a 'healthy' psychic distance from one's 'not so nice' and dangerous impulses and emotions. A lack of external social control could have this effect as well and set free these 'surprisingly unpleasant' forms of behaviour and feeling. The only way of constraining them was to keep aloof and stick to restricted and formal ways. This demonstration of little or no faith in the strength of internal (social) controls was in keeping with a strong emphasis on the dangers entailed by revealing one's inner self, one's secret anxieties and fantasies: the fear of 'falling', of losing respect and self-respect.

In the process of informalization and its 'emancipation of emotions' – their representation in the centre of personality, a shift from conscience to consciousness – many of the fears and fantasies that people were initially not even willing to admit to themselves were, at first covertly and then increasingly overtly, exchanged with others. In the process, the dangers of familiarity and of exchanging emotions and intimacies lost much of their sting. Many were recognized and acknowledged as part of a shared emotional condition. From the 1950s onwards, warnings against familiarity faded in all the countries under study.

4.4.2 Christian names and the informal pronoun

Another example of diminishing social and psychic distance is the spread of the use of Christian names. Early in the twentieth century, an **American** warning against such use was directed at boys and girls:

> The frequency with which young people of two sexes meet one another in coeducational schools leads them easily into the habit of calling one another by their first names, and into the worse one of adopting nicknames. ... Don't. Friendship does not mean familiarity. Indeed familiarity is the greatest foe. When a young girl allows a young man to call her by her first name, unless engaged to him, she cheapens his regard for her by just so much. (Harland and Water, 1905: 143)

In 1937, in the revised edition of her book, Emily Post in a new paragraph, entitled 'Today's Familiarity in Use of First Names', strongly advised against it:

> Surely there is little to be said in favour of present-day familiarity in the use of first names – because those at the upper end of the social scale voluntarily choose to do the very thing by which those at the lower end of the social scale are hallmarked. The sole reason why so many men and women who work prefer jobs in factories or stores to those of domestic employ is that the latter carries the opprobrium of being addressed by one's first name. It will be interesting to see whether the reversal will be complete. (Post, 1937: 32)

And

> The hallmark of the crashers, climbers and snobs is the familiarity with which they speak of persons in prominence in order to impress their hearers with their own importance. ... We know very well that there are countless people of middle age, and even older too, who seem to think that being called Tilly or Tommy by Dora Debutante and Sammy Freshman is to be presented with a cup of the elixir of youth. (Post, 1937: 33–4)

Considering the Americans' reputedly informal ways of addressing one another, it may seem surprising that these quotations can also be found in the 'completely revised' 1950 edition, and that, in the 1965 edition of this book, revised by the author's daughter-in-law, the same stance was taken, and even italicized:

> the pendulum seems to have swung too far in the other direction. First names, titles of respect, and descriptive phrases for members of the family have become a hodgepodge of informality and confusion. ... *It is in flagrant violation of good manners for children to call their natural parents by their first names*. (Post, 1965: 16–17)

In the 1975 edition, the italics were removed but now the sentence continued: '. . . and furthermore, it undermines the respect that every child should have for his mother and father' (Post, 1975: 18). However, italics did not help to halt the trend, nor did anything else. Increasingly informal adult manners and mentality did find their roots in more informal parent – child relationships, and were, in turn, reinforced by them. As Letitia Baldridge put it in the 1970s (in the edition of Amy Vanderbilt's manners book that she revised and rewrote): 'The parents' own attitude toward people in authority determines the mind-set of their children . . . Side by side with respect for those in authority should go respect for those who serve us . . . Harping parents make harping children who grow into harping parents' (Vanderbilt, 1978: 6–9). Baldridge continued the stance taken by Vanderbilt who, in the 1952 edition of her book, advised 'Be slow to use people's first names and try to let the other person take the initiative' (Vanderbilt, 1952: 213). This sentence is left unchanged in the 1958 and 1963 editions.

By the 1980s, even Mrs Post had resigned to the trend. Now, the practice was even called 'natural':

> Not many years ago anyone introducing two couples to each other would have said, 'Mr and Mrs Smith, Mr and Mrs Brown'. Today when the couples are contemporaries the first names are always included. This is natural, since most people – especially younger ones – call people of their own age by their first names as soon as they are introduced. (Post, 1984: 4)

In relating to older persons, advice was against the use of first names. Elizabeth Post demonstrated a kind of 'inverted ageism' similar to that of her mother, Emily:

> We all know people of middle age and older who seem to think that being called 'Sally' or 'Jack' by Tilly Teenager and Freddy Freshman will take them back to the same age level. 'Sally' or 'Jack' may suggest a camaraderie that 'Mrs Collins' or 'Mr Sears' does not. But one wonders how Mrs Collins would feel if she could hear those same youngsters calling her 'Old Sal' behind her back. (Post, 1984: 4)

The possibility that Mrs Collins would resent Freddy Freshman's boldness in taking the liberty to use first names was not considered. In contrast, the author of a manners book from the 1960s considered exactly this possibility:

> In many circles, it is custom to use first names immediately after an introduction. Some people do not care for this extreme informality, but, by today's standards, it is stuffy to make a point of the matter in most cases. However, if the point does need to be made, an older person need only address a breezy young first-name user casually by title and last name within the next few sentences, and so make clear that he or she prefers to follow the rules. (Miller, 1967: 392)

Between social superiors and inferiors, advice changed in the direction of a widening variability according to different situations and local customs, and according to different types of relationships, although always emphasizing reciprocity: 'Dr Parker should not call you Georgine unless he is happy having you call him Al' (Post, 1992: 8).

In **England**, authors of etiquette books showed less resistance to this trend. In 1939, Lady Troubridge clearly welcomed the new informality by calling the first chapter 'The New Etiquette is Informal'. A paragraph summoned readers to 'Accept the New Spirit!', which included 'sending cards with Christian names, this way: *"Michael and Sylvia are giving a party. Do come"*'. On the whole, 'Friendships are made far quicker now that the barrier of undue formality has been lifted, and Christian names follow swiftly on mutual liking in a way which would make old-fashioned people aghast' (Troubridge, 1939: 10–11).

Servants were usually called by their Christian names, a familiarity *de haut en bas* expressing a hierarchical benevolence that easily became degrading: 'Should your maid have the same Christian name as yourself, do not take the liberty of re-christening her without her consent!' (Troubridge, 1939: 71).

After the 1939–45 war, the spreading use of first names was observed rather coolly, even when an author noticed a huge change in these matters: 'our present-day manners would seem informal in the extreme to our Victorian grandparents, who, even after fifty years of wedlock, continued to address each other as "Mr" and "Mrs" instead of by their respective Christian names' (*Etiquette for Everyone*, 1956: Introduction). A few years later, the trend was reported again, but neither resisted nor applauded (Bolton, 1961: 124–5).

In the late 1960s, it was observed that

> Young people today consider you remote and formal if you do not call them by their Christian names on first meeting. This does not apply only to boys and girls in their teens, but to almost everyone who has grown up since the war. In offices too, the use of Christian names is spreading. (Edwards and Beyfus, 1969: 196)

In the first edition of this book (1956), the same observation was preceded by the following retrospect: 'People of an older generation who, after twenty years of close friendship, could be heard to say shyly, "Mrs Brown may I call you Isabel?" find it strange that young people today consider you remote...' (1956: 180).

In the mid-1950s, Harold Nicolson rightly attributed the spreading use of Christian names to ideals of equality and 'the essential requirement of avoiding anything suggestive of patronage', but he thought of it as 'an inflationary, and therefore vulgar, habit none the less' and he supposed that 'this engaging habit derives...from the United States'. This attribution may derive in part or even mainly from the modelling function of

American manners after World War II when the USA became the world's dominant centre of power. Nicolson's description of the changes, however, is informative:

> In my own youth, had I been addressed by my Christian name at my private or even my public school, I should have blushed scarlet, feeling that my privacy had been outraged and that some secret manliness had been purloined from me, as if I had been an Andaman islander or a Masai. ...In my own lifetime, as I have said, the feeling about Christian names has changed completely. My father would never have used the Christian name of any man or woman who was not a relation or whom he had not known for at least thirty years. My aunt called her husband by his surname until the day of his death. It was in the reign of Edward VII that the use of Christian names first became fashionable, and even then it was surrounded by all manner of precautions and restrictions. Today to address a man by his surname might appear distant, snobbish, old-fashionable and rather rude. ...
> I am often amazed by the dexterity with which actors, band-leaders, merchants, clubmen and wireless-producers will remember to say 'Veronica' or 'Shirley' to women to whom they have not even been introduced. (1955: 272–3)

The spread of this dexterity continued in the 1970s, and England's most formal manners book, authorized by Debrett's Peerage Limited, noticed: 'In many instances forms of address are in a transitional state from elaborate formality to considerable informality' (Debrett, 1976: iv). By the 1980s, the period of transition was over, and comments tended towards matter-of-fact-acceptance:

> Once, using someone's first name was a sign of family links, acceptance or long acquaintance, a goal for the would-be suitor, a mark of best-friendship, let alone a social signal that you yourself came from the same or a superior rank. In closed societies where interdependence had to combine with hierarchy, nicknames achieved the necessary closeness without overstepping the bounds of proper formality...
> Today, all such criteria are largely obsolete. The use of first names is no longer a benchmark of intimacy but the norm. (Courey, 1985: 19)

The custom even spread to 'formal introductions': 'Most people today are introduced by their Christian and surnames, in very informal situations by Christian names alone...' (Gilgallon and Seddon, 1988: 25).

Developments in Germany and the **Netherlands** were certainly in the same direction, but in comparison with England and the USA, the use of first names was less easy and general. Both countries lagged behind, the Germans more than the Dutch. The comparison is complicated, however, because both languages also allow for expressing degrees of distance and closeness by using, in the first case the formal, and in the second the informal pronoun. In the German language the formal you is *Sie* and the informal you is *Du*, while the verbs indicating the practice of saying *Sie* and *Du* are *Siezen* and *Duzen*, respectively,. In the Netherlands, the formal you is *U* or *u* and the informal is *jij, je,* or *jou*, while the verbs derive from the French, *vousvoyeren* and *tutoyeren*. In what follows, I will focus on both the use of first names and the use of the informal pronoun. Further examples of *Siezen* and *Duzen* are presented in Chapter 5, §§5.4 and 5.5, which offer an explanatory framework for understanding the German habitus.

At the beginning of the century, an author discussed the Dutch habit of children addressing their parents with the formal *U*. 'Confidentiality does not exclude courtesy and respect', she wrote, and proceeded to compare Dutch and French habits. French children call their parents *tu* and *toi* and the French do not view this as disrespectful, she wrote, for they also address the deity with these informal pronouns. In the Dutch language, this is very different, she continued. Here, no one will even think of addressing the deity in this way, and although some children do call their parents *je* and *jij*, 'my heart always shrinks upon hearing it, and I always fear that these children will soon also fail their parents in more serious ways'. She tried to illustrate how disrespectful this was by pointing to

> two ill-bred people, acquainted for some time although not for very long, and faithfully calling each other *u*. Between them a conflict arises, they lose their temper, enter a vehement quarrel, and soon you will hear how they instinctively, to quash one another in mutual contempt, start using *jij* and *jou*. This happens almost automatically, which proves that these pronouns have a more humiliating sound than the *u*. Actually, in Dutch one addresses servants with *jij* and *jou*. In French, however, this is carefully avoided. In the two languages, therefore, the matter is completely different. (Stratenus, 1909: 17–18)

Madame Etiquette (ECvdM, 1912: 87) provided similar information on Dutch forms of address.

In the 1920s, an author argued against the ongoing trend of children addressing their parents with the informal you. It 'appears to me to be completely unnecessary', she wrote, 'for creating a confidential relationship. ... In my opinion the convention of using [the formal] *u* can be maintained quite well and yet allow for a pleasantly intimate relationship' (Kloos-Reyneke van Stuwe, 1927: 50–1). Yet, the trend for children to *tutoyeren* their parents continued: 'Love and respect do not come or go with *jij* or *u*. The *jij* that the German and the Frenchman esteem enough to use it for addressing the Supreme Being, is also good enough, more than good enough, for the child addressing its father and mother' (Knap, 1961: 24).

Between 1939 and 1966, in all thirteen editions the sentence 'To waiters, ticket inspectors, porters, workers, hotel doorkeepers, salesmen and saleswomen, and so on, one does not say *je* but *U*' brought a short paragraph on *tutoyeren* to a close (Groskamp-ten Have, 1939: 275; 1966: 302).

Other authors gave similar advice, but showed moral indignation: 'From circles of care of the elderly it is repeatedly brought to our attention how denigrating it is to address old people as "granny" or "grandpa" and to *tutoyeren* them'; and 'many judges' were reported to be 'often guilty of this by addressing a defendant who ostentatiously was clearly not from better circles by the informal you'. An even stronger accusation is directed at 'the police, of all ranks', because, by addressing people in this way, 'they combine the expression of a pronounced power madness with a conscious attempt to intimidate' (Schrijver, 1959: 75–6). This author presented detailed instructions on who should initiate a change in forms of address and how it is done. In this context, she branded 'unmotivated' use of first names and of the informal you as lack of respect. In the USA, she claimed, this custom is a sign of infantilism rather than of a democratic spirit, and 'we should certainly guard against going down to the same level of infantilism' (Schrijver, 1959: 77–8).

In 1961, an author repeated the remarks on judges and policemen in slightly different words. He called it *discriminerend tutoyeren*, which is defined in general terms as: 'using an informal form of address in a balance of power that is unequal to the extent that the social inferior cannot possibly pay back in the same coin and is thus defenceless' (Knap, 1961: 20–2).

In the adapted fifteenth edition of Amy Groskamp-ten Have's manners book, published in1983, readers were addressed by the informal you, but in 1988, in the eighteenth edition, all these informal forms had been replaced again by the formal pronoun *u*. It signified the trend towards greater appreciation of form and formality. The 1999 edition, loudly took sides against the spread of *tutoyeren* and the use of first names. On the one hand, the new editor and author noticed that, 'it seems as if the *u* has been abolished, for almost everyone *tutoyeert* the other, regardless of age, function and background.' She fulminated against the custom: 'it only brings the semblance of equality; it is nothing more than a cosmetic trick that covers or distorts reality, for we are not always and everywhere equals' (1999: 58). Other authors of manners books took a less partisan view. For example: 'How much distance you keep from others is determined by the relation and the situation you are in. You can express distance by sticking to the formal *mijnheer* or *mevrouw*, by not *tutoyeren* or making personal remarks, and by relating little about yourself and your private life' (Eijk, 2000: 54). *Tutoyeren* and using first names have spread widely in the Netherlands, and on the whole the decision to use this or that form of address is no longer made according to a fixed set of rules, but has become dependent upon a cocktail of reflections on the relation – hierarchy, age, sex, social proximity – and the situation – time, place, public, private. The variety of possibilities invalidates any attempt to take a general position, for in this respect, too, the code of manners had become increasingly transformed from a more or less fixed set of rules into a variety of flexible guidelines.

In **Germany**, a similar process of social equalization via diminishing social and psychic distance was lagging behind. *Duzen* (the use of the informal you) and the use of Christian names remained quite restricted until the 1950s, from which time onwards repeated complaints about too hastily crossing these important borderlines signified the presence of the informalizing trend. The Nazi period did bring a few remarkable changes, such as 'That the formerly most usual "yours truly" [*hochachtungsvoll*] has been replaced by "Heil Hitler" surely is obvious' (Franken, 1937: 318), but none lasted after World War II. In the 1960s, informalization broke through, although leaving clear traces of ambivalence:

> Today, the *Du* no longer has the rarity value it had thirty or fifty years ago. Surely, in this respect, too, the shared experience of two World Wars did a lot to flatten the boundaries that the *Sie* used to erect between people. Nevertheless, the confidential *Du* should remain a decoration... only used for those with whom we are bonded in love and friendship. ... In this respect too, youth of today is much freer. They call each other by their Christian names and use the informal pronoun [*duzt sich*] directly after becoming acquainted. (Haller, 1968, quoted in Krumrey, 1984: 487)

In 1973, in a lengthy paragraph written along similar lines, an author said: 'The *Du* is the exception' (Wachtel, 1973: 98), but eight years later, precisely this sentence was deleted from the next edition. In it, the rules that had earlier been presented explicitly as inviolable – older proposes the *Du* to younger, man asks woman for the *Du* – were still rendered, but made toothless by this addition: 'these rules used to prevail. In the meantime, people no longer think so rigidly... and allow spontaneity to prevail' (Schliff, 1981: 87; for some reason the two editions have different authors). Both editions proposed the intermediate solution of sticking to *Sie* in combination to the use of each others' Christian names: 'In offices, this produces a kind of communication that is no longer so formally stiff, and yet a degree of distance is retained.' Both editions also contained a wry remark on a particular use of *Du* that is 'apparently inexterminable', the one used by

> pretentious authorities, the *Du* of cocksure *Herren* in disguise – with office workers, guest workers (in former times it used to be the serfs). This jovial *Du*, a mixture of 'you bunch of weaklings' and 'we are all travelling in the same boat', proves to be a particularly cunning form, because those addressed with this *Du* cannot defend themselves (or do not want to). (Wachtel, 1973: 97–8; Schliff, 1981: 86–8)

In 1986, an author answered a question raised by parents who wanted to address their son-in-law with *Du* and did not know how to proceed: should they offer it to him or should he ask for it? The answer was that primordial custom has it that the older one proposes to the younger, but that luckily nowadays no one is that strict any more: 'Whoever wants to propose the *Du* can do so' (Zitzewitz, 1986: 127).

Another author gave as a rule of thumb: when in doubt, *Siezen* is clearly preferred (Schönfeldt, 1987: 37). Addressing the question of whether or not to propose the *Du* at a wedding to the rest of the family, she advised that all this is voluntary, of course, for 'no one can be obliged to *duz* a relative stranger only because someone in one's own family has married someone of the other one's family'. Those who want to, however, were instructed that the proper moment to do so is after dessert when drinking a glass of champagne or Sekt. This moment was also mentioned as proper for offering to use Christian names (here, a lady offers this to a man) (Schönfeldt, 1987: 53–7).

A habitual warning in German manners books is the one against becoming too confidential and going too far by starting to *duz* at office excursions and parties. For if it happens,

> it is difficult to reverse anything. The next day, a quite self-confident man may say: Well, dear chap, yesterday was yesterday, and today I prefer to address You as Herr Soandso again! If you don't think you are capable of doing this yourself, you might withdraw to the erring tactic and fall back to the *Sie* all the time until he or she realises that the *duzerei* is not going to endure anyway. (Schönfeldt, 1987: 273)

Again and again, people were advised to gather the courage to talk honestly about it in a way 'that does not make anyone feel hurt. After all, everybody knows that a brain under the influence of alcohol functions differently than the rational "working head"' (Wolff, 1995: 45).

Similar extensive advice was given by all authors throughout the rest of the century. And although there were some small but significant changes, *Siezen* and *Duzen* remained important distinctions. This was emphasized in several ways, as for instance: 'On the day a young person is no longer indifferent whether to be addressed with *Du* or *Sie*, he has come to the full consciousness of his own personality. ... He begins to distinguish between intimates, friends and acquaintances, good acquaintances, cursory or passing acquaintances, and strangers' (*Umgangsformen Heute*, 1988: 85). The same page contains a sort of confirmation that a woman or girl had acquired the right to say to a man: 'Dietmar, please, just call me Irmela!' It was commented upon as being 'A small but real step towards female initiative.' This book is one of many of this period in which the transitional phase of using the Christian name and the *Sie* is discussed favourably.

In 1993, a return to formality and *Siezen* (the formal you) was reported: 'Today, the motto in modes of address is again "Distance and Difference"' (*Spiegel*, 1993). Indeed, in the 1990s, the authors of manners books tended to write more pages on *duzen* rather than less, and to specify a variety of relationships: when coming of age, at work with colleagues, with strangers (don't!), and with relatives (at engagements and marriage parties). An author specified the moment at which a young boy or girl is entitled to the *Sie* as lying somewhere between the age of sixteen and eighteen. At that age, 'a young person can claim equalisation' (Uffelmann, 1994: 19), an equalization that in this case means being entitled to a larger social and psychic distance. This transition was discussed at length. This author acknowledged that many young people at the university, in the Disco, and so forth, use the *Du* instantly, even before knowing each other's name, but that was depicted as something completely different from the transition from *Du* to *Sie* or from *Sie* to *Du*. In the latter case, this author saw a kernel of truth in the old saying: '*Du* and I, we understand each other so well – we should say *Sie* to each other' (1994: 258–9). The same goes for *duzen* among colleagues. A social arbiter admitted that working in a team with a good team spirit easily leads to a rather general *duzen*, but added that this should never become a group constraint. In this context, she reported that a survey comparing answers from 1980 and 1993 showed an increasing number of people who dislike to be *geduzt* by a stranger (Wolff, 1995: 64).

Apparently, a large variety of subtle differentiations of proximity and distance – of involvement and detachment – endured, even tended to increase, together with elaborate rules for transitions between public and private, *Sie* and *Du*, as is shown in the following quotation:

> The social kiss is not to be considered a step towards saying *Du* to each other … Such little kisses on the cheeks have no other significance than 'We like you and you are now recognised as one of our acquaintances!.' In these cases one might use Christian names, but they are certainly no indication that one may automatically start to *duzen*. (*Umgangsformen Heute*, 1988–90: 94–5)

4.4.3   Social kissing

From this warning it follows that social kissing was accepted, even in relatively formal Germany. In 1988, this warning may have been rather new, but the social kiss was not. In 1973, for instance, one could read: 'In circles of artists this way of greeting each other is very popular – something one should know. If one doesn't, a person thus greeted will stand there feeling a little silly and shy' (Wachtel, 1973: 47). In 1977, in a new edition of the same book, this passage was revised:

> In circles of artists this way of greeting each other *was* very popular [italics added]. In the meantime this social kiss has also become endemic at the better kind of party. In general, there seems to be a wide disposition and willingness to kiss and be kissed. The stars on stage and television show how one should do it, and even football players … give their emotions free reign, when they want to express their completely uninhibited joy. What once gave offence to the highest degree has long since become something taken for granted in our 'permissive society'. (Schliff, 1977–81: 41)

Social kissing spread in all the countries studied; here are two examples from the Netherlands:

> We do an awful lot of kissing nowadays. Much more frequently and much more easily than we used to. (Groskamp-ten Have, 1983: 175)

> In the Netherlands too, men and women nowadays exchange more kisses than ever in a thousand years of civilisation . . . The custom originated in the world of fashion, went across to the theatre, was taken up by the world of television, and has established itself today in almost every layer of society . . . The number of kisses is also on the way up: twenty years ago, one kiss would do, ten years ago, kissing twice was on its way up, and today, it has become fashionable to kiss three times – a custom that spread from the South of the Netherlands. If the present inflation continues, it is hard to predict where this all will end. (Loon, 1983: 75)

The origin of social kissing was located either in a foreign country (or, as in the Netherlands, in the South, which since it is Burgundian and Roman Catholic, is for many people in the provinces of Holland equivalent to a foreign region) or in what was called 'the world of fashion', among actors and other artists. The latter also happened to be the first people who, although they lacked any 'old family' connections or possession of wealth, were accepted in good society. Late in the nineteenth century, an American author wrote: 'Lord Chesterfield attempts to divide good society into two classes – those who lead in courts and the social world, and those who possess merit or talent and who excel in some art or science' (Bradley, 1889: 316). And a late-nineteenth-century English author wrote: 'By far the most important thing to be attended to is *ease* of manner' (Millar, 1897: 85). In the 1920s, another such indication can be seen in the observation: 'Notice the easy way in which the Stage has joined with the Peerage – obviously because the essential Stage training teaches good manners, correct speech and social actions, and also a careful toilet and a graceful walk' (Terry, 1925: 11; see also Elias, 1998 [1935]: 31). The acceptance and success of the stage in Society depended mostly on what today would probably be called 'personality', that is, their command of a 'presentation of self' that is experienced as attractive or even as irresistible. In this world, competition in self-regulation, in aristocratic ease and confidence, has probably been relatively fierce, and awareness of self-regulation stronger. The continuation of this kind of competition makes it plausible that 'social kissing' originated within these circles.

Comments upon 'social kissing' can be read as examples of an increasing pressure to avoid expressions of social and psychic distance. Apparently, this was a reversal of the nineteenth-century trend towards avoiding expressions of intimacy, at least in public. At the turn of the century, kissing in public was generally reproached. German authors were quite restrictive in their advice on the subject: 'Only when meeting or parting can a kiss be given in public. General kissing on particular occasions makes a repulsive impression' (Adelfels, 1900, quoted in Krumrey, 1984: 471). In the USA, at the end of the nineteenth century, the tide against kissing in public was strong, too: 'The kiss is empathically the language of affection, and as all public displays of affection are regarded as ridiculous, people of refinement shrink from them. . . . [I]t is generally felt that kissing in public displays both a want of delicacy and a want of sense' (Bradley, 1889: 36).

By the 1950s, however, in all the countries under study here, there was greater acceptance of kissing in public again, but its meaning as an act of affection was mixed and supplemented by another meaning, as a 'social kiss'. Social kissing had also become a demonstration of equality and intimacy: 'Oddly enough, although the English are rather reticent about shaking hands, certain of them are growing tremendously keen on saying "Hello" and "Goodbye" with a social kiss. Affectionate though this is, the gesture we are speaking of is no more than a peck on the cheek' (Edwards and Beyfus, 1956: 199).

In the 1960s, social kissing had also spread in the USA: 'The social "kiss" – a touching of the cheeks – is widely used today between people who are no more than affectionate acquaintances' (Miller, 1967: 362). The following comment placed social kissing and intimate kissing on a continuum:

> Kissing is taken so casually in some places that it is the accepted greeting among adults, and the expected 'Good night' among young people. A kiss of greeting or farewell can be anything from an affectionate nuzzle, a peck on the cheek, a tender meeting of lips, to a Hollywood production. (Duvall, 1968: 187)

These matter-of-fact observations were an exception to the rule which was to show ambivalence, a stance in between matter-of-fact reporting and a half-hearted distancing. Quite often, the ambivalence revealed the fear of rejecting others by refusing them social and psychic proximity, that is, equality. Here are more American examples:

> In the United States, there is a great deal of kissing of every imaginable kind. *Time* magazine, February 7, 1977, in an article called 'The Great Kissing Epidemic' by Lance Morrow, quoted sociologist Murray Davis of the University of California at San Diego: 'Increased kissing is a part of the general inflation of intimate signals. We kiss people we used to hug, hug people we used to shake hands with, and shake hands with people we used to nod to. Not to kiss or hug means one is not "relating". Isolated individualism is out. Today separation is not allowed. Everyone is expected to kiss everyone else.' (Landers, 1978: 671)

> Kissing has become almost *de rigueur* when greeting friends and even acquaintances. A handshake seems too formal in our informal world, and the social kiss has taken its place. (Ford, 1980: 33–4)

Miss Manners heartily joins you in deploring the debasement of both the dignified American greeting of the handshake and the intimacy of the kiss. (Martin, 1983–90: 65)

Given below are some quotations from English manners books, the first from the mid-1980s when social kissing was reported to be 'now the rule rather than the exception':

In most major metropolitan centres, the kiss has virtually replaced the handshake as the social *ave atque vale* of our times... Most favoured embrace today is the double kiss... although in some circles it is already being replaced by the triple kiss. In Manhattan they kiss on the lips – turning the other cheek to a New Yorker could be interpreted as a snub. (Courey, 1985: 21–2)

(in a chapter called *Lip Service*) Social kissing has arrived. It didn't have to wait for the Channel Tunnel to open. ... Nowadays few ask themselves 'Do we?' The question today is: 'One cheek or two?'... In my youth unnecessary kissing suggested theatrical leanings, or a flaw in the Anglo-Saxon pedigree. (Graham, 1989: 15)

Q. What is the correct sound to emit when kissing a friend by way of greeting or farewell?... A. It seems that 'Mwa!' has recently been superceded by 'Mwu!'. 'Mmm!' is currently not acceptable. (Killen, 1990: 50)

The belief that social kissing originated on the Continent and came to England from there was quite commonplace. In 1992, for instance, Drusilla Beyfus wrote: 'Social kissing has made the leap over the Channel' (Beyfus, 1992: 340). Similarly, in the USA it was believed that social kissing originated in Europe; Elizabeth Post, for instance, wrote about 'the European custom of kissing (either in the air or with contact) both cheeks. Some people even utter 'kiss kiss' as they perform this rite' (Post, 1992: 4). Placing the origin abroad, adds to the mocking, half-hearted acceptance of social kissing, as demonstrated by Dutch, English, and American authors. The ambivalence follows probably most clearly from the contrast in the genesis of social kissing, located in a world outside one's own, on the other side of national and social borderlines, whether abroad or in 'the world of fashion'.

This ambivalence can be contrasted to the positive attitude of a German author who took the ascent of social kissing as evidence for his view that 'relationships between people are being moulded in ways that are essentially more natural and less uptight' (Wolter, 1990: 10). Notwithstanding the reported return to formality, this evaluation is in line with that of most other late-twentieth-century German authors, who sincerely invited their readers to do away with uptight formalities: 'We are against empty formalities as a substitute for humane behaviour... Let us learn to have conversations with each other without having to know who and what we are! This only requires trust in all possible participants in a conversation, all fellow men, whatever their occupation or education!' (*Umgangsformen Heute*, 1988–90: 10–19).

However, no matter how one evaluated this process, most social arbiters seemed to realize that more informal codes of behaviour and feeling cannot be equated with easier codes. After the moral exclamation, 'Every authoritarian abuse of power is evil,' these German authors stated explicitly, 'We loathe constraint and drill, and with endurance and patience, we consciously choose the *difficult road*' (*Umgangsformen Heute*, 1970: 24, italics added). Not only was this choice seen as difficult, it was also interpreted as risky: 'Today's manners include a freedom for all to proceed in various ways, as far as tactfulness allows. This risk of choosing is better than being fossilised in yesterday's formalities. Formality is inhibiting. Smooth manners require a sense of togetherness between the generations and an understanding of fellow human beings' (*Umgangsformen Heute*, 1970: 16). Here, it was stated explicitly that abolishing formalities has given rise to the 'risk of choosing', and that the chances of making the wrong choice increase if a sense of togetherness is lacking, that is, when there is insufficient identification with others, regardless of age, sex, or class. The constraint to choose 'the difficult road' had intensified.

In a more theoretical formulation: informalization presupposes a fairly elevated level of involvement or mutual identification, and at the same time, if only because of an increased 'risk of choosing', an equally elevated level of detachment. Together, this means that informalization coincides with a rising level of the balance of involvement and detachment.

4.4.4   Instant intimacy and instant enmity

The examples of the twentieth-century trend towards social and psychic proximity such as the increase in the use of Christian names, familiar pronouns, social kissing, and having 'conversations with each other without having to know who and what we are' can be interpreted to a large extent as examples of intimate and private forms of behaviour 'going public', thus turning into what Goffman called 'a kind of intimacy without warmth' (1959: 83). This is why they are sometimes called 'instant intimacy' or 'anonymous intimacy', usually when these forms of behaviour are evaluated negatively. Notwithstanding negative evaluations, all these examples have become accepted and incorporated in the dominant code of behavioural and emotional alternatives, including the instant intimacy of the one-night stand.

In *Sex and Manners* (2004a), I demonstrated from manners books and other advice literature how, from the 1960s onward, the accepted code regarding the pace of getting closer and expressing further interest accelerated from a three times meeting before suggesting a 'spot of dinner', via a three times meeting before kissing and a three-date 'score', to the instant intimacy of a one-night stand. This development coincided with the emancipation of women and their sexuality, and with increasing acknowledgement of the principles of mutual attraction and mutual consent in courting. Thus, this increase in emotional and behavioural alternatives has run in tandem with rising demands on emotion regulation. Hence, this form of informalization has also occurred within the framework of an elevated level of mutual identification, which in turn occurred within the framework of increasing social interweaving and integration.

Most probably, the same holds for the other side of this coin: immediate verbal aggression or similar forms of what may be called 'instant enmity' or 'anonymous enmity'. These forms have also spread since the 1960s, particularly in the passing and anonymous contacts between strangers. Until then, respectable people adhered more automatically and unthinkingly to the social code which excluded such expressions. It is from this perspective that these expressions of 'instant enmity' are related to expressions of 'instant intimacy' such as the use of first names, informal pronouns, social kissing, and one-night stands. From that perspective, both instant intimacy and instant enmity appear to be expressions of an ongoing emancipation of emotions in public discussions, particularly in transient and volatile or anonymous contacts in the public sphere. This interpretation ends and has to be revised when an instant enmity turns into acts of violence.

4.5   Language Usage

Language usage was also involved in the processes of social integration and informalization. The formal national languages, since they were the languages of the dominant classes, spread to include more social classes and regions, a process in which the contrasts in language usage diminished and the prevailing code came to allow a more informal and varied usage. In the Roaring Twenties and even more in the 1960s and 1970s, informalization manifested itself in a growing tolerance of swear words, words referring to bodily functions such as sexuality and excretion or to primary impulses and emotions, and other 'vulgar' words and 'slang'. Manners books from before World War II, however, provide only limited evidence to document the informalization of language usage. The topic is not often mentioned, and most advice on language is restricted to forms of address, titles, the prevention of coarse words and expressions, and warnings not to talk about such topics as religion and politics because they were seen as potentially explosive. Yet the wave of informalization in the 1920s did leave some traces.

In the 1920s, the author of a Dutch manners book turned against the frankness of bluntly giving somebody a piece of one's mind:

> In many ways, the present coarseness of expression of modern young girls is beside the mark. It may, in a cheerful mood, evoke a smile when a girl utters an improper word, but generally no one really likes it, whether such loose-tongued talk is rebuked openly or not. Towards parents, too, the tone is often deficient. Exclamations such as 'You are a lying bitch!', shouted at a mother, are *not* unique events, alas. (Kloos-Reyneke van Stuwe, 1927: 50)

In the 1931 edition of her manners book, Mrs Post acknowledged the spread of slang usage in the USA by adding a separate, new paragraph under the heading *Slang*: 'The fact that slang is apt and forceful makes its use irresistibly tempting', but still she tried to steer a middle course in between no slang at all and very little use of slang: it should be used 'sparingly', she advised, because 'all colloquial expressions are little foxes that spoil the grapes of perfect diction, but they are very little foxes; the false elegance of stupid pretentiousness, however, is an annihilating blight that destroys root and vine' (Post, 1937: 92).

In a perceptive article on the development of ABN, 'Algemeen Beschaafd Nederlands' (literally, General Civilized Dutch, the Dutch equivalent to BBC English), the sociologist Johan Goudsblom wrote in 1964: 'Especially since World War II, there has been more tolerance of words that were still "unheard of" in civilised circles a generation ago' (1988: 28). Referring to Elias's comments on the development of bathing manners in the 1920s (Elias, 2000: 157–8), Goudsblom wrote: 'Just as the social order has proved capable of bearing the sight of bikinis, it can also tolerate a more candid choice of words. ... a spark of the common folk's laxity has permeated the bourgeois self-discipline' (1988: 28). It did not stop at that 'spark of the common folk's laxity'. This tendency continued, and as the 1960s and 1970s wave of collective emancipation and informalization got under way, the upward pressure of the emancipating groups expressed itself in even more direct and informal language usage, in a greater tolerance and appreciation for dialects and regional accents as well as in attempts to simplify spelling. This reflected the new esteem and greater confidence of these groups, their stronger focus on their own modes of conduct and their own ways of using language.

In the USA, this greater confidence of collectively rising groups expressed itself in the 1970s in, among other things, the novelty of a manners book for 'white folks' entitled, *How to Get Along with Black People*. At the time, Black was becoming Beautiful, as the slogan went, and a similar revolution took place in the usage of Black language. What used to be a stigma was turned upside down, or so it seemed, and Blacks were now counted as 'having a way with expressions'. One example presented is Mohammed Ali's well-known phrase: 'No Vietnamese ever called me nigger.' 'Younger blacks, sometimes out of a slightly defensive attitude about not being from the ghetto, are using the comfortable dialect. ... In the need to establish and keep ghetto credentials, they use language as a leveller and unifying force' (Rush and Clark, 1970: 19). 'Black is Beautiful' was not just a slogan: the premium on ghetto credentials also implied that the traditional skin colour hierarchy was turned upside down: 'A brown-skinned mulatto in her forties also commented on this changing colour status in the black community: "When I was a girl I wasn't light enough to be popular. Now – with all this 'black is beautiful' stuff – I'm not considered black enough!"' (Day, 1972: 254). More generally, that language was used as a leveller and unifying force within the whole of American society:

> There has been a great change in the language and the way we handle it. ... [N]ew, and rather general, forms of expression which have had, to say the least, a levelling effect upon upper-class speech.

Many things once automatically considered unshakably correct have been changed drastically under direct assault by the young, forcing the Establishment to make a second or third look at the way it was clinging to some conventions. (Vanderbilt, 1972: vii)

By analogy with the standard expression 'embourgeoisement of the working classes' and the 'trickle effect' (Fallers, 1954), which is better known as the 'trickle-down effect', the movement of modes of conduct from below to above may be called a 'trickle-up effect' and a 'proletarianization of the bourgeoisie' (see the last part of §2.2).

In **German** manners books, similar changes were welcomed. In the 1970s, an author observed that 'in a serious conversation between people of the same age, there are hardly any taboos left (except that big taboo in our culture: death)'. Family talk is no longer as chaste as before, he continued, while some swearword or other is thrown in the living room almost every night via the television. And he concluded: 'Today, an engaged style of conversation prevails, without the usual uncommitted blabla. . . . the ways of talking have loosened up. Speech is now informal, frank and sometimes unpolished. A spade is called a spade. . . . Tranquillity is gone, of course' (Wachtel, 1973: 153).

The changes in language usage were dealt with at somewhat greater length in **English** manners books. In the 1950s, it was noted that 'Once upon a time *not* making personal remarks either flattering or unflattering was a pillar of good form. Now it is an accepted ingredient of conversation'. Indeed, informalization of bourgeois or middle-class language usage also followed the route of transferring certain words from the private sector with its primary and informal contacts to the secondary and more formal relations of the public sector. The authors welcomed this change in the section headed 'The Triumph of the Personal Remark', and left all this unchanged in the 1969 edition (Edwards and Beyfus, 1969: 189).

Regarding the trend towards greater candour, in 1956, these authors at first took an unwelcoming stance by warning their readers:

People who suppose that public opinion allows the modern girl to say just what she likes when she likes should remember that the furore created by Bernard Shaw's 'Not bloody likely' in *Pygmalion* was only equalled by the furore created when Sir Gerald Kelly said 'Bloody Good' on TV over forty years later. (1956: 80)

In their next edition of 1969, this passage was deleted. Instead, these authors wrote:

It seems inconceivable that when we first wrote this book, the use of the word 'bloody' on television caused a public furore. One of the significant changes in manners over the last few years has been the liberalisation of attitude towards what can be said in mixed company. Candour, frankness and honesty in conversation have become admired attributes. (1969: 187)

Indeed, in 1991, when Prince Charles who was in Australia was heard to say, after the wind had blown away the first part of his speech, 'my bloody paper', it worked *for* him.

In their 1969 edition, these authors wrote that 'accents matter far less than they did, because more people accept others as they are'. According to them, it was a social milestone 'when the man who dropped aitches became Foreign Minister and scattered his aspirates with a bang all over the radio like Ernie Bevin in his famous passport speech, "I want to go where the éll I like"' (Edwards and Beyfus, 1969: 192). In the 1990s, accents were still mentioned as a sensitive topic,

> but much of the old snobbery has died. The essence of verbal communication is clear diction, and today few people are disparaged on grounds of their accent though they may be for acknowledged mispronunciations. Regional burrs and lilts are considered a positive asset, both personally and professionally, in many quarters. Even cockney has come into its own, in the media at any rate, though I doubt whether Cinderella would have won her Prince had she fled down the steps of the Palace bawling 'Oim orf'. (Beyfus, 1992: 313)

Next to swear words, accents, and personal remarks, four topics of conversation were mentioned in a retrospect of the 1980s as having once been 'discouraged in society that was both polite and mixed; servants, illness, religion and politics. There was a strict taboo in most circles on sex'. In contrast, the author continued, all these topics have become 'fair game, *as long as no one present is upset by what is said*' (Debrett, 1981: 104). And another author came up with a slightly different top three selection: 'The Great Mentionables... are those topics certain of fascinating anyone within earshot... sex, money – and childbirth' (Courey, 1985: 12).

In the **Netherlands**, as late as the 1950s, anyone who spoke with a dialect in the public sector was assumed to be from a 'simple' background (Haveman, 1952: 39–40). In the 1960s and 1970s, television played an important role in the rapid spread of ABN (standard Dutch), and from the early 1970s onwards a wide range of regional movements stood up for their own dialects and regional accents. The people involved were no longer embarrassed or ashamed of the way they talked; on the contrary, it filled them with warmth and pride: they were speaking their mother's – not their master's – tongue. In accordance with the rise in confidence, speaking with a regional accent became a way to play down and defy the social hierarchy, with the people who speak ABN at the top: 'Speaking one's own dialect... can evoke an atmosphere of intimacy and mutual trust: in this way, one gives voice both to the feeling of being different and to that of being amongst one another' (Goudsblom, 1988: 29).

In the 1970s, regional radio broadcasting stations gave the local dialects and accents of the various regions a respected and established outlet. This encouraged regionalists in demanding more respect. Literally as well as figuratively, regionalists argued, dialects are to a greater extent the *native* language than ABN, for ABN originated from these very dialects. On the basis of these ideas, the regionalists claimed that 'cultural minorities have a right to their own identity' (Kool, 1982, 1983: 2). They stressed their right to be 'different but equal', and the necessity for 'pluralism' rather than 'mass uniformity', whereas their opponents avoided these terms and stressed the fact that the collective or general 'clarity' (rather than 'uniformity') of the national language should not be endangered by the 'particularism' or the 'splintering' (rather than the 'pluralism') advocated by the regionalists.

In this miniature language conflict, the greatest victory for the regionalists was that, as of 1985, it has become possible to teach Friesian as a compulsory regional language at school. Their ideal, 'a country with a supra-regional standard language, Dutch, and in addition to it a wide range of languages and dialects of equivalent standing. . . . Unity and solidarity, with the preservation of diversity!' (Kool, 1983: 2) was thus granted a legal basis.

In the sections on dialects or regional accents in the manners books that were published in the 1980s, the influence of the regionalists was acknowledged and respected to some extent: 'And the use of our dialect? . . . If the company we are in is of mixed regional descent, we speak ABN, although it is perfectly all right for our intonation to let people know where we come from!' (Grosfeld, 1983: 91). Usually, however, the tone was less benevolent:

This is nothing but a trend in the field of language, like affecting a working-class accent to hide the fact that you have been to a university or come from a good family. The struggle for simplified spelling also attests to this desire for a candid way of life without any frills. . . . Affecting a working-class accent has gone out of fashion again, as is apparently also the case with simplified spelling. (Eijk, 1983: 34)

Another author called it 'a strange tendency towards ordinariness, a desire to adapt oneself to the language usage and the vocabulary of the masses'. She took a quite negative stance: 'Unfortunately it is too frequently overdone, and then easily degenerates into the deliberate use of vulgar language, coarse words and an abundance of expressions that happen to be fashionable' (Bakker-Engelsman, 1983: 111).

Paradoxically, the emancipation of regional languages seems to have run in tandem with changes in these languages in the direction of the standard language. Since the 1950s, the number of people who take pride in speaking their regional accent has increased, while, simultaneously, their accents have become less distinct in comparison to the standard language. The same development has been noticed in other countries; the various varieties of Austrian German, for example, have all changed in the direction of the language spoken on television (Kuzmics, 2002). In this process, contrasts in language usage diminished while a more informal and varied usage came to be accepted within the dominant code. It is a continuation of a development that was also perceived by Norbert Elias in the period he studied and which he summarized as 'diminishing contrasts, increasing varieties' (2000: 382–6).

Emancipation of regional language usage does not only presuppose a strong regional identity but also a highly developed national identity. When national integration and identification are not established firmly enough, regional identification is soon considered as a threat, branded as treason and, as such, suppressed. Only from a critical moment in the process of national integration and identification onwards can a revival of subnational identification occur without any trouble. A striking example is the fate of the Kurdish language in Turkey. In 1984, the Turkish ambassador to the Netherlands was so offended by the term 'Kurdish East' in a Dutch newspaper that he publicly expressed his 'surprise' that such a thing had been possible. In a letter to the editor he wrote 'This term is not only erroneous, but it is also extremely misleading,' and then went on to note that the population of Turkey constitutes 'an indivisible whole' and that it 'absolutely could not be tolerated' that Turkey should be divided into regions 'with arbitrary names' (*NRC-Handelsblad*, 30 May 1984). Right up until the end of the twentieth century, the Turkish authorities would not admit that there were Kurds living in Turkey, only Turkish citizens. Use of the Kurdish language in public was not allowed. Kurdish first names were not accepted in the register of births. In 1999, a few days after Turkey became a candidate member of the European Union (EU), the Turkish minister of Foreign Affairs declared that all Turkish citizens should have the right to speak in their own language on television. Increased cultural rights for the Kurdish minority, particularly the right to a television station and to teaching the Kurdish language at school, ranged among the conditions for Turkey to become a member of the EU. In 2001, the Turkish parliament accepted the EU demand for the removal of the term 'forbidden languages' from the constitution. A year later, after months of bitter debate, Turkey's parliament accepted an obligation to expand minority rights, including the right to speak the Kurdish language in radio and television broadcasts and in education. On the same day, parliament decided to abolish the death penalty (in peacetime), another major precondition for being considered as a candidate for EU membership. Apparently, the fear of Turkey's politicians of being missed out in international integration has overruled the fear of the Kurdish minority. In this case, international integration into the EU functioned as an incentive for national integration and for the emancipation of the Kurds and their language: what earlier had been branded as treason, was now legalized.

4.6   The Constraint To Be Unconstrained, At Ease, Authentic, and Natural

The examples of the twentieth-century trend towards social and psychic proximity described in this chapter – the increase in the use of Christian names, familiar pronouns, social kissing, instant intimacy and enmity, and in the use of more evocative and informal language – are examples of the process of informalization that is directly related to increasing social equality and sensitivity to inequality, to processes of social emancipation and integration. These developments have been compelling; no one was able to ignore or withdraw from its inherent constraints completely. On the other hand, many people may not even have experienced or recognized any constraint, as it is a constraint to be unconstrained. As status competition intensified and the art of obliging and being obliged became more important as a power resource, demonstrations of being intimately trustworthy while perfectly at ease also gained importance. In this sense, processes of democratization, social integration, and informalization have run parallel with an increasing constraint towards developing 'smooth manners'. The expression 'a constraint to be unconstrained' seems to capture this paradoxical development.

This expression resembles the one used by Norbert Elias: the social constraint towards self-constraint. Indeed, the two constraints are hardly distinguishable: the constraint towards becoming accustomed to self-constraint is at the same time a constraint to be unconstrained, to be confident and at ease. Almost every etiquette book contains passages that emphasize the importance of tactful behaviour, rather than demonstrative deference, and of 'natural' rather than mannered behaviour. However, in processes of emancipation and informalization, some ways of behaving, experienced previously as tactful deference, came to be seen as too hierarchical and demonstrative, just as what had once been defined and recommended as natural came to be experienced as more or less stiff and phoney and branded as mannered. It then became so obvious a 'role' in which so many traces of constraint could be 'discovered' that 'playing' this role would provoke embarrassment. People who stuck to these old ways of relating were running the risk of being seen as bores, as lacking any talent for 'the jazz of human exchange' (Hochschild, 1983). Hence, new forms of relaxed, 'loose', and 'natural' behaviour were developed.

Some writers of manners books seem to be at least vaguely aware of this process, if only because they took it for granted that 'natural behaviour' had to be learned. Full awareness was prevented, however, because of status anxiety (see the first section of Chapter 1) and 'hodiecentrism' (Goudsblom, 1977), the glorification of the actual definition of tactful and natural behaviour as the end of the history of learning to act naturally. Here is an example from 1923:

> It is essential to *learn* to appear just as much at ease in one's dress suit in the presence of Royalty as one does in one's crêpe de chine pyjamas in one's dressing room in the presence of a Persian cat. And it is necessary to *learn* to walk as if in sandals and not as if in tight boots on soft corns.
>
> *Be natural.*
>
> Go to a good tailor, even though he may seem a little more expensive... (*Etiquette for Gentlemen*, 1923: 21)

In all the countries considered in this book, this emphasis on ease and easy-goingness tempered the emphasis on 'reserve' or avoidance of familiarity.

In Britain, both sides of this tension-balance were highly developed. As was noted, 'anything that smacked of effort, awkwardness, or forethought was itself bad manners: above all things, one must be self-confident and at ease' (Curtin, 1987: 56–7). This demand clearly derived from the aristocratic tradition. Lord Chesterfield referred to 'ease' as 'the last stage of perfection of politeness'. At present, and not only in England but all over the Western world, this still remains the case, only more so.

As 'ease' and 'naturalness' gained importance and demands for individual authenticity and a socially more meaningful personal identity rose, to behave according to a set of fixed rules of manners increasingly came to be experienced as rigid and stiff and their performance as too obvious and predictable, as 'insincere', even as a 'fraud' or as 'deceit'. In its wake, for example, the mourning ritual was minimized (Wouters, 2002: 7). This means that traditional ways of behaving and regulating emotions lost part of their 'defence' or 'protective' function. The former formal codes had functioned as a defence against dangers and fears which were now diminished or could be avoided or controlled in more varied and subtle ways – ways in which both social superiority and inferiority were less explicitly and less extremely expressed. Increasing numbers of people pressured each other to develop more differentiated and flexible patterns of self-regulation, triggering a further impetus towards higher levels of social knowledge, self-knowledge, and reflexivity.

In its basic form, this observation has been made quite regularly, for example, by the author of a historical study of American manners: 'Actually, the easier manners of today, it may be argued, call for finer tact, a surer taste, than did the stiff conventions which once held sway in the citadels of privilege' (Carson, 1966: 296). Another example is from an English manners book. After having stated that 'social customs are greatly simplified and remarkably flexible; expressions of courtesy are more informal, often gaining spontaneity because of it', the author adds: 'But easing conventions does not mean that "anything goes." The ground rules are as important now as ever, perhaps more so when so many social encounters are haphazard' (Debrett, 1981: 10). In his book *Battle Ground of Desire*, subtitled 'The Struggle for Self-control in Modern America', social historian Peter Stearns concluded: 'In sum, manners became more informal while demands for systematic emotional control became more stringent. . . . Americans were told to become less stiff but more cautious' (1999: 154).

Pressure to develop a keen eye for 'the latent meaning of apparently insignificant details', for instance by examining 'the most trivial details . . . involuntary gestures, slips of the tongue' (Kasson, 1990: 94–5),[7] was part of the continued pressure in social competition and collaboration to develop the presence of mind based upon keen awareness and sensitivity for social and psychic processes and power balances. The rise of these pressures was accompanied by heated discussions about the distinction between a 'false self' and a 'real self', or between 'phoney' and 'natural' or 'authentic' behaviour and feelings. Together, rising awareness of a 'self' or an 'inner self' and growing awareness of (and pressures towards) impression management have created the experience of a distance from one's 'self' that was interpreted as a loss of one's 'true self'. Many adherents to this interpretation embarked upon the quest for a 'real' and 'enduring substance' in the self, for universal and eternal realities *behind* all these changing and changeable appearances, a quest as old as religion and metaphysics. Some came to take what might be called a zero-sum perspective on emotion regulation, a perspective which also has a long tradition; for instance, as outlined by Georg Simmel at the beginning of the twentieth century: 'punctuality, calculability and exactness become part of modern personalities *to the exclusion* of those irrational, instinctive, sovereign traits and impulses which aim at determining the mode of life from within' (quoted in Krieken, 1990: 353, 371; italics added).

The mode of life 'within' came to be seen increasingly as determined or even dictated from 'without'. However, as the management of appearance rose in importance, *both* inward and outward signals and signs have come to be scrutinized more severely and in ways more sensitive to shades and nuances. On the one hand, in the attempt to retrieve the real and natural 'true self', overt expressions of, and references to, social constraints, status differences, and status anxieties have come to be experienced increasingly as embarrassing, particularly in face-to-face contacts. On the other hand, people's sensibility to social constraints and external pressures has been rising. Either way, they exerted pressure towards developing a more intense presence of mind, and in this process, many inner rules of conscience were stripped bare or 'uncovered', made subject to consideration, and applied less automatically. It increasingly became a prerequisite to develop 'the capacity, without forcing ourselves, to have understanding for other people in the most widely divergent situations', as the authors of a Dutch manners book called it (Grosfeld, 1983: 347). Indeed, smoother and subtler navigation in social relationships, particularly through the tensions and frictions of inequalities in power and status, came to demand a controlled decontrolling of emotional controls, a self-regulation that is more highly controlled as well as more reflexive and flexible.

4.7 Levels of National Integration and Mutual Identification Compared

During the twentieth century, manners books came to address and represent more and more social groups and classes. The change seems to validate the words of the author of a 1930s German manners book:

> It would be a mistake to think that these forms and manners are the invention of one single class who, by the factitious development of certain forms and formulas haughtily aimed at some splendid isolation. These conventions have developed naturally, namely from the pursuit of eliminating areas of friction...and preventing even the possibility of quarrels or disputes emerging from them. (Dietrich, 1934: 5)

At the beginning of the period of research, however, most members of the established classes did aim at splendid isolation. Where possible, they tended to avoid the lower classes. When and where these possibilities disappeared, areas of friction and social hostility appeared, triggering accommodation processes. Accordingly, the power and the range of 'the pursuit of eliminating areas of friction' will vary with levels and degrees of social integration. On the whole, it tends to grow or shrink as networks of interdependence grow or shrink.

In her annotated bibliography of twentieth-century American manners books and articles, Deborah Robertson Hodges reported that it was not before the 1940s that an article was written on manners in the relationship between 'Negroes' and 'whites'. The fact that such a topic surfaced in this literature was indicative of the rise of a black bourgeoisie and also of a rising sensitivity to a new area of friction and social hostility between these rising outsiders and people from the more established classes. The article was called *Courtesy Across the Colour Line*. It focused on forms of address, and its author, J.H. Marion, a southerner, wrote he was 'disturbed and saddened by this tradition of racial discourtesy that is unworthy of the best in southern people'. He complained that the 'most cultured and law abiding Negroes among us are usually compelled to endure the same searing and contemptuous indignity . . . as that of the prostitute or prisoner' (quoted in Hodges, 1989: 11).

In the 1950s, as this sensitivity spread, an interest in 'interracial etiquette' emerged. In manners books, however, this interest had not yet surfaced. Amy Vanderbilt, for example, totally ignored the existence of different classes or ethnic groups in her best-selling etiquette books of the 1950s and 1960s. The situation was summarized in the early 1960s. In his popular *First New Nation*, S.M. Lipset claimed that the USA was 'a new nation which successfully developed . . . a relatively integrated social structure (*the race issue apart*) . . .' (1963: 17; italics added). At that time, this description seemed adequate: more groups of people – WASPs (White-Anglo-Saxon-Protestants) and European Americans from various social classes – had orientated themselves to the same national code of behaviour and feeling, and it was still possible to put the 'race issue' in brackets.

By the end of the 1960s, the position of Negroes, by then called Blacks, had become a national issue and social integration a national objective. Authors of manners books, however, continued to show no concern what-soever for 'interracial etiquette'. One of the rare references to Black Americans is found in *The Ann Landers Encyclopaedia* (1978), written and edited by Ann Landers, a well-known author of manners books. For this encyclopaedia, the late Senator Hubert H. Humphrey had prepared a little contribution in praise of American freedom and democracy, in which he swept this area of social hostility under the carpet of history: 'Today problems of overt discrimination and segregation based on race are relegated to the history books' (Landers, 1978: 869).

Only in the second half of the 1980s did prejudice and Black Americans come to be mentioned, although only briefly, as in an *A-to-Z Guide* under Black:

To be called 'Black' is the preference of most persons of Negro ancestry. To persist in calling them 'Negro' or 'coloured' is to risk giving offence, and is indeed probably a subtle form of racism. People have every right to be called what they wish, and polite and kind persons abide by those wishes. (Stewart, 1987: 25)

By the end of the 1980s, most etiquette books did contain some small reference to prejudice, ethnic jokes, ethnic insults, and bigotry. The 1984 edition of Mrs Post's book already reflected some significant changes by including a new section entitled 'With People Not Like You'. It contained cheering sentences such as: 'The disabled have been invited into the mainstream of life. Homosexuals are allowed to emerge from the closet. Mixed marriages are taking place every day. We have come a long way in recognising that people are individually created, not stamped from a mould in the shape of a majority group.' At this point the next section, on 'How to Deal with Prejudice,' begins, advising readers to say, 'I don't like jokes that belittle people,' or alternatively 'If you prefer, you may simply get up and take your leave' (Post, 1984: 146). Obviously, the reader is not supposed to belong to the group of belittled people. That the victims of these insults and jokes were not supposed to read these manners books was the rule, and Jews were the only exception.

In the edition of 1992, the whole section 'With People Not Like You' was deleted. Now, on just one of the almost 800 pages, the possibility was mentioned that someone *not like you* might be among the public reading the book: 'If you yourself belong to a minority group under attack, you have two courses. One, you can ignore it...Or two...Just say, "You must be talking about me, I am [whatever it is]." ' (Post, 1992: 90).

The author of one etiquette guide, 'a blond, WASP-looking, East Coast, outwardly elitist etiquette teacher' at a school 'in the heart of the highest crime-area' in Philadelphia, seemed to have succeeded in building a cultural bridge. She reported that,

unless I carefully explain that every American greeting includes a handshake and direct eye contact, my Latin American students will be lost. Neither is part of their culture and, in fact, this greeting runs counter to everything they've been taught about greetings. Once they learn that cultural greetings differ, they adjust without embarrassment and use the proper method in the proper circumstances. (Mitchell, 1994: xiii, 19–20)

Judith Martin had her successful creation of 'Miss Manners' – quite a character, judging from book titles such as *Miss Manners' Guide to Excruciatingly Correct Behavior* and *Miss Manners Rescues Civilisation* – deal with bigotry and racism briefly but efficiently. If someone tells an 'off-colour racial joke', her advice was to take control and 'to be simultaneously smooth and firmly in charge', for example, by looking

> unsmilingly around the room, finally allowing your eyes to rest on the person who told the joke. The room goes silent. Slowly, and in a conversational tone, you ask, 'Do you find that amusing?' ... Before the teller of the joke can recover enough to attempt self-defence, you say, 'But I'm sure Brian didn't mean any harm by it.' Then you turn to him and engage him in innocent social conversation that has nothing to do with what just happened. (Martin, 1996: 376–7)

Miss Manners also depicted the rather characteristic swing of the pendulum from avoiding certain people by stigmatizing them to avoiding even the smallest trace of that stigma:

> This way of talking – 'See that black gal up front?' 'You mean the presiding judge?' – was so racist in its presumption that society finally got around to recognising how rude it was. You may well argue that avoiding any such mention, when it obviously is a conspicuous identifying characteristic, is also racist. If race weren't so much on your friend's mind, she wouldn't be going that far out of her way to avoid mentioning it when offering a physical description. (Martin, 1996: 387)

This swing of the pendulum seems an initial stage in the process of social avoidance being internalized, a transformation from avoiding classes of people to avoiding layers of feeling: feelings of superiority. It signifies an early stage in a process of social integration. By the end of the 1980s, a small rejection of prejudice or bigotry had become 'politically correct'. Apparently, groups of outsiders had succeeded in forcing the established to take more of their feelings and interests into account (Elias and Scotson, 1994).[8]

Another symptom of a particular phase in a process of emancipation and social integration was the emergence of a separate specialized genre of manners books for 'multicultural' situations and relations, with titles such as *Different Worlds* (Bode, 1989), *Multicultural Manners* (Dresser, 1996), and *Basic Black*. *Basic Black* addressed the black community as 'our community', and provided 'good old "home training"' (Bates and Hudson, 1996: 3). Usually, the tone of introductions into these specialized manners books was quite matter of fact: 'This book is based primarily on talks I had with teenagers across the country. Nearly all are dating someone whose race or background is different from their own' (Bode, 1989: 11), and: 'Our title, *Swaying*, suggests both the problem, the instability of these intercultural relationships, and its provisional solution, flexibility. It suggests a bending between different realities, different worlds, a movement that is graceful but suggests uncertainty, insecurity, even trouble' (Grearson and Smith, 1995: xv). In 1999, *Race Manners: Navigating the Minefield Between Black & White*

Americans was launched as the first book of its kind, namely a manners guide written for all Americans, black and white (Jacobs 1999). It was reviewed at the Amazon Internet site by someone from San Diego who wrote: 'Sad to say, but I found this book ONLY in the African-American section of a bookstore. This is an ironic twist for a book designed for all people, regardless of color.'

The fact that a segregated genre of manners books had come to exist next to mainstream manners books may be seen as a continuation of segregation, but it certainly was a segregation by different means. It points to the rise of a middle class of African Americans and their leap forward in the processes of emancipation and social integration. This was sharply contrasted, however, by the withdrawal of companies, public institutions, and most functions of the American state from several neighbourhoods, thus stimulating the formation of groups of urban outcasts living in ghettos. In the 1990s, in addition to the growing segregation of the unemployed ghetto poor, the spread of multiculturalism created an impression of a process of disintegration, a 'disuniting of America'. In his book of that title, Arthur M. Schlesinger Jr mentioned the relatively open competition in the USA as one of the 'disuniting' forces: 'Mutual suspicion and hostility are bound to emerge in a society bent on defining itself in terms of jostling and competing groups' (Schlesinger, 1992: 60). However, as these competing groups had become increasingly interdependent, the *balance* between mutual suspicion and hostility on the one hand, and mutual confidence and sensitive understanding on the other – between detachment and involvement – was under constant pressure in both directions, disuniting as well as uniting. The latter pressure has a good chance of getting the upper hand: as mutual interests expand, emotion regulation will follow.

Schlesinger feared the 'separatist impulse': 'The bonds of cohesion in our society are sufficiently fragile, or so it seems to me, that it makes no sense to strain them by encouraging and exalting cultural and linguistic apartheid' (1992: 138). On the contrary, I believe that these bonds of cohesion had expanded to the extent that an 'emancipation-via-segregation' outlook and strategy (Stolk, 1991) had become both conceivable and to some extent socially possible. This outlook and strategy are symptomatic of a particular moment or phase in an integration process. Similar phases can be discerned in the emancipation movements of women, homosexuals, and speakers of 'regional' languages (see the above discussion on the Friesian and Kurdish languages). In my book *Sex and Manners*, this strategy of 'emancipation-via-segregation', as propagated and practised by the women's movement, is also presented as symptomatic of a particular phase in a process of emancipation and integration (Wouters, 2004a).

In her *War-Time Supplement* to the 1942 edition of her etiquette book, Emily Post expressed the Janus-faced pressure towards both uniting *and* disuniting, or, as she saw it, the pressure to simultaneously develop a higher level of mutual trust *and* distrust. Although she addressed a specific wartime problem, her formulation would need little change to be

97

generally applicable to the established–outsider relations within and between nation-states:

> Because in us Americans flows the blood of every race and creed, there is no other country in the world where there is so great a need of wise appraisal; of sensitive understanding of our fellow Americans. The Janus-faced difficulty of this most important aspect of wartime etiquette is on the one side, the need for alertness lest enemy wolves in white lamb's clothes take us unawares; on the other side is the equally great need to avoid mistrusting those who are completely loyal. (1942: 877)

Most probably, since World War II, the development of the prevailing balance of mutual trust and distrust – and of involvement and detachment – has been related not only to America's history of open competition, but may be even more strongly to its comparatively low level of social integration. The latter and its correspondingly relatively high level of mutual distrust have permeated and fuelled both McCarthyism and the Civil Rights Movement, and, more generally, the American habitus and identity (see §§5.15–5.18, also Wouters, 2004a: §8.1).

In response to a 'gentle reader' who had experienced an hour of America bashing (of unspecified provenance and content), Miss Manners came up with nine polite and possible reactions, for example: 'I'm sorry you feel that way. You ought to have the American experience while you're here, and that involves a certain attitude of easygoingness and tolerance and openness. I'd hate to have you go home never having really been here' (Martin, 1990: 700). None of the reactions suggested by Miss Manners was related in any way to class or ethnicity; that part of the USA is cut-off from polite discussion and polite consciousness, or rather, it is 'compartmentalised', as Anna Freud and Abram de Swaan would have it (Freud, 1966 [1936]; Swaan, 2000). The concept refers to a psychic *apartheid* that corresponds to a degree of social *apartheid*; it is a psychic defence mechanism that develops when and where direct attacks and other openly displayed ways of social defence are subjected to shaming processes in which they eventually become counterproductive and more or less automatically avoided and/or compartmentalized. In a book on the history of American manners, Judith Martin provided more characteristic examples of compartmentalization. With one hand, she wrote: ' "All men are created equal" ... The people who signed on to that phrase certainly did not intend "all" to mean *everybody*. Slaves and Indians failed to make the cut'. And with her other hand, she wrote: 'We also have vigilant forces to keep the hoity-toity in line, although the weapon used to spread fear has never been the guillotine or the gulag, only the sharp edge of American satire' (Martin, 2003: 99, 21).

The European countries under study have had far fewer immigrants, although the numbers of them have been growing rather rapidly since the 1960s. However, I know of no similar genre of separate emancipation books for ethnic minority groups. In Britain, the Netherlands and Germany, most immigrants have arrived since the 1960s. They came from former colonies and/or relatively poor countries on the fringe of Europe. Moreover, as slavery was not practised in Europe itself after the eighteenth century, there are few descendants of imported slaves among its inhabitants. Nor is there much of a 'minority' or 'residue' of indigenous peoples defeated in colonizing processes. It seems significant that since the 1970s, most German and Dutch best-selling manners book have paid some attention to guest workers and other recent immigrants by providing information on specific differences in behaviour and emotion regulation in a separate section or chapter. Until the end of the century, however, authors of English manners books have largely avoided writing about ethnic minorities. One English author did include some information – five sentences – on Moslem rites in a chapter on first and last rites (Beyfus, 1992: 141–2). And in the chapter on marriage, after having mentioned the freedom for people to choose their own spouse, Beyfus wrote: 'It is a Western idea which is still questioned today by Islam's adherence to the custom of arranged marriages' (1992: 40). That is all. Until 2002, when a new volume of *Debrett's Correct Form* appeared with a synopsis that said: 'there is recognition of the more multicultural nature of society today'.

Some of the Dutch manners books of the 1980s and 1990s contained no reference to immigrants at all (Groskamp-ten Have, 1983, 1988, 1999). Others had a whole chapter (Grosfeld, 1983; Eijk, 2000) or several paragraphs (Eijk, 1983) on the subject. The information concerned the manners and customs (giving presents, visiting, family, eating, conversation, expression of emotions), religions, and holidays of Turks, Moroccans, Surinamese, Moluccans, Indonesians, and political refugees. German authors often opposed addressing 'guest workers' or 'our colleagues of foreign descent' with the informal *Du*: 'Although we are usually rather reserved in this matter, here the *Du* springs from our lips without difficulty. How shameful!' It is called rude, and the defence that it is 'only a habit' is severely questioned. 'Oh no, my dear colleagues, claiming the right to address foreigners in this way springs entirely from our own arrogance' (Löwenbourg, 1987: 71). This author also has a little discourse on chauvinism:

> For quite a few years now, one has unfortunately been able to observe a steady growth of regrettable chauvinism in our midst. Today, we have to put up with slogans like 'Turks go home', and with fanatic football fans using the Hitler salute while furiously setting on and beating up any foreign-looking individual. Slowly but surely the ground is being prepared again for the kind of chauvinism that brings the crest of evil. Was it really not enough what we did in the past? (1987: 64)

Another German book contains two pages on 'guest worker colleagues', which includes the sentence: 'To *duzen* a guest worker or even his wife without being friends with them may have very nasty consequences' (*Umgangsformen Heute*, 1988: 237–8). Another author deplored 'discouraging remarks' towards 'foreign fellow citizens' and claimed that the German culture obliges people to engage in 'tolerance, not bigotry, and sensible benevolence' (Wolter, 1990: 57–8).

Systematic comparison of what has been written – and what not – about on the one hand these 'new' lower classes in the European countries, and on the other what was written on the 'old' lower classes throughout the twentieth century, is beyond the scope of this book. But it would certainly bring more detailed knowledge of the many phases of emancipation and accommodation in established–outsider relations (Elias, 1994). To read (and translate) the words 'sensible benevolence', for instance, immediately reminded me of similar words being used in similar unequal balances of power between social superiors and inferiors, both in the nineteenth and first half of the twentieth century. To the ears of people who are involved in rather explosive emancipation and integration battles, such as Turks and Turkish Kurds or European Americans and African Americans, an expression such as 'sensible benevolence' may sound either like naïve meekness, or like blatant conceit, depending on which side they are on.

5

Introductions and Friendships, Forms of Address, and Other Differences in National Habitus Formation

5.1 **General Outline of National Developments**

The comparison of American, Dutch, English, and German manners books reveals several significant national differences not only with regard to a variety of specific topics but also to the genre as a whole. In this chapter, a few of these differences will be discussed, particularly those that illuminate specifics in national habitus formation.

Since the USA was a 'new nation' with an enormously varied population, ranging from black slaves to rich landowning and commercial patricians – but no formal, hereditary aristocracy – its integration processes differed in many ways from those in 'old nations'. Usually, the lack of any hereditary ruling group is held to account for the easy-going conduct that is so often portrayed as typically American. This conduct, however, originated from court society:

> While our [American] rejection of the magnificent and the grandiose and our preference for ease and informality are probably influenced by levelling and democratic ideas, the fact remains that the easy style was an invention of an aristocratic age and was meant to exalt its possessors above his fellows, not to bring him down to their level. (Curtin, 1987: 110)

In Chapter 4, the development of the easy style was presented as a product of a courtly civilization. It was suggested that it continued to function as a means for demonstrating and attaining social success. Easy-going conduct was sought-after in all the countries under study; it was at most more conspicuous in the USA. As a 1992 advisory on success puts it, 'Yes, there are little "tricks of the trade" in meeting and greeting people and learning to become at ease and casual in social situations' (Cunningham, 1992: xi). This is a twentieth-century example of a process-continuity; it is in fact similar to the process that occurred in the late eighteenth century, when 'the middling sort repudiated the basis of aristocratic power even as they seized the aristocratic armour of manners and remade it for their own purposes' (Hemphill, 1996: 321). In each country under study, appropriating the manners of superior groups has again and again facilitated the rise of subordinate groups.

Comparisons between new and old nations have often been ideologically inspired to the extent that all old nations are lumped together after the model of England and France. Thus, the fact that countries such as Germany and the Netherlands also have strong middle-class characteristics in their national habitus is generally neglected. In the Netherlands, rich merchants became the ruling class at a very early date. In 1581, their separatist movement succeeded in freeing the country from king and aristocracy. It has been reported that both the contents and the history of the Dutch freedom charter, het *Plakkaat van Verlatinge* (Declaration of Secession) of 1581, contain striking similarities to the American *Declaration of Independence* of 1776 (Coopmans, 1983). Since 1581, merchant patricians have been the dominant class in the Netherlands, although this ruling group had come to function more or less as an aristocracy by the end of the seventeenth century when they attempted to regard themselves 'as the equals of Crowned Heads'. This 'process of aristocratisation' (Spierenburg, 1981) was not unique to the Netherlands. In the USA, too, after the decline of a 'Southern aristocracy' before and during the Civil War, ruling classes again attempted with some success to function as an aristocracy (Baltzell, 1964). The Dutch patricians, however, continued to keep close ties to the world of commerce, and consequently, the Dutch national code of manners and emotion regulation is highly permeated by middle-class characteristics. As early as the 1850s, the American historian John L. Motley compared the Dutch struggle for independence with that of the United States; and in 1968, Johan Goudsblom went so far as to suggest that S.M. Lipset (1963) was wrong in calling the United States *The First New Nation* (1967: 154).

In what was to become Germany, bourgeois classes and aristocratic circles remained highly segregated until the unification in 1871; accordingly, different habituses developed in the two groups. Particularly from 1871 until World War II, the bourgeois habitus amalgamated with certain elements of the aristocratic code into a German national habitus. However, lacking one central court and the development of a pacified courtly code like those in England or France, these elements were more directly related to an aristocratic warrior code than to an aristocratic courtly civilization. As Norbert Elias observed,

> it is military values which have once again grown deep roots in the German tradition of behaviour and feeling. In regard to his own honour, the honour of his country, his Kaiser, his Führer, the officer cannot make any compromises. ... Complete determination, absolute loyalty to principles, uncompromising adherence to one's own convictions, still sound particularly good in German. (1996: 296; also on compromising: 113, 133, 163, 199)

An American manners book from 1943, addressing German Americans and Germans who were trying to become Americans, contained significant information on this subject:

> Americans on the whole are less likely to be *rechthaberisch* and to ride principles than Germans. They frequently appear to be, and frequently are, less interested in WHO was right or WHAT was

right in a given situation, right ethically and morally, than in getting on with the job at hand – if by a set of principles agreed upon, well and good – if not, by compromises that are arrived at by various methods and devices. Such behaviour, which is common also to the British, is often described by Germans as hypocrisy. . . . Discussions in American professional groups are as a rule characterised by much less intensity in the stressing of one's point of view, and often by an avoidance of the real issue. The manner of debate is usually suave, even when vital issues are at stake. When a decision has been reached, both sides of the contesting groups are likely to accept it in good spirit. (Whyte, 1943: 146)

At this point, the argument turned into a lesson in the principles of democracy, and compromise was declared to be central in this regard. A few pages further on, the author again stated that 'Germans are normally more reluctant than Americans to compromise,' and continued to explain the advantages of compromising:

The spirit of compromise which is characteristic of American (and British) legislative bodies and political life may . . . be considered either a pillar of strength of American civilisation or its glaring structural weakness. The overwhelming American opinion is that the disposition to compromise makes in the long run for a rough kind of justice and safeguards democracy. . . . Everywhere there is the disposition to avoid head-on collisions and to reach compromises before bitter feelings are aroused or serious wounds are inflicted. (Whyte, 1943: 153–4)

Since World War II, the uncompromising attitude, this element of a warrior code, has receded, and a 'revised' middle-class habitus has become the German national habitus. A clear example of this process is found in the frequently reprinted *Good Manners are Back Again* (*Man Benimmt Sich Wieder*). After depicting a skilful negotiator as a *'typischer Kompromißler'* [typical compromiser], the author continued:

This expression *'typischer Kompromißler'* is used deliberately because it is taken to be a reproach in our country, whereas a 'good compromiser' to most other peoples is a highly respected and very esteemed man, whose person and *'kompromißliche'* abilities are in demand and praised. As against what once used to be the case, we have to become clearly aware of this sharp contrast between German and foreign views on the importance attached to 'partly giving in'. We view, or used to view, rigid insistence upon a total claim as proud, brave and masculine, whilst the rest of the world views it as foolish and destructive, because it blocks any negotiation from ever producing results that are satisfying for both parties, while it generally rules out living together harmoniously. (Meissner, 1951: 242)

In England, an early development of a parliamentary regime during the eighteenth century implied the development of a readiness to compromise. A relatively high level of this readiness is presupposed for ruling classes to come to peacefully hand over ruling power to opponents, trusting them to abstain from using this power to humiliate, oppress, or destroy them.

> In England, the parliamentary regime not only allowed open contests between rival factions but made it *necessary* that they should come out into the open. Social survival and most certainly social success in parliamentary society depended on the capacity to fight, but to fight, not with dagger or sword, but with the power of argument, the skill of persuasion, the art of compromise. (Elias in Elias and Dunning, 1986: 37)

Throughout the nineteenth century, rich middle-class newcomers were allowed into the centres of power and their good society, provided they knocked at the appropriate doors in the appropriate ways. This way of integrating *nouveau riche* helped make good society a unified and strong social and political centre. Thus, the integration of new classes into society coincided rather with collective and non-conflicting changes in the English national code of conduct and affect-control:

> In the making of this English code, features of aristocratic descent fused with those of middle-class descent – understandably, for in the development of English society one can observe a continuous assimilating process in the course of which upper-class models (especially a code of good manners) were adopted in a modified form by middle-class people, while middle-class features (as for instance elements of a code of morals) were adopted by upper-class people. Hence, when in the course of the nineteenth century most of the aristocratic privileges were abolished, and England with the rise of the industrial working classes became a nation state, the English national code of conduct and affect-control showed very clearly the gradualness of the resolution of conflicts between upper and middle classes in the form, to put it briefly, of a peculiar blend between a code of good manners and a code of morals. (Elias, 2000: 428)

The sociologist Kuzmics similarly concluded that: 'Knightly-aristocratic reserve and an autonomous single individual suiting the market seem to be fused together to warrant the high degree of affective control that is often viewed to be "typically English"' (1993: 124).

5.2 The German Habitus in Comparison with the American Habitus: Public and Private

Particularly in comparison with its German counterparts, the American (and English) national habitus has been characterized by an open and confident attitude towards the public (including the political) arena, which has been widely penetrated by informality. In contrast, the Germans have tended to distinguish rather sharply between public and private, formal and informal. In the words of Stephen Kalberg, 'the public realm is generally characterised by social distance and purely functional exchanges with only formal involvement. Conversely, all "impersonal" values –...such as achievement, competition, and goal-attainment – are strictly banned from the private sphere' (1987: 608; also Lewin, 1948). In Germany, political power and the associated public sphere remained dominated by an aristocracy for about a century longer than in most other Western countries. Representatives of the middle classes remained by and large excluded. The aristocracy and the bourgeoisie in Germany had largely separate centres of power: the noble courts and the universities. Their aristocracy had kept more of the warrior code and they obliged the bourgeoisie to exhibit either subservient behaviour or to adopt the aristocratic code. Germans still behave rather formally in the public arena, as if they distrust it, particularly in the absence of a clear hierarchical setting with clearly designated superordinates and subordinates. In private, however, relationships tend to be experienced as highly personal and as 'immediate, not domesticated by general rules, intent on honesty and profundity' (Dahrendorf, 1969: 300), which implies they may involve almost unlimited rights and obligations (Peabody, 1985: 113). These characteristics can be interpreted as a process-continuity derived from a distinction made by the bourgeois intelligentsia in eighteenth-century Germany. Blocked from the political centres of power, they emphasized their 'depth of feeling', 'honesty', and 'true virtue' as against the 'superficiality', 'falsity', and 'mere outward politeness' of the nobility (Elias, 2000: 15–23).[9] A similar social inheritance of the German bourgeois habitus is evident in behaviour in public, where a kind of formality is demanded that varies with hierarchical differences:

> the greater attentiveness and even, in some circumstances, extreme sensitivity to status of middle-class educated Germans erects obstacles to a free mixing from group to group, even if the social skills for doing so are present. This is the case simply because each new social situation requires an assessment of relative status and the assumption of either a posture of deference or leadership, an exercise that is far too stressful to be repeated frequently. (Kalberg, 1987: 616)

Accordingly, in the public sphere Germans tend to cling more strongly to hierarchically differentiated formal rules, whereas in private and informal situations, they allow themselves to let go to a greater degree. Throughout the twentieth century, German manners books contained questions such as *Ehrlich oder höflich?* (honest or polite? – a chapter title in Oheim, 1955: 29) as well as many warnings against confiding too much and against *duzen* (using the familiar you). Their formality–informality span has remained wider than that of the other countries (Elias, 1996: 28).

This span seems to be smallest in the USA: Americans tend to be relatively informal. From observations like 'Americans invite people once to check them out; it's the second invitation which is a compliment' (Bremner, 1989: 20), it follows that the American dividing line between private and public is less sharply drawn (see Lewin, 1948, his drawings in particular). With regard to national symbols and ceremonies, however, Americans tend to be more formal, if not very formal, which is probably related to the making of Americans out of immigrants. Moreover, many formal aspects of American behaviour are not directly recognizable, for instance, the relatively intense pressure towards conformity through a variety of social controls on individuals as members of communities and organizations (Riesman, 1950; Dahrendorf, 1968). At this point, too, the book explaining *American Words and Ways Especially for German Americans* makes a sharp observation: 'many a foreigner conscious of this social pressure can only shake his head over the paradox of living in a politically free and democratic America and having to conform to rigid local mores' (Whyte, 1943: 152). S.M. Lipset viewed these strong pressures to conform as resulting from relatively high levels of competition, status uncertainty, and status-striving (1967: 127–9).

5.3   German Forms of Address: Titles and Occupational Denominations

Throughout the twentieth century, the authors of German manners books have shown themselves to be aware that the demands in their country on forms of address are exceptionally high; a wide range of titles and occupational denominations that resemble military and semi-military ranks remained in demand:

> In Germany, the title phenomenon is still of major importance, and, in order to avoid hurting neither here nor there, one has to track down and remember all the professional, hierarchical and living relations of the persons one meets socially. ... it is, for example, extremely embarrassing when titles cannot be indicated, or only falteringly and incorrectly. (Ebhardt, 1921, quoted in Krumrey, 1984: 417)

In the 1930s and 1950s, the awareness that there were easier forms of address elsewhere continued: 'Whereas abroad one has long since come to address everyone by his name, even in the highest circles, ... we continue to torment ourselves with the title question, and quite often we get most awkwardly embarrassed because of talking to someone whose exact title we don't know' (Meister, 1933, quoted in Krumrey, 1984: 421–2). And: 'In our country, it is still a common custom in social intercourse to address people by means of occupational and academic titles' (Franken, 1951, quoted in Krumrey, 1984: 425). Sometimes, advice in this matter was given in a rather factual way: 'One has to consider whether one prefers to write "Lieber Herr Doktor," "Sehr geehrter Herr Doktor" or "Hochverehrter Herr Doktor"; that depends on the age difference and the nature of the relation with the receiver' (Elwenspoek, 1952, quoted in Krumrey, 1984: 456). At other times, this kind of advice was rather moralistic and nationalistic:

> Titles provide distinction and generate veritable colour and variety in our lives, ... Therefore, we had better guard ourselves against the swift imitation of American manners that have reduced all different forms of address to the monotonous Mr. and Mrs X. Our cultural heritage is infinitely more opulent, colourful, hierarchical, and it would only signify further impoverishment if we allowed the diversity of our forms of address to subside to the most prosaic petty forms. (Andreae, 1963, quoted in Krumrey, 1984: 428, 430)

In the 1980s and 1990s, the authors of manners books showed a degree of half-hearted resistance to this tradition:

> In the matter of addressing with title, academic degree, or occupational denomination, I am in fact quite stubborn. Too often I have observed titles being used with some presumption. They create a (needless, I think) distance, because many people allow themselves to be intimidated by them. Neither do I understand those women who still want to be addressed by the title or academic degree of their husband. ... Nowadays, I think, social relations – particularly private ones – would be so much simpler if all were to be addressed soberly by their name. (Zitzewitz, 1986: 76)

The way in which this author turned against the use of presumptuous titles still betrayed resignation. It seems a form of wishful writing, expressing an ideal with an acquiescent sigh. In fact, this style of writing was also used in expressing a similar ideal, captured in the sentence 'Anyone who abstains from formal authority, gains real authority' (*Umgangsformen Heute*, 1970: 48; 1988: 41). For this exclamation was followed by the example of a *Generaldirektor* who indeed proposed to omit this title. His move should not be trusted at face value, the authors warned, because as much as his proposal may impress you, 'this impression will fade, of course, if his secretary tells you the next day that her boss insists on being addressed as *Herr Generaldirektor*' (1988: 41–2). In the 1990s, German forms of address still featured among the often-reported difficulties of foreigners working and living in Germany. A Dutch businessman who worked as a manager for *Deutsche Telekom* in those years, is reported to have said:

> 'Once a number of managers of large German corporations were invited by a bank, and over lunch someone suddenly said: our company has abolished all titles. I thought he meant they would no longer address each other as Herr Doktor and Frau Doktor, so I shouted out: Hear! Hear! Finally!'

The memory has him laughing again. 'Everyone around me dropped silent. And you know what? It turned out to be only the *Geschäftsbereichsleiter* and *Fachbereichsleiter* and I don't remember all the six or seven semi-military ranks they had there, and *those* were the ones they had abolished. Herr Doktor and Frau Doktor remained, so you had to find out somehow whether someone had a doctoral degree from a university or not. At first, I thought, well, I'll keep it simple, I just call everyone *Doktor*. But that, too, was completely wrong. Then it was: I am not a *Doktor*.' (Erik Jan Nederkoorn, interview: Jannetje Koelewijn, *NRC Handelsblad* 4-4-1998).

The following section aims at interpreting this persistent and uniquely German custom by placing it in a wider historical and sociological framework.

5.4 Friendship in Germany and England

Compared with the manners books of the other countries under study, German ones are also unique in their emphasis on friendship. They presented extensive accounts on the subject, often as extensive as those on marriage and the relationship between spouses. To rank a friend even higher than a spouse was not exceptional: 'All poets have sung the praises of friendship. ... Goethe ranks friendship "more holy, pure, and spiritual than love"... No blood ties, no constraints of external relations determine the friend. In love, human beings also follow a natural urge. The friend is chosen freely!' (Weißenfeld, 1951: 42–4). This praise of friendship stands in a long tradition. In Knigge's famous manners book, for example, the chapter on manners in relating to friends was longer than the one on relating to women:

> Everything that belongs to your friend, his possessions, his civilian happiness, his health, his reputation, the honour of his wife, the innocence and upbringing of his children, all that should be holy to you, and subject to your care and your caution. Even your most intense passion, your most extravagant craving should respect this impassibility. (1977 [1788]: 221)

German manners books have continued to present elaborate advice on friendship. Nearly always the topic is directly connected to *Duzen*, which may partly explain why English and American manners books have been much less prolix on the subject. But not altogether, for in comparison with even Dutch manners books, the German ones paid far more attention to friendship and *duzen*. An obvious reason for this difference is that neither *Bruderschaftstrinken*, the ritual drinking that marks the transition from *Sie* to *Du*, nor the kind of brotherhood (*Bruderschaft*) that is associated with it, ever existed in the Netherlands. This is related to another difference, already indicated by the term *Bruderschaft*, namely, that in Germany the term *Du* has been primarily, and remained, a kinship term, much more than the Dutch *je* and *jij*. But more importantly, in discussing the topic *tutoyeren* (using the personal pronoun), Dutch manners books never contained lengthy remarks nor the short essays on friendship that were common in

German books. Nor did Dutch authors warn people not to start using familiar personal pronouns at an office party. In the German books, however, the topic of the office party and this warning always went hand in hand. The authors always insisted that, at the office, the next day such an offer – indeed, the *Du* is 'offered', not given or requested – will surely be regretted. Apparently, the transition from *Sie* to *Du*, marked by a special *rite de passage*, retained a special social meaning in Germany. It was related to a much stronger sensitivity regarding the public–private distinction (see Wouters, 2004a: §5.c).

In twentieth-century English manners books, intimate relations were hardly ever discussed; apparently the intimacy of friendship and love was considered to be private and delicate, and therefore not really a topic for an etiquette book. English etiquette rules of the nineteenth century occasionally referred to friendship, distinguishing degrees of intimacy that corresponded to the public–private distinction (Curtin, 1987: 8), but these distinctions were not repeated in the twentieth century. Authors usually referred to 'friends and acquaintances'. What counted was the protection offered by privacy, the certainty of being in each other's good company. Further distinctions were important, of course, but not *socially* important, and there was accordingly no need to discuss them.

The different connotations of the expression 'to be in good company' is another case in point: the English would tend to think of a social gathering in good society, whereas the Germans would think of being among friends, that is, behind the scenes of good society, in private. *Duzen* means friendship (or kinship), and only among friends is one among equals. In all other relations, the Germans search for and find hierarchy, inequality. Therefore, friendship is a very serious matter and the familiar second-person pronoun *Du* is equally important. A section on *Duzen* from 1893 says: 'The word "friend" offers many and high rights. Therefore one should carefully deliberate to whom to grant that title' (Schramm, 1893: 172). The choice of words in this formulation of friendship was quite principled, the words 'title' and 'high rights' even suggesting a precedence akin to aristocratic rights and title. A century later, this very attitude was still alive. A Dutch journalist, for many years a correspondent in Germany, reported that he had rarely come across politically mixed friendships, because Germans who would reject a political stance tended to reject the whole way of life that it implied (Meines, 1989).

At this point, the question of the sociogenesis of this kind of friendship arises. Is this friendship more a bourgeois than an aristocratic social heritage, or perhaps a mixture of both? Friendship in the old sense of the warrior nobility was a friendship that implied enemies. It was something to fight for, an alliance or a treaty that, if broken, branded you as a traitor and turned you from a friend into an enemy. As the sociologist Allan Silver (1990) observed, up to the eighteenth century, the space between friend and enemy was not occupied. Friend and enemy were part of a language of war. It was based upon war as a 'normal' condition. This is backed up by the common etymology of the words friend and fiend, and also by the related fact that medieval concepts of meeting all had strong connotations of fighting *and* sexual intercourse, thus depicting both ends of the continuum of possibilities when people get closer: they tend to make love or war (Vree, 1999). These extreme connotations correspond to relations characterized by rather unrestrained enmity *or* congeniality, possibly in rapid alternation. They also correspond to the knightly and aristocratic stance of standing by your man, being uncompromising, willing, and able to fight for him, and to challenge to a fight, a duel, if offended. It is an uncompromising attitude. At the same time, as part and parcel of this warrior code, this friendship had many characteristics of the treaty and the alliance: the bond was never as absolute and universal as the bond of a contract. It was always dependent upon changing power balances, and therefore pragmatic and opportunistic (see Chapter 2, §4.2). It was a bond in a warrior world in which violence ranged among the accepted power resources. This made for harsh human relations.

In contrast, bonds in the world of business were far less dependent on the personal bonds of alliances and treaties. The bonds of contracts were far more universal in the sense of being based upon 'rules for all' (see §3.4) and backed up by the force of a state monopoly over the use (and the means) of violence. Friendship in the entrepreneurial bourgeois sense departed from a nation-state society with a market. In their contracts and contacts, people largely came to take it for granted that the use of violence was excluded. It was this universalism of contracts which allowed for the possibility of a friendship formation with no other strings attached. As Allan Silver has put it:

> strangers in commercial society are not either potential enemies or allies, but authentically indifferent co-citizens – the sort of indifference that enables all to make contracts at all. ... commercial society makes possible a distinction, without extensive precedent in fact or culture, between sympathetic relationships that normatively exclude the ethos of calculation and utility and relationships oriented to instrumentalism and contract. This development both enhances the moral quality of personal relationships and frees them from exclusivistic solidarities expressing pervasive competitiveness. ... Only with impersonal markets in products and services does a parallel system of personal relations emerge whose ethic excludes exchange and utility. (Silver, 1990: 82–94)

To a large extent, marriage was also a contract, a marriage contract, and words such as marriage market and marriage broker further illustrate the point. Marriage was (and is) perceived as a practical solution for many reasons, including sexuality and children. Knigge accentuated this contract character of marriage by writing that love is reputedly blind, and instinct driven, but that friendship is based upon harmony in principles and affections (1977 [1788]: 207). Indeed, the bourgeois ideal of friendship was a relationship that transcended the world of treaties and contracts, violence and money; and in that sense, it transcended the bonds of politics and commerce.

Around the turn of the nineteenth to the twentieth century, when the English centres of power and their good society opened up to the new rich, what happened was an extension of a long tradition of gentrification in which the aristocracy, industrial classes, and intellectual and artistic strata had blended. In the process, the uncompromising part of the old aristocratic code vanished as the treaty-based warrior code and the contract-based market code were synthesized. Norbert Elias has argued that codes have blended in such a way that 'British formality became in general more informal and British informality more formal than their German counterparts' (1996: 50). 'Gladstone's peculiar mixture of absolute and unswerving righteousness in principle with expediency, opportunism and compromise in practice' (1996: 169), for example, was related to the fact that the safety of the British population did 'not primarily depend on a standing army officered by men who stood in the traditions of the old warrior estate, of the landed nobility, but on a military formation specialised for warfare at sea, on a navy' (1996: 164). The warrior code of the navy was less uncompromising. Commanding a ship and a fleet demanded less ruthless manners of command than did commanding an army, if only because of the smaller social distance between the ranks and the vital importance of the crafts and skills of sailing (Elias, 1950). Moreover, ships are 'total institutions' (Goffman, 1968) and so, in a way, are the British Isles. Both made for a greater 'permeability of stratum barriers between different estates, particularly after the virtual unification of England, Scotland and Wales in the seventeenth and early eighteenth centuries, compared with that of the corresponding barriers in continental European societies'. And this 'greater interpenetration of neighbouring social strata facilitated a specific fusion of their codes of norms and a general inclination towards pragmatic compromises' (Elias, 1996: 163–4).

In Germany, aristocratic good society did not open up to the middle classes but – after the unification under Bismarck in the victorious war against France, the pride of the middle classes, traditionally attached to intellectuals and artists in a good society centred on universities – increasingly shifted in the direction of pride attached to the army and the warrior nobility that had accomplished both the unification and the victory over France. It stimulated a blend of codes cherished by the university and the military – which was also expressed in manners books: 'The Prussian soldier's maxim: Breast forward, head high! should serve every young man in the street for guidance, even when he has never been a soldier' (Marschner, 1901: 91). Military values spread, and universities, the traditional centres of middle-class good society, became permeated by an awe for the army and its (aristocratic) officers. In this development, the meaning of friendship is likely to have been included. It is as likely, however, that the meaning of friendship before the war of 1871 had been predominantly middle class.

In Part One of *The Civilizing Process*, Norbert Elias shed light on earlier, particularly eighteenth-century developments of Germany's two good societies, the courts and the universities, and their relation to the development of the German habitus. He describes a veritable class conflict between the middle classes and the court nobility. Elias depicts the comparatively low level of social integration in what was to become Germany, and he connects this, on the one hand, to the mass of the rising middle classes being completely cut-off from political activity or power, and, on the other hand, to the formation among these middle classes of a habitus that strongly rejected aristocratic attitudes and values, and instead emphasized learning, education, *Bildung, Herzenbildung* (education of the heart), inner values and virtues. It was middle-class *Kultur* versus the nobility's *Zivilisation*, the university versus the court. Because the carriers of *Kultur* were cut-off from political power, German culture was actually a counter-culture (to use a popular term coined to capture the social movements of the 1960s).

In the introduction to the late-eighteenth-century book that made his name a brand name of the whole genre, Freiherr von Knigge gave a range of examples from which he drew the conclusion: 'All these observations seem to tell us that the most learned of men, if not every now and then most incompetent in all worldly affairs, are at least unlucky enough, due to the lack of a certain dexterity, to be discriminated against.' On the next page he presented the example of a stiff, highly respected university professor going 'to the residence or to some other city' where people have hardly heard of his name, and where he, in a fine company of about twenty people, is ignored completely or 'is taken for a valet by some stranger' (1977 [1790]: 19–22). In sum, Freiherr von Knigge was addressing a middle-class public and he struck out at them right on their weakest spot by turning their hero, the learned professor, into a scholarly recluse, and worse, into a social nobody at court. Knigge did say 'or some other city', of course, but it is the court capital which sticks in the mind.

Knigge's celebration of friendship was a celebration of equality. Time and again, he repeated that everything that undermines equality among friends will harm their friendship (1977: 206–24). And he goes further:

> Why have high-ranking and rich people so few sincere feelings of friendship? They are less in need of the spirit. All they are engaged in is to satisfy their passions, to rush after intoxicating, stunning pleasures, to enjoy without interruption, to be flattered, praised, honoured... They are used to keeping lesser and poorer people at such a great distance from themselves that they are unable to accept any truth from them or bear the thought of putting themselves on a par. In even the best among them, sooner or later the idea awakens that they are made of superior material, and that then kills the friendship. (1977: 208)

What has been presented thus far suggests the hypothesis that, among the German middle classes, friendship cut across the heavy ranking characteristic of their own social circles and also supported their sense of pride and human value in relation to people who closed their ranks to them and kept them from rising into the political centres and their good societies, the courts. Their bonds of friendship functioned in rivalry to political bonds, and were experienced as based upon the solid and profound inner, that is, non-utilitarian values of kindred souls and hearts, whereas the bonds of friendship among courtiers were depicted by them as not being *real*, as superficial, and as merely based upon ever-changing and never-lasting pragmatically calculated political interests.

Friendship is an ideal of youth, an ideal of bonds more pure and opposed to the utilitarian bonds of adult professional or business life. Therefore, middle-class ideals of friendship will have found an additional thrust by being adopted and internalized by young people, and particularly by students at the universities. Students came to the university from the various politically autonomous parts of the German lands. They were in need of developing new forms of bonding, and *Freundschaft* was able to transcend regional differences.[10]

During the course of the nineteenth century, there seems to have been an ongoing penetration of the norms and attitudes of the warrior and courtly class. Many student fraternities [*Studentenverbindungen*], particularly the duelling ones, developed military attitudes and ideals, as attached to words such as discipline, honour, toughness, ruthlessness, and iron will, the will to power [*Wille zur Macht*]. As modernizations of the army also implied a functional democratization and the *Offizierskorps* (with the exception of some elite regiments) opened up increasingly to non-aristocrats, the student fighting fraternities and the officers' messes formed a model-setting good society.

> The code of the students and officers was the German equivalent of the code of the 'English gentleman', in function if not in substance. ... It can be said that these upper classes, different as they were in the many states and cities of Germany, in fact formed a single large society of men who were *satisfaktionsfähig* – able to demand and give satisfaction in a duel. ... In this way, types of relationships which have always been characteristic of warrior societies...persisted into the twentieth century in Germany and some other societies as a sign of membership of the establishment. (Elias, 1996: 50–1)

Whereas the Germans rated being *satisfaktionsfähig* – qualified socially to take part in a duel – as the main criterion for belonging to good society, the English had *vorstellungsfähig* – qualified socially to take part in an introduction – as their main criterion, the boundaries of the latter being comparatively fluent and flexible. Although a highly elaborate and rigid formal social life developed in England, it was embraced by the aristocratic and middle classes in both town and country, and it left open the possibility 'for upwardly mobile individuals and parts of families to gain access to new groups if they had the necessary qualifications' (Davidoff, 1973: 27). In Wilhelmine Germany, both the university and the military could give access to good society, but the code of honour that was formalized – the rules of duelling – was military. This also implied that ideals of manliness tended towards the military code: 'Our army, the navy included, has of course proven in every respect to be such a precious school for manliness that it would have to be invented anew if it didn't exist already' (Gurlitt, 1906: 4). This author directly connected German unification (and the victory over France) to what real manliness meant. It was the will to power, and a real man, Bismarck, had set the example, for he had proven 'what true male worth' is, and that 'it is not the masses, not conference resolutions and political organisations, but predominantly the clear will of single men that takes the world forwards. ... If Bismarck had contented himself with the fame of being an obedient monarchical servant, we would have no German empire' (Gurlitt, 1906: 48). Next to Bismarck, this author exemplified the English gentleman, for England's success in colonizing foreign countries was credited predominantly to the gentleman. However, in this context, too, what was in fact idealized is power, and the will to power. Even dissident voices of the time testified to the codification of the iron will and the will to power:

> In Germany, in certain circles that imagine themselves to possess a highly distinguished sense of honour, although in reality it is in many cases an entirely false idea of honour, it is the regrettable custom to have insults followed by duels. ... In England and America, the ludicrous duel has since long receded from the public mind, and in Germany, too, the time will come when duels will be abolished and one will generally live up to the legal ban on them, circles of officers included. (Eltz, 1908: 444)

Elias's finding, reported in *The Germans*, that after Germany's unification its many local good societies also tended towards unification, is backed up and supplemented by a study of the German gymnastics movement [*Turnbewegung*]. Drawing on Elias, the sociologist Michael Krüger has reported how this movement via a multitude of schools and clubs functioned as a good society for the German middle and lower classes, just as student fraternities functioned in that way for the upper classes. The habit of *duzen* in the gymnastic good society was an imitation of the same habit among the officers, and it had roughly the same function: '*das offiziersbrüderliche "Du"* created the solidarity feeling of a brotherhood. Quite a few members of this lower good society tried to move upwards into the higher one by becoming a reserve officer. This was possible by volunteering for a one-year military service, called: 'the servants' entrance to the *satisfaktionsfähigen* upper classes' (Krüger, 1996: 425–6).

Throughout the nineteenth century, but particularly in Wilhelmine Germany, the middle-class ideal of friendship blended with the military and aristocratic codes of male bonding, making friendship look and sound like a serious wartime bond with survival value, but not with much warmth. This hardening of friendship was limited, however, if only because friendship remained an ideal of equality and of transcending or escaping the necessary bonds for making a living. Whereas the English had succeeded to a far greater extent than the Germans in locating their ideal of equality *in* good society, allowing them, ideally, to treat others either as equals or as strangers, the Germans had located their ideal of equality outside good society, to some extent even outside society. In this respect, therefore, the English ritual of 'being properly introduced' and the German ritual of *Bruderschaft trinken*, marking the transition from *Sie* to *Du*, despite their many great differences are functional equivalents in the sense that both mark a similarly significant change in the balance of involvement and detachment: the transition from a rather formal relationship to a more equal and informal one, an important decline in social and psychic distance, and an equally important rise in equality and warmth:

> When two acquaintances intend to continue their relationship on *Du* terms, they drink a 'brotherhood' or *schmollieren*, as the student language has it. Only the older one of the couple can propose the *Du*, or, if both do not differ much in age, the one in a more privileged station in life does it; for example in the form of 'May I propose *schmollies* to you' ['you' written as *Sie*, the formal pronoun]. If accepted, one should put one's glasses to one another three times and shake hands, saying words such as 'Be my friend!' and 'You shall live!' Students are in the habit of emptying their glass with arms inter-twined and of giving the brotherly kiss to each other. (Adelfels, 1900, quoted in Krumrey, 1984: 470)

The importance of this drinking ritual and of the change from *Sie* to *Du* implies that access to the back rooms of friendship's equality in Germany were as well-guarded and ritualized as the drawing rooms of introduced equality in England.

These differences between England and Germany do not only largely explain why friendship and *duzen* appeared so prominently in German manners books; they also account for the differences in the *formality–informality span* or *gradient* of the two societies. They explain why, comparing like with like, this synchronic span is much larger in Germany, why formal behaviour in that country is far more ostentatious, but also why the chance of informally letting oneself go is comparatively greater in Germany than in Britain (Elias, 1996: 28–31).

The importance of friendship as a way of transcending or escaping a world where rank used to be all-pervasive, becomes even more poignant for understanding that these differences in rank used to be expressed in hard and commanding ways. This is another social inheritance of the Wilhelmine era. Not only was Wilhelmine Germany a strongly hierarchical society, but direct and plain expression of status differences and the related feelings of superiority and inferiority was also expected:

> Anyone who revealed himself as weak counted for nothing. Basically, people were brought up here to lash out hard whenever they realised they were confronted with a weaker person, making him immediately and unambiguously aware of their own superiority and his own inferiority. Not to do so was weakness, and weakness was contemptible. (Elias, 1996: 107)

In the 1940s, this attitude was still clearly recognized and addressed by the author of the book addressing German Americans:

> Many Germans and Austrians, particularly those of the older generation, show too great deference to their superiors. ... they sometimes lay themselves open to the charge of servility and obsequiousness. While Americans are expected to show proper deference to those above them, their manner is likely to be much more straightforward, direct, and man to man. Conversely, Germans in authority are apt to make a greater show of their authority in dealing with their inferiors, to order and command, instead of to suggest and direct. Americans in inferior positions are likely to resent the *tone* of authority, the 'you have to do this' attitude. Their co-operation on a job, an assignment, or an enterprise can normally be much better enlisted by a suggestive kind of authority. ... The American employer's 'I'd like to have you finish that for me tomorrow, if you can', is probably the equivalent of the German 'Ich muss das unbedingt morgen haben' [I absolutely need that by tomorrow]. (Whyte, 1943: 136–7)

Late in the twentieth century, a correspondent in Germany could still report a similar habitus to his Dutch readers:

> Friendliness and a serious commission do not match. Anyone who has received the commission will feel it is not being taken seriously enough, and 'consequently' they will not fulfil it seriously. If you start off by being too friendly, things hardly ever go well straight away. First, the commission has to be expressed clearly and distinctly, and particularly in a slightly brusque tone. Once this seriousness ritual has been performed, another tone of communication becomes possible, but even then one should carefully measure friendliness in order not to undermine the arrangement just made. (Meines, 1989)

Now *duzen* and introductions are perceived as functionally equivalent in opening the door to (greater) equality. Presenting a sequence of examples on *duzen* in Germany and one on introductions in England seems an obvious next step to take. Both topics clearly stand out as particularities of these societies and they show a similar curve of attention in manners books. However, in between the next sections on *duzen* in Germany and the section on introductions in England, I will present a few other topics that are uniquely German.

5.5   The Informal Pronoun: Duzen

Throughout the twentieth century, warnings against too light-heartedly *duzen* abounded. The next quotation, from the 1930s, is quite typical:

> The customary *Siezen* is a very useful convenience, which in all courtesy and friendliness keeps people at a healthy distance from each other. Before giving up the *Sie* in favour of the *Du*...one should consider the matter seriously, because a *Du* is irreversible. If you were to meet your new friend [*Duzfreund*] again, would you really feel good about having to treat him as your own brother even though he is – as you learn only now – actually quite alien?...Because the *Du* does not come out truly as a matter of the heart, the result is that you evade a contact that becomes somewhat embarrassing. Thus, instead of having sealed a friendship, you have lost a good companion or acquaintance. (Dietrich, 1934: 79–80)

The rules about who takes the initiative in proposing the use of *Du* and in introductions were similar: 'the older or higher ranked lady, the older or higher ranked gentleman proposes brotherhood [*Bruderschaft*] to the younger one' (Dietrich, 1934: 80). The comradely spirit of working or playing sport together may lead to a *Du* 'used without any formality and without special statements', but this is the *Du* of comrades, colleagues, or companions, and has to be clearly distinguished from the *Du* between friends. The English equivalent of this kind of *Du* is the old 'acquaintance for the nonce': an introduction that only counts for a moment.

The author of an East German (DDR) manners book of the 1950s wrote that, in Germany, the brotherly *Du* had been an age-old expression of solidarity among workers who realized they were in a similar position in relation to their exploiters. He continued that this does not mean that all members of the work unit, from the director to the apprentice, should *duz*:

> The order of a company owned by the people [*volkseigen*] is a *classified* order; why should our manners obscure this? The *Du* among company workers is no longer an expression of class solidarity among the exploited against the exploiters. Therefore, it is about time to *privatise*, so to speak, the *Du*. *Du* is the form of address expressing the confidentiality and connectedness among relatives, friends and comrades. The sooner we get used to limiting the use of *Du*, the quicker it will regain the charm that it has lost by its use en masse. (Kleinschmidt, 1957: 108)

Coming from a DDR author, this is painfully reminiscent of Orwell's *Animal Farm*. But West Germans could not have agreed more with his argument that the general *Du* was senseless and a form of disrespect for polite manners. During the 1950s, this was a typical statement:

> Without the *Du*, everything works out fine, too. Many a friendship has even been stranded because of the confidentiality that came with it. On the other hand, friendships that only knew the *Sie* have lasted a lifetime. *Faith*, not confidentiality, should be the basis of a friendship in which *Du* is used as an expression of a special bond. Anyone who gives away the *Du* lightheartedly forgets altogether that, together with this *Du*, an obligation is to be accepted: to be a real friend, who will also prove himself as such in bad times. (Oheim, 1955: 133)

The authors of the best known manners book of the 1950s and 1960s clearly conveyed their impression that, in the 1950s, the *Du* was used much less thriftily than before, and they continued:

> Outside the nuclear family, the *Du* used to be something like a decoration that had considerable eccentricity value. It was the pledge of an imperturbable friendship that transcended the outer societal framework, beyond which it also contained inner, spiritual-mental bonds. Recently, this precious background has become more and more flattened. Surprisingly, countless numbers of people take the stand that their relations to others only receive a hallmark of real warm heartedness if also conveyed outwardly via the use of *Du*. And they forget all too lightly that, together with the *Du*, they give up a healthy distance, which is essentially more favourable for attaining harmonious relations than the cumbersome confidentiality that so easily develops. The *Du* leads to temptations that the *Sie* never confronts us with. ...the *Sie* is a continuous admonition not to let oneself go. (Graudenz and Pappritz, 1956, quoted in Krumrey, 1984: 485–6)

In their 1967 edition, these authors had added several qualifications to this topic, as for example: 'When one day we feel convinced that we are armed against all the temptations that the *Du* engenders, then – only then *verbrüdern wir uns*' (Graudenz and Pappritz, 1967: 440). This formulation means 'only then will we make ourselves brothers' and refers to the *rite de passage* from *Sie* to *Du*. These authors insisted that it is much better not to rush in on a flush of alcohol and friendship, but even – indeed especially – then, one should say something like: 'I think far too highly of You already to want to say *Du* to You...cheers!' (1967: 439).[11] These warnings against *duzen* as a curt familiarity, as merely a shallow demonstration of closeness, actually implied that *duzen* was in danger of becoming the very external superficiality that it once transcended. A *duz*-friendship should continue to reveal the deep spiritual ties of the soul as superior to the outer societal framework.

The 1967 edition of this book also contains the following remark: 'Etiquette is in fact international...Therefore, it is not coincidental that 'kindred spirits" recognize and find one another everywhere, despite their different languages' (1967: 28). Here, 'kindred spirits' were depicted as dependent upon kindred etiquette, and at the same time as a group within international good society. The same expression was also used in the title and in the text of a section on giving a dinner party: 'Far more important [than lobster, champagne, gold plated tableware, and a large troop of servants] are *kindred spirits*. This is to say that it is always more important to first consider the composition of the guests, and only in the second instance the composition of the meal' (Graudenz und Pappritz, 1967: 392). This emphasis on kindred spirits sprang from a sanctified ideal of love and friendship as primary to all other ties; once again it reflected a hierarchy of (inner) honesty as superior to (outward) civility.

In the habitual presentation of the case of people who had been drinking and had given in to the impulse of *Bruderschaft* feeling, an author advised the female, the younger, or the social inferior to return to *Siezen* again when that feeling got drowned in the morning-after hangover. Only 'if the other then protests "But last night we…," is the *Du* saved. Otherwise, one has to give it up and, if you are keen on the *Du*, … wait for the next occasion' (Schönfeldt, 1987: 37–8). In many ways, this advice resembles the English 'right of recognition', that is, the right of a social superior after being introduced not to 'recognize' a social inferior on a second meeting. In both countries, the social inferior was apparently expected not to 'recognize' or 'acknowledge' the preliminary abandonment of social and psychic distance, although in English good society this had been transformed into a specific right for social superiors and a corresponding specific rule for social inferiors: do not take the initiative but wait for recognition.

At about the same time, the authors of *Umgangsformen Heute* vehemently turned against the *Gruppen-Du*, the *Du* used by whole groups travelling together on a holiday, at work, or playing sports:

> If it were to come to a members' meeting [of a tennis club] and a general *Du* were imposed by a majority vote, I would resign from the club!…The question of an esteemed or even revered television presenter [to the people taking part in his show] – 'Why don't we all say *Du* to one another, so we can understand each other even better?!'– actually isn't a question, but, to put it mildly, an indecent assault under mitigating circumstances. …Quite a few foreigners envy us for our discerning capacity – if only because of the better handle we have for teaching our children to discriminate between the false uncle and the real one. (1988: 88–9)

Together with the other examples of opposing real and true to phoney and false, this German pride in the capacity to discern between the real or true uncle and a false or phoney one shows how deeply this social heritage of the eighteenth century has become ingrained in the German habitus.

Whenever *Duzen* was framed in an international context, which happened regularly, it seemed as if the German middle classes had replaced their traditional opponent, court nobility, by some vague international community in which this distinction between the formal and familiar pronoun is not made (this community is the English-speaking global one, of course):

> I think our German *Sie* is beautiful, and I am glad about being able, purely by linguistic means, to create a distance from people whom I do not want to come closer, or to whom I feel so much awe that I can perceive a *Du* that is offered as a gift. (Schmidt-Decker, 1995: 118)

The habitual warnings against office parties for their danger of getting too close too soon testify to a relatively large formality–informality span or gradient in Germany, but probably an even more striking symptom of this gradient is the absence of a word for 'party' in the German language: 'If we translated the word "party" literally as "company" [*Gesellschaft*], we would not capture its essence. One could rather designate them as "informal gatherings", but that would be quite laborious, and therefore we prefer to stay with the "party"' (Weber, 1956: 168). Parties are formal–informal gatherings of a kind where Germans on the whole tend to feel far less comfortable than the English. For Germans, a party soon confuses public and private. If the guests expand a circle of *duz*-friends, it will be perceived largely as a formal occasion to which formal rules apply, as for instance rules about 'who gives... the sign for parting?' (Schliff, 1977, 1981: 292). And what should one do if, at a party, standing in a group of people among whom the host is not present, the waiter has just handed out a glass to each person: who then takes the initiative to raise the glass and start drinking?

> Who actually has the responsibility to do this? Quite simply: the oldest gentleman in the circle. If one is of about the same age, any gentleman may say 'cheers!' and give the signal to drink... If none of the gentlemen takes the initiative, then, after a small pause, a lady may say directly: 'I think we all have a glass now,' upon which the gentleman whom it concerns quickly apologises: 'Our conversation has been so interesting that we almost... Well then, let us drink to the health of our attentive ladies!' (*Umgangsformen Heute*, 1988: 175–6)

5.6   Introductions in Germany

To effect an introduction is important in all countries, of course, but compared with the English manners books of the nineteenth and first half of the twentieth century, it was not of *great* importance in Germany. Regularly, there was even reluctance expressed in the tone of writing:

> We already had to mention it a couple of times, for it is completely unavoidable in social intercourse. Wherever two people who do not know each other meet, they introduce themselves or they are intro- duced to each other. Although they do not know each other any better

than before, they thus at least know how to address one another. . . . Probably the custom is related in some way to the primordial magical significance of a name to its bearer. The true meaning is lost. The custom lingered on, becoming an obligation for everyone who wishes to belong to good society. (Dietrich, 1934: 70)

These words were followed by advice on how to make an introduction, including a discussion on how to cover up for having forgotten the name of one of the people you are introducing. Apart from the dislike of empty formality – true meaning is lost – it is also quite clear that what mattered was not to know each other's names, but to 'really' know each other.

The rules of introduction were quite simple: 'One is to be introduced to people to whom we owe deference (older and social superior people); to people of equal age and social position we can introduce ourselves' (Martin, 1949, quoted in Krumrey, 1984: 423). The view that it is only a ritual, a simple *rite de passage*, remained: 'Communications between people start with an introduction. One may sit for days at the same table of a holiday hotel or boarding house – only after one has introduced oneself, does personal communication start' (Weber, 1956: 104). The same mocking reluctance against this superficial and dreary formality was apparent in the following remark: 'If all people were really as equal as they should be according to the law, then introductions would be simple, and neither sequence nor manner would play any part. . . . Inequality regarding age, sex, and social rank have become embodied in the rules governing introductions' (Wachtel, 1973: 49–54). In 1970, and again in the new edition of 1988, these formalities were regretted with renewed force:

What our society lacks most is the generosity to talk freely and without the prickly formalisms of elaborate rules. . . . [in train or plane:] Let us learn to converse with each other without knowing who and what we are! All we need is to trust any possible conversation partner, any fellow human being, of whatever occupation or education! If we really get to each other, it is always possible to introduce your-selves at a later time. (*Umgangsformen Heute*, 1988: 19)

5.7 The Formality–Informality Span: FKK and Camping as German 'Social Escape'

From what has been reported above, we may conclude that social dividing lines in Germany have tended to be rather sharp and extreme. The passport for the switch from formal to informal is called friendship, and the span between the two has remained relatively large: only gatherings of friends and relatives were perceived as informal, that is, gatherings behind the social scenes. In all other settings, one needed to know the many details of rank, age, sex, occupation, and education, before one was able to move about confidently. Acquiring the details of rank provided the comfort of knowing the degree of deference, the terms of address, and other related details of the manners considered appropriate. This pointed formality may partly explain why most German authors of manners books in the second half of the twentieth century wrote with such obvious involvement about camping. Campsites must have loomed up as havens of informality in a formal world. The same part-explanation goes for the *Nacktkultur*, *Freikörperkultur* or FKK, all simply meaning nudism, which at an early stage was more popular in Germany than anywhere else. Nudism was discussed in German manners books but not in those of any other country under study. Around the turn of the nineteenth to the twentieth century, the word naked received connotations and meanings that were clearly extensions of the old university versus court contradiction, *Kultur* versus *Zivilisation* – and this is another part of the explanation: in connection with asceticism, nakedness became dignified, a sign and symbol of truth; it now referred to what was pure, natural, simple, in short: utopia! The FKK movement used arguments referring to good health, beauty, harmonious living and training, the moral effects, and forces of nakedness. Throughout the twentieth century, the FKK movement was alive and kicking (König, 1990). Yet, in manners books, most references to FKK were found in those from the second half of the century. In the 1980s, for example, under the heading *Bathing, Naked Bathing, FKK*, an author wrote: 'There, where people are no longer constituted by their clothes, everything depends on a pleasant face and good behaviour' (Schliff, 1981: 35–7). Later in the 1980s, the popularity and spread of nude sunbathing was discussed as something particularly German:

> Today in Germany, it has become customary to sunbathe in the nude not only at the seaside and lakeside, at swimming pools and nude beaches [*FKK-Strände*], but also near springs and in public parks. Anyone who takes offence is loudly charged with stale repressive prudery. Usually, such charge brings the protest to an immediate halt.

This author continued with a warning that this is exceptional, so please beware: 'You may do that in Germany, but not everywhere' (Schönfeldt, 1987: 302–3).

Another manners book also contained a long piece on FKK with similar contents. It mentioned an enormous spread in recent years: 'To be naked is "in," anyone who still wears a bikini top has herself to blame.' The park in Munich, famous at the time for its nude sunbathing, was mentioned, and this piece, too, was concluded by stating: 'Not all holiday countries appreciate the sight of nakedness, so you may do this in Germany but not everywhere' (Löwenbourg, 1987: 87).

In the 1950s, when camping became popular and affordable for widening circles of the population, camping trips were perceived and experienced to some extent as a continuation of nudism. This very connection was made in a manners book of the 1950s, in a section entitled *On a Camping Tour*: 'Wherever you find the arrangement of a "Nackedunien" or an "Abessinien," enjoy the possibility of giving in a hundred percent to the practice of *Freiluftkultur* [literally: free air culture]', and the author continues by warning her readers not to look down, however, upon anyone who doesn't doff her bikini (Oheim, 1955: 346).

The author of a highly popular manners book of the 1950s addressed topics such as a liaison between people who are not willing to give up their occupation and freedom. The bonds between them were not considered as lasting, while attempts at stopping the couple going on holiday together were branded as foolish: 'In the era of camping trips, it is a folly to try to stop them' (Graudenz and Pappritz, 1956, quoted in Krumrey, 1984: 370). The conception of the campsite as a place for lovers was also implied in the remark that: 'In an era of unprejudiced camping, travelling, all night dancing, and going for a car ride, values that warrant a lasting marriage are sacrificed to "love"' (Andreae, 1963, quoted in Krumrey, 1984: 373). Another argument that was repeated again and again referred to the spirit of companionship and solidarity that was said to prevail while camping. At the end of the 1950s, camping was also mentioned in a chapter on sports:

> Camping is not really a sport; it rather is a way of travelling and touring... but as this also demands a sporting spirit, a proper inclination, and a sense of companionship, it is mentioned here. Camping neither externally nor morally means a retreat to some human primeval condition. It actually demands a special degree of consideration and decency. (Franken, 1959: 269)

In the 1970s, a similar conclusion was derived via quite a different route:

> The companionship among campers, the experience of community: again and again one hears these arguments in discussions about camping in an era that has long said goodbye to any authentic experience of nature and is orientated towards expecting exalted convenience; the term 'Hilton-Camping' has been heard already. It is of the utmost importance, therefore, not to enervate this spirit of solidarity too much, or to exaggerate boisterously the alleged independence. (Wachtel, 1973: 85)

Exactly how the alleged companionship and independence of campers were to be harmoniously related was not explained. Later in the book, however, an explanation was offered for the preference of young unmarried couples for going camping: problems with parents and hotel managements were mentioned as fostering young couples' decided preference for 'camping, where everything happens in a more uncontrolled way' (Wachtel, 1973: 326). Apparently the discussion continued at least until the end of the 1980s, for in a manners book of 1987 a section on camping opened as follows: 'Here, the word is simply: "you are either for or against camping."' In this book, the spirit of companionship was also mentioned as one of the 'pet arguments for camping', but the reader was reminded that 'camping only functions as such if everyone gives tender care to this spirit' (Löwenbourg, 1987: 64).

Camping as an activity was never typically German, but the excitement about it certainly was. In the English and American manners books I have found no discussion of camping, while Dutch ones usually contained only a few lines on the subject. Moreover, they radiated quite a different message. Whereas German authors emphasized the spirit of comradeship and informality, Dutch authors warned people to spare one another. They emphasized privacy and the necessity to avoid inconvenience (Eijk, 1983: 73; Grosfeld, 1983: 203). A typical opening sentence was: 'On a cramped camping site you are more directly dependent upon your neighbours than in a tower block apartment' (Eijk, 2000: 209).

5.8 Introductions in England

In the 1850s, an author advised 'Consider seriously before you accept a new introduction'. In Germany and the Netherlands, to ask someone in advance whether he or she would accept an introduction did not become the rule. In England this rule continued to prevail, only its motives ceased to be formulated as bluntly as this: 'Ever bear in mind, that acquaintances are more readily formed than discontinued; and that character may be compromised by contact with the worthless and dissipated, even if no particular intimacy subsists' (*Etiquette*, 1854: 43). Strong words like these were destined to disappear. But all manners books would repeat: 'Introductions should never be indiscriminately made – that is to say, without a previous knowledge on the part of those making introductions as to whether the person introduced will be likely to appreciate each other, or the reverse, or unless they had expressed a desire to become acquainted' (*Manners and Tone*, 1879: 40). By the end of the nineteenth century, the rule still was: 'It is bad manners to introduce people without permission', but readers were informed of an exception: 'The only exception to this rule is at a dance or ball, where introductions need not be regarded as leading to acquaintance-ship. They are only for the dance, and may be ignored next day' (Humphry, 1897: 16). This is a characteristic of the 'acquaintance for the nonce'. Except at a dance, a private one, of course, such acquaintances should be prevented:

> If you are walking down the street in company with another person, and stop to say something to one of your friends ... do not commit the too common, but most flagrant error, of presenting such persons to one another. ... If you should be so presented, remember that the acquaintance afterwards goes for nothing; you have not the slightest right to expect that the other will ever speak to you. But observe, that in all such cases you should converse with a stranger as if you knew him perfectly well; you are to consider him an acquaintance for the nonce. (Millar, 1897: 43–4)

A large variety of advice concerning a wide spectrum of situations and relations all served to prevent people from making mistakes in the important matter of introductions. For instance, what to do if you had one guest at your house who was of a markedly higher rank than the others? Well, 'you would only present to her the most distinguished of your other visitors, or anyone he or she might particularly wish to have introduced' (Klickman, 1902: 60). The following example also unobtrusively shows that women were the gatekeepers of good society:

> A man may have acquaintances, however, whom it is necessary for him to know in the course of business, and yet they may not be by any means men whom he would care to introduce into his own family circle. In such a case, he would merely salute them in passing, but would not introduce them to his wife. (Klickman, 1902: 60)

This is reminiscent of a well-known remark by the American tycoon J.P. Morgan: 'you can do business with anyone, but only sail with a gentleman' (quoted in Baltzell, 1964: 119).

The following advice was mentioned in many a German or Dutch manners book as an example of the rigid formality of the English: 'It is supposed to be an unwritten law that one person does not speak to another at a garden party without an introduction, even though the fact that all are guests of the host and hostess should be sufficient guarantee of the social status of each one.' The author of these words added a touch of informality in her next sentence: 'Happily it is often broken' (Klickmann, 1915: 84). From most advice in this book, however, informality was lacking. This author addressed upwardly mobile women and tended to present them with rather strict rules. When staying in a hotel abroad, for example, women and girls were advised:

> With English people it is certainly wise to make inquiries before becoming intimate. The world is really a fairly small world, and it is nearly always easy to find out something about any acquaintances one may make when travelling, before becoming really intimate. It is nearly always possible to write home and make inquiries. In the meantime be courteous, but no more, till you know that you stand on safe ground. (Klickmann, 1915: 57)

The advice to write home served 'to place acquaintances mentally and morally' (1915: 59). At home in England, too, 'she should avoid making chance acquaintances':

> The skating-rink, the lawn tennis courts of pleasure gardens, even the seats round the bandstand, may all bring her into proximity with strangers; ... they should receive neither recognition nor encouragement. ... It is possible that the girl or the young man will ask, 'But why assume this stand-offishness?' ... Firstly, there is no means of knowing that the persons met without credentials of any sort may be all what they represent themselves to be. Secondly, those from well-ordered homes know that it is far from desirable to have

acquaintances that would not commend themselves to parents or relatives of greater discrimination. Thirdly, to be willing to accept the friendship of a chance comer suggests that a person moves in social circles in which the rule of 'Hail fellow, well met' obtains, rather than that of exclusiveness as to those with whom one associates.

The conclusion of this argument was that, 'at the risk of appearing stiff and formal it is better to wait for the fulfilment of formalities before accepting the acquaintance of all and sundry' (Klickmann, 1915: 72). Introductions needed a policy, a strategy, timing and proper gradation; not to have them was regarded as fatal: 'The problem of how, when and whom to introduce frequently exercises the mind of the novice in society. He soon discovers that it is as fatal a mistake to effect too few introductions as too many, and that this social responsibility calls for considerable tact and discrimination' (*Etiquette for Gentlemen*, 1923: 27). In the 1920s, 'unwelcome introductions' did occur, for an author admitted that:

it is really difficult to decide what to do on suddenly meeting a person who has been introduced by an acquaintance and who you do not desire to know. It is strict etiquette to bow; but prudence demands reticence, and however mean it may seem, it is wiser to appear oblivious of the presence of the person concerned than to convey the impression that you wish the intimacy to progress. (*Etiquette for Ladies*, 1923: 18)

Here, the word 'intimacy' is telling. A German or a Dutch author would never have even thought of using a word like this to indicate the consequences of an introduction. In England, introductions provided access to intimacy, friendship, and elevated equality. From appreciating how directly introductions and social recognition in England were connected to friendship and equality brings an additional layer of meaning to George Orwell's 'All animals are equal, some are more equal than others.'

In the 1920s, warnings against introducing 'two people to each other, and then leav[ing] matters in the hands of Fate' continued: 'Unless you feel certain that both parties wish it, you will be wise to leave matters alone' (Terry, 1925: 20). However, it was admitted at the same time that times had changed, that friendships between a man and a woman spring up without an introduction, at a dance, through business affairs, 'or under even still less formal circumstances'. Indeed, 'Convention is less severe on a friendship of this kind than was formerly the case', but this should not lead a man to step on to a slippery slope: 'Although the formality of an introduction has been waived, the man should not relax any other of the conventions in his treatment of the girl' (Devereux, 1927: 119). Another author even wrote a lengthy piece under the heading of 'Friendships without introductions', in which she said that 'girls in various grades of life admit to their acquaintance, and accept as escorts to theatres, dances, etc., men with whom they have become acquainted in the course of their business or professional interests, without ever having had any actual formal introduction effected by anyone who knows them well' (Burleigh, 1925: 233). This may no longer be considered to be a serious breach of etiquette, but that does not mean, she warned, that this delicate matter can be dealt with light-heartedly; one should be very careful.

In 1926 and 1931, Lady Troubridge's popular etiquette book still was quite traditional on the subject of introductions: ' "To introduce or not to introduce" is often a puzzling question. It requires a great deal of tact and a certain knowledge of the world' (Troubridge, 1926–31: 66). After a few pages she came up with the same golden rule as that applied in Germany with regard to *Duzen*: 'don't, unless certain'. In the case of introductions, this meant 'certain that both like it' (1926: 70). With regard to *Duzen* this meant 'certain to last a lifetime'. Her warnings against making acquaintances in hotels also kept the old asperity: 'one can feel lonelier in an hotel than anywhere else', she wrote, and, 'consequently, there is a very strong temptation to forget all about conventionalities' and simply speak to strangers. 'But every one, and women especially, should be extremely careful in making friends and acquaintances in hotels. . . . Strangers still remain strangers, even though you sleep under the same roof with them'. Yet people were no longer advised to write home in order to get all the required mental and moral details. Now, a somewhat less solid way of checking was mentioned: 'Since the War the hotel visitor's book has become of far greater importance than it was formerly as a registration of identity. For this reason it is essential that the guests should enter their social status before their names' (Troubridge, 1931: 302–3).

By the end of the 1930s, Troubridge's stance had changed considerably: 'Friendships are made far quicker now that the barrier of undue formality has been lifted', she wrote, and also 'Remember you are of your day, and of your time, and therefore you will not be doing the wrong thing if you accept this new spirit, and waive any petty, cramping little rules which were intended for another, and far more formal, age' (1939: 10–11).

After the war, the old rules governing introductions were still presented, but they either lacked the power of conviction or they were now taught to new and broader social classes, for what had been obvious before was now explained: 'the etiquette of introducing is a safeguard, since if someone is presented to you via a known and trusted friend there is less likelihood of them turning out to be, in the old-fashioned parlance a "Wrong-'un" ' (Bolton, 1955: 20). A few years later, in the early 1960s, this author explained these changes:

In this country we are often considered to be ultra formal in respect of not speaking to strangers unless we are formally introduced. Since the Second World War, this insistence upon formality has largely slipped away with the result that, especially among young people, there is a tendency to be too slap-happy about seeking acquaintances and friends. . . . people who were thus non-introducible in polite circles were known as persons who were 'not received', and anyone associating with them clearly did so at their peril. Nowadays introductions are the merest formality and do not carry any recommendation with them other than the fact that the person being introduced is known, by name at least, to the introducer. (Bolton, 1961: 50)

The merest formality was now presented as necessary for other reasons: 'The first duty of a hostess is to introduce her guests. The English are a shy and diffident race, and can sometimes be seen looking lost and lonely at parties because they do not know the other people in the room and are too timorous to introduce themselves' (Debrett, 1981: 143). Throughout the rest of the century, the topic was treated rather casually. It meant that formal introductions had lost much of their gatekeeping functions to good society. In the 1990s, even the memory of introductions functioning as opening the doors to elevated equality seemed to be lost: 'As a race we are not particularly adroit at the art of introductions and tend to hope that the parties know one another already and require no formalities.' This observation is part of a section on introductions that contains only five other sentences (Beyfus, 1992: 313).

5.9   To Greet or Not to Greet: The Right of Recognition is the Right to 'Cut'

In the late nineteenth century, the question on how to greet others was dealt with in the manners books of all four societies under study. How deep to bow, when, how high, and for how long to raise one's hat, were considered important because these details were expressions of rank and precedence. Only in England, however, were the questions of whom to 'recognize' by greeting and whom not, who had the 'right of recognition' and was, therefore, the one to greet first, were considered important enough to be dealt with extensively. Already in the middle of the nineteenth century, not to recognize someone to whom one was introduced was called a 'cut'. The author of *Habits of Good Society* disapproved of the habit, although he thought it was sometimes necessary and ought to be done as inoffensively as possible:

> There are some definite rules for cutting. A gentleman must never cut a lady under any circumstances. An unmarried lady should never cut a married one. A servant of whatever class – for there are servants up to royalty itself – should never cut his master; near relations should never cut one another at all; and a clergyman should never cut anybody, because it is at best an unchristian action. Perhaps it may be added that a superior should never cut his inferior in rank; he has many other ways of annihilating him. (*Habits*, 1859: 279–80)

Later in the century, one only finds less scrupulous remarks: 'If she has any reason to disapprove of his character, she is perfectly justified in "cutting" him, as it is termed' (*Etiquette for Ladies*, 1876: 2). And a later differentiation was the 'cut direct': 'To call anywhere on an "At Home" day, and simply hand in your card, is more than a slight – it almost amounts to a cut direct' (*Woman's Life*, 1895: 59). Mrs Humphrey formulated these niceties as part of teaching her readers 'the gentle art of snubbing': 'This is an accomplishment which some women never acquire. They cannot firmly repress the unduly officious or the over-eager without adopting harsh measures or losing their temper. Where they should simply ignore, they administer the cut direct' (1897: 72). Apparently this was written from the perspective of the social superior. Other authors addressed social inferiors, and told them to accept the class boundaries: 'If you meet a lady with whom you have become but slightly acquainted, and had merely a little conversation (for instance, at a party or a morning visit), and who moves in a circle somewhat above your own, it is proper to wait till she recognises you' (*Etiquette for Ladies*, 1900: 64). Regarding men, however, a lady was always the one who decided about recognition: 'When meeting a gentleman whom a lady has no objection to numbering among her acquaintances, she denotes it by bowing first' (*Etiquette for Ladies*, 1900: 64–5).

Alternative practices to 'cutting' existed, as formulated by an author who said that an unwelcome introduction means that a person 'may feel compelled to cut the other, or to maintain a frigid demeanour, at variance with his nature' (*Etiquette for Gentlemen*, 1923: 27). And next to alternatives, degrees of cutting were discussed: 'It is extremely rude and unkind to "cut" an acquaintance publicly by staring coldly in response to a courteous bow and smile. There are many other more dignified ways of ending an undesirable acquaintanceship. One has only to keep one's eyes averted if one wishes to avoid greeting' (Troubridge, 1931: 312).

In order to understand the social significance of this right of recognition and greeting first, a small comparative excursion to German manners will prove instructive. Here is what a German author wrote in 1885 about greeting: 'One's social superiors are greeted deferentially, one's equals heartily and in a friendly way, one's social inferiors affably and benevolently' (Höflinger, 1885, quoted in Krumrey, 1984: 443). Another author was more tolerant of superiority gestures, for social superiors 'need not comply with the greeting of members of lower strata' (Berger, 1887, quoted in Krumrey, 1984: 442). At times, the comparison with English manners was explicit:

> That in our country, contrary to English custom, gentlemen greet first, is well-known. But it would appear strange and pretentious if girls who had just been confirmed or even schoolgirls of the first grade were to expect to be greeted first by a clergyman or by their teachers. That is not in the book of good manners, on the contrary; the book says it would suit the newly grown-up little ladies well to greet these gentlemen first, and if one of them happens to be exceptionally young, he will know how to meet his pupils in a way that makes it hard to distinguish who was the first to greet. (Schramm, 1893: 245)

These lines make perfectly clear that to greet first was a gesture of deference in Germany, that by greeting first, the social inferior acknowledged his lower position. In England, however, greeting first was not a symbol of deference, it was a right: the right of recognition. These differences were directly connected to the whole English class system. Together, these rules of introducing, of 'cutting', or who greets first and has the right of recognition, open a window to the technicalities of gatekeeping and boundary-maintenance between the social classes in England. The 'right of recognition' found optimal expression in the joke about the lady who refused to 'recognize' a man by saying 'sexual intercourse is no social introduction'. It was 'absolutely vulgar to force recognition' (*Etiquette for Ladies*, 1923: 16).

In her manners book of 1939, celebrating the new informality, Lady Troubridge no longer discussed 'cutting'; nor was greeting any longer a topic of interest. She did refer to letters of introduction, and called them 'travelling passports to friendship'. One was advised to leave these letters open, 'so that your friends can see exactly how you have introduced them'. The words of caution expressed about letters of this sort were no longer as harsh and rigorous as before:

> Don't be too free with them, for obvious reasons; and, if you decide to do this kindness for a mere acquaintance, you are justified in saying so, as follows: I have not had the pleasure of knowing the Blanks very long, but I am very glad to write this letter for them – a sentence which will artfully combine truth and diplomacy, and let you out if the two families thus introduced do not 'cotton' to each other. The same caution is wise when writing to some influential person in the hope of getting a job for a friend or a relation. (1939: 151–2)

After World War II, in each one of the four societies under study, the levelling forces of status competition and increasing interdependence made for a strong acceleration of the trend from rules of precedence and rank towards rules for all. By the middle of the twentieth century, advice no longer focused on how to distinguish manners according to differences in rank or status but on how to treat everyone in an equally respectful way. A Dutch manners book said: 'Usually, the truth can be formulated in a friendly way' (Groskamp-ten Have, 1983: 33), and a German one warned 'Do not allow rank to influence your way of greeting, but greet your social inferiors as courteously as you do your social superiors' (Franken, 1951, quoted in Krumrey, 1984: 447).

5.10   The English Habitus

As was indicated in §4.1, the comparison of changes in the manners books of the four countries under study is complicated by the fact that the English ones that were published in the period of research no longer contained open references to class. From reading these books, one often gets the impression that, except for an occasional parvenu, all readers belonged to the same class – good society – and all were expected to participate in the 'Great Events' of 'the Season'. Within good society, differences in rank were extremely important, of course, but references to their existence had become a delicate matter. The same goes for references to those outside good society. Even at a time when many 'new people' with 'new money' were entering good society, as was happening around 1900, this style of writing remained dominant. Yet the appeal to status anxiety could remain quite strong, as was demonstrated by Mrs Humphry who wrote in 1902 'that "by omitting or ignoring the usual forms" [of card-leaving], one supplied "information quite unconsciously" and told "the social world" that one was "outside its borders" ' (quoted in Curtin, 1987: 58). References to upward mobility were also scarce and the ones I have found were dressed up in the disguise of geographical mobility and fashionableness: 'circumstances made it necessary to move to a new neighbourhood. . . . Local ways vary slightly . . . Then the wretched thought suddenly comes to her: Is she doing the correct thing? This is a more fashionable neighbourhood than the one she has left . . .' (Klickmann, 1915: 1).

It seems likely that the scarcity and delicacy of references to class differences in English manners books is related to the development of a rather intense feeling of community among the English. During many centuries of relative freedom from external threats, England had become a highly urbanized, unified, and homogeneous country, with a high degree of national integration and London as the great centre of a national culture (Elias, 1960, 1962; Davidoff, 1973: 16–17). Yet England had remained a strongly class-segregated society. This continuity in being a society with a strong class segregation as well as a high level of social integration helps to explain the nineteenth-century development of a system of introductions, cards, and calling that functioned quite effectively to screen newcomers into good society and to close their ranks against others. This system of gatekeeping functioned not only to identify and to exclude undesirables, but also to ensure that the newly introduced would accommodate to the prevailing code of manners and emotion regulation. The system was completed and complemented by the development of an important means of seclusion: the maintenance of 'reserve', that is, the avoidance of exactly the kind of manners and emotion regulation required when one was 'in company'. The elaborate, highly formal, and hierarchically differentiated system of screening and restricting those one met 'in company' functioned as a necessary condition for the development of 'the requirement that a gentleman treat those he met in company on the basis of equality', and this was, as Curtin observed, 'one of the commonest and most frequently reiterated principles of etiquette' (Curtin, 1987: 121).[12] And the same system of rules helped to identify situations in which the practice of 'reserve' was prescribed. Thus, the gatekeeping system of the English also helps to illuminate why and how they developed a tendency to behave either with 'reserve', which 'implies that everyone is to be treated alike as a stranger' (Peabody, 1985: 99), or 'on the basis of equality', which implied that everyone 'in company' was to be treated alike as an equal. As a whole, the high degree of social integration and the existence of a strong, unified, and unifying centre, in combination with the possibility of treating everyone alike, either on the basis of equality or as a stranger, allowed and obliged the authors of manners books to keep silent about problems connected with the social mingling of different classes, whereas these issues were openly and frequently discussed in manners books from other countries.

An unobtrusive insight into the significance of the elaborate and rather rigid system of manners of the English can be derived from the following warning against the 'visiting card trick', published in a 1906 English magazine:

> To bring this trick to a successful issue the beggar must be a man of respectable appearance and some address, for it is essential that he should gain access to your drawing room. . . . If he is fortunate enough to be admitted to the drawing room, he asks, before going, if you will oblige him with a glass of water. Should you leave him . . . he takes the opportunity to pocket any visiting cards he may see lying about. Presently one of the cards comes back to you. It is presented by another caller, and on the back you read: 'Bearer is a thoroughly deserving man. He is on his way to (some distant town) to obtain work. I have given him ten shillings. Can you help?' . . . Some of the other stolen cards will be similarly presented to other friends of the people whose names they bear. Thus, the vicar's card will be presented to one of his churchwardens, the town councillor's to one of his colleagues on the council, and so on. Visiting cards are a recognised article of commerce in some of the common lodging houses, where they are sold at prices ranging up to five shillings according to the supposed value of the card as a bait. (Quoted in Porter, 1972: 24–5)

This confidence trick demonstrates the importance of visiting cards and, at the same time, the high degree of seclusion and integration, the strength of the sense of belonging and protectedness that good society provided; without these, a con game like this could not have been successful. Only within such a protective environment could tact and consideration be developed more fully. The certainty of being more or less equals 'in company' may also explain why many English people, to this day, tend to behave in a rather easy and informal way in formal situations, whereas on the other hand, in informal situations where this certainty is lacking, they tend to cling to a relatively greater formality. To put it in theoretical terms, the English adhere to a code of manners and emotions regulation characterized by a relatively small formality–informality span.

A clue to the roots of the process-continuity of avoiding references to class can be found in the ideal of being a gentleman. Most nineteenth-century etiquette writers mentioned as the first and foremost of a gentleman's qualities his egalitarian manners: 'His egalitarian but independent manners were well-calculated to abolish various forms of patronage and condescension that the Victorians rejected when they overturned the traditional society of fixed orders and ranks' (Curtin, 1987: 289). At the same time, the gentleman was closely associated with manners that are 'easy', *un*self-conscious, and yet self-confident, as well as to owning land, and both are clearly derivatives of court life. In this way, the ideal of the gentleman combined middle-class and aristocratic characteristics; the gentleman personified both, thus symbolizing that strength of English political continuity: the social integration of new groups coming into political power. In fact, the gentlemanly ideal demonstrates the way in which the English aristocracy had entered into agreement with the rising middle classes. This ideal of egalitarian manners amounts to a class-society, consisting of layers of equals. And the upper layers of equals, 'High Society', as the English called it, was quite different from court society and much larger, but clearly a good society. It was in the wake of these changes that the functions of boundary maintenance and gatekeeping, and of including the new rich with 'proper social credentials' and excluding 'undesirables', developed into a complicated and highly formalized system. And an important reason for its becoming so complicated was that it should never smell of patronage and condescension, or any other feeling of superiority. This ideal had been integrated into the English habitus:

> We English people are apt to think that there is no other country in the world quite like our own. There is, of course, no reason why we should not believe this, but it is bad form and poor judgement to show by action or speech in other countries that such is your opinion. ... And even England is not perfect enough to warrant a great deal of boasting. (Troubridge, 1931: 347)

This attitude towards other countries is likely to derive from a similar relation to lower classes; regarding that relation, indeed, the same argument could equally be applied to class (although too embarrassing to be overtly expressed): there is, of course, no reason why we should not believe that there is no other class quite like your own, but it is bad form, poor judgement, and too embarrassing to show it.

The relatively high level of integration and seclusion of English good society may also explain, at least partly, why the English have developed a taste for understatement and self-mockery; this demonstrative 'cool' is connected with a relatively strong inhibition of anger. 'In company', some are more equal, of course, but by developing the custom of not accentuating these differences, the English habitually prevented and contained tensions, conflicts, and loss of decorum. To a considerable extent, individual idiosyncrasies were allowed, but only if expressed within a rather strict social definition of modesty. Even with regard to dressing, 'etiquette writers worried more about over-dressing than they did about under-dressing' (Curtin, 1987: 107). For example, 'In the morning, before eleven o'clock, even if you go out, you should not be dressed. You would be stamped a *parvenue* if you were seen in anything better than a respectable old frock coat' (Millar, 1897: 32).

Another source of evidence for this part of the English habitus and for the corresponding 'English Condition' of living in a class-society that consists of layers of equals, is the kind of literature that explains the stiff upper lip as a 'genuine attempt not to sneer when talking about the Lower Classes' (Gammond, 1986: 63; see §4.1). In the next example, both manners and class are ridiculed:

> *Plate and Knife Licking*. This is a satisfying ritual. . . . Should less well bred folk show surprise at you and ask 'Where the hell were you brought up' come right out with it 'Sir I was raised in poor and humble circumstances and I regard your question as an insult to all those still in sacred embrace of deprivation.' (Donleavy, 1976: 145)

This genre of literature, ridiculing or 'sending up' its topic, is typically English. It is part of a tradition of self-irony and self-mockery: 'To be able to laugh at yourself is the surest sign that you have an acute sense of humour. But to laugh at others shows that you have very little' (Kandaouroff, 1972: 7). This tradition betrays a strong feeling of national community, a high level of mutual trust. The English may live in worlds that are quite apart, a class-society indeed, but these worlds are nearby, sometimes even close: together they form a nation; for it is exactly this imperturbable security about the worth of themselves and their nation, which allows them to laugh at themselves (Elias, 1960).

The same overall process in which direct references to the lower classes and differences of rank came to be tabooed, also accommodated a trend in which references to 'lower instincts' (emotions related to bodily functions and body control, particularly sex and violence) were tabooed. In the nineteenth century, the latter came to be experienced as embarrassing and branded as vulgar: they would betray lower-class origin. No such references have been found in pre-1970 twentieth-century English manners books. Victorians in each other's 'good' company could be friends, equal and intimate, but they would prefer not to discuss bodily needs, functions, and longings. English 'cool' implied a relatively strong inhibition not only of anger, but also of the emotions and impulses connected with the body, with the 'animalic' or 'first-nature' layer of human beings (see §§4.1 and 6.7).

At this point, the word 'relatively' needs to be emphasized because, as is argued in this book, in all four countries under study people came under mounting pressure to develop a similar habitual and thus rather automatic kind of control over the body and its urges. The trend to bring emotions more strongly under social and psychic control, particularly those related to sex and violence, can be observed all over the industrialized West. The English, however, have been unique in the extent to which these particular topics were banned from the public scene, and even to some extent from the psyche, from consciousness. Even to touch or shake hands when meeting was banned almost completely: 'In this country, this custom is very much bound up with the etiquette of introductions. In Britain, people shake hands on being introduced, and may never do so again; but in other countries, hand-shaking is done much more frequently – often daily' (Bolton, 1969: 49). Indeed, in the first decades of the twentieth century, the Dutch custom, for example, was exactly the opposite: 'You bow when you are introduced to a stranger, someone you know you shake hands with' (ECvdM, 1911: 32). Shaking hands on being introduced was apparently the English equivalent of the German *Bruderschaft trinken*, both being rituals that marked a *rite de passage* from social distance to social proximity and equality.

During the Expressive Revolution, the 'emancipation of emotions' included the rise to popularity of such topics as the loo, but nude and topless sunbathing remained excluded. In the mid-1980s, most Britons were reported to 'have no home experience of toplessness to act as a yardstick', for 'British beaches are better known for their acreage of uncompromising Lycra' (Courey, 1985: 138–9).

The introduction to a study of *Etiquette, Rules & The Victorians between 1830 and 1890* opens with the following observation: ' "The English, more than any other people, not only act but feel according to the rule", John Stuart Mill wrote that in 1869' (St George, 1993: xi). And Michael Curtin observed an 'obsessive concern of the etiquette writers to establish criteria by which to identify and to exclude undesirables' (1987: 420). Both observations are obviously related: the quest for criteria did result in more precise rules that to a large extent became internalized and yet functioned to externalize class discrimination: no longer was it the individual who discriminated, it was the rules of good society. In manners books published in Germany and the Netherlands such an obsessive concern with rules and criteria 'to identify and exclude undesirables' was absent. It also remained absent from American ones, but in that country the English attempt 'not to sneer when talking about the lower classes' was taken to the extreme of an ideology of a classless society (an ideology on which Russians under Lenin and Stalin tried to improve). The USA was, of course, too big and diverse for power elites there to develop a unified good society together with a complicated system of rules for entrance and exclusion. From the countries under study, this left the German and Dutch books to contain relatively more open and direct references to class differences and avoidance behaviour. Towards the end of the nineteenth century, the established in Germany and the Netherlands, authors of manners books included, most probably did not fully understand the connection between the English obsession with rules and procedures on the one hand, and their fear of intruders and undesirables on the other. For them, although for the Germans more than for the Dutch, to concentrate so strongly on rules and procedures as did the English was to concentrate on superficialities; they themselves tended to focus more on the people playing the game than on these – in their view – exaggerated rules which governed it. The development of relatively strict and effective rules for inclusion and exclusion in England implied a relatively powerful, persistent, and enduring external social control towards developing a corresponding type of self-control – a typically English regime of manners and emotions, characterized by the paradox of having preserved a rather hierarchical class-society, which went hand in hand with relatively high degrees of tact, consideration, and tolerance.

5.11   A Note on Royalty and the Season

In 1992, the book with a paragraph of only six sentences on introductions, nevertheless, contained a long chapter called 'Great Occasions'. It opened with five pages on royalty, and another twenty pages on 'the Season', on all occasions at which royalty is present, and on other great events such as dances, balls, banquets, and diplomatic occasions. The title page of the chapter on Great Occasions contains this preview:

> Prevailing standards of informality meet their come-uppance at certain grand occasions. Among these are the cultural, sporting and other events that make up the Season; balls and banquets; royal garden parties; all examples where festivity walks hand in hand with formality. Relaxed as the affair may seem on the surface, a sense of protocol is never very far away. (Beyfus, 1992: 238)

These sentences reveal the English to be informal on formal occasions on the basis of a generally accepted broad layer of mutually expected formalities: English informality as an art that bloomed on a ground of secure social dividing lines. Davidoff's description of how the Royal Family at the top of good or high Society underpinned its boundary maintenance (1973) was still broadly conveyed in this 1992 paragraph. All the great occasions mentioned, festivities, sports, nightlife, and other great events, were known intimately, announced in the court pages of newspapers, reported extensively, and followed by a large majority of the population. In effect, the function of these Great Occasions had remained much the same: 'public enough to raise hopes for all, but private enough to thwart those of most' (Curtin, 1987: 71). Traditional gatekeeping at the boundaries via introductions had become a thing of the past; yet England had indeed remained a highly integrated society with a generally accepted and admired upper class and with, at its top, a sparkling upper crust of royalty and aristocracy.

After World War II, particularly in the 1950s, the authors of manners books conveyed a number of important changes. At first, English royalty tried to widen its appeal and to include the growing number of people and strata that had become 'introducible' to high Society and court circles: 'General society is now very frequently brought into contact with Royalty' (*Manners and Rule*, 1955: 115). And: 'Now that more ordinary people than ever before are meeting the Royal Family on public occasions, it is important to know Royal rules of etiquette. For the pervading spirit of informality is not compatible with the dignity of the Palace, and a great deal of formality still hedges the Royal Family' (Edwards and Beyfus, 1956: 277). At Royal Ascot, where 'the Royal enclosure is the smartest place to be' and some other places 'are open to the public for a fee', newcomers, of course, 'do not get to the prestigious No. 1 car park; they have to make do with No. 7' (Lansbury, 1985: 36). Somehow the Royal Family managed to stay in touch with the democratic times, as this quotation apparently concludes:

> An invitation to a Royal garden party is an honour. The parties grew out of the demise of débutante presentations at Court in 1957. The Palace announced that instead, the Queen would hold additional garden parties. It was thought that the presentation of a small group of society girls was out of touch with the democratic times, and accordingly, guest lists for the garden parties were enlarged and widened. Three royal garden parties are held at Buckingham Palace in July and one at Holyroodhouse, Edindurgh, also in July. About 12,000 guests are invited and about 8,000 acceptances are received, in all. Invitations are sent to people across a broad swathe of the populace. (Beyfus, 1992: 242)

5.12 The Formality–Informality Span: Gatecrashing, Watering Places, and Cruise Ships

The strict and highly detailed gatekeeping regime of English good society may help to explain why, from the 1920s onwards, gatecrashing was highly popular in England while completely unknown in the other countries. Gatecrashing was (and is) the 'sport' of getting through the well-kept gates in the high walls and hedges, or whatever was needed to appear at a party or other social occasion without introduction or invitation. Davidoff sees its origin in the merging of Society with the great 'show-biz' community: 'Cocktail parties and large public balls given by the new rich were not the places to control entry to this new breed of elite' (1973: 69). Gatecrashing is arguably a playful continuation of a game that was reported to have become popular as early as the first decade of middle-class politics, the 1830s: 'The English are the most aristocratic democrats in the world; always endeavouring to squeeze through the portals of rank and fashion, and then' – here comes a playful reversal – 'slamming the door in the face of any unfortunate devil who may happen to be behind them' (*Hints on Etiquette and the Usages of Society*, 1836: 54, quoted in Barnes, 1995: 117–18). In the 1980s, the game of gatecrashing was reported as still rising in popularity, and it even came to be written as one word: 'gatecrashing is rising to one of life's most irresistible challenges' (Courey, 1985: 29). Its joy is in the playful contravention of rigid rules and borderlines.

Another such escape from the strict regime of manners consisted of going to places which offered more latitude: the watering places, holiday resorts at the seaside or abroad. Later in the twentieth century, going to these and other places by aeroplane gave rise to the term 'jet set'. Before that era, the people of good society gathered at watering places and on cruise ships. There, secluded in each other's good company, they experimented with laxer ways and manners. For this reason, these places can be interpreted as laboratories of informalization. There, acquaintanceships could be only temporary and needed not be acknowledged later, so making contact was relatively easy, and flirting and flirtatiousness abounded: 'The seaside season is prolific in these chance acquaintanceships – "flirtations" as they may perhaps be called. Bicycling is well known to favour them' (Humphry, 1897: 21).

Manners books contain many warnings. In 1915, the opening sentence of a chapter on introductions started out with telling one: 'Never does the holiday season fail to be followed by a little aftermath of unpleasant consequences, leading even to law-suits, due to the indiscriminate acquaintances made at the sea-side, when travelling, or under the circumstances which may be defined as those of semi-public occasions.' And the examples given were quite graphic:

> It is common knowledge that there are men and women who regard a few weeks in a boarding house during the summer as a kind of speculation from which they may derive advantage. The man nearly at the end of his resources can ... induce a widow with means to marry him ... The unscrupulous woman, living by her wits, ... unless he pays her handsomely to keep quiet. ... the chance-made acquaintance of the boarding house might prove a very unwelcome hanger-on afterwards. (Klickmann, 1915: 71)

These warnings are absent from German manners books. 'In a watering place meeting and living with strangers actually proceeds quite effortlessly. Also becoming acquainted with them is hardly avoidable, if at all' (Marschner, 1901: 218). In Germany, social life at the seaside or at a spa or lake in the country was praised for allowing greater freedom, as in England, but manners books contained hints, no warnings. 'Nowhere else', the same author puts it, 'can one give in as uninhibitedly to the *Dolce far niente* [sweet lazing about] as at a lake', but examples of this 'giving-in' do not exceed gentlemen walking around on a warm day with their jacket on their shoulder, and ladies entering the beach barefooted (Marschner, 1901: 229).

In the 1920s, the generation of pleasurable tension in English holiday resorts was indicated as follows:

> There is not the same harm in dancing with a strange partner at a public hotel dance, because everybody else is doing it, and there is safety in the presence of numbers, but it is a questionable matter when a girl disappears for two or three hours with a seaside acquaintance, even if she honestly intends a walk. Undesirables are more easily encouraged than choked off. (Terry, 1925: 116)

The cruise was as typical a topic for English manners books as the FKK and nude sunbathing were for their German counterparts. As early as 1915, it was observed that 'No form of holiday has advanced more rapidly in popularity than that of a cruise' (Klickmann, 1915: 85). From the following warning, typical of the 1920s, one may understand why:

> One is likely to drift into an occasional chat as the days go on – but no more, let it be at once said, till you have satisfied yourself that an extension from courtesy to intimacy is really desirable. The unconventional *does* happen on board ship, but it is to be held in check by all who desire to enter and to be retained by the 'best set'. (*Etiquette for Ladies*, 1923: 92)

Probably, 'the likelihood of drifting into the unconventional' was a pretty adequate description of what made the cruise attractive, taking for granted, of course, that the 'cruise set' is the 'best set'. Unlike with a stay at a hotel abroad, writing home was not possible, so one simply had to resort to one's own resources in satisfying 'yourself that an extension from courtesy to intimacy', which in all other circumstances would depend completely upon formalities and inquiries, 'really' is 'desirable'. Apparently, occasional chats were directed at finding out whether intimacy is 'really desirable', and from there the unconventional could only bring more excitement.

The pretty formal Lady Troubridge of the 1920s mentioned the cruise as a most unconventional place: 'The only place where formal introductions are not necessary is at sea. Life on shipboard is more or less free from conventionality' (1931: 358). Her book, however, contained no further information than: 'When there is a dance on board, the woman who is travelling alone may accept an invitation to dance from a gentleman to whom she has not been formally introduced' (1931: 360). At the end of the 1930s, she had not become more specific, but she certainly invited the reticent English to open up: 'So, on your cruises, or when staying at a pension or seaside hotel, if really nice people look like getting friendly pretty quickly, don't draw back for lack of introduction, or hesitate overmuch to respond' (1939: 11).

Apparently, the building up of relatively strong external social controls on internal social controls or self-controls corresponded in England to the development of a relatively high sensitivity to rules and procedures, boundaries and fences, and to a longing for informality, whether at watering places, on cruise ships, or via the pleasurable tension of gatecrashing.

5.13 Introductions in the Netherlands

As in the German language, in Dutch, too, effecting introductions (*voorstellen*) and getting acquainted (*kennismaken*) can be used synonymously. From Dutch manners books, introductions appeared as an important formality without indications that they were considered to be superficial and dreary, as in Germany. Similar in both countries, however, was a typically casual tone: 'We may get acquainted with people in two ways: through mediation of some go-between, or under our own steam' (Groskamp-ten Have, 1939: 168).

Introductions were considered far less important than in England. In the second decade of the twentieth century, an author compared making introductions in the Netherlands to the English way:

> With regard to the matter of introductions we are less strict than the Englishman who will never address someone to whom he is not properly introduced, that is, formally and according to all the rules of the game. ... After being introduced, one of the two parties will have to break the ice. This is what a Dutchman postpones as long as he can. He rather starts a competition in keeping silent. Usually the highest in rank or the oldest starts speaking. (Viroflay, 1916: 23–4)

The following passage was added to the third edition of this book:

> It may happen that someone, for lack of tact or out of ignorance, introduces two people to each other who absolutely do not want to know each other. What should these people do? In the first place, they should spare their mutual acquaintance the feeling of having blundered. Consequently, they should behave like anyone else who is introduced to someone he does not know. Later, they will simply forget this introduction and pass each other without recognition. Without a very valid cause, however, one should not ignore someone to whom one is introduced; to do so is insulting. On the other hand, it is folly to continue infinitely to greet someone to whom one is formally introduced only once. (Viroflay, 1919: 22–3)

During the 1950s, when manners books found a much wider public among the rapidly expanding middle classes, an author observed 'a veritable mania' of introductions. Any host or hostess at any party considers it their 'solemn duty', she wrote, to introduce each guest to all the others, one after another. After having presented some examples of what is called 'our national habit of introducing ourselves in and out of season', she concluded: 'we may understand this introducing mania as a residue from a time (at least half a century ago), which has trickled to lower circles of society, as all remnants of manners that have gone out of fashion' (Schrijver, 1959: 68–9). The following addition to the fourth edition of this manners book was placed right before this conclusion:

> A mistake often made in our country is that men who pay a visit somewhere do not wait for the host or hostess to introduce them to those already present, and introduce themselves directly after entering. To do so is very unpleasant for the host or hostess, who in these times of no servants perhaps are still occupied with helping his spouse out of her coat or galoshes. (Schrijver, 1962: 72)

In the 1980s, several authors confirmed: 'With increasing frequency, people introduce themselves. This holds true for women as well as men' (Groskamp-ten Have, 1983: 269). In some respects the recent code of introduction was presented as a synthesis of the old, traditional modes of conduct and their individualized and informalized versions:

> Nowadays modern women stand up when they are introduced to someone, just as men do, although officially women can remain seated if they prefer. They do not even have to extend a hand...but can make do with a nod of the head. However, even the sweetest nod is now viewed as being very aloof and cool, and the other person thinks: why doesn't she shake my hand? Am I not good enough? So it can seem impolite and that is why as women we stand up and shake hands. (Grosfeld, 1983: 32)

5.14   The Dutch Habitus

What probably stands out most as specifically Dutch in the comparison of manners books is a relatively outspoken class-consciousness and open discussion of class differences until the mid-1960s, which was followed by a gap in the publication of manners books in the late 1960s and through the 1970s. During the publication gap, only two books were reprinted and one new book published. One of the two reprints was published in 1969 (Breen-Engelen). It was an unrevised reprint of a 1959 edition. The new book was published in 1972 (that by Loon), and both books were soon available at discount shops at sharply reduced prices. The other reprint appeared near the end of this long decade, in 1979; it was an unrevised fourteenth edition of Groskamp-ten Have's manners book that had dominated the period from 1939 until the late 1960s. The earlier edition had come out in 1966, so this 1979 reprint was not a serious attempt at reopening the market in search of a new public. Only from 1982 onward, did manners books become popular again. They sold well.

During the publication gap of about fifteen years, quite a different type of book flourished, in the Netherlands as in the other countries under study – there was an upsurge of books on liberation and self-realization, coupled with a relative loosening of codes and ideals. This type of book stimulated emancipation and informalization. The question of the 'right way' was replaced by the question of how to treat each other as equals. Starting in the mid-1960s, this self-actualization and emancipation literature was also studied at schools of social work and universities. In this sense, the question of 'good manners' and the 'right way' was discussed in the centres of the social sciences and caring professions, although in different jargon. At the time, peace and wealth seemed to have solved the problems of physical safety and material security to an extent that social emancipation and personal growth could become main targets of public interest. Emancipation literature even became so popular that, as an outgrowth, a new academic discipline flourished in the Netherlands; it was called *andragologie* and was even recognized as an independent branch of study in the universities. The *raison d'être* of this adult educational theory was the claim that it could transform the knowledge acquired by the social sciences into practical and comprehensible recommendations for a better society. Just about the time when etiquette books came back into fashion, however, *andragologie* was closed down as an independent branch of study. These features will be interpreted with the help of a brief historical sketch.

The seventeenth-century Dutch Republic is an early example of a state in which the nobility lost their leading position as they became subordinate to merchant patricians. The new leading groups had to treat differences of opinion and conflicts with greater care and discipline. In contrast to monarchies in which the king had the power to separate conflicting factions, any such higher authority was absent in the Dutch Republic. The States-General were a type of parliament where words counted, not weapons. Even the Stadholder of the States of Holland in his position as commander-in-chief of the army and navy was officially a servant of the States, because the army and the fleet (along with the whole central official apparatus of the Republic) were financed largely by taxation and loans provided by the politically autonomous provinces. The very decentralized organization and control of the monopolies of taxation and physical force prompted members of the States-General to use stratagems of negotiation, persuasion, informal discussion, the despatch of delegates, threats of economic sanctions, and buying others off. All important decisions were made in meetings of people who had received their directives from meetings taking place at lower levels of integration. The replacement of a monarchy by a government of a relatively large group of mandated and, in principle, equal participants thus promoted predominantly peaceful, more business-like, and less personal negotiating and meeting manners. A profound study by Wilbert van Vree (1999) shows how these manners, as they developed in parliament, came to function as examples, and how 'parliamentary' behaviour also came to mean 'polite' behaviour. Thus the model-setting classes of urban merchant patricians took their art of governing with the help of negotiation and compromise from the city to the state, from where it was passed on into the Dutch habitus. The early Dutch Republic was a relatively highly integrated country despite, or rather because of, its large regional and religious variety. Its people fostered tolerance and equality earlier and to a greater extent than the people in countries where aristocratic and/or military models prevailed. In 1966, the Duke of Baene, a former Spanish ambassador to the Netherlands,

> approvingly cited the description of Dutch moderation given in the seventeenth century by Sir William Temple. The Duke speaks of a 'hymn to moderation' and adds: 'Anyone can live more or less happily in Holland if he is a moderate person, and by using the term "moderate" I mean no exaggeration, no ostentation, no glamour, nothing visibly superior: for what the Dutch do not like and will not take is *superiority*.' (Quoted in Bruin, 1989: 218)

Throughout the nineteenth century, the typically Dutch pluralistic kind of state continued to exist: negotiations at the top, prepared for by negotiations on lower levels of integration, and lots of commissions and informal deliberations for doing preliminary work. Leaders developed a rank and file support according to differences of class and religion. This centre of power, the institutions of the state, however, hardly functioned as a good society. It did not radiate power and glory, or provide many career chances. The state was not loudly present, and the same went for the newly established royal court. In comparison with England, the royal court in the Netherlands was rather remote from the public and not very lively or active in functioning as a good society. Nor was there any other such centre. In 1899, a visitor from abroad formulated his view as follows: 'In Rotterdam you make your fortune, in Amsterdam you consolidate it, in The Hague you enjoy it' (quoted in Aerts and Velde, 1998: 195). Today, together with Utrecht, these cities are considered to form one large urban conglomeration, which shows how close to each other these cities are. Their proximity and the compact smallness of the whole country allowed the bulk of social life to be spread over into small-scale *coteries* as they were called, consisting of tight and overlapping networks. They had all the characteristic social controls of a good society, most of them functioning via multifarious gossip channels, making and breaking the vital social capital of a good reputation (Aerts and Velde, 1998: 278).

From, at the latest, the beginning of the nineteenth century onwards, *deftigheid* was a characteristic attitude of Dutch elites. '*Deftigheid* constantly engendered an atmosphere of a somewhat condescending, liberal and sober stiffness' (Aerts and Velde, 1998: 172). To be *deftig* was the way to be. Closely related was a constant preoccupation with distinctions of *stand*, a word that formally translates as estate and actually refers to class and rank, but was used in ways similar to how the English used 'station in life'. The Dutch preferred and continued to use *stand* instead of class until somewhere in the 1960s: 'Probably in no other country in the world does one worry so much about differences of *stand* as in the Netherlands' (Knap, 1961: 19). One did not consort with people of a lower *stand*, and *standsbesef* or *stand* consciousness implied moral superiority, but that was a public secret one preferred not to admit. The traditional emphasis on equality did not collide in serious ways with this preoccupation with class and rank, because equality before the law and in terms of business contracts was taken for granted. On that basis and within those limits, rank and reputation were always contested and competition was fierce.

Among experts, it appears to be undisputed that nineteenth-century manners lingered on longer in the Netherlands. Among the reasons for this was the comparatively late political awakening of the working classes, and a working class movement that, from its beginning, was rather strongly bourgeois-orientated. This coincided with the preservation of a relatively homogeneous middle class for longer and with the absence of a social revolution in the Netherlands. Highly important in this context is the fact that the Netherlands did not participate in World War I. Before this war, a trend towards greater distinction and *deftigheid* was observed among the upper crust of the traditional Dutch establishment, probably in defence against rising groups of the newly rich, and probably also because *stand* and *deftigheid* were the criteria for entrance into the 'first circles' – as they called themselves – of the Dutch patriciate. These ranks were open to newcomers, provided they had proved themselves to be *deftig* enough to be accepted in these 'first circles'; it proved them to live *op stand*. Notwithstanding significant changes after the war in suffrage and lifestyle in line with what the 'roaring twenties' stood for, the Dutch ruling classes, hardly affected by the war, soon resumed control of the country according to pre-war codes. In countries that had participated in the war, this was simply impossible.

The Dutch authorities continued to be *deftig* and to believe in *tucht*, a word that translates as discipline, but has a more specific meaning because it refers only to the discipline to which people are subjected by social superiors. It refers to external constraints, whereas the word discipline, which also exists in Dutch, refers in general to the result of obeying *tucht*: disciplined behaviour and self-discipline. That the Dutch ruling classes believed in *tucht* also implied they continued as before to control people via *tuchtmaatregelen*, disciplinary measures. In this, as in a whole range of habits and sensibilities, they showed an almost nineteenth-century type of obsessive penchant for order and regularity, for calmness and exact schedules: 'Anyone who was seen running had committed an offence, or was someone's servant' (Montijn, 1998: 121). In other words, the preoccupation with and competition about rank and reputation remained, and representatives of the working classes joined in. However, their sticking to relatively conservative codes and ideals about *deftigheid* and *tucht* could not prevent the gap between these codes and widespread practices behind the scenes from growing particularly, of course, in matters of sexuality (see Wouters, 2004a).

And yet, in 1936, a foreign observer such as Karl Landauer could report (in a series edited by Max Horkheimer) a strict morality regarding premarital sex in the Netherlands:

> My impression is that today's strict sexual morality in the groups I have observed (sociologically limited, for sure) may be interpreted as a symptom of the continuation of the strong authority of all societal institutions. For in other countries, where sexual morality has loosened up, the complete traditional cultural fabric is usually corroded as well. (Rothe, 1991: 283)

Regardless of how wide the gap between appearances and reality was at that time, these words certainly convey the observation that the whole traditional cultural fabric remained intact. Yet Landauer overlooked the distance between codes (or appearances to be kept up) and the practices of everyday life at least a little, judging from evidence such as an article in the 1920s in which an increase in venereal diseases was observed. Next to prostitution, still the main cause, the author mentioned 'promiscuity' as having recently reached a good second position (Mooij, 1993: 120). In 1930, a dermatologist described the new category of girls coming in for consultations as middle class: 'I refer to the thousands of young girls who used to stay at home and help in the household, who today have got a job in a shop or an office, earn some money that helps support the household, but also provides them with a basis for getting themselves more leeway' (quoted in Mooij, 1993: 124).

In comparison to German manners books, some of the Dutch ones that appeared before the 1960s were more openly class-ridden. On the whole, German authors seemed to write more cautiously about differences in class, rank, and status, while their reading public was in fact more in need of this information because these differences corresponded more closely to differences in manners such as form of address. In a book published in 1937, the author, a German immigrant to the Netherlands, turned a Dutch 'joke' about a German stage director who called a stagehand [*toneelknecht*] 'Mister Lighting Inspector' into an illustration of how status-ridden the Dutch were:

> Until recently it was a general custom simply to call one's employees by their Christian names, and to address them with the informal you. In order to ridicule the German urge for titles [and occupational denominations], which certainly is a ridiculous matter, someone told me the following joke. Max Reinhardt was directing at the Amsterdam Theatre and held a final rehearsal. He was not pleased with the lighting of a particular scene. Therefore he called: 'Herr Beleuchtungsinspektor!' His call was not answered, nor was it when he repeated his call for the 'Herrn Beleuchtungsinspektor'. His Dutch assistant came out to help him. 'Kees!' he called, and the man in question appeared in the floodlight: 'What is it, Sir?' (Schreiner, 1937: 173)

Another story characterizing the humiliating status-related pressures towards conformity concerns the charitable work that any woman living *op stand* was obliged to do.

> It wasn't done with discreet bank accounts and neutral collections, no, neediness had a face. ... The subscription register, which mentioned each donor by name and stated the exact amount of the donation, visualized how strong *standsbesef* [*besef* = awareness] and charity were tied together. If the baroness in the grand house had given two guilders, then the wife of the doctor should give at least one guilder, and then the wife of the notary could not fall short, of course, so she also contributed a guilder – while the wife of the industrialist possibly dared to follow the example of the baroness. All this for the benefit of the poor fatherless family X, whose name and address were also mentioned on the list. (Montijn, 1998: 28–9)

After World War II, representatives of the pre-war establishment aimed at restoration of the old order. In fact, both progressives and conservatives shared the opinion 'that the war had damaged the Dutch people not only materially, but also morally, and that reparation in both areas was needed. ... On this point the parties fully agreed and the labour unions resolutely subordinated their traditional opposition to employers and their associations to the national cause' (Dunk, 1994: 112). And they were quite successful. Traditional hierarchy, *tucht* and *deftigheid* returned and prevailed again until the latter half of the 1960s, although many of their sharpest edges had been removed. Many humiliating aspects of pre-war charity, such as subscription lists, for example, did not return. In 1965, a social security law was presented and accepted. The authorities introduced 'Welfare' [*Bijstand*] to the public with the slogan 'Welfare is not a favour, it is a right!,' and in this slogan, the word favour still captured the smell of the shaming process that stuck to charitable work, and of the disgrace in receiving charity.

This whole world vanished, so to speak, behind the smoke curtain from a smoke bomb pitched in 1966 at the royal carriage and parade for the wedding of Princess Beatrix and Prince Claus in Amsterdam. The metaphor of the smoke curtain conveys the success of the Dutch variant of an international youth and protest movement in attacking the narrow-mindedness and seriousness of bourgeois culture: the whole world of *tucht* and *deftigheid* disappeared from sight. The word *tucht* has been extinct since the 1960s, and so are all composite words with *tucht* such as *tuchthuis*, *tuchtschool*, *tuchtraad*, *tuchtcommissie*, *tuchtmaatregel*, or *tuchtwet* (respectively prison, reform school, *tucht*-council , *tucht*-committee, *tucht*measure, or *tucht*-rules). They have all been washed away in the 1960s flood of democratization and informalization. The same goes for *knecht* – as in *toneelknecht* (stage hand) and in 'anyone who was seen running was either a thief or a *knecht*' – which translates as servant, but derives from *knechtschap*, which translates as 'living in subjugation or even bondage', and which became unbearable for its strong connotations of social inferiority. The same change in sensitivity made words with strong connotations of social superiority intolerable. The old displays of *standsbesef* were despised to the extent that, in the late 1960s and throughout the 1970s, the word *deftig* was not heard, or only as a curse: to call someone *deftig* would brand him or her as stiff and arrogant, as claiming superiority not on the basis of some personal merit but on the basis of socially inherited privileges that had lost their validity. In circles where the word was still used, a *deftig* person counted as a ridiculous fossil from a world that had ceased to exist.

In such a cultural climate, it seems almost self-evident that manners books would not sell. The large formality–informality gradient had come to be experienced as intolerable: what formality had demanded now seemed unjust, and informality was brought out from behind the scenes into the open. The swing of the pendulum went from manners that breathe hierarchy to manners that breathe equality. In the second half of the 1960s and throughout the 1970s, authority, etiquette, and rules in general became and remained so suspect that manners books became complete commercial flops, and they were not published for more than a decade.

In his study of the 1960s in the Netherlands, the American historian James Kennedy shows how the leaders of parties and religious organizations were overtaken by their grass-roots support. His outlook was American in the sense that he was struck by the fact that the established did not offer full-scale resistance. They even used their power to accommodate and facilitate the smooth flow of the tidal wave of democratization and informalization. Indeed, these elites were Dutch in the sense that their habitus, particularly their conscience, was to a large extent on the side of the protesters. The latter claimed civil rights, demanded democratic procedures, and broke through stiff formality and haughty stateliness, in short through *deftigheid*, in ways that made almost all authority appear absurdly unjust, oppressive, and corrupt.

One could say that the people in authority were to some extent defence-less, namely to the extent that their conscience was on the side of their opponents. This made them unable and unwilling guardians of old-fashioned stiff and class-ridden formality. They were prepared to negotiate and compromise. In fact, often unknowingly, functioning as a second-nature reflex, they shared a common ground of basic trust with their opponents, a shared level of mutually expected self-restraints. And, furthermore, they had remained merchants in the sense that they saw the profit of remaining in power by investing in the strategy of accommodation and cooperation. In this sense, the Dutch managerial elites did what they had always done (Kennedy, 1995).

What is sometimes called the long nineteenth century had resulted in a growing gap between public appearance and private daily practice as well as in a growing gap between existing ideals of equality and existing inequality. That these gaps had grown larger in the Netherlands than in the USA, England, or Germany may also explain why generational differences in the Netherlands were experienced as larger. In all these countries, whole generations had been growing up in conditions of physical safety and material security to the extent that some of them could become relatively insensitive to traditional sanctions. This enabled them to take action against all sorts of authority defined as oppressive (Wouters, 1972). Leaving existing differences in habitus formation aside, the main reason why the clash of the generations had deeper and more lasting effects in the Netherlands was again the gap of hypocrisy that had grown between a front stage of stiff pretence and backstage realities. In the 1960s, when the Dutch caught up, it was exposed as a big lie.

If existing differences in habitus formation *are* taken into account, however, they may help explain why the Dutch took the lead in several moral and legal respects. The argument may be presented as building upon Kennedy's argument that 'the habits, sensibilities and ideologies of the pre-war generation – however different from those of their children – helped contribute to the relative lack of conflict in Dutch society during the 1960s' (Kennedy, 1995; 1997: 367–8). The old authorities and the new ones coming to power continued to take the issues of protest and individual rights seriously, to set up committees, to negotiate and compromise.

The high level of social integration in the Netherlands provided the necessary basis for committing themselves to a greater extent to all this negotiating and compromising than in most other countries. It provided a relatively high level of mutual trust which allowed for a comparatively early conditional permissiveness towards legal marriage for homosexuals, prostitution, abortion, euthanasia, and soft drugs. In no other country did manners books contain advice concerning such matters as requests for homosexual marriage, abortion, or mercy killing; and among the countries where the books have dealt with (soft) drugs, only in Dutch manners books is their use still discussed in the same spirit of conditional permissiveness as in the 1960s:

> Drugs, if used sensibly, may be a great impetus to your social abilities. If used insensibly, they may cause enduring and complete alienation of all your social contacts. Drug use is not generally accepted. In itself, this may not amaze anyone. It is a fact, however, that especially those who think drugs should be exorcised at any price would profit most from taking a little dope. It would widen their horizons. (Klanker and Vries, 1999: 65)

This was written in an attitude of trust; it is 'yes, if...', rather than the less trusting or even suspicious 'no, unless...'. An unconditional yes or no would both be rejected immediately. The issue was not either controlling or decontrolling, but both: it was controlled decontrolling, socially as well as individually.

The 1980s, and particularly the 1990s, saw the spread of an appreciative interest in tradition, the lifestyle of the upper classes, including the nobility, and a constantly rising concern for manners and morals. One can detect the contours of a network of political managers and managing politicians; there are many centres, circles, and coteries, and the television is loud, but nothing looks like a functioning good society. In the meantime, status competition and hierarchy have come fully into being again, but the *knecht* and *tucht* have remained dead, buried in the dictionary. *Deftig* is used sometimes, but mostly as an alternative for chic and elegant, and there is a ring of glamour, which used not to be *deftig* at all; it means that the word, as used by a new generation, has not inherited some of its most significant old connotations, and attacks on superiority have persisted:

> Many people who *claim* to belong to Old Money have a dictionary full of 'wrong' words and expressions at their disposal: fridge (should be refrigerator), costume (suit), 'enjoy your meal' (nothing), and 'sleep well' (nothing). Style-terrorists who stumble over these linguistic *faux pas* expose themselves as *nouveau riches* who, just like parvenus, seek to spread the gospel of the elite. For the same reason it is rigorously forbidden to label something or someone as 'bourgeois'. To do so is a poor business, seeking to bring one's superiority feelings into the limelight. Such a type of hubris is improper. (Regteren *et al.*, 2002: 127)

5.15   Class and Good Society in the USA

The reception of European manners books in eighteenth- and nineteenth-century America, particularly of Lord Chesterfield's *Letters of Advice to His Son* (1826 [orig. 1775]), instigated the creation of American codes and ideals of behaviour and emotion regulation. In close connection with the changing power structure, this revolutionary period saw the transition from a courtesy genre to an etiquette genre. In the latter genre, inherited status and class deference were no longer emphasized. As 'the manners game was open to all who could compete' (Hemphill, 1996: 333), these were more openly books for status-conscious social climbers on a social ladder, the rungs of which were pretty unclear and unstable.

Throughout the twentieth century, certainly in comparison with England and the Netherlands, American good society has been far less an integrated and secluded whole. The American upper classes were more spread out and more strongly divided among themselves, the country being much larger and characterized by much greater differences between North, South, East, and West, without a unifying and dominant centre such as London or Paris. This coincides with a larger rather than a smaller interest in manners: 'In a country like America where there are no castes ... and where the intermingling of the different classes is so general – there is a constant and almost universal desire to know what the social laws or rules of etiquette of the best society really are' (Bradley, 1889: 15). Indeed, such a class structure, characterized by open competition and uncertainty of status, may explain the continued popularity of manners books in the USA. 'There is no country where there are so many people asking what is "proper to do," or, indeed, where there are so many genuinely anxious to do the proper thing, as in the vast conglomerate which we call The United States of America' (Hanson, 1896: v).

The open competition and status insecurity may also explain why, in such a setting, 'those who felt they were eligible for entry on the basis of wealth and achievement but who were excluded on grounds of religion, ethnic background or race, formed their own Society' (Davidoff, 1973: 102). This may sound reassuring, but as Digby Baltzell remarked in the introduction to his classic study of America's upper classes: 'A crisis in moral authority has developed in modern America largely because of the White-Anglo-Saxon-Protestant establishment's unwillingness, or inability, to share and improve its upper-class traditions by continuously absorbing talented and distinguished members of minority groups into its privileged ranks' (1964: x). Apparently, the Anglo-Saxons, who dominated the British Isles for almost a millennium, also dominated the English colony in North America, both before and after independence from England. At the end of the nineteenth century, the country club and the country day school became the main fortresses of exclusiveness: good society centres. In the decades following 'the founding of The Country Club, at Brookline, Massachusetts, in 1882, ... similar clubs sprang up like mushrooms and became a vital part of the American upper-class way of life. ...Along with the business and suburban boom which marked the twenties, the country-club movement went through its period of most rapid growth' (Baltzell, 1964: 122, 355). It soon acquired most characteristics of a good society centre, one of them being the ideal that there, in each other's good company, one was among equals, and guarded against the manners of (obvious) social climbers and other intruders: 'In no place is the climber, male or female, more offensive than in the club' (Wade, 1924: 289). Another study typically views the 'country club' as 'an American improvisation, now about eighty years old, [which] provides a rough equivalent of the English weekend, adapted to American conditions' (Carson, 1966: 244). To elaborate on Gabriel Tarde's metaphor: there were many competing 'social water towers' in the USA (although not as many as there were 'country clubs'), but a real centre was lacking. No doubt, some of these many good societies were more nationwide than others, and as such observed by Society reporters, but most were more local and all were competing. In New York alone, for instance, there has been a more or less constant competition between 'two Societies, "Old New York" and "New Society." In every era, "Old New York" has taken a horrified look at "New Society" and expressed the devout conviction that a genuine aristocracy, good blood, good bone – themselves – was being defiled by a horde of rank climbers' (Wolfe, 1970: 35). In comparison with New York, Los Angeles has been far more diverse. In the 1960s and early 1970s,

> The Wasps ruled the centre of town . . . and Pasadena. The Westside of the City, stretching from Hollywood to Beverley Hills to the coast, was dominated by Jews, many of them in the film business. Property developers, aerospace corporocrats, oil magnates and savings-and-loan sharks all had their own empires. These groups were separated not only by physical distance – the greater Los Angeles area encompasses 33,210 square miles – but also by social and religious snobbery. Blackballed by the Wasp oligarchy, the Jews set up a rival establishment, with their own country clubs and political networks. The result was a 'headless city' that found it hard to build the civic institutions – art galleries, concert halls and the like – that most other cities take for granted. (*The Economist*, 12 July 1997: 31–2)

At the close of the twentieth century, the city of Los Angeles still remained 'headless', or, better, 'multi-headed', with dozens of competing ruling groups. Often, America's openness has been emphasized for ideological reasons, while the other side of the coin, its strong competitiveness, was played down. For instance, in the 1960s the author of a historical study of American manners claimed that 'no other civilisation can show so many orders, associations, fraternal lodges, . . . where it was possible to "meet people," "make contacts" and find a place' (Carson, 1966: 240).

In America, the open competition between many good societies explains to a large extent why, throughout the twentieth century, good society as a whole has had a weaker political significance than in England or the Netherlands.

Davidoff has pointed out that this 'lack of access to real power through Society meant that its reward and entertainment function was stressed' (1973: 102). This has been expressed in many ways, for instance in the subtitle of Crowninshield's 1908 book *An Entrance Key to the Fantastic Life of the 400*, and in American words such as 'the smart', 'fashionable set', 'jet set', and 'socialites', words that are closely associated with 'conspicuous consumption' and 'showing off'. In other words, whereas the English tended to tone down social differences, Americans tended to accentuate them. The weaker integration and seclusion of America's good society has also prevented a comparably advanced development of the English habit of keeping one's distance or 'reserve'. It has made the dominant code of manners and emotion regulation in America more universal than the English type, but at the same time, it prevented the American code from becoming as unified and yet subtly differentiated as the corresponding English code. The range of accepted behaviour in the American code allowed for extremes that the English, according to their code, would experience as disgusting. A nineteenth-century example is spitting indoors; in 1859, an English author called this an American 'national habit' (*Habits*, 1859), and in 1884 an American author, addressing English readers in a special preface, wrote that 'Spitting upon the carpet naturally comes in for severe condemnation; and the authority of Dr. Wendell Holmes seems necessary to prove that a hand-kerchief should be used in blowing one's nose' (Censor, 1884: 5–6). By the end of the nineteenth century, extremes like these had faded, but the differences in national codes and their perception of each other remained, as this English example shows:

> I should be glad to exhibit to the host of American *parvenues* their own broad, glittering cards – bearing upon them names reeking with plebeianism, sewgawed with some paltry title, the synonym and pass-port of insignificance – in contrast with the plain and modest cards of some of the highest peers of the British realm. (Millar, 1897: 53)

This example also shows that national differences between the old country and the new one were experienced as class differences. However, hardly ever would an English author even address *parvenues* in his own country, let alone with strong words like these.[13] Half a century earlier, de Tocqueville had observed that 'the English make game of the manners of the Americans' (Tocqueville, 1945: II, 229). The Americans on their part cultivated the Pilgrim Fathers ideology in ritualized resistance to the English. This resistance was not only to the English. This ideology also formed a barrier of conservative resistance to the cultural changes of the 1960s, a barrier that consisted of clinging to the belief 'in the almost timeless stability of American institutions and values, given to them by the Founding Fathers for all time' (Kennedy, 1997: 371).

In the 1960s, the term WASP (White-Anglo-Saxon-Protestant) was introduced to help identify the dominant group in the USA (Baltzell, 1964). These Anglo-Saxons had 'founded' the USA, and considered it to be 'theirs'.

Until the 1960s, the hyphen and 'Americans' were rarely used. One simply spoke of 'the Germans' (or Krauts) and 'the Irish,' not 'Irish-Americans'. At that time, the feeling that it 'is needless to say that all full Americans are considered naturally superior to all whose Americanism is incomplete' (Gorer, 1948: 195) may have been weakening, but it was expressed often enough without being considered to be arrogant and shameful. Since the 1960s, other groups of Americans than WASPs integrated into the American establishment to the extent that the term WASP became too narrow, too offensive to use in front of all the other groups in need of being represented when speaking of the American establishments. Most of these recently integrated groups were also of European descent. At the same time, since the 1960s, immigration into the USA has changed to include increasing numbers from Latin America and Asia. In relation to the changed composition of newly immigrant Americans, Americans from European descent came to experience themselves as the older, that is, as the established Americans. This experience would have been inspired also by their integration into the centres of power and into American country-club good societies. And although they are not WASPs, in the 1980s and 1990s, together with the WASPs, the European-Americans have indeed become the dominant group, the established. Thus, it was in an ongoing process of social integration that the term WASP became too narrow and outdated.

5.16 American Status Insecurity as a Function of Both Class and Nationality

Despite all their resistance to the English, the WASPs stayed Anglo-Saxon in the sense that, for them, English manners retained their function as a model and continued to be their main standard of comparison. 'In the USA, calling cards never functioned as they did in England. The custom was imitated but, without its function, it soon became too demanding and too English. Often, the Americans found the English model empty, but they kept accepting it as a model' (Schlesinger, 1946: 40–1). Indeed, America's open competition and class structure left some English manners without a clear meaning other than 'jolly old English', especially those manners functioning to back-up the particularly English class structure such as calling cards. They were also imitated in Germany and the Netherlands, but never fully accepted, and hardly anyone took all the complicated subtleties seriously. In the first half of the twentieth century, nowhere was the English model more fully accepted than in the USA, which can be interpreted as a symptom of status insecurity related to both class and nationality. The status insecurity was related to the open competition between the classes and would have provided an additional breeding ground for the experience of relatively strong status insecurity as a nation, which in turn fuelled the love–hate relation with the English.

This part-identification with the fathers of the Pilgrim Fathers and with a distinguished and established world power – until World War II, Britain ruled its Empire and was still a superpower – can be compared, for instance, with the part-identification of the German middle classes with the aristocracy. Both followed a similar mechanism: identification with the established. For as much as the German middle classes have a history of experiencing political frustration and humiliation in relation to the German nobility, judging from the large number of aristocratic authors of manners books – starting with Freiherr von Knigge – they must have also partly identified with them. During the first half of the twentieth century, the many editions of manners books written by authors with an aristocratic name (or pseudonym) such as von Franken and von Weißenfeld sold in their hundreds of thousands. And in more recent decades, the manners books written by Graf Wickenburg (1978), Rosemarie von Zitzewitz (1986), Gräfin Schönfeldt (1987, 1991), Gräfin von der Pahlen (1991), and Sylvia Lichem von Löwenbourg (1987) appear to have dominated the market. If not, they came close.

In the USA, particularly in the first half of the twentieth century, the Declaration of Independence was kept vividly alive by continued comparison, or rather competition with the 'old world', an expression that also captures the love–hate relation, for its connotations form a mixture of respect and disdain. A recent example is: 'Social distinction based on jobs has not only continued to prevail throughout America but now, centuries later, has found its way to the Old World' (Martin, 2003: 90). An older example is Mrs Post's chapter on the 'Growth of Good Taste in America', printed in every edition between 1922 and 1942. She went beyond a renewed Declaration of Independence straight to patriotism (as Americans prefer to call their form of nationalism):

Certain great houses abroad have consummate quality, it is true, but for every one of these there are thousands that are mediocre, even offensive. In our country beautiful houses and appointments flourish like field flowers in summer; not merely in the occasional gardens of the very rich, but everywhere. And all this means – what? Merely one more incident added to the many great facts that prove us a wonderful nation. (But this is an aside merely, and not to be talked about to anyone except just ourselves!) At the same time it is no idle boast that the world is at present looking toward America; and whatever we become is bound to lower or raise the standards of life. The other countries are old, we are youth personified! We have all youth's glorious beauty and strength and vitality and courage. (Post, 1922: 619; 1937: 859; 1942: 859–60)

Of course, Mrs Post did not mean that there are no old people in America; she expressed a we-identity that will last longer than a few generations. It is this we-identity of the We–I balance that is youthful and will live on, and a bit of its imagined immortality spills over to the I-identity. Vehement nationalism usually indicates a strong we-ideal in combination with a contested and insecure we-identity, a combination that usually blocks a deeper sense of mortality, for in defence of both we-identity and we-ideals, I-ideals are subordinated, sacrificed, and the use of violence is accepted more easily. At the same time, the value of an individual human life is impeded from rising. The death penalty can be taken as a criterion. As national integration expands, the gap between we-ideals and we-identities declines, and as the we-identity becomes more secure, the value of an individual human life usually rises together with an individual's sense of mortality. From the end of World War II onwards, the Americans seem to have continued the remarkable combination of a weak we-identity and a show of strength as a superpower.

The ritual renewal and thus acute significance of the Declaration of Independence is also demonstrated in the old American conviction that nationality is an act of will. This probably dates back to the time when those who decided to go to the colony needed to convince themselves that they were doing the right thing. In 1948, the mood was captured, although probably in somewhat exaggerated form, by an English researcher of American ways:

> The fact that the Germans and Italians were Germans and Italians was a sign of their (and their ancestors') weakness of will and their contumacy; by not *choosing* to be American they had wilfully rejected the best condition known to man and all its attendant advantages; they had shown individually their contempt for and their rejection of Freedom, Opportunity, Democracy and all the other civic virtues embodied in the American Constitution and exemplified in the American Way of Life; from weakness of spirit they had chosen to be inferior, and should therefore be so regarded. (Gorer, 1948: 168)

5.17 American Introductions, Snubbing, and Ways of Addressing Readers

In the nineteenth century, according to the social historian Hemphill, 'visiting was important because it served the crucial (but inadmissible) function of defining one's acquaintance by class. Visiting was a ritual performed with social equals, and one's visiting circle constituted a social set defined by class'. This intimate equality was captured in the saying 'A visit and an umbrella should always be returned' (1999: 151–2). Another example concerns introductions: 'Caution in introductions was indispensable because, once properly introduced, others had a claim on one's goodwill and could not be slighted' (1999: 149). Hemphill concluded:

> The similarity of British etiquette reminds us that ... economic forces were the insistent cause of the role of manners in antebellum America, despite the democratic assertions of the authors. ... [It] also reminds us that, however tenacious the hold of the aristocracy on the British social imagination, the forces behind manners were clearly those of bourgeois assertion. (1999: 148)

In the early twentieth century, many American authors still explicitly presented the English code as an example without any sign that they found it empty: 'If we could learn to treat the English people as they treat us in the matter of *introductions*, it would be a great advance. The English regard a letter of introduction as a sacred institution and an obligation which cannot be disregarded' (Sherwood, 1907: 359). In this tone of writing is regret: we would if we could, but we can't. Even when the English code was not explicitly mentioned, it was often implicitly there: 'If not friends from childhood, acquaintance between young men and young women begins with an introduction, and this matter of introduction is one rather too lightly considered on our free American soil' (Harland and Water, 1905: 123). In this example, the authors started out to prescribe introductions in an almost commanding tone, only to withdraw in the same sentence by appealing to the American dream. This quotation demonstrates a typical American ambivalence which could be found in most American manners books from around 1900. It is an ambivalence with regard to social usages such as introductions and chaperonage which functioned to keep strangers and 'intruders' at bay. These were considered important by some authors and disputed by others, but many were just ambivalent. Taking the matter of introductions 'rather too lightly' implied that the ranks of American good society did not close as efficiently as those of English good society. This also implied that protection against strangers or intruders was less efficient. This relatively weak protection from strangers, another aspect of America's rather open competition between many good societies, served to make these ranks more dependent upon external social controls and prevented the level of mutual trust from rising, which is another connotation of a remark quoted earlier (in §4.1): 'There are unfortunately many persons abroad in the land without proper social credentials, who seek new fields of adventure by the easy American manner of beginning a conversation' (Wade, 1924: 28). The ambivalence in etiquette books regarding introductions accordingly reflects yet another ambivalence: between trust and suspicion, or between the inclination to 'converse amicably with strangers about private things' and the need to be evasive and keep a protective distance. This ambivalence might explain another difference (also in §4.1):

> in fashionable London society a hostess takes it for granted that her guests understood that she would invite none but well-bred persons to her house, and that, therefore, they are safe in addressing strangers whom they encounter in her drawing-room. Americans, however, have not generally accepted this custom; and consider it better form for a hostess to introduce her guests. (Holt, 1920: 9)

Here, it is implied that Americans were not safe in addressing strangers whom they encountered in a drawing room and that they therefore had not accepted this custom. Instead, they preferred to leave the prime responsibility for new acquaintanceships to the hostess. This subtle difference was significant, because around 1900, people in American good societies still more or less tried to live up to the ideal that

> one individual introducing another becomes responsible for his good behaviour, as if he should say, 'Permit me to introduce my friend; if he cheats you, charge it to me.' Such must be the real value of an introduction among all people who expect to take a place in good society. In the course of business, and under various circumstances, we form casual acquaintances, of whom we really know nothing, and who may really be anything but suitable persons for us to know. It would be wrong, therefore, to bring such characters to the favourable notice of those whom we esteem our friends. (Hanson, 1896: 45)

This ideal never died out completely, but it did fade considerably. In the revised 1937 edition of her etiquette book, Emily Post abandoned former, more formal claims by writing, 'Under all informal circumstances the roof of a friend serves as an introduction.' Her explanation was quite explicit, 'Yesterday believed in putting the responsibility on the protector. ... The idea of protection, as it existed then, is out of tune with the world of today' (Post, 1937: 10, 353). The vanishing of protective rules of etiquette implies that the external social control they had provided was to be taken over by the people themselves, by self-controls: in these matters people increasingly had to protect themselves, and, correspondingly, came to expect exactly that capacity from each other.

As social dividing lines in America were less sharply drawn, people wanting to cross these lines were accordingly presented with a much more direct kind of advice than anything to be found in the English sources. Two examples of American advice are: 'If a person is more prominent than ourselves, or more distinguished in any way, we should not be violently anxious to take the first step' (Hanson, 1896: 38) or 'Too much haste in making new acquaintances, however – "pushing," as it is called – cannot be too much deprecated' (Sherwood, 1907: 2). These would have sounded much too crude in the ears of English social arbiters of the same period. They took the avoidance of such intruding manners more or less for granted. Consequently, English authors felt no need to point to the sanctions imposed upon such conduct. American advisors did: 'there is the tyranny in large cities of what is known as the "fashionable set," formed of people willing to spend money ... If those who desire an introduction to this set strive for it too much, they will be sure to be snubbed; for this circle lives by snubbing' (Hanson, 1896: 38–9).

This quotation demonstrates another characteristic difference: American authors of manners books regularly wrote from the perspective of outsiders – people wanting entrance into good society – into 'smart circles', *Who's Who* or the *Social Register*. In contrast, most English authors took their perspective rather exclusively from within good society. They revealed a confidence and a degree of identification with the established that is virtually absent in American manners books. Whereas the English would emphasize that 'it takes three generations to make a gentleman', most Americans would tend to agree with the author who had protested against this maxim as early as 1837: 'This is too slow a process in these days of accelerated movement' (quoted in Schlesinger, 1946: 20). In this vein, many authors were quite explicit about the class and status gaps their readers were hoping to bridge. In 1905, for example, the readership of a manners book was described in its introduction as:

> Men and women – women, in particular – to whom changed circumstances or removal from secluded homes to fashionable neighbourhoods involved the necessity of altered habits of social intercourse; girls, whose parents are content to live and move in the deep ruts in which they and their forebears were born; people of humble lineage and rude bringing up, who yet have longings and tastes for gentlehood and for the harmony and beauty that go with really good breeding – these make up the body of our *clientèle*. Every page of our manual was written with a thought of them in our minds. (Harland and Water, 1905)

With thoughts like these in mind, the identification of social arbiters with any particular 'fashionable set' or good society could only have been half-hearted, balancing an identification with rising outsiders against an identification with the established.

A peculiar position was taken by Emily Post. Edmund Wilson contrasted her book to Lilian Eichler's successful etiquette book, published a year earlier (1921); Eichler, he wrote, 'makes social life sound easy and jolly. But Mrs Post is another affair.' She 'always assumes that the reader wants to belong to Society' and 'to believe in the existence of a social Olympus'. Moreover,

> What you get in Emily Post, for all her concessions to the age's vulgarisation, is a crude version of the social ideal to which the mass of Americans aspired after the Civil War: an ideal that was costly and glossy, smart, self-conscious and a little disgusting in a period when even Mrs Oldname reflected the lavish Gildings in stimulating her visitors to realise that the clothes she wore were 'priceless' and her tableware and furniture museum pieces. (Wilson, 1962: 382)

This perspective may partly explain why, in 1922, Mrs Post still strove to gain greater acceptance for an elaborate system of introductions. A social Olympus cannot be climbed without pull. Although she admitted that 'about twenty years ago the era of informality set in and has been gaining ground ever since', she remained rather strict in presenting specific shades and boundaries for introductions. For instance, she wrote: 'A lady who goes to see another to get a reference for a servant, or to ask her aid in an organisation for charity, would never consider such a meeting as an introduction, even though they talked for an hour. Nor would she offer to shake hands in leaving' (1922: 81, 15). And, according to Mrs Post, when people were introduced, this did not necessarily bring recognition: 'if Mrs ... and Mrs ... merely spoke to each other for a few moments, in the drawing-room, it is not necessary that they recognise each other afterwards' (1922: 10). At the most, such a conversation could establish a 'bowing acquaintanceship', as it was still called in the late nineteenth century, but only if the lady of higher rank took that initiative (Hanson, 1896: 38–9). Although all this was relatively formal, and very English, Mrs Post was not really exceptional: *Social Usage in America* presented similarly strict rules for introductions (Wade, 1924).

In a few years, these formalities crumbled. In Post's revised 1931 edition, this kind of advice was omitted. By that time, in all the countries under study such conduct was branded as too formal and artificial. Such a view was typical of the 1920s, when the rise of whole social groups and an acceleration of processes of emancipation and social integration were reflected in the shape and volume of the social water-tower. The expansion of business and industry, together with an expansion of means of transportation and communication, gave rise to a multitude of new and more casual relations. These made the old system of introductions too troublesome. It was an era in which many newly wealthy families were jostling for a place within the ranks of good society, bringing about a formidable spurt of informalization. It is then that the often-observed American characteristic of social promiscuity was more sharply profiled than elsewhere, not only in the eyes of foreign observers, but also by Emily Post. In her 1931 edition she wrote: 'Fashionable people in very large cities take introductions lightly; they are veritable ships that pass in the night. They show their red or green signals – which are merely polite sentences and pleasant manners – and they pass on again' (1931: 15). And in her revised edition of 1937, Mrs Post wrote explicitly that 'introductions in very large cities are unimportant' (1937: 16). In a new section on introductions, she also wrote that, in the modern fashionable world, the titles Mr, Mrs and Miss are literally never said, except to outsiders.

> To be called 'Miss Stranger' (or Mrs Stranger if she is in her early twenties) announces that she is not a member of the group ... she does not 'belong'. Obviously, then, introductions among our younger groups are titleless ... Also, if Muriel were not really a friend to Sally Stranger, she would introduce her – and her own friends as well – by their titles of Mrs, Miss or Mr, as formally as her mother would. (1937: 9)

Another new paragraph – 'Young woman to man at dinner' – clearly demonstrated how unimportant introductions had become:

> When a young woman finds herself next to an unknown man at dinner, she more likely than not merely talks to him without telling her name. But if he introduces himself to her, she perhaps says in turn,

'I'm one of the Smiths that live on X /10/ Street.' She can't very well say, 'I'm Miss Smith,' unless she is at least approaching the mid-thirties, and she might not want him to call her 'Mary', which he would be quite likely to do were she to say 'I'm Mary Smith.' (Post, 1937: 9–10)

5.18 The American Habitus

Quite a few typically American manners, mentalities, and modes of self-regulation have been dealt with already, in this chapter and also in Chapter 4 (§§4.1 and 4.7; more examples in Wouters, 2004a: §8.1). Other differences and manners, which reveal further parts of the same overall American habitus, are business etiquette, superlatives, popularity, and 'race' or ethnicity. They will be discussed in this section.

The decline of formal rules for 'getting acquainted' was characteristic of all the countries under study. The trend implied the increased importance of individual social navigational abilities, the greater capacity to negotiate with ease and lack of friction regarding the possibilities and limitations of relations. This shift also implied that formal and external rules and constraints had to be taken more into individual custody. Social interweaving also exerted pressure towards an increased avoidance of conflicts, and in conflicts, to increased attempts at de-escalation through 'role-taking' and by using diplomacy and compromise, not anger, shouting, and ridicule. In the USA this trend was stimulated and reinforced by approaches like the 'Human Relations' school of Elton Mayo. An indication was the spread of industrial relations departments in American business. During the 1930s, 31 per cent of all companies maintained such services (Stearns, 1994: 125). This had spread earlier and much more widely in the USA than elsewhere. As to why this was, economic profitability is not likely to be the only explanation. An additional answer is related to America's class system of open competition and to its corresponding relatively high levels of coercion and violence in this competition, which were also a social legacy of the 'frontier society'. This resulted to a larger variety of codes of conflict management and their lesser predictability functioned as a barrier to a further rise in the societal level of mutual trust or mutually expected self-restraints. Americans had accordingly remained more dependent upon external social constraints. In this relational context, Americans developed 'social engineering' into a kind of security system in order to control conflicts and the dangerous emotions involved. Industrial relations departments provide one such form of external social control. They lubricate, supervise, and pacify, and it is this function of providing a social constraint towards self-restraint, lowering the levels of insecurity, mutual fear, suspicion, and hatred, which helps to explain why industrial relations departments spread so early and widely. Social engineering was also popular among politicians and others who believed it could produce a 'great society', a belief also demonstrated in number of successive 'wars', from the War Against

Alcohol (Prohibition), via the War Against Communism (McCarthyism, the Cold War, and Vietnam) the War Against Drugs to the War against Terrorism. In turn, this belief and these 'wars' indicate relatively high levels of fear and suspicion.

5.18.1   Superlatives and popularity

Americans tend to use superlatives – overstatements, judged according to not only the English standards but also to those of the Netherlands and Germany – and relatively open displays of feelings of superiority. Wide use of exaggeration and superlatives is symptomatic of uncertainty of rank, of porous and changing social dividing lines. This characteristic is connected in explanatory ways to the process-continuity of the absence of a unified and centralized good society. In the USA, a relatively open competition between a large variety of centres of power and good societies, and also a stronger reliance upon supervision and other forms of external social controls have formed a barrier to the development of lower-pitched or subtler forms of expression and negotiation; they continued to stimulate more pronounced and accentuated forms of impression management. In societies and circles where social positions are more stable and established, the use of super-latives tends to diminish. 'Bragging and boasting', 'exaggeration', 'national self-consciousness and conceit' appeared as generally recognized American characteristics in a 1941 review (Coleman, 1941). Irving Berlin dealt ironically with this tradition in his lyric 'Anything you can do, I can do better. I can do anything better than you.' A later example is a 'line' used by businessmen: 'You're a real pro; you can charm a monkey's balls! But there's a difference between you and me: I can do it *all* the time.' And Judith Martin, who joined the tradition by choosing titles for her books such as *Miss Manners Rescues Civilisation*, told me in 1992 that the use of super-latives in negotiations leaves many with the question, 'What's the bullshit degree?' (Wouters, 1998a). The question has penetrated all spheres of life. In courting and dating, it was raised in connection with the 'line', as for instance in *A Girl's Guide to Dating and Going Steady*, published in 1968:

> The first person tells the other how attractive and desirable she (or he) is. The receiver of the 'line' then faces the task of deciding how much is true and how much is false . . . [W]hen a boy with a fast line meets a girl with a gullible disposition, she sometimes falls for him hook, line, and sinker. A line is basically flattery. . . . Few dating expe-riences could be more painful than falling for a line, believing a boy truly loved you, giving him your own love, and then discovering that he was only fooling. (McGinnis, 1968: 100–1; see also Wouters, 2004a: §6.7.b).

In circles where social positions are more stable and established, the use of superlatives tends to diminish. Another example besides good English society is the Republic of the Netherlands in the eighteenth century. In the first part of that century, it had become a civilized custom in Dutch good society to outbid each other in mutual compliments. According to the historian Spierenburg, customs like these 'reflect the fact that within the patriciate there was often no certainty about rank'. In the second half of the eighteenth century, when this uncertainty had diminished, 'the higher strata in the Republic dropped these forms of ceremonial altogether... [and] the dropped habits came to be regarded as characteristic of the middle class' (1981: 30).

Open competition and its related status-striving may also explain why Americans are more directly and more openly concerned with social success in terms of popularity. In American etiquette books, manners and popularity are closely linked. The manners books from the other countries under study use the term 'success' or 'social success' in the sense of gaining respect and appreciation, but the term 'popularity' is entirely absent. The close link in American manners books seems to be another symptom of relatively high status insecurity and status consciousness.

As Karen Halttunen has vividly described it, in the antebellum period, Americans developed a high sensitivity to confidence men and a fear of hypocrisy that were countered by developing a system of 'sincerity'. In her view, it 'expressed the deep concern of status-conscious social climbers that they themselves and those around them were "passing" for something they were not'. After 1870, as she points out, 'a new success literature was emerging that effectively instructed its readers to cultivate the arts of the confidence man in order to succeed in the corporate business world' (Halttunen, 1982: xv, 198). As the expansion of this world stimulated both status insecurity and the circuits in which confidence men could operate successfully, Americans more or less started to beat confidence men at their own game, a peculiar example of 'if you can't beat them, join them'. This change implies that the link between manners and popularity was established when social manipulation was openly embraced as an art. It was a transformation that can be interpreted as a conciliating mix of middle-class and aristocratic patterns of emotion regulation: middle-class 'sincerity', 'honesty', or 'true virtue' was mixed with aristocratic 'ease', 'grace', 'charm', or, from a middle-class perspective, 'outward politeness'. This mix implied a higher level of awareness or reflection than the former, more or less automatic reliance upon being principled and sincere. Book titles such as *The Secret of Popularity: How to Achieve Social Success* were in themselves clear demonstrations of this nexus. The opening sentence of this book, published in 1904, stated that it 'has been written to the especial benefit of those men and women who wished to be liked and admired and are not', while its basic message was, 'popularity, like charity, begins really at home' (Holt, 1904: 241). This was a clear attempt to give success-striving a basis of sincerity.

In 1922, Emily Post also combined old-time sincerity with modern social manipulation. Focusing on young girls, she wrote 'Instead of depending on beauty, upon sex-appeal, the young girl who is "the success of to-day" depends chiefly upon her actual character and disposition. ... the secret of popularity? It is unconscious of self, altruistic interest, and inward kindliness, outwardly expressed in good manners' (1922: 287). Here, Post echoed the nineteenth-century demand to demonstrate 'perfect sincerity' or 'transparency of character'. At the same time, the twentieth-century competitive 'rating' aspect of popularity was quite outspoken, as has been explained in my *Sex and Manners* (2004a). The connection between the dating system and social engineering can also be seen from a change made in a later edition of a book on dating; a section in the 1958 edition headed 'How To Be Popular' was changed into 'Learning Social Skills' in the 1968 edition (Duvall and Johnson, 1958, 1968: 17).

Dale Carnegie directly connected popularity and friendship to success in business, and he brought this out straightforwardly in his book's title, *How to Win Friends and Influence People* (1936). This open emphasis on social manipulation as an art, presenting its author as some sort of 'charm-school' director, was typically American; in other countries such a title probably would have been banned as too embarrassing to be commercially sound. For instance in the Netherlands, a translation of Carnegie's book was entitled *'How to Make Friends and Establish Good Relations.'* Earlier as well as later American book titles, for instance *How to Make Friends and Deal Effectively in the Global Marketplace*, indicate a tradition of connecting friendship, popularity, and business success (i.e. Hopkins, 1937; Copeland and Griggs, 1986; Cunningham, 1992). In the countries under study, particularly in Germany, this was often experienced as a tradition of insincerity and hypocrisy (also in France, see Carroll, 1989). Indeed, in some cases this American tradition of wanting to be liked and to seek validation from everyone did go over the top. Take, for example, the following introductory words:

> Too often many of us feel like Willy Loman did in Arthur Miller's classic play, *Death of a Salesman*. Willy said: 'Oh, I'm liked, I'm just not *well* liked'. We want to be well liked, we want to be able to meet new people without a trace of nervousness or a queasy stomach, we want to know how to be casual and friendly, know how to turn strangers into friends. In short how to unlock the 'real you' and have people like you. That's what this book is going to do for you. (Cunningham, 1992: xi)

Ironically, these lines are an example of exactly that American death-denying mentality – 'Winning is not the most important thing, it is the only thing' – against which Miller's play is directed. (On the connection between American death-denial, class-denial and insecure national we-identity: see §5.16).

5.18.2 'Service' as profitable and pacifying

In the 1930s, the rise of 'social promiscuity' in the USA, or in other words the declining importance of introductions and other such hierarchically differentiated ways of establishing relations, coincided with an increasing concern for manners in the business world, that is, business etiquette. Large numbers of books, newspaper sections, and articles on the subject appeared. In the other countries under study, apart from a few translations from American books on the subject, this concern reached comparable intensity only in the 1980s and 1990s. According to Deborah Robertson Hodges, one of the authors of business etiquette books, Joan Wing, 'created a niche for herself by proving that improved manners among employees would mean improved efficiency in business' (1989: 8). Thus, what Emily Post had formulated rather casually about social navigation in fashionable society – 'they show their red or green signals – which are merely polite sentences and pleasant manners' – was taken more seriously, adopted, and further developed in offices and other places of work. In the words of Schlesinger: 'And so, by a strange juxtaposition of circumstances, stereotyped politeness, having been ejected from the drawing-room and the dance floor, found an unforeseen asylum in the marts of trade' (1946: 61). According to Hodges, 'Even the railroads jumped on the courtesy bandwagon, as the 1937 article 'Smile School: Teaching Courtesy and Service to Railroaders, U.P. Trouble-Shooter's Job' would indicate. The trouble-shooter's job is 'instructing railroad employees on the best ways to avoid getting angry at finicky passengers' (1989: 8–9).

A little later, via Dale Carnegie's famous book, the smile-school message was spread widely; it has been further developed in literature and campaigns ever since: 'no "attacking or defending" behaviours, please' (Stearns, 1994: 310). This literature prescribed the behaviour that Arlie Hochschild analysed in *The Managed Heart* (1983). She interpreted this kind of smiling and troubleshooting as a 'commercialisation of human feeling'. A rival interpretation would see it as the commercialization, or rather as the 'trickling down', of the pleasant manners of good society via the expansion of commercial classes. It was this 'waterfall of imitation descending from the social water-tower' that has resulted in the type of civility for which Harold Nicolson expressed his deep admiration: 'They call it "service," but we should describe it as a universal gift for being unfailingly helpful, hospitable and polite. It is not a virtue confined to any class; it comes as naturally to a porter at a railway station as it does to the president of a fresh-water university' (1955: 16). This 'public virtue' did not come naturally, of course, but resulted from the particular development of American society, in which good manners had a specific function in the integration process. A casual anecdote on snobs (in its old meaning of lower-class people trying to pass as higher class; see §3.6) in *How To Be Happy Though Civil*, published in 1909, illuminates this function:

> The greatest snob is polite when he knows that it is safer or more to his interest to be so. 'The idea of calling this the Wild West!' exclaimed a lady, travelling in Montana, to one of the old hands. 'Why, I never saw such politeness anywhere. The men here all treat each other like gentlemen in the drawing-room!' 'Yes, Marm, it's safer,' laconically replied the native, with a glance at his six-shooter. (Hardy, 1909: 279)

Taken more broadly, this anecdote suggests that the waterfall of imitation was also enforced by America's history of violence, and by the syndrome of 'American Tough' (Wilkinson, 1984).

In the absence of effective rules of procedure for avoiding 'strangers' and situations that might be dangerous (avoiding anger), both 'American Tough' and 'have-a-nice-day' manners can be interpreted as functional alternatives and successions to the protection provided by introductions, cards, and calling. The same goes for the multitude of American expressions such as 'take it easy', 'no sweat', or 'keep your shirt on'. This 'take-it-easy' custom has been interpreted as evidence of the desire of Americans 'to avoid mental and physical irritation and the strain that follows it' (Whyte, 1943: 131). In contrast to the tough-guy tradition, the 'take-it-easy' and 'have-a-nice-day' customs not only function to lubricate social intercourse but also to pacify it. They are another form of external social control, a kind of security system, preventing and containing conflicts and the dangerous emotions involved. They formed a social constraint towards self-restraint through which the level of insecurity, mutual fear, suspicion, and hatred was lowered. In a country where so many 'tough guys' of so many diverse groups were fiercely involved in open competition, where the state has rather incompletely monopolized the use of violence – where there are so many weapons around (and used to kill and wound people) – the need 'to avoid getting angry', not just at 'finicky customers' but in all situations, has been quite pressing. This necessity illuminates Peabody's observations that 'for Americans, a tradition of violence exists side by side with a desire to be liked by everyone' and that Americans in particular try to avoid public hostility and get 'along with others without friction by smiling affably' (Peabody, 1985: 174–211).

5.18.3   Stalled social integration

As was explained in §4.7, American social integration processes have lagged behind compared to those in England, Germany, and the Netherlands. From this chapter it appears that the development of a specifically American cultural structure – particularly America's relatively open competition between various centres of power and their good society – helps to shed light on several aspects in the development of the American habitus, such as a smaller formality–informality span, 'American tough', 'take-it-easy', and 'have-a-nice-day' manners, the use of superlatives, a preoccupation with popularity, and social manipulation or engineering. The relative absence of a strong and unified good society, protected against intruders via formalized and internalized rules regarding entrance and mobility, appears to be connected in explanatory ways to a relatively high level of (status) anxiety, a correspondingly lower level of mutual trust, and a comparatively strong reliance upon external social controls. These higher levels of social competition and mutual suspicion have been directly related to the tensions and conflicts among classes, ethnic groups, the sexes, and the generations, and more specifically to the relatively strong domination of European-Americans over other Americans. In the words of Judith Martin: 'With an occasional truce for however long it takes to clean up after a natural or unnatural disaster, we have been living in a state of low-grade mutual suspicion, subject to sudden outbreaks of hostility' (2003: 292).

For a major part of the history of the USA, African-Americans had been excluded from the 'open' competition, but from the 1950s onwards, the rise of this social group as a whole once more changed the shape and volume of the social water-tower. They remained excluded from good society and virtually absent from the genre of manners books until a middle class developed within their midst, a 'bourgeoisie' with enough economic and social capital to claim and receive more respect (see Dunning, 1972, 2004). In the early 1970s, they surfaced as Blacks in the margin of the genre, in the form of special books with special titles such as *How to Get Along with Black People: A Handbook for White Folks*. Over these decades, however, the processes of emancipation and integration coincided with the development of a class of unemployed 'ghetto poor'. In these contrasting processes, America's relatively high level of segregation 'on grounds of religion, ethnic background, or race' had to be increasingly faced and its history and appreciation of 'open' competitiveness reconsidered. When it came to African-Americans, the American process of social integration slowed down and stalled. America's history of colonization, slavery, and segregation partly provides an explanation: the frictions and conflicts inherent in this rather recent and rapid emancipation process tended to function as a barrier to further increases in the level of mutual trust and thus seemed to lead to a stalled process of nation building. For additional elaboration of this interpretation, see my *Sex and Manners* (2004a), pp. 140–7 in particular.

At the same time, the tensions and conflicts inherent in the process of emancipation and integration of African-Americans and other ethnic groups provided additional motives for avoiding public hostility and anger. In this respect, multiculturalism had a function. For example, the author of *Multicultural Manners* claimed to have written the book 'because I wanted to ease the conflicts and misunderstandings that happen to all of us every day'. By emphasizing its commercial advantages the author clearly connected to American tradition: 'It's all quite pragmatic: Having information about other people's expectations and taboos can improve human relations and increase financial benefits' (Dresser, 1996: 7–8). Thus, high levels of sensitivity and insecurity or uncertainty were combined.

5.19 Concluding Remarks

In this chapter, I have focused on ways in which the authors of manners books in each of the four countries under study have addressed readers, how they have drawn such social dividing lines as those between public and private, formal and informal, and what they wrote about social introductions. In addition to these differences, special attention has been paid to topics in manners books that stand out as specifically German, English, Dutch, and American. The illuminating power of these topics was enhanced, I believe, by placing them in a wider international comparative context, focusing on connections between differences and changes in national class structures and differences and changes in specific patterns of emotion regulation. The study of dominant manners opens a window on these connections not only because they enable one to sketch the characteristics of the groups who are included and of those who are excluded, but also because most changes in manners are related in some way or another to the representation of new groups in the centres of power and in good society. Apparently, codes of manners function to include some groups and to exclude others, but they also function to allow newcomers in. No group of established people has ever been able to keep its ranks entirely closed. The opening of the ranks of the established, the particular mix of ways in which these openings were to some extent forced and to some other extent offered, and the demands that newcomers had to meet – demands of social position, wealth, lifestyle, manners – have been different processes in each country under study. But in each country, the particular course of this process of social integration has provided a major key to the understanding of processes of national habitus formation. It appears that each particular course corresponds to changes in the forms and levels of competition and cooperation, to changes in the relative power-chances of the rising and falling strata. In summary: the specific processes of social integration in each country, particularly the ways in which the ranks of the falling strata of social superiors have been opened up *by* the rising strata – emancipation – and *to* the rising strata – accommodation – appear to have been decisive for the ways in which their distinctive codes of manners and self-regulation have influenced the type of mixture that finally resulted as the national habitus. A still shorter summary is found in an aphorism on 'National character: how in a particular country the people of different social classes relate to each other' (Goudsblom, 1998: 106).

6

The Spiral Process of Informalization: Phases of Informalization and Reformalization

Reduced inequality of power and power chances will have always gone hand in hand with various types of informalization, some of them more conspicuous than others. But it has only been since the end of the nineteenth century that the hitherto dominant formalization – the trend towards more extensive, more detailed, and stricter regimes of manners and emotions – has been overshadowed by a long-term process of informalization.

Informalization has not been a unilinear process; it has proceeded in several waves or spurts, through which the general trend accelerated. In all four countries under study, this general trend towards less formal and rigid regimes of manners and emotions became dominant in what is called the 'Fin de Siècle' or the 'Belle Époque'. It accelerated in the 'Roaring Twenties', and then again in the 1960s and 1970s, the period of the 'Expressive Revolution'. In each wave or spurt, in each round of the acceleration of this trend, more people of increasingly broader social classes became involved. This chapter opens with a sketch of the phases of informalization and reformalization in the period of research as observed by the authors of manners books and by a few authors *on* manners books. Later in the chapter, I shall connect these short-term phases in the long-term informalization process in explanatory ways to phases in the processes of social emancipation and integration.

6.1　The Fin de Siècle

At the end of the nineteenth century, according to Davidoff, 'enlargement and segregation of various "sets" within Society allowed a certain relaxation in the rigid codes of behaviour that had been demanded at mid-century' (1973: 66). This process of informalization was also observed by many authors of manners books. In 1899, for example, a German author wrote:

> The careful observer will have noticed that, in comparison to earlier times, social relations have gradually become much more informal, that is, more natural. . . . This is undoubtedly due to the general trend in art, science, and living, to strive after nature. . . . Nowadays one often hears elderly people say: 'In my time, one would not have dared to say or do this.' (Adlersfeld, 1899, quoted in Krumrey, 1984: 413)

Among the examples mentioned is the liberation of women from the judgement that a woman should wait for a man to speak the first word before she is allowed to say anything (Adlersfeld, 1899, quoted in Krumrey, 1984: 354–5).

In America's so-called Gilded Age, when the owners of the new 'regal fortunes – or, more accurately, their wives – helped to set the social pace of the times', and 'the "gold rush" crashed the portals of exclusive society' (Schlesinger, 1946: 28), Florence Howe Hall noticed:

> There is a form of folly quite prevalent in New York which seems to be peculiar to the place. It is for women who are entirely respectable and well-behaved members of Society to imitate the dress of a fast, loose class, because they think it is rather knowing to do so. Thus, one will often see a middle-aged, quiet looking woman resplendent with gold-dyed hair and a very showy costume, the incongruity between the garments and the wearer often quite startling. (Howe Hall, 1888, quoted in Miller, 1967: xi)

Florence Howe Hall ranged among the authors who came to present etiquette as an art: *The Art of Pleasing* and *The Art of Being Agreeable*. Arthur M. Schlesinger comments:

> Etiquette conceived of as art acquired an aura that had been lacking when it was viewed more prosaically as a species of unofficial law. With the maturing of American civilisation people were coming to pay greater deference to cultural concerns, were growing increasingly sensitive to the fact that in the graces of living their own great country lagged behind the Old World. (Schlesinger, 1946: 34–5)

Conspicuous consumption in the USA (Veblen, 1979 [1899]) and attempts at imitating aspects of the leisure classes in Europe may indeed have been 'often quite startling'. Its ideals may also have tended more towards the aristocratic than the 'natural', but in its emphasis on art and play, the trend displayed many of the characteristics of informalization.

Early in the twentieth century, an English author not only observed the same kind of trend, but also expressed a concern that accompanied the whole twentieth-century process of informalization:

> A great change has passed over us of late years with regard to the manners of daily life. The boy of early Victorian days was a ceremonious little creature. He called his parents 'Sir' and 'Madam', and would never have dreamed of starting a conversation at table, and scarcely in joining in it... One would not wish to see the ceremoniousness of those times revived, but it is possible that we... err in the opposite direction. (Armstrong, 1908: 187–8)

These examples are a selection from among many which indicate that the process of informalization became more and more clearly evident as the nineteenth gave way to the twentieth century.

6.2   The Roaring Twenties

The following quotation from a Dutch manners book does illustrate the 1920s wave of informalization and the author was rather positive in her answer to the question whether we are 'erring in the opposite direction':

> Half a century ago, the position of a woman was very different from nowadays; the relations between parents and children differed vastly from that of today; and the result of these enormous changes has been that manners have also changed completely. All stiffness and mannerism vanished from society and was replaced by a carefree abandon. It should be rebuked as strongly as the former exaggerated formality. ....
>
> After the stiff formality of the last century, the reaction is tending at present towards the other extreme. The natural person strikes a happy medium without difficulty, even spontaneously. (Kloos-Reyneke van Stuwe, 1927: 6, 9)

Through these words, the spirit of freedom is still speaking, but concern for the limits to that spirit tended to get the upper hand. What in the 1920s was still called 'carefree abandon' was toned down in the 1930s and for the rest integrated in the dominant codes.

In Germany, more than anywhere else, the 1920s saw widespread social misery, rising crime, and suicide rates. Not many German authors referred to the 'Golden Twenties'. One manners book referred to the war as having been a lever towards more freedom. The author explained its influence by the fact that the different classes had come to know each other in the trenches. Through these war experiences the 'external differences of rank' had diminished, he wrote, while the importance of 'knowledge of the heart' had increased (Weißenfeld, 1927: 131, 116).

An English author also referred to the war but remained on a more general level: 'The war has changed many of our long-cherished conventions. In certain respects very much more freedom is allowed now than was considered permissible up to the opening of the present reign' (Cassell's, 1921: v). Another author observed a *possible* influence of the war,[14] but was not so sure that it was positive:

> The custom of men giving up their seats in crowded trains or buses to women is not so marked as it was a decade ago. Perhaps the War and women's changed status may have something to do with it. Perhaps it may be the lack of courtesy with which many women accept this deference to their sex. Or it may be just a 'coarsening of manners'. (Troubridge, 1931 [1926]: 319)

Opposite to this interpretation of a 'coarsening of manners' was one viewing the same behaviour as an expression of heightened sensitivity. This author admitted that 'fashions to-day are much more elastic – or shall we say "loose" – than was the case a few years ago' (Terry, 1925: 18). She pointed to the fact that women's new freedom had been acquired only very recently and that it may almost be taken as a rule 'that those who appear to care least, are in reality the most sensitive – the rough rugged exterior is merely a cloak to hide the real feelings. This is frequently seen in young people, who are, in fact highly self-conscious and nervous' (Terry, 1925: 10). Here, the 'coarsening' is interpreted as an outward cover of increased sensitivity. Throughout the century, both these views accompanied the process of informalization.

Another author avoided both extremes, striking a more factual tone: 'It is true that much of the old formality of speech and action has disappeared' (Burleigh, 1925: xi). This author appeared to be well informed about good society, and just a bit worried:

> [B]etween those already established within the 'charmed circle' there is a camaraderie which permits much that would cause a new-comer to be looked at askance. It is only a familiar, assured standing in any grade of society which allows the taking of any liberties with its own particular social customs and concerns. . . . Never should the 'elasticity' of modern conventions be made the excuse for overstepping the bounds of good taste or for the neglecting to be chivalrous, courteous and considerate to one's fellow-men and women, no matter what their station in life may be. (1925: xv)

This concern about 'elasticity' was also based upon the view that this greater freedom often means perplexing complexity:

> Life in general has become freer for the modern woman, yet in some ways it is more complicated and perplexing as regards conforming to the rules of convention, than it was when her activities, both social and otherwise, were more restricted, and the decrees as to what it was correct or incorrect for her to do were so clearly defined that few perplexities arose. (Burleigh, 1925: 229)

These perplexities also resulted from the velocity of changes, making for a veritable spurt of informalization: 'In these days social affairs are conducted in a rather less formal and conventional manner than was the case even a few years ago' (Devereux, 1927: 11).

In the USA, Mrs Post observed in the first edition of her manners book that 'about twenty years ago the era of informality set in and has been gaining ground ever since' (1922: 81). Schlesinger Sr characterized Lilian Eichler's 1921 manners book quite well. Eichler, he wrote,

> saw good from the start in the revolution in manners. . . . she flayed 'the stilted formalities of another age', declaring that the simpler ways were 'sane and wholesome, creating a sense of ease and comfort in social intercourse rather than a feeling of stiff formality and restraint'.

Furthermore, she emphasized, 'The new etiquette does not "lay down the law." It offers suggestions that are based upon modern tendencies and that are subject to changing conditions and circumstances'. (1946: 53).

In a manners book of 1924, a vivid picture of the changes which took place in the Roaring Twenties' is found in a section entitled 'The Girl Who Smokes and Drinks':

> The young girl who smokes, who drinks cocktails either in public or private, who dances all night and takes breakfast with a gay party at an all-night café, or in the home of some member of the gay set, is not the well-born, well-bred girl of America's best society, even though a debutant of a fashionable circle well-known to the illustrated supplements, and sometimes of a family of great prominence. She should never be taken as a model by newcomers in society, school-mates of small towns, or the sub-debs of the cities. There have always been occasional wild birds in well-regulated families, just as there have been black sheep, but it is when society condones the actions of these trouble-makers and attributes all irregularities of conduct to the passing craze for jazz, that the parents of really nice girls become insecure and the tone of polite society is reduced to the lowest terms. ... The nice girl ... from seventeen to twenty-one ... This girl does not smoke in public, does not drink cocktails, does not indulge in 'petting parties', never listens to a vulgar story, much less tells one, but at the same time refrains from criticism of those weaker or more foolish sisters who may believe 'the good time' that youth demands is to be found in the transient if alluring features of the jazz age. (Wade, 1924: 278–80)

This conception of the 'good time' and of 'fun morality', as it was called in a later generation (Wolfenstein, 1951), was still rejected, but its allure was clearly recognized. But first came the Depression and then World War II.

6.3   From the 1930s to the 1960s

In the 1930s,

> Women no longer tried to look boyish, but emphasised their difference from men ... The neo-Victorian fashion ... expressed the contemporary nostalgia for the secure social life of the Victorians, and was accompanied by a sudden fashion among well-to-do women for having as many children as they could afford: to be prolific had been vulgar in the Twenties. (Graves and Hodge, 1941: 278)

These authors, British historians, speak of a 'Victorian revival' and, indeed, the 1930s brought some integration of new forms into old traditions, a reformalization after informalization. Here is an example of this reconnecting to tradition from a Dutch manners book: 'these days, now that for so many civilisation is all that could be rescued from the shambles of perished glory, greater importance is again being attached to correct manners than in the golden era after the war' (Haeften, 1936: 10). In this period, some authors tended to focus on continuity in the trend towards informalization, and others rather on discontinuity. And there was plenty of both. An American author wrote: '[E]veryone knows that styles have changed in the past thirty years. Not so many people, however, realise that the last six have also made a difference' (Eldridge, 1936: 177). Troubridge, as mentioned earlier, opened her new manners book in 1939 with a chapter called 'The New Etiquette Is Informal'. In her English manners book of the 1920s, she had still contemplated the possibility of a 'coarsening of manners', but by the end of the 1930s, she obviously saw that informalization was continuing, that there was more continuity than discontinuity. Troubridge observed how some people allowed 'etiquette to become a sort of bogy in their lives', and she referred to 'our grandmothers – poor dears' for whom etiquette

> *was* a bogy, you see, and in the gay 'nineties it was really little better, with taboos everywhere, and card-leaving a perfect infliction! But, nowadays, quite a new spirit has crept into those unwritten laws which we know as etiquette until, in this year of grace, one is almost tempted to say 'Anything goes!'. Not quite, of course! In the country especially, a certain formality still holds sway, but, on the whole, it can be safely said that to be informal is often, nowadays, to be correct. (1939: 7)

The chapter contains a small paragraph on '*Simplicity* – that's the key-word for social demeanour nowadays' and ends with the summons 'to steer a course nicely blended between old-fashioned courtesy and new-fashioned informality, so that we shall always be right' (1939: 11). Troubridge mainly mentioned the disappearance of stiff little formalities such as 'gilt-edged menus, carefully written out beforehand, and revealing at least six courses', and 'no arm-in-arm business, but the guests just streaming to the dining room in any order they please'.

> That last stronghold of Edwardian formality, the card-case, still plays its part, and an important one in social life, but even here the strictness has been quite definitely relaxed a bit. Don't worry, for instance, if something prevents you from returning a call within the prescribed fortnight, or if some lady on whom you have left a card is a little slow in returning it, or jump to the conclusion that she doesn't want to know you! Those who practise the new etiquette are troubled by no such fears, nor do they elevate their eyebrows if anyone drops in to leave a card after strict calling hours (three to five), or stays longer than the conventional quarter of an hour or twenty minutes. (1939: 10)

None of this may seem so informal to many present-day readers, but all readers of this book, however, will sense the almost tangible joy of liberation. Moreover, this relaxation may have been welcomed with greater joy in England because of the country's relatively strict and elaborate regime of gatekeeping and its rather rigorous social control.

6.4 Periodization Matters: The Two World Wars

In his book on the history of American manners, Schlesinger reported the assertion of an authority on social usages that immediately after World War II, 'formality was pushed aside with a barbaric shout' (1946: 62). As his book was published in 1946, this observation probably illustrates mainly how impressive the relief from wartime behaviour and feeling had been. From a somewhat greater distance and surveying a longer period, however, it seems that World War II functioned predominantly as a catalyst. Arguably, in terms of changes in the codes of manners and emotion regulation over the twentieth century, both major wars and their aftermath seem to have had little independent lasting effect on the overall trend.

This perspective of overall continuity rather than discontinuity also appears to be inherent in the periodization of the history of courtship in the USA discerned by Ellen Rothman. She described a rapid erosion of taboos between 1910 and 1930, followed by a more gradual change from 1930 to 1965, and a renewed burst of informalization after that (1984: 287). A similar periodization can be found in the studies by Cancian (1987) and Cancian and Gordon (1988). The latter two sociologists noted: 'Public opinion surveys...show that modern norms accelerated in the 1920s, fell during the depression and World War II, and then accelerated again in the 1960s and 1970s' (1988: 330). Their conclusion from an analysis of a random sample of marital advice articles from 1900 to 1979: 'The long-term trend to modern norms in the United States during the twentieth century is linked to a broad cultural shift to greater tolerance of diversity' (1988: 333). This long-term trend of informalization is seen to be connected with collective emancipation:

> If we consider the entire twentieth century, instead of recent decades, we find a zigzag pattern of change associated with waves of political liberation and oppression, not a linear trend to modernity. When the authority of the government and established institutions was challenged, the authority of husbands over wives was also challenged. (1988: 337)

Their specification of the time of these waves as 'during the 1920s and the late 1960s' (1988: 313) implicitly confirms the conclusion that the barbarity of the wars was of small significance for overall developments in regimes of manners and emotions.

6.5   The Expressive Revolution

The 1960s and 1970s provided almost innumerable examples of challenged authority in combination with a critique of the 'inauthenticity', 'superficiality', and 'falsity' of 'icky old' manners. **American** examples from the 1960s are what was called the counterculture, comprehending the civil-rights movement, the Black Panthers, blue jeans and work shirts, long hair and mini skirts, the 'Fuck the Draft', and other 'dirty speech' protests. Kenneth Cmiel studied rulings of the US Supreme Court since the *Chaplinsky v. New Hampshire* (1942) rulings, a case in which the defendant was convicted for calling someone a 'damned racketeer' and a 'damned fascist'. Free speech gradually won the upper hand over the demand for verbal niceties in civil society, and Cmiel concluded that this was 'the legal version of the informalization going on in American society at large' (1994: 284).

Of course, among those in the front lines of the 1960s movements, manners books were not popular. They were perceived as representing the authorities and inauthenticities that were under attack during that momentous decade. Most authors of manners books, however, tried to strike a happy medium, although in a different tone of voice.

A factual **German** voice of the late 1960s said: 'Much that to our grand-mothers still counted as inadmissible and "indecent" no longer gives any offence to us, and parts of the teachings and good advice of our own childhood have also lost their validity' (Haller, 1968: 93). A book published in 1970 contains a similar observation, only the tone is more strongly emotionally involved:

> Suddenly, a youth appeared on the stage who no longer put up with the rules that were 'issued from above and, therefore, to be accepted'. They demanded sense and meaning: the question 'Why should we?' had to be posed... Consideration, complaisance and humanity in particular are more necessary at present in all social contacts than the hollow formality of an outdated etiquette. (*Umgangsformen Heute*, 1970, quoted in Krumrey, 1984: 186–7)

The author of a book published in 1973 also seemed under the influence. In the preface, he first presented some examples of recent changes, such as state ministers who in a discussion with students sat unabashedly on the floor, couples in love frankly exchanging gestures of tenderness in public, and ministers of religion on television addressing their audience without wearing a tie. Then they exclaimed:

> Freedom, freedom above all [*Freiheit, Freiheit über alles*]... Change wherever we look... Hollowed out conventions and formalities turned stale are bid farewell – now, the meaningful, sensible forms stick out all the more clearly. For without this basic framework of manners, human relations simply cannot be organised.... Youth protest has brought a shot of ease and informality, even uninhibitedness into the lives of each one of us. (Wachtel, 1973: 10)

By comparison, **English** authors were more restrained. Take, for example, this one:

> Television, films, certain newspapers and weekly magazines, novels and plays and autobiographies have for many people broken down the taboos on what can be discussed in public. Particularly this relates to the old indiscussibles, intimate sexual experiences, detailed descriptions of violence and every kind of physical experience and emotion. (Edwards and Beyfus, 1969: 187)

A book representing that typically English custom of 'sending up' institutions or people, contains the following example of romanticizing the lower classes:

> Try and get out of your usual world, to meet people other than the ones you have been brought up to know. Everyone has something to give... A gypsy, for instance, ... Even beggars and tramps are frequently fascinating. There is always a story about how they became what they are. Circus people are delightful. (Kandaouroff, 1972: 25)

Giving in to this fascination was acknowledged to demand confidence and strong emotion regulation: 'You can do anything, however outrageous, if you know how to carry it off. If you keep your dignity, nothing you do will ever make you feel ashamed of yourself' (Kandaouroff, 1972: 27). In these words, keeping your dignity and avoiding shame are presented as a necessary condition. Any attempt 'to get out of your usual world' is an attempt at decontrolling and unwinding, indeed, but it should certainly remain controlled. It clearly is a *conditional* 'anything goes': a '*controlled* decontrolling'.

One of the 'old indiscussibles' that became a fascinating topic, a topic representing not the lower classes but the lower 'animalic' functions, was defecating and urinating. Under the heading of 'Getting away to the lavatory' was now written: 'The technique of getting away has changed considerably. ... A number of middle-class euphemisms, such as "the can," "the John," the "loo" are still current, but we note an increasing number of people who simply ask quite straightforwardly where is the lavatory' (Edwards and Beyfus, 1969: 192). More than a decade later, in a paragraph on welcoming guests, it was still deemed necessary to write: 'Be sure all guests know where the lavatory is as shy folk may not care to ask' (Penelope, 1982: 12). And even as late as 1990, the taboo may have ended but the fascination lingered on: one of the chapters of a manners book was called 'Lavatories', and it raised the question 'What is the current protocol about going to the loo?' (Killen, 1990: 130). There was no such interest in the other countries under study.

Dutch voices representing the spirit of the era of informalization were in short supply. The reason is simply that in the years 1967 to 1982, hardly any manners books appeared in the Netherlands. Only in one book, published in 1967, were there the sounds of a prelude to the expressive revolution:

> Our grandmothers and great grandmothers groped about with *The Code of Madame Etiquette*. That code contained a lot that now appears silly to us. After Madame Etiquette there have been other zealots for correct ceremonial, and again, there is a lot that now appears silly to us. But one thing is forgotten, namely this: we should not cling to the letter of the law and forget its spirit. Someone who is tough and rigid in following Madame Etiquette through life, who does not budge an inch from the path she has pointed out, is – to put it mildly – a marionette. (Eyk, 1967: 3)

6.6 The 1980s and 1990s: Reformalization

In all four countries under study, the spurt of informalization came to an end between the end of the 1970s and the start of the 1980s. In the new phase, certain informalization offshoots remained operative, but on the whole *reformalization* gained the upper hand: dominant regimes of manners and emotions tended towards greater strictness, hierarchy, and consensus. There was renewed respect for discipline, for law and order, and the sexual revolution was pronounced over and done with.

In **England**, new interest in manners was verbalized with typically English 'send-up' humour in book titles and subtitles such as *Etiquette for Very Rude People* and *Bad Form, Or How Not To Get Invited Back*. The author of *Bad Form* wrote in a serious tone that 'there seems nowadays to be as much uncertainty in matters of etiquette as there has ever been', and he proceeded to turn the world upside down by giving 'advice on the appropriate misbehaviour' (Brett, 1984: 7). The introduction to the first book said: 'The world is going to hell. All we can do is behave in a way that makes us look good on the trip' (O'Rourke, 1984). Another author wrote:

> It is precisely in trying situations that we need our manners most, so a guide to good manners in a time of apocalypse may be appropriate. The fact that someone may drop The Bomb in the middle of our mad tea party should in no way deter us from serving the best tea and the best conversation in our best manner – for ever. Formality should be maintained from the cradle to the grave – and beyond. (Crisp, 1985: 11–12).

The slowing down of the spurt of informalization was noticed as factually as its beginning: 'Our aim is to construct an improved framework that will increase opportunities for convivial interchange without restricting the pleasures of self-expression and individuality' (Debrett, 1981: 10). An observation that seems to build on this idea is that manners have changed from fixed rules to flexible guidelines – an observation made in more than one country under study. Here is the English version:

> the guidelines given here, on points of etiquette, shouldn't be taken as absolutes. For a central point of this book is that there *are* no absolutes and that it is necessary to get away from the absolutism which bedevils most books on manners and etiquette. . . . Good manners are creative and allow change and adaptation. (Bremner, 1989: 5)

Indeed, in a more strongly differentiated world in which a larger variety of social circles had a modelling function, a degree of changeability or flexibility came to be demanded:

> [N]ew employees are expected to adapt to the 'manners of the country'. For example, the worlds of the arts and the media are traditionally informal, both about dress and address, while the worlds of banking and the civil service tend to be conservative in dress and strictly hierarchical in behaviour. But even within these broad outlines, firms differ and the advice given below should be modified and adapted as appropriate. . . . The basic, and frequently offered, social advice holds good in this area also – that one should behave in a relaxed and natural manner as far as possible, and play difficult situations by ear. (Debrett, 1981: 251)

In the 1980s, some authors of manners books tried to find some new 'organizing principle' that could function as a supportive hold on contacts allowing for – and also demanding – many more alternatives and options than the old comparatively simple and fixed rules offered. For example, in a chapter called 'Gay Guidelines', one reads:

> If you could master the mores of the class immediately above you, ran the theory, you stood a good chance of climbing into it. Today, it isn't so much class that moulds behaviour as category . . . shared experience creates the strongest bonds of all. In the world of natural science, this form of grouping by similarities is known as cladistics. Social cladistics sees a shared pattern of behaviour as arising from common experience, each 'species' posing different problems of etiquette or manners. (Courey, 1985: 7–8)

All in all, English authors of manners books wrote with considerable detachment about the changes in the waves of informalization and reformalization that were occurring. Their detached tone of voice made these waves seem less high, more gradual, and/or more moderate and/or received with more moderation than in the other countries under study. Each one of these possibilities was closely connected to the English habitus of being rather 'imperturbable', as the cliché puts it, as well as to the strong English tradition of socially integrating new groups coming into political power.

In the adapted and rewritten edition of a **German** manners book that was published first in 1970, moralizing remarks such as 'If young people have difficulty in coming to terms with the world, this usually results from their bad upbringing' (*Umgangsformen Heute*, 1970: 34) had been deleted. Much advice characteristic of informalization was left unchanged, for example, 'Anyone who abstains from formal authority, gains real authority' and 'Fear really is the instrument of false authority' (*Umgangsformen Heute*, 1988: 41–3), and:

> *Fewer formalities – more tact!* At present, prevalent manners allow each person a freedom to apply other forms to the extent that this is tactfully feasible. To choose this risk is better than to stiffen the formalities of yesterday. Formality restrains. Flowing manners encourage the solidarity of the generations and the understanding of fellow human beings.

After a few remarks on the reception of the first edition of this book, the new edition offers a retrospect trying to explain some of the changes:

> The 1970s showed how a sceptical generation (as Helmut Schelsky called them) again learned to appreciate the feeling for human contacts. To find strength in this feeling of solidarity again became a desirable goal. The tragedy of this generation is that, by the 1980s, hundreds of thousands of them became unemployed or did not find an entry to professional training. Thus, young people in search of a job recognised the advantages of the security which ensues from good manners. (*Umgangsformen Heute*, 1988: 16)

A similar explanation was given by another author in her preface: 'For anyone who wants to make headway, professionally and socially, good manners will be required. Thus, it is far from accidental that just in recent years good manners are highly appreciated again' (Löwenbourg, 1987). The back of another book contains in capital letters: MANNERS ARE BACK AGAIN (Wolter, 1990). Another author coolly polemicizes:

> Are manners back again? The question is rather silly. People always have manners. Neanderthal people already had manners, not to speak of the ancient Romans. Only very different manners. All who ask this question deem only themselves and their own manners (or those of their group) worth mentioning, and thus 'manners' or 'good manners' only marks what is familiar . . . This is static behaviour. . . . We are changing all the time, and our manners change along. (Schönfeldt, 1987: 13)

These insights were explained in a mechanistic way, as if there was a 'law' of 'ever alternating conditions: strict and restrained formality and then again freedom without borders' (1987: 18). Only in recent decades, she added, has this alternation become less extreme, for in the public world of today, people have a choice: 'Informal or correct, that is the question.' In this formulation, she avoided the word formal – probably because former attacks on formality were still well remembered, and also because the word no longer seemed to correspond to the rise in complications that choice had brought. For, 'whereas a few years ago . . . informal behaviour was to be found among the informal people and correct behaviour among the correct ones, this practical division of the world is gone. Left wing people wear ties and right wing people open shirts' (Schönfeldt, 1987: 213). These changes imply an uncertainty that was also connected with the disappearance of a clear centre with a modelling function: 'We no longer have a Society for developing our collective desires and our expectations of each other, only television' (Schönfeldt, 1987: 26).

In the USA, the end of the last spurt of informalization was noticed and commented upon in many different, including quite factual, ways: 'I am aware that etiquette relaxed enormously in the Sixties and has only recently begun a swing back to more formality' (Young Stewart, 1987: xii). More formality implied that, in the 1980s, manners books sold well: 'we may say that over the last ten years or so, there has been in America something of an etiquette boom' (Barrows and Weiner, 1990: ix). It also implied that several authors observed a lack of discipline. One of them, Mrs Post, blamed psychologists:

> During the 1960s and early 1970s, psychologists went overboard in recommending that parents be their children's 'pals', and promoted the idea that disciplining a child would inhibit the growth of his character and personality. Children called their parents by their first names, were never required to shake hands when meeting older people, to say 'please' or 'thank you' nor to adhere to any other social conventions. Instead of becoming mature, independent adults, these children grew up as lazy, confused individuals, lacking respect not only for their parents but for all society. Fortunately, young parents today have seen the results of that lack of discipline, and have reversed the trend. If you, as parents, lead your youngsters to believe that your experience, your education, and your attitudes are worth emulating, respect will follow of its own accord. (1984: 288)

The new star of the manners boom, usually defending tradition in a playful way, was 'Miss Manners'. What Miss Marple is to the murder mystery, Miss Manners is to the etiquette mystery. Judging from sentences such as 'There must be a solution to all of this, and Miss Manners has it' (Martin, 1983: 290), and from a book title such as *Common Courtesy, in which Miss Manners Solves the Problem that Baffled Mr. Jefferson* (1985), the comparison is intended. An early example of her attack on informality is: 'The widespread use of first names, sports clothing, audio recreation, and other attributes of "informality" in the work world has assisted in the illusion that no-one really needs to perform a service for anyone else' (Martin, 1979: 417). In the 1990s,

Judith Martin's partisanship for good manners was assessed as 'the closest thing to a call for a revival of... the notion that civilities must precede civil rights' (Cmiel, 1994: 290).[15]

Whereas Miss Manners radiated a negative appraisal of informality, the author of a 1988 book on *Service Etiquette* used the term informality more descriptively to encompass the social changes of a century: 'In the past there have been definite times of social change – for example, the Victorian Age and the Jazz Age. Perhaps one could say that today is the age of informality.' Negative connotations were removed immediately by adding: 'Informality does not imply a barrier to gracious living' (Swartz, 1988: ix).

In the **Netherlands**, after a publication gap of about fifteen years, nine new etiquette books were published in between 1982 and the end of 1984 (Wouters, 1987). The demand was sizeable and the tone of writing conveyed a self-assured good society:

> Unlike the legal world, the social world has no coercive measures to put people on the right track and keep them there. But society does see to it that anyone who does not adhere to the proper rules of conduct – whether due to ignorance, a lack of understanding or even unwillingness – puts himself outside the bounds of society. He is out of the running, he barely counts any more. (Groskamp-ten Have, 1983: 5)

Yet, in comparison with the older ones, the newer etiquette books clearly revealed an almost casually formulated tolerance. In one introduction, it was noted that, in reaction to some of the rules, the younger generation will say: 'That might be the done thing, but this is how we do it!' and the author continued by stating 'That is everyone's perfect right, of course' (Bakker-Engelsman, 1983: 8). There were no such *escape clauses* in the older etiquette books.

Another common characteristic of the new manners books is that they all bore traces of a process of *social equalization*, the decrease in power differences between the classes and the sexes:

> It used to be the task of 'the attentive hostess or host, whichever the case may be' to see to it that everyone had a good time. Now that the host or hostess, besides being the much-appreciated organiser of a party, has become more a *primus inter pares*, a pleasant course of events depends much more on the entire group. And on each member of it individually. (Grosfeld, 1983: 312)

Another novelty in comparison with older manners books was the variability of manners according to *different relations and situations*, a development most clearly formulated and elaborated upon by the authors already quoted for their effort to provide 'flexible guidelines that everyone should be able to interpret depending on the situation' – a change from altimeter to plane geometry. Another example is: 'Then we have the dinner party at home with friends or relatives or with the firm's managing director as the guest. The word "or" might indicate a shift from strictly informal to somewhat more formal behaviour, depending on the relation with the boss (or with some other special guest)' (Grosfeld, 1983: 223). Other authors also bore witness to this development: 'But giving examples is still risky. Here again, everything depends on the occasion, the environment and the situation. And what might be witty in one person can become coarse in another' (Bakker-Engelsman, 1983: 85). And: 'Unfortunately cut-and-dried answers cannot always be given. Sometimes one has to apply one's own norms and ask oneself in which situation one would feel most comfortable' (Eijk, 1983: 7).

6.7   A Spiral Process of Informalization

In the 1960s, especially, the process of informalization spread to increasing numbers of people to include most layers of the societies under study. Both the spurt of social integration and of informalization became conspicuous: 'emancipation' (of the working classes, of women, of homosexuals, etc.), 'equality', 'permissiveness', and the 'permissive society' became hot topics in public debates. This eye-catching power brought the sociologist Michael Schröter to the paradoxical conclusion: 'Perhaps the present informalisation is just bringing previous processes of formalisation... into the field of view' (1985: 2). Indeed, the long-term process of informalization is inconceivable without the preceding long-term processes of formalization. In the twentieth century, currents or short-term phases of informalization were followed by currents of formalization, and after some turmoil accompanying the change, a synthesis of currents and counter-currents apparently tended in the direction of a code of manners in which informalization held the upper hand. There has been a zigzagging spiral process of informalization.

The following visual images may illustrate this spiral process. The continued relaxation and differentiation of manners can be observed in photographs: the traditionally stiff studio poses of serious looking people, dressed in their Sunday best, were replaced in the 1960s and 1970s by spontaneous *snapshots* of relaxed and smiling people, dressed according to (spare) time and place (Oosterbaan, 1988). In the 1980s, in addition to a continued appreciation of relaxed and informal pictures, the presentation of self became somewhat more serious and reserved, and many changed (back) from sweater and jeans into suit and tie – a return to old traditions, while integrating new ones.

The 'soft look' bra, introduced in the 1970s, when some women had given up wearing bras altogether, may be taken as another, playful illustration of the same process. This bra supports the breasts, as did the old type of 'hard look' bra that was still common in the 1950s and early 1960s, without removing the image of 'free' flesh and the visual suggestion of nipples. This triplet – hard look bra, no bra, soft look bra – also illustrates the 'dialectical' change from formal via informal to a synthesis of both. At the same time, the hard-look bra symbolizes the rigid second-nature type of control over 'first nature', while no bra and the soft look bra symbolize the attempt to reach back to first nature.

A similar sequence can be seen in the history of corsets. Wearing a corset spread from Spanish aristocratic women in the sixteenth century to other strata and other countries, and it flourished in the nineteenth century. The spread of the corset symbolizes the spread of increasing control over the body – loose clothes came to indicate loose morals. Towards the end of the nineteenth century, as for instance in the movement for reform of clothing, ideals of naturalness amalgamated with ideals of beauty. From that time onwards until the 1960s, the boned corset came to be used only as an orthopaedic gadget for female bodies gone out of control, ones that burst the bounds of the prevailing standard of beauty. This standard increasingly contained ideals of naturalness, but not without control: much female flesh that was not quantitatively excessive remained controlled by corset-like underwear, girdles, straps, corselets, and bras. Only at the end of the 1960s did women succeed in liberating their bodies from this kind of control. However, it was not a full liberation. It was clearly a controlled decontrolling, while the control of the corset over the body was continued as self-control: women turned heavily to diets, sports, aerobics, fitness, home trainers, and other forms of 'working the body' such as plastic surgery (Steele, 2001; see also Finkelstein, 1991, and Davis, 2003). Since the 1980s, the corset has reappeared: 'the visible corset has become a socially acceptable form of erotic display'; its 'subversive charisma' was exploited by performers and designers such as Madonna and Gaultier (Steele, 2001: 168–70). As it is taken for granted that the women who wear one do not need such a corset for controlling their bodies, the visible corset can also be taken as a symbol of how ideals of beauty, naturalness, and self-control have merged with each other.

The 'working-the-body' trend seems more marked in the USA and England than in Germany and the Netherlands, a difference which may be related to a history of more puritanical repressive control of the body in the former two countries. A hint in this direction is found in an English manners book of the mid-1980s. The book introduced and discussed a new word for a new trend: 'Body-people: those whose goal is some platonic ideal of absolute fitness', and for whom the 'body is not so much a sex object, more a way of life. ... All Body People look at, and talk about, their bodies incessantly' (Courey, 1985: 115–17). The same author provided a key for understanding the Body-People trend when writing:

> The British pet, moreover, holds one compelling psychological card that is missing from the paw of the average Eurodog or cat. In this country, we are not on the whole a culture of touch – especially where men are concerned. In Europe, men touch anyone within reach as naturally as they laugh or smile; for the British male, permissible

touching is confined to his wife and his dog. And on the whole, the
dog does better. (Courey, 1985: 137)

This graphic extension of the metaphor of the stiff upper lip to the whole
body was the visible expression of a rigid kind of second-nature self-control
(see §5.10). Liberation from this stiffness and rediscovery of the first-nature
body has given Body-People cause for celebration, and cause for cerebration
among Body-Intellectuals (those connected with journals such as *Body &
Society*, established in the mid-1990s, and with national and international
conferences such as *Controlling Bodies* (24–26 June 2002, University of
Glamorgan, Wales).

My last visualization of these short-term phases of informalization and
reformalization and their spiral movement consists of changes in popular
dancing. At the beginning of the twentieth century, the popular waltz
visualized the prevalent ideal of relations of harmonious inequality
between the sexes: the man led, the woman followed, and together they
created harmonious figures. Each movement on his part presupposed one
on her part and vice versa. In the 1920s, the waltz came to be seen as a
manifestation of an old-fashioned and more inhibited way of dancing.
But, at the start of the century, the waltz still represented a break from
earlier group dances such as the cotillion. Accordingly, as a dance for two,
the waltz was a clear step in the direction of individualization. Actually, the
waltz was a prelude to the individualized dancing of the 1920s. Moreover,
because it involved closeness and touching, the waltz was also a harbinger
of the eroticization of dancing. At that time, however, the waltz was
scorned and new dances (among which the Charleston is best remembered)
were welcomed as 'liberation from the constraints of earlier patterns of
dancing..., in one word: one dances individually' (Viroflay-Montrecourt,
[*c.*1920] II: 68). From the end of the 1920s onwards, the waltz and other
such dances regained popularity and they prevailed until somewhere in
the 1960s, when individualized dancing again became popular and even
dominant. In individualized dancing, each individual tries to adjust his or
her movements to the music as well as to those of a partner. The dancers
follow less of a set pattern; their movements are more informal and more
varied. It is less easy to see who is leading and who is following, and it is
less predictable. Different shades and gradations of leading and following
are possible. If the two partners are well-matched, there can very well be
moments when all the separate, loose movements seem nevertheless to
flow together into joint harmonious figures. This would seem to be the lofty
ideal of individualized dancing. During the 1980s and 1990s, there was a
revival of the older type of dance styles, and popular dances such as salsa
fit the description of the waltz again. Many other dances involved sticking
to the style of individualized dancing, and thus the whole twentieth-
century trend in dancing runs parallel with the spiral movements in the
process of informalization: more variation, enlarged choice of acceptable
alternatives.

6.8 Spiral Processes of Informalization and Social Integration: Two Phases

To a large extent, the spiral process of informalization can be understood from alternating accelerations and decelerations in the emancipation and integration of increasingly wider social groups – their representation in the centres of power and its good society. Writing about the period after World War II, and inspired by two phases or waves that Norbert Elias distinguished in expanding networks of interdependencies (Elias, 2000: 430–4), Bram van Stolk and I distinguished a *phase of accommodation and resignation* that went on up to the mid-1960s, after which there was a *phase of emancipation and resistance* up to the end of the 1970s (1987: 152–61). Up to the mid-1960s, we noted a tradition of *harmonious inequality* as the prevailing relational ideal: even in more controversial unequal relations such as those between employers and employees (and their organizations), this ideal of relating in harmonious inequality prevailed over the more radical ideals which held (class) struggle to be inevitable. Ideally, conflicts should be avoided. In the mid-1960s, the pressure on established groups to justify their authority began to build up. At the same time, the strength of ideals of harmonious inequality underwent a rapid decline. A new phase of collective emancipation and resistance had commenced. It was also a phase of social integration that embraced more groups of people than ever before. Relations between men and women, parents and children, older and younger people, professors and students, employers and employees, all became clearly marked by out and out tensions. In the early 1980s a new phase of accommodation and resignation manifested itself with increasing clarity. Old and new established groups became increasingly successful in asserting their power and distinctness through a return to greater formality, including forms of accepted informality. Members of all strata again orientated themselves principally around the example of the more formal manners and lifestyles of good society, and virtually all groups focused more strongly on stabilizing and asserting their power and their distinctness. Thus formalizing tendencies again gained the upper hand (Wouters, 1986).

During the phase of emancipation and resistance, it was the lessening of power inequalities between social groups that was conducive to greater informality, while in the phase of accommodation and resignation, the stabilization or even increase of power inequalities triggered formalization and more open displays of distinction. In turn, these phases in the spiral processes of social emancipation, integration, and informalization were connected principally – and have fluctuated along with – alternating dominance in the twin processes of the differentiation and integration of social functions. When differentiation of functions and social groups had the upper hand, the change in the balances of power eventually allowed for chances of collective emancipation, for a phase of emancipation and resistance to emerge, and for informalization to prevail. Indeed, on a general level of understanding, the transitions of all these phases may be understood as expressing the twin processes of differentiation and integration of social functions and groups, together amounting to expanding and denser networks of interdependence.[16]

The long-term process of informalization became dominant when large groups with 'new money' emancipated themselves by forcing 'old-money' establishments to open up. The expansion of business and industry, together with an expansion of means of transportation and communication, gave rise to a multitude of new types of relations for which the old formality was too troublesome. This happened again in the 1920s, when many newly wealthy families were jostling for a place within the ranks of the centres of power and their good society. According to Leonore Davidoff, the social integration of new groups that were claiming political power has always been the strength of English political continuity, but particularly in the 1920s, the social absorption of new groups was becoming a problem:

> At the end of the nineteenth century it had been relatively easy to integrate the small number of trade unionists and labour leaders via the mechanisms of formal Society. It was obvious to the new-comers that there were political gains to be had through social contacts while the more perceptive social leaders realised that there were important new elements in the nation's life which ought to be absorbed. ... But after the war, when there were so many more working-class representatives and when, above all, their attachment to working class culture formed their primary tie with their constituents, many refused the blandishments of upper- and middle-class social life. (1973: 69)

In the new phase of emancipation and resistance of the 1960s and 1970s, with entire groups rising socially, practically all relations became less hierarchical and formal. The emancipation and integration of large social groups within welfare states coincided with informalization: the regime of manners rapidly lost rigidity and hierarchical aloofness. Many modes of conduct that formerly had been forbidden came to be allowed. Sexuality, the written and spoken language, clothing, music, dancing, and hairstyles – all expressions – exhibited the trend towards informality.

In the course of the 1960s, it gradually came to be taken for granted by more and more socially rising groups of outsiders – workers, women, children, teenagers, homosexuals – that changes for the better were to be expected. Their position within the existing set-up were no longer mainly perceived as something acquired as a result of a long and hard struggle in the past, as had been the case in the previous phase. From then on, their positions were subjected to a critical comparison with utopian images and expectations for the future of greater and lesser magnitude. For many people, it became increasingly difficult to picture any kind of unequal relation as being harmonious. In the minds of most of the gradually rising, the relational ideal of harmonious inequality was repressed by their preoccupation with humiliation, whereas in the previous phase they would have tried to repress exactly these feelings of humiliation. Now, on the grounds of their preoccupation with their humiliating experiences, they put a great deal of emphasis on the solidarity within their own ranks regarding their 'justified demands' pertaining to 'unjust' differences.

It is striking that in the social sciences, at the beginning of this phase of emancipation and resistance, the distinction was first drawn between a *harmony model* and a *conflict model*, a distinction that rapidly became a matter of general usage. In the Netherlands, the two terms became common among politicians, trades union leaders, the spokesmen of liberation movements, and so on all the way down to schoolchildren. The distinction gave outsiders the opportunity to formulate the legitimacy of their opposition to inequality; they were simply 'choosing the conflict model', a respectable strategy. The dangers and fears that were previously perceived in such conflicts and tensions, a perception reflected in the figurational ideal of harmonious inequality, had strongly diminished and the more rigid and formal ways of controlling these dangers and fears were attacked as being too stiff, showing conceited superiority and exaggerated anxiety for loss of power, status, and self-control.

In the 1980s, the collective emancipation that had flourished in the 1960s and 1970s disappeared. The rising classes stopped rising, and a market ideology spread. This reflected a new phase in the process of global interweaving. A change in the world economy coincided with a change in national power structures: politicians and governments came to side less with unions and social movements, and more with commercial and managerial establishments. From the 1980s onwards, the prevailing power structures allowed for only individual emancipation. Individuals aspiring for respectability and social ascent came to feel strongly dependent again on the established elites and they adjusted their manners accordingly. Thus the sensibilities and manners of the established again came to function more unequivocally as a model. This shift was reinforced in the 1990s by the collapse of the Soviet Union and the Iron Curtain. In the USA, the only remaining 'superpower', feelings of superiority strengthened both we-identification with the established and demands to conform to the dominant regime of manners and emotions. In Europe, the events following the collapse of the Iron Curtain – breaking out into violence in some cases, such as in former Yugoslavia – intensified feelings of fear, insecurity, and powerlessness. Increased awareness of the lack of control that European nation-states could exercise over global processes stimulated a tendency to identify with the established order and to focus with greater concern on anything perceived as a threat to it – crime and bad manners in particular (Wouters, 1999a and 1999b). Accordingly, the whole regime of manners became somewhat more compelling. To a large extent, however, informal behaviour that had become socially acceptable in the 1960s and 1970s remained so, through their endorsement by, and integration into, the standard, dominant code of manners and human rights.

6.9   Social and Psychic Changes in Spiral Processes

A major driving force of the ongoing differentiation of functions, shifting balances of power, and greater interdependence was (and is) the competitive struggle for greater freedom and independence. In the course of this ongoing process, shifts in power balances at times offered collective power chances to groups of relative outsiders, and these chances came to be realized and expressed in social ranking, but usually not without some delay. The process of realizing collective power chances has a psychic (mental) and a social side. Individuals need to become aware of these chances and to shake off the submissiveness that the old balance of power demanded. This is not as easy a process as it may sound because this submissiveness is usually ingrained rather firmly in the personality. It triggers a fear of rising (see §3.5). In order to make their latent power manifest, the individuals concerned needed to get organized and collectively demand what cannot be refused to them for much longer.[17]

Part of the process in which latent power was transformed into manifest power consisted of emphasizing and 'discovering' of an increasing number of *conflicting interests* by groups of outsiders. In the 1960s, more than ever before, social integration amounted to national integration, and this also brought about the 'discovery' of conflicting interests on the national scale. Whereas previously there had been a nationally accepted stock of *common interests*, in this phase of emancipation and resistance, several of these interests came to be rejected as one-sidedly favouring established groups. Manners and ideals based upon the rejected definition of common national interests came to be interpreted as being based on oppression on the one hand and a 'slave mentality' on the other. In many negotiations where the established had been able in the past to appeal successfully to such general interests as national welfare and national solidarity, they now met resistance.

In negotiations on a national scale, under the continuous upward pressure exerted by rising groups on the established in the world of commerce and industry, the power range of the latter was restricted while that of governments widened. The less unequal balance of power between established groups and rising outsiders allowed governments a larger area of play for tipping that balance. Moreover, with public spotlights mainly focusing upon all kinds of conflicting interests, a great deal of injustice loomed up that governments were expected to 'do something about'. In the 1960s and 1970s, these conditions created a favourable 'government climate'.

In the phases of emancipation and resistance, collective emancipation tended to stimulate rather positive expectations of the future, rising levels of confidence and declining levels of fear and suspicion. In the phases of accommodation and resignation in which social integration and formalization had the upper hand, the tide flowed in the opposite direction: visions of the future became more modest, expectations diminished, hopes faded, the mood turned gloomy, the level of fear and suspicion went up, and confidence was in need of restoration.

In theoretical terms, this trust or confidence can be conceptualized as *mutually expected self-restraint* (MES for short), an expression that was introduced by sociologist Johan Goudsblom (1998: 78). People restrain themselves in the expectation that others will restrain themselves, too, and the degree of (mutual) confidence among them can be analysed and expressed in terms of the level of their MES.

Another change connected to the alternation of one phase to another is the change that takes place in we-identification. In phases of reformalization, the dominant downward pressures as exerted by the established stimulated 'identification with the established';[18] while in a phase of informalization, the upwards pressures exerted by emancipating groups stimulated 'identification with outsiders', with 'the underdog'.

In the 1960s and 1970s, strong examples of 'identification with outsiders' can be found in the 'Black is Beautiful' and the Civil Rights movements in the USA. With the rise of these movements, for example, the perspective on interracial marriage was turned upside down: 'Lately, as white resistance has lessened, black opposition has increased' (Rush and Clark, 1970: 40). Another example concerns education: 'In the past, education was used by blacks to differentiate themselves from other blacks' in the competition for 'entry into white-oriented elite black groups':

> Now, however, well-educated blacks, especially younger ones, appreciate what they regard as the survival mechanism of uneducated blacks. These are the humour, the mother-wit (wisdom), the conscious putting-down of 'Whitey' without his knowing it (otherwise it was the lynching rope), and a way with expressions. . . . Education is now less used by blacks to scale the ladder to 'whiteness'. (Rush and Clark, 1970: 18–19)

In a way, this identification with uneducated blacks was similar to the example (described in §4.5) of Dutch academics affecting a working-class accent in an attempt to establish progressive leftish credentials. The scope of the we-groups differs, of course. The Beautiful Blacks in the USA restricted the scope of their we-identification to black people. Their use of ghetto language was intended to evoke the symbolic unity of all black people as distinguished from all white people. In the Netherlands, this identification with the working classes by affecting a working-class accent was intended to evoke the symbolic unity of all progressives as distinguished from all conservatives. Another difference was the duration. In the Netherlands, this example of we-identification with the lower classes is now almost completely forgotten (almost no one under thirty has ever heard of it), while in the USA, the importance of ghetto credentials and of the attempt of blacks – now African Americans or Afro-Americans – to establish symbolic unification in ghetto-behaviour has remained important throughout the century: 'Even criminal behaviour has been cited as an expression of cultural authenticity. . . . A student who committed armed robbery in his hometown during a vacation pleaded that he did it to prove that despite attending an Ivy League school, he was still loyal to his roots' (Martin, 1996: 383).

In both the USA and the European countries, this identification with outsiders was probably strongest in the case of psychiatric patients and, to a lesser extent, criminals: 'anti-psychiatry' and other similar social movements of the 1960s and 1970s tended to view them as people like themselves, with feelings that are perfectly understandable, and with an almost 'healthy' reaction to 'unhealthy' and oppressive social conditions. Not only psychiatric patients but also people living in relatively unprotected and dangerous social conditions such as 'working-class heroes', hoboes, beatniks, and other non-conformists were granted more prestige and respect. It was an extension of an orientation that was already exemplified in George Orwell's romantic description of 'the proles' who had 'stayed human' and had 'not become hardened inside'. During the 1960s, as the protective function of keeping a distance or reserve came to be suspected, this romanticization spread. Avoidance behaviour was suspected of being largely superfluous. It was the dynamic vitality of *street sense*, the ability to react alertly to the perils and opportunities of the street that were praised in many ways, particularly in 'youth culture'. An example is the group around Ken Kesey, author of *One Flew Over the Cuckoo's Nest* (1962). Tom Wolfe described how they invited and 'entertained' the Hell's Angels, and he commented:

> it once and for all put Kesey and the Pranksters above the category of just another weirdo intellectual group. They had broken through the worst hang-up that intellectuals know – the *real-life* hang-up. Intellectuals were always hung up with the feeling that they weren't coming to grips with real life. Real life belonged to all those funkey spades and prizefighters and bullfighters and dockworkers and grape pickers and wetbacks. *Nostalgie de la boue*. Well, the Hell's Angels were real life. It didn't get any realer than that, and Kesey had pulled it off. (Wolfe, 1968: 158)

The expression '*nostalgie de la boue*, or romanticising of primitive souls' is explained as 'a nineteenth-century French term that means, literally, "nostalgia for the mud"' (Wolfe, 1970: 32). In his essay *Funky Chic*, Wolfe described clothing fashions of the 1960s as another example of this nostalgia. In the early 1960s, 'well-to-do whites began to discover the raw-vital reverse-spin funk thrill of jeans' and other 'prole gear', whereas the 'hard-core street youth in the slums...were into the James Brown look...so that somehow the sons of the slums have become the Brummels and Gentlemen of Leisure, the true fashion plates of the 1970s, and the Suns of Eli dress like the working class of 1934' (Wolfe, 1976: 182–9). This idealization of street sense was one side of a coin which had a straightforward or hidden contempt for the established (and their *real-life* hang-up) as its other side. This was the side Bob Dylan was on:

> You've been with the professors, and they've all liked your looks
> With great lawyers you've discussed lepers and crooks

You've been through all of F. Scott Fitzgerald's books
You're well read, it's well known
But something is happening here and you don't know what it is
Do you, mister Jones? (Bob Dylan, *Ballad of a Thin Man*, 1965)

In the Netherlands, 'Mister double-barrelled name' shared the fate of
'Mister Jones':

> When, after World War II, the roots of the class system were being
> seriously disturbed in the joyful illusion that the tree of class would
> now finally succumb to being felled, the aristocracy wanted to be as
> inconspicuous as possible. Everything bearing a slight likeness to class,
> had become extremely delicate. Double-barrelled names, even non-
> aristocratic ones, sometimes were a burden at work, in social contacts,
> and they were particularly disadvantageous when applying for a job.
> (Pauw van Wieldrecht, 1987, quoted in Eijk, 1991: 40–1)

This retrospective view, written in the second half of the 1980s in a book
entitled *The Dialect of Nobility*, bears traces of satisfaction: 'nowadays, the
aristocracy seems to be climbing out of a deep ravine again', an observation
that was corroborated by the book's success (Pauw van Wieldrecht, 1991: 29).

Indeed, from the early 1980s onwards, there was a sharp rise in the
model-setting function of good societies. As profits and investments diminished in the late 1970s, the commercial climate declined, and businessmen
came to have less confidence in business prospects. They brought about an
exodus of capital and a declining supply of venture capital, thus contributing
to a stagnation in economic growth. State revenues stopped increasing or
dropped, obliging governments to cut budgets. The power chances of trade
unions and other groups that had been rising now deteriorated. This was also
a result of automation and of the transfer of production processes requiring
large labour forces to countries where labour remained cheap and plentiful –
an acceleration in the globalization process, which would become a major
issue in the 1990s. To promote confidence or trust between the government,
the business world, and the rest of the population was to accept and
emphasize their common interests again. Thus, representatives of governments and others again came to refer to general interests when they defended
and instituted budget cuts and other measures to promote the commercial
and the 'labour' climate. Policy measures increasingly tended to de-regulate
state organizations and functions, and to stimulate the 'free market'.

With the growing tendency to envy established groups and to distinguish oneself downwards, there was a rapid and collective change in
we-identification – from identification with groups of rising outsiders to
identification with the established. *Salon sense*, the subtle intimation that
one is *not* a person of the street, increasingly became (and remained) the
focus of interest and appreciation.

These examples may suffice to suggest the conclusion that the alternating
phases in the twentieth-century process of informalization were characterized

by radical collective social and psychic changes. They concerned people's orientations and identifications. They involved a revision of prevailing images: self-images, we- and they-images, and images of the present and the past. The dominant images of past and present came to be increasingly viewed in terms of the people who actively embodied these processes. During the last phase of emancipation and resistance, the image of what was happening at the time was predominantly based on a 'minority of the best' (Elias and Scotson, 1994) participating in social experiments and liberation movements. In the 1980s and 1990s, in a phase of accommodation and resignation, the image of the 1960s and 1970s increasingly came to be based on a 'minority of the worst', the 'hedonists', 'softies', and 'profiteers' of those years. Under the direct influence of such a transition, some people saw the most drastic offshoots in one direction or the other as representing radical changes in mentality. Examined in a more comprehensive processual framework, however, these offshoots prove to be quite a bit less radical. From a more detached long-term perspective, *spiral* movements and *overall* trends become apparent.

6.10   The Spiral Movement of the We–I Balance: Individualization

At the beginning of the twentieth century, the I-identity of individuals was highly subordinated to their we-identity, but throughout the century there was a trend towards emphasizing personal identity rather than group identity: 'Nowadays, every individual is a family to themselves' (Schönfeldt, 1987: 41). Phases of differentiation, emancipation, and informalization have apparently run in tandem with spurts in the process of individualization, tilting the We–I balance towards the I. In the phases of integration, accommodation, and formalization, the We–I balance was tilted towards the we since the significance of coordinating and integrating social functions and institutions stood at the centre of interest and attention. Thus, in the 1980s and 1990s, the longing for more stable and secure manners, we-groups, and we-identities intensified. In the meantime, however, most of the old we-groups – groups such as family, sex or gender, city, religion, class, or nation that in the previous phase of accommodation and resignation had provided a solid sense of belonging – seemed to have crumbled or lost cohesion. They merely seemed to provide a rather limited and insecure sense of belonging, and the same went for we-groups on a transnational plane, only more so. Moreover, as the We–I balance of individuals was tilted towards the we, the trend of individualization continued in the sense that the emotive charge of the I-ideals and I-identity of individuals did not lose strength. I-ideals and we-ideals seemed to have lost the harmony they once enjoyed. This begs for a closer look from a wider perspective.

Particularly from the second half of the nineteenth century onwards, Western states gained strength, resulting in growing military and police forces and a vigorous and unquestioned monopoly of state power. This development involved many processes on a national as well as on an international plane.

And in practically all these processes, the differences between people based on nationality gained importance in relation to other differences between them, such as those on a basis of class, region, or religion. Up to and during World War II, the rising power of states went hand in hand with a strengthening of national group identity, until the nation-state became the highest-ranking reference group for the we-identity of individuals. On the international or global plane, international competition between states contained strong incentives in that direction – particularly the forms involving violence. On the national plane, in processes such as internal pacification and the integration of previous groups of outsiders into the nation-state structures, individuals increasingly directed themselves in terms of a unified national code of behaviour and feeling. In this process, their we-identity in relation to the state strengthened and their scope of identification widened. These changes implied that their We–I balance was tilted towards the we. However, it was tilted towards the I as well, because these more highly integrated multiparty states offered greater personal freedom of choice and wider scope for self-control. Many relations such as those between family members or between workers and employers became less of an obligatory, lifelong, external constraint. Within limits, but to a growing extent, these we-relations became voluntary and interchangeable, putting all the more emphasis on the I, on the decisions of individuals about the forms and continuity of their relations. Thus, as chances for individualization grew and demands on the capacity for self-regulation rose, the We–I balance was tilted towards the I. In sum, the We–I balance of most individuals changed in both directions; their we-identity and their I-identity were simultaneously strengthened.

During and shortly after World War II, states of a new order of magnitude, the 'superpowers' that were the USA and the USSR, moved to the top of the hierarchy of states, pushing the smaller European states with their more limited military and economic resources into a second-rank position. Accordingly, their inhabitants' old we-identity in relation to the state came under pressure, a pressure that was increased when these states 'lost' their colonies. Under this pressure, more and more individuals and countries in the world took sides with one or the other of the superpowers, which implied a widening of perspective, if not of identification. It was a spurt in the globalization process. To a large extent, the implications of the weakened position of the European states for the we-identity of their individuals were warded off, mainly by concentrating on post-war reconstruction, on the expansion of industries and commerce as well as on further national integration via welfare state institutions. All over the West, relations of cooperation and competition expanded and intensified, and with them the networks of interdependence.

Particularly from the early and mid-1960s onwards, as entire groups were rising socially and the most striking social pressure came from below, a strong shift of the We–I balance towards the I took place. Relations between political, administrative, and commercial authorities and their subordinates became less hierarchical and formal. As practically all relations became less unequal, more open, and flowing, even more of the we-relations, which were once taken for granted to last a lifetime, became more or less voluntary and interchangeable. The traditional submission of the interests of individuals to those of their groups and their honour diminished further; most people were expected to have more individual means of defence at their disposal. They developed many different part-identities, as well as the flexibility to switch swiftly between various situations and relations. Accordingly, the kind of identification with we-groups that is complete, blind, and automatic was substituted increasingly by more varied, more differentiated, and, to some extent, also wider circles of identification (Swaan, 1995, 1997). The latter was expressed in a relatively strong ideal of equality and in a sense of belonging to an expanding social universe. Although only partly and vaguely attached to national and transnational organizations, these we-feelings and we-ideals had a wide scope. Some of them clearly crossed national borders and were shared across those borders, thus also representing a shift in the We–I balance towards the we.

In the 1980s, the change from an optimistic view of the future to a feeling of greater uncertainty and insecurity opened a perspective in which the disintegration of old we-groups and the loss of old we-feelings and I-feelings loomed large. The voices expressing concern about the corrosion of social cohesion and solidarity became louder and more numerous. It was a concern about more encompassing we-ideals and we-identities, representing a shift in the We–I balance in favour of the we. But what we? The groups people used to refer to as 'we' had both expanded and become more differentiated, resulting in a multitude of multilevel we-groups, we-identities, and we-ideals. The concern about social cohesion also revealed that many people were experiencing difficulties in satisfying their longing to belong, particularly in the big way of belonging to a large and strong social unit.

In the USA, identification with the nation-state was strengthened by an intensified feeling of belonging to the world's better 'superpower', the other one being an 'evil empire'. In the 1990s, being a member of the only remaining superpower appears to have revitalized that old feeling, expressed in Emily Post's manners book, that it 'is no idle boast that the world is at present looking toward America; and whatever we become is bound to lower or raise the standards of life'. (Post, 1922: 619; 1942: 859–60). A more recent example is *Star-Spangled Manners*, in which Judith Martin glorifies the American Etiquette of Equality, which 'like other American forms of culture... has become the most influential force of its kind in the world' (2003: 39).

In Europe, identification with the nation-state was strengthened, too, but in quite ambivalent ways as this type of we-identity had also become constrained and threatened. It was constrained by the perception of nationalism as a major incentive to large-scale annihilation and humiliation, and it was threatened by the pressures of continued international competition in which the weakened world position of European states had come to be realized more fully.

A modest example of changes in the We–I balance from the early 1980s onwards comes from a study of changes in letters to an agony column in a Dutch weekly (Post, 2004). The study shows that between 1978 and 1998, we-feelings and 'collectivism' were increasingly expressed in these letters and also presented as a motive for writing them. From the early 1980s onwards, more discontent was related to broad societal topics such as the economy, employment, unemployment, and crime. A similar shift towards the perspective of a we-group was discerned in the new sources of discomfort mentioned. They included such broad, general, and abstract references as 'the future', 'an indefinable sense of doom', 'life', and 'the world'. At the same time, with regard to form, style, and the way in which the problems were presented, these letters continued to become more individual, more direct, and personal. Taken together, this study illustrates how individuals increasingly turned to their we-identity and we-ideals, while they continued to attach unrelenting importance to their I-identity and I-ideals, and also that the longing to belong was directed at rather unspecified we-groups.

In the economy, as lifetime jobs had largely become almost an anachronism, identification with one's organization was restricted in accordance with the rising demands of flexibility. To some degree the longing to belong was satisfied by the formation of 'neo-tribes', as Maffesoli has called the rise of a multitude of small groups 'with splintered but exacting intentionalities', favouring 'the mechanism of belonging', yet fundamentally 'unstable, since the persons of which these tribes are constituted are free to move from one to the other' (1996: 83, 140, 6).[19] Yet although joining these groups, organized around the catchwords, brand names, and sound bites of consumer culture, did give a sense of belonging, they merely provided (additions to) a patchwork of part-identities. Robbed of the feeling of belonging to an expanding social universe and stuck with this feeling of insecurity, increasing numbers of people appear to have come to experience their many part-identities, even the whole 'post-modern orgy of community-chasing' (Bauman, 1992: 199), as somewhat problematic. Particularly in moments of life and death, their longing for a more encompassing and secure sense of belonging was not satisfied, or only in part. In addition, the formation of part-identities that can be almost instantly and flexibly assembled and dismantled may well have increased the freedom to move, but in the 1980s this greater freedom was experienced increasingly as a pressure of having to comply with increased demands on self-regulation.

Indeed, this greater freedom was at the same time a greater pressure to perform. These are two sides of the same coin. Sometimes, particularly in celebrations of postmodernism, the side of greater freedom was emphasized: 'No authoritative solutions to go by, everything to be negotiated anew and ad hoc' and ideally 'all structures . . . light and mobile so they can be arranged at short notice . . .' (Bauman, 1999: 26–7). But who's ideal is this?[20] Certainly not Michel Foucault's and the people he represents, for usually their eyes are fixed upon the other side of the coin, that of the constraint to perform. In what he describes as the 'new capitalism', Richard Sennett (1998) has taken a position close to that of Foucault. Against those who claim that the new flexibility gives people more freedom to shape their lives, Sennett argues that the new order and 'the new regime of time' threaten to rob the modern person of his feeling of social continuity and community; they threaten to 'corrode his character, particularly those qualities of character which bind human beings to one another and furnish each with a sense of sustainable self' (1998: 27). However, whether the stances and descriptions favoured greater freedom or greater captivity, looking at both sides above all, highlighted the rising tension in the We–I balance of individuals, between their we-ideals and I-ideals. The same goes for the balance of involvement and detachment.

During the 1990s, the feeling that social cohesion and solidarity were lacking was intensified, and so was the feeling of insecurity. The events that followed the collapse of the Soviet Union and the Iron Curtain implied changes, tensions, and conflicts, from which perspective the period of the 'Cold War' and 'Peaceful Coexistence' suddenly seemed relatively stable. The existence of an 'enemy', a clear they-group, obviously had provided a we-group to hold on to. Now that hold had vanished. Shortly afterwards, the only remaining 'superpower' engaged itself in an intense debate on the 'disuniting of America' (Schlesinger, Jr, 1992). Without a common enemy, the maxim 'United We Stand' suddenly seemed incomplete and in need of the supplement 'Sitting We are Divided'.

In addition, nation-states had become quite noticeably involved in continental and global integration processes, from which perspective most national countries are in fact little more than regions within global networks of interdependence. Particularly in Europe, it has increased the awareness that most nation-states, including one's own, have but little control on the course of these global processes. On the one hand this awareness has stimulated the formation of a we-identity in relation to humanity at large, to 'human rights' and international justice. It was a widening of circles of identification, exemplified in a growing interest in activities of global organizations such as the United Nations, the World Bank, the International Monetary Fund, the World Health Organisation, and the World Trade Organisation, as well as in the growing support of global organizations such as Amnesty International, Greenpeace, and Médicins sans Frontières. To some extent, we-identification was extended to life on the planet (motivating social movements such as environment organizations, animal liberation, and vegetarianism). On the other hand, however, the curtailing of national power and sovereignty was experienced as a threat to people's we-image and we-identity. This was expressed in many ways, for instance by crying out for more powerful state rule – governments and politicians are inclined to feed on this demand (Garland, 1996). About the people who experience the trend towards integration into a larger unit as a threat to their we-image and their identity, Norbert Elias observed that their defence against such integration arises from the fear of a kind of collective dying. He concluded: 'As long as no feelings of personal identity, no we-feelings are associated with the higher-order unit, the fading or disappearance of the lower-order we-group appears in reality as a kind of death threat, a collective destruction and certainly a loss of meaning to the highest degree' (1991: 225).

The desired feeling of new communal solidarity was also sought via the detour of creating new enemies and scapegoats. The scapegoating of an entire population such as the Austrians and the 'sanctions' against Austria since about 1986 can be seen as an expression of an integration conflict on the level of continental (European) integration (Kuzmics, 2003). On the level of nation-states, this way of seeking communal solidarity was sought in scapegoating foreigners or immigrants and criminals. From this perspective, Richard Sennett claimed that 'we' had become 'the dangerous pronoun'. In a chapter with this title, he argued that 'today, in the new regime of time, that usage "we" has become an act of self-protection. The desire for community is defensive, often expressed as rejection of immigrants or other outsiders...' (Sennett, 1998: 138). Indeed, in the 1990s, the rise of populist movements and the rising popularity of concepts such as 'civil society', 'civic responsibility', and 'communitarianism' also expressed this longing for a more encompassing and solid we-identity. The popularity of these movements and concepts practically all over the Western world can be taken as an indication that the shift towards continental and global integration has been relatively rapid in comparison to the pace of the corresponding change in the we-image, the we-identity of the majority of people. For most, states have remained the highest-ranking reference group for their we-identity. Their 'we-image, the whole social habitus of individuals, is immovably tied by a strong affective charge to traditional group identity on the plane of the nation state' (Elias, 1991: 220). We-identifications and we-ideals have been lagging behind, thus creating the impression that I-ideals and we-ideals had lost their harmony. The 'War on Terror' has provided a vague new enemy, but without repairing any of this harmony because the 'war' was not accompanied by any support for we-ideals and we-identifications above the plane of the national state. On the contrary, the USA government ridiculed them. However, seen from a longer-term perspective, it seems likely that the spiral movement of the We–I balance will keep running in tandem with the spiral processes of social differentiation, integration, and informalization, but now on a global scale.

7

Connecting Social and Psychic Processes: Third Nature

7.1   Three Regimes in Change

In 1998, an Islamic primary school in Amsterdam was reported never to allow teachers to leave their pupils alone in the classroom. Children were not allowed to wear short sleeves or trousers, nor tight clothing. Officially, corporal punishment was banned, but what about 'having to stand for an hour in a corner on one leg', a teacher wondered. According to another teacher, school management had no faith whatsoever in discussion or consultation, 'only in authority and intimidation' (*NRC Handelsblad*, 5 December 1998). Here, an omnipresent, austere supervision and checking of authoritarian rules prevailed in strict hierarchical relations. Bodies should be covered, their presence not even suggested. Trust in internalized codes was small. This strict pedagogical regime was, of course, closely connected with a strict regime in the families of these children and to the strict regime of the state in the country of their (parents') origin.

Many people today will find it hard to imagine that regimes of comparable hierarchical strictness used to prevail all over the Netherlands and over all the other countries under study here. Particularly from the second part of the nineteenth century onwards, Western regimes of state, family, and personality gained in strength, resulting in (among other things) sizeable police forces, the legally defined power of heads of family, and in the formation of an authoritarian personality. This type of personality is characterized by an 'inner compass' of reflexes and rather fixed habits which function as a 'second nature'. A vigorous and unquestioned state monopoly of power over the means of violence and taxation thus ran in tandem with an equally inviolable paternal authority within families and an equally unquestioned reign of the personality over individual impulses and emotions. The pedagogical regime was 'rigorous but fair', and it did not excel in producing confiding relations and intimacy. Children growing up in such authoritarian circumstances usually developed an authoritarian conscience, with a strong penchant for order and regularity, cleanliness, and neatness. Righteous life started, so to speak, with a straight parting of the hair. Negligence in these matters indicated an inclination towards dissoluteness; without rigorous control, 'first nature' might run wild.

In the 1960s, relations between family members rapidly lost their rigidity and hierarchical aloofness as they became attuned to a more flexible and varied social traffic. Unthinking or imposed compliance was replaced by 'made-to-measure' pedagogical forms. Couples had fewer children, and those they had were for the most part consciously desired. Affective investments by parents in their children mounted, thus bringing family ties to higher levels of warmth, mutual trust, intimacy, and intensity. Social experiments to allow children a wider scope for living in accordance with the emotional and libidinal urges of the moment – treating them more as equal human beings – strongly accelerated in the 1960s and 1970s. In fact, this trend in the relations between parents and children can be discerned from the last decades of the nineteenth century onwards. During this trend, the extremes of what counted as authoritarian standards of upbringing and what as negligence or *laissez faire* diminished. Simultaneously, on the basis of mounting affective investments, increasingly large groups tended towards a pattern that came to be known as a 'love-oriented discipline' (Bronfenbrenner, 1958; Klein, 1965). Commanding children and presenting them with established decisions, came to be seen as plainly damaging. Anxious acceptance of authority – 'you obey because I tell you' – came to be perceived as a symptom of blind submissiveness, estranging children from their own feelings. In a more equal and affective regime, parents (and others) appealed more strongly and compellingly to affection and reflection, thus teaching their children to direct themselves more according to their own conscience and reflections than to simply obey the external constraints of adults. The new ideal in raising children is aptly summarized in the dialogue:

'Even when we were angry, we never punished you.'
'Your anger was punishment enough' (Goudsblom, 1998: 84).

These changes in family regime ran in tandem with changes in the regimes of state and personality. In each of these three regimes, relations came to be more equal, open, flowing, and flexible. On the level of the personality, a 'second-nature' type of authoritarian conscience made way for a conscience attuned to more equal, flowing, and flexible relations. This attuning did not automatically engender a weaker conscience, rather the opposite – just as parents who never punish, whose anger is punishment enough, do not automatically lose any power over their children in comparison to more authoritarian parents.

At the same time, the conglomeration of political, administrative, and commercial authorities opened up as contacts became more flowing, just as the relations between them and their supporters or subordinates became less hierarchical and more open. This development would have been impossible without the far-reaching integration of all social classes, including the lower classes, into society. These more equal and open relations in the political and economical domains were extended to the domains of education, upbringing, and personality, allowing for more open and less formal regimes.

In growing up, children are at first mainly preoccupied with their own feelings and impulses. Only gradually do they internalize the commandments and prohibitions of parents and others upon whom they are dependent. In this process, their fear of being punished is transformed into a fear of being ashamed, a shame-fear that, after transgressions, may manifest itself as a feeling of guilt. The shame-fear of a tender conscience manifests itself in rather authoritarian ways: for a while, children live up to the newly learned rules in a rather rigid way. Only after having gained fuller command of these rules, at a time when they are also better able to take the feelings and experiences of others into account, do they learn to apply the rules in more flexible ways. In the relatively complex societies of the modern West, they learn to do this from the age of 11 or 12 onwards.

A similar sequence, 'learning to control' precedes the possibility of 'controlled decontrolling', can be discerned in the broad social and psychic processes of recent decades. The transformation from rather formal to more informal and flexible manners depended upon a relatively high level of integration of all social classes in welfare states. On this basis, in the 1950s and 1960s, the level of mutually expected self-restraints rose to a point allowing for more open and flowing family and personality regimes – a controlled decontrolling.

As most social codes became more flexible and differentiated, manners and emotion regulation became the more decisive criteria for status or reputation. People have pressured each other to become more conscious of social and individual options and restrictions, and this has put social and self-knowledge in greater demand. The same goes for the ability to empathize and to take on others' roles. Respect and respectable behaviour have become more dependent upon self-regulation, particularly on the functioning of internal social controls. Thus, the pressures of social controls on each individual have intensified, which means that the fulcrum of the balance between external and internal social controls has moved in the direction of the latter. In this sense, self-controls have increasingly become both the focus and the locus of external social controls.

In a lecture in 1970, Norbert Elias used the expression 'controlled decontrolling of emotional controls'.[21] Various experiments in allowing children a wider scope for living in accordance with their emotional and libidinal urges of the moment tended towards such 'controlled decontrolling'. They were part of a wider process in which people were becoming aware of deeper feelings and learning to surmount hidden fears, a prerequisite for an 'emancipation of emotions' – a representation of these deeper layers at the centre of personality or consciousness. They increasingly became conscious of emotions that, as a rule in the past, had been either ignored or concealed for fear of parents and others on whom they were dependent.

As a rule, most parents who took part in the social experiments of raising children in an affectively warmer parental regime that was more tolerant of 'animalic' or primary urges and impulses had themselves been raised in more rigid and severe regimes. To a greater extent, they had learned to control their own primary urges and impulses more strongly via the auto-matically functioning counter-impulses of a rather rigorous conscience. This second-nature type of personality had resulted from shaming processes which fuel the shame-fear of being unable to constrain affects in accordance with the prevailing regimes of manners and emotions. This shame-fear concerns social degradation, loss of respect and self-respect, with total social expulsion and loss of all meaning in life as an extreme. To avoid these sanctions, most people in the generation of these parents developed the habit of avoiding certain parts of themselves. They developed counter-impulses that discharged the potentially connected affects and at the same time kept them from becoming conscious. Thus, the fear of others was changed into the fear of parts of themselves. What was kept in the dungeons of their inner life might break loose, so they also feared being tempted. In this light, participation in these social experiments, as is the case in informalizing processes in general, involved voyages of discovery into one's own closer or more distant past, in pursuit of the reasons why and the ways in which impulses and emotions were led into the paths they took.

The attempt to raise children in affectively warmer parental regimes, more tolerant of their primary urges and impulses, signifies also that parents had come to expect more emotional gratification from family life. Throughout the century, but particularly since the 1950s, the bond that may turn couples into parents had been developing in the direction of greater equality, mutual trust, and emotional warmth. And in the 1960s and 1970s, within the borders of family life, the relational ideals of being close and frank intensified. The more these ideals spread, the more immediately was the exertion of authority – in the sense of issuing commands or expecting special treatment on the grounds of some claim to superiority – experienced and exposed as an unnecessary humiliation. Increasingly, traditional ways of 'pulling rank' or 'playing the authority card' were soon made ridiculous and thus became counterproductive. The growth of the desire for closer and emotionally more satisfying bonds thus heightened the sensitivity to whether manners show personal qualities, merits, and respect, or whether they reveal 'remnants of the power and status aspirations of established groups, and have no other function than that of reinforcing their power chances and their status superiority' (Elias, 2000: 446).

7.2 Connecting Social and Psychic Processes

During the twentieth century, a dominant process of informalization followed the long-term trend of formalization which had dominated in previous centuries: manners became increasingly relaxed, subtle, and varied. The turn of the twentieth century, the Roaring Twenties, and the Expressive Revolution of the 1960s and 1970s were periods in which power differences sharply decreased. They were also periods with strong spurts of informalization. In the present book, these developments have been placed in the wider framework of expanding and intensifying competition and cooperation, which operated as the main driving forces towards continued social differentiation and integration, a social interweaving in which networks of interdependence between various groups of people expanded, becoming denser and more multilevel. This process expanded and became increasingly tangible and visible at the global level, particularly from the 1970s onwards.

In the four countries under study, as more and more groups of people came to be represented in the various centres of power and their good societies, the more extreme differences between social groups in terms of power, ranking, behaviour, and regulation of emotions diminished. Depending upon the extent that power inequalities lessened, the Golden Rule and the principle of mutual consent became expected standards of conduct among individuals and groups.

As power and status competition intensified, and sensitivities about social inequality increased, demonstrations of an individual's distinctiveness became more indirect, subtle, and hidden. References to hierarchical group differences, particularly to 'better' and 'inferior' kinds of people, were increasingly tabooed; social superiors were less automatically taken to be better people. Yet it was not until the 1960s that the once automatic equation of superiority in power and superiority as a human being declined to the point of embarrassment. It was also only in the second half of the twentieth century that the dominant mode of emotion regulation apparently reached a strength and scope that enabled most people to admit to themselves and to others to having 'dangerous' violent and/or sexual emotions and impulses, without provoking shame, particularly the shame-fear of losing control and giving in to them. Whereas previously, sexual and violent emotions, like emotions in general, had come to be viewed as dangerous – for example, it was considered dangerous to 'covet thy neighbours wife' – from the 1960s onward, to covet was no longer perceived as dangerous, nor was acting upon this longing perceived as such, if only the principle of mutual consent were to be respected.

To the extent that expressions like 'to become emotional' still have the connotation of a lack of control over emotions, of being swept away by them, they are reminiscent of this very danger *and* of the rigid social control that served to counter it. Until the 1950s and 1960s, emotions in general were predominantly seen as a source of transgression and misbehaviour. Since then, emancipation and integration processes in most Western countries have apparently reached a level at which the dangers of becoming overwhelmed by 'dangerous' emotions have become small enough for emotions to gain acceptance as important guides for orientation and behaviour (Wouters, 1992). Such a high level of mutually expected self-restraints can only develop in societies with a correspondingly high degree of interdependence and social integration.

As bonds of cooperation and competition blended, power inequalities decreased and former outsider groups integrated into welfare states (Swaan, 1988), the people involved felt increasingly compelled to identify with others. The expanding and intensified cooperation and competition prompted them to observe and take the measure of themselves and of each other more carefully, and to develop a greater willingness to compromise. Social success became more strongly dependent on a reflexive and flexible self-regulation, upon the ability to combine firmness and flexibility, directness and tactfulness (see McCall *et al.*, 1983; Mastenbroek, 1989, 2002). In sum, the emancipation of the lower classes and their representation in the centres of power and good society have run in tandem with an 'emancipation of emotions' and their representation at the centre of personality, that is, consciousness. This is a characteristic of the process of informalization: it breaks through social and psychic dividing lines as they open up and social groups as well as psychic functions become more integrated. Some groups of people, formerly excluded, came to be recognized as fellow human beings, just as some impulses and emotions the humanity of which was denied, came to be acknowledged as such – it was a social as well as a psychical de-hierarchization, opening up, or levelling.

As manners and relations between social groups became less rigid and hierarchical, so too did the relations between psychic functions such as drives, emotions, conscience, and consciousness, altogether opening up a larger and more differentiated spectrum of alternatives and more flowing and flexible connections between social groups and psychic functions. In the course of this informalizing process, to paraphrase and contradict Elias, 'consciousness' becomes *more* permeable by drives, and drives become *more* permeable by 'consciousness'. In informalizing societies, elementary impulses again have an easier access to people's reflections. At the time of writing his book on the civilizing process, Norbert Elias did not perceive this and other characteristics of informalization, which led him to attribute characteristics of the long-term formalizing phase to the entire civilizing process:

> What is decisive for a human being as he or she appears before us is neither the 'id' alone, nor the 'ego' or 'superego' alone, but always the *relationship* between various sets of psychic functions, partly conflicting and partly co-operating levels in self-steering. It is these relationships *within* individual people between the drives and affects that are controlled and the socially instilled agencies that control them, whose structure changes in the course of a civilising process, in accordance with the changing structure of the relationships *between* individual human beings, in society at large. In the course of this process, to put it briefly and all too simply, 'consciousness' becomes less permeable by drives, and drives become less permeable by 'consciousness'. In simpler societies elementary impulses, however transformed, have an easier access to people's reflections. In the course of a civilising process the compartmentalisation of these self-steering functions, though in no way absolute, becomes more pronounced. (Elias, 2000: 409–10)

In the long-term informalizing phase of the twentieth century, however, the latter process was reversed: this compartmentalization diminished. Social emancipation and integration demanded psychic emancipation and integration, a more strongly ego- or I-dominated self-regulation. This kind of self-regulation implies that drives, impulses, and emotions have become more easily accessible while their control is less strongly based upon an authoritative conscience, functioning more or less automatically as a 'second nature' (Wouters, 1998b).

The German sociologists Blomert (1991), Engler (1991, 1992), and Waldhoff (1995) have argued convincingly that Elias focused mainly on 'automatic inner anxieties', 'automatisms of self-control', and 'more or less automatically functioning fears and self-constraints', and thus in most cases refers to the constraints of conscience, or to superego constraints, when writing about self-constraints. Waldhoff has accordingly suggested that there is a need to disentangle some of the connections Elias made between social and psychic processes. A decisive first step was to distinguish two types of superego-dominated self-regulation: in addition to an authoritarian superego-dominated self-regulation – an authoritarian personality with a strong inclination or a compulsion towards reduction, repetition, imitation, cleanliness, law and order – he conceptualizes a type of personality with a self-regulation dominated by a *we-less superego*. The latter was often described by Elias as a *homo clausus* or a *we-less I* (1991). The self-regulation of this type of personality allows for a broader spectrum of behavioural and emotional alternatives, and is correspondingly more ego- or I-dominated, but a person of this type suffers from a loss of we-feelings, as if separated from others and from his or her emotional life or 'true self' by an invisible wall, more or less desperately trying to force a breach in it.

From here, it was relatively easy for Waldhoff to take the next step and distinguish between five types (he calls them 'ideal types') of self-regulation: (1) dominated by drives and impulses; (2) dominated by external social controls, that is, by constraints from others; (3) dominated by the internal social control of an authoritarian conscience or superego; (4) dominated by a 'we-less' superego – the *homo clausus* type, and, as more and more people become involved in processes of informalization and emancipation of emotions, their self-regulation may become; (5) ego-dominated, developing not simply a stronger or more wide-ranging control of affects, but a different pattern of control, one that involves more flexible, more individually malleable, and more easily accessible emotions.

On the basis of these distinctions between forms of self-regulation, Waldhoff further differentiates in the balance of controls – the balance between external social controls and internal ones (or between external constraints and self-constraints) – and he connects this differentiation to the two phases in 'civilizing' processes. Until the end of the nineteenth century, most Western countries were involved in a disciplinary or formalizing phase in which the central tension of self-regulation was between external social controls and the internal ones of superego or conscience. This tension tended towards a change in the direction of an authoritarian superego-directed personality. In the twentieth-century phase of informalizing processes, as more and more people developed a type of self-regulation that is more ego-dominated, the prevailing tension shifted to the balance between conscience and consciousness, or, between superego and ego. In Waldhoff's terminology, the tensions in self-regulation came to arise predominantly from the 'superego–ego' balance.

In the following three sections, I will sketch the theoretical framework of these types and phases with few direct references to their empirical basis, which is to be found in earlier chapters of this book.

7.2.1 Formalization and the balance between external social controls and the internal control of conscience: the rise of an authoritarian superego-dominated personality

In the disciplinary phase of formalization, people exerted increasing pressure upon each other to reject everything that seemed wild, violent, dirty, indecent, or lecherous, in order to better control or cope with these impulses and urges. In this phase, the austere and inexorable repression of urges and affects can only be accomplished, so it seems, by effacing them both socially and individually from consciousness and by warding off everything that is reminiscent of them with a rigour similar to that which was demanded in the original process of suppression. This process of compartmentalization, in which all kinds of emotions and patterns of behaviour are removed behind the scenes of social life – a trend towards social *apartheid* – has a socio-psychical counterpart in the societal production of unconsciousness – a trend towards psychic *apartheid*. As these urges, impulses, and emotions, are repressed and sink into the unconscious, an emotional 'estrangement' is created. 'Thus', writes Waldhoff, 'the strange and the unconscious have come to appear as belonging to the same incomprehensible rebus of an intangible *nature*' (1995: 82). This fits into both a rigid way of relating to strangers and to one's own feelings of strangeness. As the authoritarian personality type is not aware of desires and fears that have become compartmentalized and thus strange to the self in processes of repression, denial, and other forms of defence, its own 'strangeness' tends to be projected on 'strangers'. Thus strangers came to personify bad company because they (as explicated in §§2.3.3 and 3.3) could endanger the self-control of the respectable, prompting loss of composure in response to repulsive behaviour or, worse, the succumbing to temptation. Particularly in this long-term phase of disciplining and formalizing, there is a strong tendency to discharge the problems inherent in this process by projecting them on to they-groups of 'strangers' and on to weaker social groups, who might otherwise function as a reminder of one's own weaknesses. This largely explains why the social dividing lines keeping weaker classes and other 'strangers' at bay are usually as rigid as the psychic dividing lines keeping one's own weakness and 'strangeness' at bay.

In the more extreme moments of a disciplinary phase, primary impulses and emotions can come to be denied and placed outside one's personality with such forced rigour that social classes in which (some) members yield to these weaknesses may even be considered to be less than human (Elias and Scotson, 1994: xxvii). All kinds of humiliation and annihilation have occurred on the basis of such an anxiety-ridden orientation and pattern of emotion regulation. Colonialism is full of examples. Another example is the way the bourgeoisie, including the petit bourgeoisie, in nineteenth-century Europe took it for granted that the lower classes were to be avoided because 'the Great Unwashed' counted as coarse and rude, as dirty and smelly. In this way, social and psychic fears – of loss of status and loss of self-control respectively – were moulded in physical terms and transformed into physical repulsion (see §3.2). Thus, the lower classes were socially excluded as 'strangers', just as strange feelings (meaning 'not mine') were excluded from consciousness.

Waldhoff presents the example of 'gypsies' in Nazi Germany: on the one hand they exerted a certain attraction because of what counted as their freedom or independence and their animalic or instinctive naturalness ('in full radiance and colourful wildness'), while on the other hand, they caused alarm, especially to the authorities (and to the psychic functions representing the authorities within the psychic make-up of individuals), because of exactly the same attributed characteristics and qualities. It was precisely because 'these creatures still live in complete dependence on nature and fate...driven by their originally inherited instincts', that Oberarzt Robert Ritter, leader of the 'rassenhygienische und völkerbiologische Forschungsstelle des Reichsgesundheitsamtes', demanded 'an elimination of primitives, who are determined by their predisposition'. Waldhoff sighs: 'This is how close the romanticisation and extermination of a group can get' (1995: 73).

These examples illustrate Waldhoff's thesis that socially produced patterns of relating to 'strangers' (i.e. *they*-groups in contrast to *we*-groups) *mirror* psychically produced patterns of relating to one's own 'strangeness' – that is, to the part of oneself that one no longer recognizes, fenced off as it is by the counter-impulses of conscience. It is the part or layer of personality that has become 'unconscious', defended from consciousness by inner fears like shame.

Authoritarian superego-dominated personalities tend to react to the tension-balance of attraction *and* repugnance by closing themselves off from the attraction. Such a reaction betrays their lack of confidence and their fear of losing self-control if they were to admit, even to themselves, that they were tempted by what they one-sidedly prefer to see as 'dangerous behaviour': they are afraid to set the fox – in themselves – to watch the geese. Their displays of superiority in controlling these temptations demonstrate how small and rudimentary their newly gained control actually is. As a result, in this disciplinary phase in the 'civilizing of emotions', the established group's feeling of being threatened by *they*-groups of 'strangers' and other outsiders remains explosive. As long as these they-groups maintain a looser and what the established perceive as more dissolute lifestyle, they are experienced as a threat to the more or less automatically functioning self-restraints, the 'superego' of the established. Further to this, the more the lifestyle of the members of the they-group becomes 'impeccable', the greater is the threat they pose to the we-ideal and self-image of the established.

In established–outsider relations, the established reflect their capacity to endure their own feelings of 'strangeness' and to procure an 'emancipation of emotions': to work through their own history of emotion regulation, particularly through the processes of repression, denial, and other forms of defence, in which particular desires and fears have become strange to the self. Therefore, the fate of outsider groups such as immigrants also depends upon the degree of emancipation of emotions among the established groups, that is, upon the degree of informalization in the society in which they come to live, for it determines the extent to which the established can possibly identify with outsiders.

Similar processes may still occur as a phase in growing up, on the level of individual formalizing processes. For example, as a boy I was often impatiently irritated by the 'clumsy' progress of my brother, eighteen months younger than myself, in a new phase or a new field in his life, precisely because I was painfully reminded of my own clumsiness in a very recent past. Quite often I would have simply preferred to deny that I had been just like him. I had overcome 'tyro-fears' and succeeded in bringing the chances and dangers of moving to new fields or new levels largely under control, but 'regression-fears' were still prominent. Often the latter remained strong enough to form a barrier to feeling attracted to or being moved by my brother's experiments. Regression-fears soon led to my feeling and showing repulsion and conceit. Displays of superiority often show a lead in manners and emotion regulation is only small and incipient.

In the West – in most European countries and their successful former colonies – the collective formation of authoritarian superego-dominated personalities occurred primarily in the nineteenth century (see §2.5). The 'stiff upper lip' is a colloquial symbol of this, and a well-known representation in social science is Riesman's 'inner-directed personality' (1950). However, twentieth-century examples can also be easily found, as I will demonstrate by comparing a 'global' example with a Western one.

Towards the end of 1995, the authorities in Vietnam started a national campaign against what were called 'negative foreign influences'. 'American cultural imperialism', in particular, was considered to be a serious threat to 'traditional morals'. In the 1920s and 1930s, many European authorities used to speak a similar language. A Dutch government committee, for instance, warned against the 'demoralising Americanisation of Europe'. The poison was localized predominantly in the lower abdomen of America: under the influence of 'Negroes and popular Negro music, the most primitive feelings might gain the upper hand in our country, too':

> In a country with a disconnected mass like the Americans, bonding has to resort to the sphere of instincts, and this determines the essence of American culture. That Negroes set rhythm and tone in dance and music is no coincidence, because as far as their instinctual life is

concerned, Negroes have maximum vital force at their disposal...
[this music] is pre-eminently suitable for bringing about the flush
that makes life easy for those whose way of life prevents them
developing a deeper conception of life. (*Rapport*, 1931: 12)

Whereas authorities in the twentieth century – recently in Vietnam,
earlier in the Netherlands – perceived 'instinctual life' as a threat, many
others had a contrary view and saw it as vital and attractive. In the 1920s
and 1930s, for example, in the Netherlands, 'Negroes' were in demand
as musicians because of their 'natural feeling for rhythm', that is, as Negroes.
Announcements such as 'Negro duo' or 'Negro orchestra' on posters, names
of jazz bands such as 'The Black Devils' and of jazz cafés such as 'Negro
Palace Mephisto' clearly attracted many people. It was precisely for that
reason that the authorities perceived a social virus threatening 'our' girls and
morals. In 1936, a chief inspector of police in Amsterdam wrote in a report:

> The performance of the bandleader in particular makes the audience
> think it is at the zoo. While one might still enjoy the pranks of the
> apes in that paradise of animals, in The Negro Kit Cat Club, however,
> watching the act of these 'apes' is disgusting. Coloured foreigners are
> a danger for white girls. Quite a few young girls have been sexually
> debauched by such people, and children born from such relationships
> usually have to be maintained at the expense of the poor law.
> (Quoted in Openneer, 1995: 27)

During the war (early in 1942), his successor wrote:

> I judge the performance of these Surinamese as musicians in public
> places to be a great moral danger to the female youth of the
> Netherlands. In actual practice it has been sufficiently proven that
> these Surinamese have a fatal influence on young females, who are
> partly attracted by the black skin of these folks and partly carried
> along by their barbaric music. In perfect agreement with the Mayor
> of Amsterdam, I have therefore summoned the owners of the
> following establishments to dismiss their Surinamese musicians.
> (Quoted in Openneer, 1995: 33)

The conceptualization of long-term trends of formalization and informalization as phases in long-term 'civilizing' processes helps to illuminate
a common characteristic of the Dutch authorities in the inter-war years
and the Vietnamese authorities in the 1990s: Both perceived a threat to
'traditional morals' in the lifestyle of people who belonged to subordinate
classes, as well as in the lifestyle of people who belonged to more powerful
states ('a demoralising Americanisation'). Both took disciplinary measures to
prevent the population from becoming 'estranged' or 'alienated' from tradition and from concluding a treacherous union with the 'strangers' or 'aliens'
from abroad. In this respect, these authorities were in a similar phase: their
own 'strangeness', defended by the inner fears of their rather authoritative

conscience, was mirrored not only in the lifestyle of people who seemed less confined by the 'iron cage' of a rigid conscience, but also in the more informalized lifestyle of people with a more flexible and ego-dominated self-regulation. Usually, the latter threat is conceptualized in terms of morals and branded as decadence.

This 1995 example of the Vietnamese authorities trying to defend 'traditional morals' is one of many. Globally known groups such as the Taliban and Al-Qaeda feed on the same 'cause'. These examples show that, in twentieth-century processes of informalization, this type of 'second-nature' defence against the dangers and problems of a more reflexive and flexible kind of self-regulation has expanded from the West to the global level. Whereas in former centuries the threat as well as the vitality and attractiveness of 'instinctual life' or 'unrefined spontaneity' was only perceived and located in lower classes and outsiders such as 'Negroes' or 'gypsies', in the twentieth century both this threat and this attraction came also to be perceived and located in globally established they-groups or nation-states.

7.2.2 Informalization and the 'superego–ego' balance: the sociogenesis of a we-less superego-dominated personality

In contrast to the authoritarian superego-dominated personality, the we-less superego-dominated personality no longer allows itself the simple solution of projecting its own weaknesses upon they-groups of outsiders. In terms of the tension-balance between attraction *and* repugnance – as before but rather more strongly – they feel attracted to representations of the 'free', the 'authentic', and the 'natural', whether experienced in themselves or in others, but they now suffer from the repugnance, alarm, and irritation they experience about the 'animalic', the 'primitive', the 'dangerously wild'. As they no longer deny their own dangerously wild (in)side, the tensions of ambivalence are no longer acted out, but '*acted in*', leaving the tensions of this tension-balance of attraction *and* repugnance to remain unresolved. The same goes for the tensions between consciousness and conscience in these matters. Although already more strongly I-directed than the personality dominated by an authoritarian conscience, this type of personality suffers especially from a degree of ego- or I-weakness in integrating antagonistic psychic functions: 'What the bearers of the human image of the we-less I appear to suffer from is the conflict between the desire for emotional relationships with other people and their own inability to satisfy this desire' (Elias, 1991: 201).

The whole quest for a 'true self' appears to be a manifestation of this we-less I condition or phase. Such a quest usually betrays the belief that, at some point in time, people had not yet lost their 'true selves', which in fact was a time when they still were unaware or hardly aware of the complexity of themselves and their motives. Indeed, the feeling of a distance from one's 'self' as well as a distance from others emerged with a rising awareness of a 'self' together with mounting pressures to develop impression management and a dramaturgical perspective on life. On the level of the individual psyche, this distance was and continues to be interpreted as loss of 'true self'; and on the we-level of the group it is interpreted as alienation. Overall, it amounts to a sense of living in a world where each person is cut-off from others, as if separated from the world 'outside' by an invisible wall. This is the experience and interpretation captured in the concept of a we-less I or *homo clausus*.[22]

The twentieth century is full of examples. The concept of alienation is one; during the 1960s and 1970s it was very popular in circles of social and cultural critics. Elias and Waldhoff have presented literary examples: Sartre and Camus by Elias, the Turkish author Demir Özlü by Waldhoff. My own focus tends towards examples of romanticization in cultural criticism, in its inherently irritated nostalgia or nostalgic irritation. As dreams and ideals, these romanticizations appear to mirror the anxieties that arise from mounting pressures to scrutinize both inward and outward signals and signs of emotion regulation and the presentation of self, front of stage and backstage. Goffman's dramaturgical perspective was rejected bitterly by the sociologist Alvin Gouldner, who characterized it as the 'sociology of soul-selling'. In parenthesis Gouldner relates an anecdote that, I think, characterized him at least as much as it characterized Goffman:

> I remember one occasion after a long negotiating session with a publisher for whom Goffman and I are both editors. I turned to Goffman and said with some disgust, 'These fellows are treating us like commodities.' Goffman's reply was, 'That's all right, Al, so long as they treat us as *expensive* commodities.' (Gouldner, 1970: 383, quoted in Materman, 1986: 22)

The romanticization inherent in the suggestion that 'real', 'true', 'authentic' people should be able to do without the dramaturgical perspective was heard throughout the century, and it remains quite popular, particularly in the USA. In his study of American manners, the historian Kasson, for example, has written that authors like Dale Carnegie, 'urging the cultivation of manners, deportment, and emotional management as essential to success in social and business dealings alike, have further encouraged readers to regard their very personalities as commodities to be sold' (Kasson, 1990: 259). Abram de Swaan has characterized the bulk of this kind of cultural criticism in the jeering remark: 'What is socially permitted only serves to exploit and control the people better – a continuation of Marx – and what is socially allowed can never be essential, a nod to psychoanalysis' (1979).

Cultural criticism was flying high in Arlie Hochschild's popular book *The Managed Heart: Commercialisation of Human Feeling* (1983). Hochschild's theoretical stance was a combination of Goffman's dramaturgical perspective with an American branch of Marxism: it was capitalism and commercialization that threatened the 'real self' and 'a healthy sense of wholeness'. The 'commercialisation of human feeling' forced people in particular 'to accept as normal the tension they feel between their "real" and their "on-stage" selves' (1983: 185). This tension was also seen as being at the roots of 'The Search for Authenticity' – the title of her book's concluding chapter. Indeed, 'people are made increasingly aware of incentives to *use* feeling' (1983: 198), but with the help of this greater awareness, I argued, their *ability* to use emotions and emotional regulations as instruments for orientating and manifesting themselves has also increased. Moreover, as networks of interdependence expanded and the inherent cooperation and competition intensified, the pressures to develop a higher-level balance between direct-ness *and* tactfulness have continued to rise, making emotion regulation more important as well as more highly appreciated (Wouters, 1989).

In the twentieth-century, particularly from the 1960s onwards, as the emancipation and integration of 'lower' social groups in Western societies permitted, and soon demanded, the emancipation and integration of 'lower' impulses and emotions in personality, the perception of emotions and impulses increasingly came to be seen in terms of a tension-balance: as both dangerous *and* vital. They were viewed as potentially dangerous because they may get out of control and bring the miseries of imprisonment and committal in an asylum, *and* they were seen as vital for being a source of pleasure and for their signal function in finding harmony between the 'domestic policy' and the 'foreign policy' of emotion regulation (Elias, 2000: 416). Similarly, the presentation of self has come to be more and more experienced as both a burden *and* a pleasure. Such a perspective, and the need for it, may explain the rising popularity of and demands for 'reflexivity' both as cultural and personal capital. The romanticization in cultural criticism, however, tends to one-sidedly emphasize the burden, which is rather typical of a we-less I.

In the process of social interweaving, the groups about which individuals have learned to say 'we'– we-groups – change, forcing them to adjust their we-identities and we-feelings. This kind of change, in many respects similar to the changes inherent to the process of growing up, may draw people into a tug-of-war between old and new we-feelings; it affects different layers of the personality and often creates ambivalence. This too, has been conceptualized as 'estrangement' or 'alienation'. If this ambivalence finds expression in the romantic way, the changes in groups and society at large are easily inter-preted as predominantly oppressive, and irritation dominates. In these cases, the changes seem to have robbed individuals of their we-feelings or identi-fication with some cohesive we-group. In their nostalgia, that 'melancholy yearning for a sense of belonging which is often seen as being in the past' (Bailey, 1988: 31), the emphasis is on the loss of we-feelings and on the oppression of a particular kind of intense I-feelings, while the other side of the coin, namely increasing possibilities of expressing I-feelings of another kind – more managed ones, but still relaxed and informal – is neglected. This type of nostalgia, or the romanticization of some imagined past, is therefore also a way of expressing a we-less I.

The experience and interpretation of these changes as increased demands is justified: extreme expressions of superiority and inferiority came to be banned and gradually vanished, while respect and self-respect came to require a more individual articulation and profiling, still expressing inner authenticity or authentic profundity. Increased sensitivity in these matters made for a presentation of self that is soon experienced as artificial and superficial. At the same time, people have found themselves more often in situations where they feel obliged to create and endure differences, even contradictions between their emotions and their emotion regulation. As hierarchical differences diminished, people increasingly pressured each other to strike a more subtle and harmonious balance between all kinds of opposing motives and behaviour, such as directness and tactfulness, simplicity and sophistication, compelling and being compelled, attracting and repelling, being charming and being daunting. Simultaneously, the art of producing and maintaining a gratifying and harmonious balance, one that to a certain extent surpasses or sublimates these tensions, has become more demanding. Ambivalences and insecurities intensified, together with the wish to be liberated from them.

These changes have often been interpreted as predominantly oppressive, and ambivalence has often found expression in an irritated romantic way. Both feelings of irritation and idealization, romanticization or nostalgia occur as a pair – no nostalgia without irritation and vice versa – and, depending upon the balance between the two, the reaction may be called irritated nostalgia or nostalgic irritation. As a pair, they express the we-less I version of the tension-balance of attraction *and* repugnance, thus showing the relation between constraints and dreams of liberation or ideals. Any investigation of the history of utopias and romantic ideals can be used to illustrate this connection. Passions and anxieties mirror each other, as do utopias and 'dystopias', ideals and spectres. Whether projected into the past or into the future, they always betray the social and individual tensions of the figuration in which they were created. A familiar example is the process in which knights lost sovereignty over their domains and became courtiers. In this process, the imaginative form of literature called romance was born. Courtiers found an outlet for the social and psychic tensions of living at court in the dream world of Arcadia; in pastoral romances and plays, the unrestrained simplicity and relaxed directness of country life was romanticized (Elias, 1983).

Again, the tradition of cultural criticism in the social sciences provides many examples. For instance in Philippe Ariès's work on attitudes towards dying, irritation with the present 'taboo' on death is combined with a nostalgia for some past in which death was thought to be 'both familiar and near, evoking no great fear or awe' (1974: 13; Wouters, 1990b). And in Christopher Lasch's *The Culture of Narcissism* (1979) irritation with the present 'culture of narcissism' is combined with nostalgia for some past in which fathers were thought to be still righteous and demanding. Inherent in this tradition is a tendency to think in terms of dichotomies rather than balances: 'Hedonism . . . originates not in the pursuit of pleasure but in a war of all against all, in which even the most intimate encounters become a form of mutual exploitation'. The hedonistic side of the balance is explicitly rejected as 'false': 'this hedonism is a fraud; the pursuit of pleasure disguises a struggle for power' (Lasch, 1979: 125–7). Eleven years previously, Bennis and Slater had made a similar statement in their *The Temporary Society*, one that was not so dichotomous, although it remained rather one-sided: 'More play in work also means more work in play, until all acts become both playful and instrumental, public and private, and no sphere of human expression is altogether uncontaminated by duty' (1968: 88). Had these authors continued this sentence by adding 'nor unrelated to play and pleasure', they would have fully acknowledged the balance and the intensified ambivalence of work *and* pleasure.

Feelings of being cut-off, typical of a *homo clausus* or a we-less I, and feelings of ambivalence, insecurity, and disorientation will to some extent have accompanied each new round in the process of self-distanciation and reflexivity. And although articulating and emphasizing one's distinctive features has become increasingly important and inescapable, it seems at the same time to have become a form of play and an art: more and more people seem to have become increasingly aware both that they have to put their minds and hearts into it, and of how it is to be done. Moreover, as the longing for a simpler and more passionate kind of life intensified, the function of self-control as a weapon in the status struggle was simultaneously reinforced, which means that the meaning and justification of one's life, one's respect, self-respect, and identity have become more dependent upon this capacity for control.

As long as processes of differentiation and integration continue in the same direction, ensuring that social and psychic bonds will continue to expand and intensify, the social and psychic tensions of these bonds will also increase and with them the intensity of the longing to defy these tensions in spontaneous, authentic, relaxed, and informal conduct. On the other hand, unrealistic expressions of this ideal will tend to be brought under control more strongly. Becoming simple and innocent again is impossible anyway; the road back is blocked. Only ambivalences and balances, like '*sophisticated* simplicity' or '*noble* authenticity' (*controlled* decontrolling) are open as realistic ideals. [23]

7.2.3   Informalization and the 'superego–ego' balance: towards a more ego-dominated self-regulation – a 'third nature'

Continued expansion and intensification of social competition and cooperation triggered further social and psychic emancipation and integration: drives, impulses, and emotions have tended to become more easily accessible to consciousness while their control has come to be less strongly based upon an authoritative conscience. This implied a decline of unthinking – more or less automatic – acceptance of all sorts of authority. As this unthinking acceptance decreased, the respect and self-respect of all citizens have become less directly dependent upon external social controls and more directly upon their reflexive and calculating abilities, and therefore upon a particular pattern of self-control in which the 'unthinking acceptance' of the dictates of psychic authority or conscience also decreased. Thus, the emancipation of impulses and emotions has been accompanied by a shift from conscience to consciousness (to use this shorthand expression). In this way, the social processes of relations and manners between social groups becoming less rigid and hierarchical have been connected with psychic processes: less hierarchical and more open and fluent relations between the psychic functions of people's emotions and impulses, their regulation via the counter-emotions and counter-impulses of conscience, and their self-regulation via consciousness. As social and psychic dividing lines opened up, social groups as well as psychic functions became more integrated – that is, the communications and connections between both social groups and psychic functions have become more flowing and flexible. Lo and behold: the sociogenesis and psychogenesis of a 'third-nature personality'!

I have introduced the terms 'third nature' and 'third-nature personality' as sensitizing concepts to illuminate these changes (1998b, 1999a, 1999b, 2004b). The term 'second nature' refers to a self-regulating conscience that functions to a great extent automatically. The term 'third nature' is indicative of a development from this 'second-nature' self-regulation in the direction of a more reflexive and flexible one. Ideally, for someone operating on the basis of third nature, ego functions have become dominant to the extent that it becomes 'natural' to attune oneself to the pulls and pushes of both first and second nature as well as the dangers and chances, short term and long term, of any particular situation or relation. As national, continental, and global integration processes exert pressure towards increasingly differentiated regimes of manners, they also exert pressure towards increasingly reflexive and flexible regimes of self-regulation. The term 'third nature' refers to a level of consciousness and calculation in which all types of constraints and possibilities are taken into account. It is a rise to a new level on 'the spiral staircase of consciousness' (Elias, 1991).

Development in this direction can be discerned more clearly from the 1950s onwards. Since then, 'inner-direction' – as Riesman called these internalized controls of a rather fixed kind – has definitely changed from being an advantage into being a handicap; automatisms became too predictable, too rigid and stiff. Expanding and intensified cooperation and competition have put people under pressure to calculate and to observe themselves and each other more sharply, while showing flexibility and a greater willingness to compromise. In this process, almost everywhere in the West, the once highly elevated ideologies and great ideals – and with them great conflicts and wars – have been superseded to a large extent by more pragmatic and flexible points of departure in containing and solving conflicts. This process brought with it a continued relativization of the once rather narrow and blind – that is, more or less automatic – identification with one's own group, one's family, religion, nationality, race, class, and sex, for which a more varied and wider circle of identification was substituted.

From the 1950s and 1960s onwards, there arose an increased necessity to be more open to all kinds of extreme and 'deeper' impulses and emotions. The fear of the slippery slope of having to give in was turned upside down: 'Where formerly there was felt to be the danger that, in seeking fun, one might be carried away into the depths of wickedness, today there is a recognizable fear that one may not be able to let go sufficiently, that one may not have enough fun' (Wolfenstein, 1955: 174). Many people participated in social and psychic experiments searching for the limits of self-regulation and the pleasure of sniffing the dangers on the other side of the boundaries. Many demonstrated a 'quest for excitement' (Elias and Dunning, 1986), even a craze for taking risks in more or less dangerous situations and relations. This provocative and experimental attitude is characteristic of a new level of social and psychic integration: before the 1950s the social and psychic authorities would have banned it as too subversive and too dangerous.

This 'quest for excitement' and taking risks can also be understood as a direct counterpart to the 'equanimity of the welfare state': the greater personal security and confidence that was generated by increased wealth and the provision of 'social security' by the state (Stolk and Wouters, 1987). In the relatively long period of peace and rising 'social and personal security' since 1945, the arrangements of a caring welfare state were increasingly taken for granted, and this 'peace' in material respects functioned as a breeding ground in which much relational and individual unrest took root, including an enhanced quest for excitement, tensions, and risks. Young people in particular became fascinated by new questions such as 'What follows freedom and prosperity?' and 'What lies beyond the boundaries set by conscience and morality?'. The latter question is characteristic of the development towards a 'third nature', a more ego-dominated type of personality.

In the 1960s and 1970s, the 'emancipation of emotions' and the shift from a second-nature towards a third-nature type of personality involved a different function for and appreciation of guilt. In comparing the three types of persons that he distinguished – tradition-directed, inner-directed, and other-directed – Riesman wrote about the inner-directed type: 'He goes through life less independent than he seems, obeying his inner piloting. Getting off course, whether in response to inner impulses or to the fluctuating voices of contemporaries, may lead to the feeling of *guilt*.' In contrast, 'the other-directed person, must be able to receive signals from far and near; the sources are many, the changes rapid. ... As against guilt-and-shame controls, though of course these survive, one prime psychological lever of the other-directed person is a diffuse anxiety' (1950: 24–5). These words can be read as a harbinger of the widespread attack on guilt and guilt feelings in the 1960s and 1970s, expressed in the widely used words 'guilt trip' in exclamations like 'Don't lay that guilt trip on me!'. Ralph Turner observed that 'guilt becomes an evil thing. It becomes the impediment to individual autonomy and to an individual sense of worth. Guilt is the invasion of the self by arbitrary and external standards' (1969: 402). This social movement was mirrored in changing opinions about guilt in criminal law and punishment, as well as in a critique of blame attribution as a means of orientation (Benthem van den Bergh, 1986), and in the 'self psychology' of Kohut (1977).

Guilt feelings came to be experienced more strongly as indicative of a conscience-ridden personality make-up and, therefore, as an anxiety to be mastered. They came to be seen as a symbol and a symptom of an authoritative and rather automatically functioning conscience. In comparison, shame feelings refer more directly to other people, to external constraints, and in addition also to the fact that one's conscience is at least partly in agreement with these others. From this perspective it becomes understandable why the shift from a superego-dominated personality in the direction of an ego-dominated personality has coincided with a decline in the status of guilt, both as a feeling and as a concept, or, to use this shorthand expression, why it coincided with a shift from guilt to shame.[24]

Over this same period, an important characteristic of informalization and the development of a 'third nature' has been a strong decline in social as well as psychic censorship. Until the 1960s and 1970s, many thoughts were generally branded as dangerous, out of the prevailing conviction that they would almost automatically lead to dangerous action. Because of this direct, second-nature connection between thoughts and actions, a relatively high degree of social and psychic censorship was common practice (see §2.5). Rigorous and violent censorship in stricter and more authoritarian regimes demonstrates to what extent authorities and others have believed in the danger of thoughts, imagination, or fantasy. In most Western countries, especially since the 1960s, both the fear and awe of fantasy or dissident imagination have diminished together with the fear and awe of the authorities of state and conscience.[25] These censorships have decreased in the course of the integration of 'lower' social groups within Western societies and the subsequent emancipation and integration of 'lower' impulses and emotions in personality. As 'third nature' – this more ego-dominated pattern of self-regulation – spread, there was a significant spread of more and more unconcealed expressions of insubordination, sex, and violence, particularly in the realms of imagination and amusement.

A harbinger of these changes was George Orwell's essay 'Raffles and Miss Blandish,' in which he compared two types of detective novels. The first was a series of stories, written in the early twentieth century, about a gentleman crook, Raffles, for whom 'certain things are "not done," and the idea of doing them hardly arises' (1972 [1944]: 66).

Raffles...has no real moral code, no religion, certainly no social consciousness. All he has is a set of reflexes – the nervous system, as it were, of a gentleman. Give him a sharp tap on this reflex or that (they are called 'sport', 'pal', 'woman', 'king and country' and so forth), and you get a predictable reaction. (1972: 79)

There are 'very few corpses, hardly any blood, no sex crimes, no sadism, no perversions of any kind' (1972: 67). All these are, however, central to the Miss Blandish novel, about an American type of detective, published in 1939. In this book, the pursuit of power is a pervasive motive, and 'if ultimately one sides with the police against the gangsters, it is merely... because, in fact, the law is a bigger racket than crime' (1972: 71). 'In *No Orchids* anything is "done" so long as it leads to power. All the barriers are down, all the motives are out in the open.... there are no gentlemen and no taboos. Emancipation is complete. Freud and Machiavelli have reached the outer suburbs' (1972: 75, 79).

Since Orwell wrote this essay, the emancipation he refers to as being complete has in fact continued. In the 1970s, Tom Wolfe, a fellow writer and trend-watcher described this continuation as the rise of a new kind of pornography, 'pornoviolence':

> Violence is the simple, ultimate solution for problems of status competition, just as gambling is the simple, ultimate solution for economic competition. The old pornography was the fantasy of easy sexual delights in a world where sex was kept unavailable. The new pornography is the fantasy of easy triumph in a world where status competition has become so complicated and frustrating. (Wolfe, 1976: 162)

A few more examples of popular 'pornoviolence' from later in the twentieth century are novels such as *American Psycho* by Bret Easton Ellis, movies such as *Natural Born Killers* and *Pulp Fiction*, and Nintendo and other expressions of violence and sex in 'virtual reality'. From the popularity of this kind of imagination, it would follow that the 'pursuit of happiness' has turned into a pursuit of power.

On the whole, this development implies that this 'second-nature' type of fear of being inevitably 'carried away into the depths of wickedness' by indulging in these 'dangerous' imaginations can be faced and controlled. In fact, much of the pleasurable excitement found in reading or seeing these products derives precisely from facing and controlling these dangers. This also means that the dividing lines *and* the increasingly complex and subtle connections between imagination and reality have come to be more sharply perceived.

But there is more to it than that. It is much less well perceived that this imagined pursuit of power has also allowed for the experiencing of emotions that had become tabooed in actual social life: feelings of superiority and inferiority. Only in the realm of imagination (and to a lesser extent in sports and games) are these feelings still allowed to come to the surface, that is, in 'sublimated' ways. In mimetic triumphs and defeats, whether in the world of sex or money, the daily pressure of having to repress and conceal these emotions was released. Here, in the realm of imagination and fantasy, the pleasure in expressing these kinds of feelings had regained dominance over the discontent it provokes. Thus, these feelings of superiority and inferiority have become subjected to a controlled decontrolling, to a balancing act between restraint and expression – and the same applies to constituent emotions such as pride and shame, anger and anxiety, aggrandizement and jealousy. This leads to the question of how strange these feelings actually are?

7.3 Towards a Controlled Decontrolling of Superiority and Inferiority Feelings?

The period after World War II was characterized by decolonization, global emancipation, and democratization. It was a period of expanding inter-dependencies and rising levels of mutual identification, in which ideals of equality and mutual consent spread and gained strength. On this basis, avoidance behaviour came to be less and less rigidly directed at 'lower-class' people and 'lower' emotions, and on the whole, in most Western countries, behavioural and emotional alternatives expanded. There was one important exception: the social codes increasingly came to dictate that overt expression of inferiority and superiority feelings be avoided. The avoidance of these feelings and of behaviour that expressed them was a confirmation of social equalization and a necessary condition for informalization to occur. Thus, there was a further curbing of emotions in relation to the display of arrogance or self-aggrandizement and 'self-humiliation'. These were either banished to the realm of imagination, games, and sports, or compartmentalized behind the social and psychic scenes. Displaying such feelings increasingly came to provoke moral indignation and shame, and thus seriously damaged a person's status and self-esteem. This avoidance could only be accomplished by either keeping it a secret or by doing it unconsciously and automatically, that is, by turning it into the product of a 'second nature'. In the shaming and banning process involved in developing such a 'nature', however, the insight that feelings of superiority and inferiority are inherently provoked by status competition tended to be shamed and banned as well, and the same went for the insight that part of any encounter or gathering is a 'trial of strength', a power and status competition. Thus, during the same period in which many emotions were allowed to re-emerge into consciousness and public life, and in which second-nature habits were discovered and loosened up as 'third nature' developed, the emotions connected with triumphs and defeats were simultaneously becoming 'strange' to the self.

The banning of these emotions from the social and psychic scene may help to explain why discussing differences in levels of development in self-regulation between individuals and groups easily provokes negative reactions; it soon came to be understood (or misunderstood) as ranking their human value. In the period since World War II, only with regard to small individuals – children – has thinking in terms of phases in (individual) processes of self-regulation remained acceptable, as the accounts of developmental phases by Kohlberg or Piaget may demonstrate. In other contexts, it was (and is) promptly condemned as a demonstration of superiority feelings, as ethnocentrism or racism.

These words, superiority and racism in particular, suggest that these reactions to distinguishing developmental phases are triggered because of their being reminiscent of World War II, and, perhaps even more important, of the colonial era. In addition, there is an older and deeper level from which these negative reactions stem: to think and write in terms of phases in social and psychic processes is linked to the old habit of equating differences in power with differences in human value (Elias and Scotson, 1994: xv). Within the spectrum of first nature and second nature, this old habit may even range closer to first nature than to second, for it prevails both in the history of humankind *and* in the history of each living human being. Up to a certain age, children seem to take it for granted that smaller and less powerful children are second rate: *vae victis*, might is right, and the mighty are better people. It has 'survival value'. It belongs, so to speak, to their 'logic of emotions' to identify with stronger and established people, and to dis-identify with weaker and subordinate ones. Today, in growing up, most children will to some extent develop a second-nature type of counter-habitus. Throughout all the centuries of the long-term formalizing phase, however, among all age groups, the assumption that the socially weaker necessarily also had weaker characters, that second-rate citizens were second-rate people, was completely taken for granted.

Although in every emancipation movement this assumption was attacked, it was only after World War II that it lost its dominance. This occurred in a period of accelerated democratization (including decolonization) and diminishing power differences – a period, moreover, in which many painfully realized that the superiority feelings inherent in this old habitual assumption had been a basis and a motive for the mass killings under Stalin and Hitler as well as for the exploitation, annihilation, and humiliation of colonial regimes such as Churchill's (Goudsblom, 1992: 184–5; Lindqvist, 1997) or that of the King of Belgium Leopold II (Hochschild, 1998). This formed a strong motive for intensified shaming of these feelings and for putting a stricter ban on them, in which process they disappeared further into deeper layers of personality. Thus, they were transformed into inner fears, more or less automatically countered by a person's conscience. In the development of this counter-habit, everything that was reminiscent of the old habit of equating social power with human value came to be warded off with a rigour similar to that which was demanded in the original process of suppression.

Up to the early twenty-first century, however, the taboo on discussing phases in social and psychic processes and the interconnected inner fears have quite often led to overheated attacks on perceived racism, ethnocentrism, or 'political incorrectness'. In those instances, the rather blind force of such attacks seemed to indicate that the struggle against 'we are better, they are inferior people' is not only being fought on the social battlefield but also in the psyche, against parts of oneself. The ongoing psychic battle of individuals, in this particular disciplinary phase in the 'civilizing' of these emotions, usually prevents any discussion of their relations with people of different skin colour, class, or sex from going far beyond multiculturalist banalities like 'they are just different, we are not better'. In these instances, discussions in terms of phases in social and psychic processes soon get tense and come to an end, or progress into an evaluative dispute about plus and minus points. Of course, the study of developments and developmental phases is not directed at drawing up and balancing the disadvantages of any lead against the advantages of any backlog. Such an endeavour would greatly confuse analysis with evaluation (see Goudsblom, 1996). However, exactly this kind of confusion quite often results from the workings of a rather authoritarian conscience formation regarding these emotions. Between the 1950s and the twenty-first century, this type of conscience formation was more the rule than the exception.

It was rather early in this period, in 1976, that Tom Wolfe observed that the emancipation of some emotions coincided with a continued shaming and banning of others: 'We are in an age when people will sooner confess their sexual secrets – much sooner in many cases – than their status secrets, whether in the sense of longings and triumphs or humiliations and defeats' (1976: 189). This observation is in keeping with a widening gap in public discourse: as the principle of proceeding by mutual consent gained acceptance, the possibilities of discussing sexual impulses and emotions grew, making these discussions more open and detached, whereas the possibilities of discussing the impulses and emotions connected with triumphs and defeats have become more narrow, more restricted and evaluative.

To some extent, anger or aggressive impulses have come to be recognized as normal aspects of emotional life, and more and more people have also taken the liberty of venting them in cursing, calling each other all sorts of names, and making allusions to violence in flushes of 'instant enmity' (§4.4.4). However, the spread of allusions to sexuality and of 'instant intimacy' seems to be much wider. This is in keeping with the fact that, through psychoanalysis and other forms of psychotherapy, a rich tradition of recalling and interpreting sexual impulses and emotions has come into existence and spilled over into all walks of life. By contrast, there is hardly any tradition of analysing and interpreting emotions and impulses connected with the struggle for power and status, particularly feelings of inferiority and superiority. And yet, again and again, from the suicide attacker to the 'president of war', these feelings appear to be directly and highly significant for understanding why social and psychic conflicts erupt in violence.

As it is highly improbable that the emotions connected with longings and triumphs, humiliations and defeats will ever disappear from emotional or social life – it is just about as improbable as the disappearance of sexual impulses and emotions – the extent to which they will lead to annihilation and humiliation will depend on the level of social and individual control over these emotions. I therefore think, that it makes sense to specify the task of 'working through feelings of strangeness', as Waldhoff has called it, and particularly to direct this 'working through' to feelings of inferiority and superiority. In this context it might also help to bring racism, sexism, ageism, nationalism, ethnocentrism, etc., under the new conceptual umbrella of 'superiorism', because this concept brings all these 'ism's' onto a higher level of generalization, highlighting their common characteristic: equating power superiority with superiority as a human being.

Since the 1980s, the level of social and individual control over the feelings of inferiority and superiority has gained importance because, in and between most societies all over the world, tensions about they-groups of 'strangers' and the particular 'strangeness' related to feelings of superiority and inferiority, have intensified. This intensification was related to rapidly increasing migration into Europe, and to a change in migration into the USA, which involved increasing numbers of Americans being of non-European descent. This intensification also stemmed from the fact that collective emancipation chances vanished, as was indicated by a wide range of budget cuts. As the collective social ascent of whole groups came to an end, collective identification shifted from the social groups that had been rising towards the established. This shift was reinforced in the 1990s by the tensions, conflicts, and insecurities associated with the collapse of the Iron Curtain. Accordingly, social protests were no longer mainly directed at the establishment, as had been the case in the 1960s and 1970s, but towards anything perceived as a threat to the established order, including 'strangers' and 'strangeness'.

It is in this social climate that in most rich countries the tensions surrounding immigrants and other they-groups have been rising. The attack on the Twin Towers and the Pentagon on 11 September 2001, followed by the 'War on Terrorism', has led to rising tensions between we- and they-groups at a global level, and brought about significantly higher levels of mutual fear and suspicion. This 'War on Terrorism' (which may turn out to be more an overheated authoritarian reaction than a reflexive and accommodating one), may lead to a fear-ridden hardening of feelings of (Western, American) superiority, increasing the dangers of annihilation and humiliation. On the other hand, if these tensions do not rise to the level of a major explosion, it seems likely that national, continental, and global processes of differentiation, interweaving, and integration will continue, and that the interconnected psychic processes of an 'emancipation of emotions' and controlled decontrolling will also continue, coming to include more feelings of superiority and inferiority.

As national, continental, and global integration processes exert pressure towards increasingly differentiated regimes of manners, they also exert pressure towards increasingly reflexive and flexible regimes of self-regulation. The level of reflexive 'civilizing' of social and psychic authorities may also continue to rise, strengthening informalization processes and the development of a 'third-nature' type of personality. This would imply that feelings of inferiority and superiority will be further admitted into consciousness, while, at the same time, they come under a stronger, a more comprehensive, more stable, and subtle internal (ego) control, one that is sharply scrutinized and thus backed up by external social controls.

Appendix 1: Informalization of Manners and of Labour Relations

In the 1990s, expressions such as the 'informalization of the economy' or 'informalization of labour', or 'informalization of the labour market' have surfaced in connection with the deregulation of labour relations in Third World countries, competing for the investments of transnational or multinational corporations (Parry *et al.*, 1999). The informalization of the formal codes of the labour market is quite a different process, of course, from the informalization of formal codes of manners and emotion regulation. However, there is an important similarity, which forms the focus of this appendix.

In the 1970s and 1980s, the transfer of labour-intensive production processes to countries where labour was cheap and plentiful strongly accelerated. In rich countries where wages were high and protected by various regulations, this transfer was accompanied by increasing competitive pressures to develop a policy of greater wage moderation, to stimulate the 'free market', and to deregulate state organizations and functions. The transfer also shows how national and international labour markets were directly involved in the process of expanding networks of interdependence to the global level (Wouters, 1990a; Smith, 2006). In low-income and low-wage countries, the transfer was welcomed for the chances it brought of providing work and raising income, but it also placed these countries in competition with each other. Thus, governments in poor countries came under rising competitive pressures to enforce the kind of wage policies that would attract companies and capital investors to come to their country. In many cases these measures involved abolition of earlier regulations of the labour market which had served to provide a degree of protection against severe forms of exploitation (Hart, 1973). Increasingly large areas, eventually called *free trade zones* or *export processing zones*, were designated to attract investments from multi- and transnational corporations, and in these areas workers are explicitly declined the right to form unions. According to *Human Development Report* 2000, these workers amounted to 50,000 in 1975 but by 1999 their numbers had risen to 27 million in 845 zones. According to this report of four years later (2004), there were 43 million of these workers in 2002 (in about 3.000 zones in 116 countries). Doing away with formal restrictions and rules regulating labour market relations led to the expansion of a dark sector in the economy with rather exploitative labour conditions and multifarious illegal practices.

Thus, in high-wage Western societies as well as in low-wage societies, globalization has stimulated deregulation (allowing private enterprises a wider range of operation) and weakened the position of workers in the labour market. The trend manifested itself much more strongly at the bottom of the world economy, where unions were weak or non-existent. In the Western welfare states, the deregulation of labour relations – and labour conditions generally – was accompanied by a tightening of many remaining formal rules, combined with sharpened control over their application and over the application of all welfare state arrangements and institutions. In these societies, the deregulation of economic relations usually coincided with new and revised regulations of the relations between government organizations and 'the market', meaning business organizations and unions. It was a 'regulated deregulation', an informalization of labour relations in the sense of a 'controlled decontrolling'.

In these high-wage countries, the 'regulated deregulation' or 'informalization of labour relations' was preceded by a substantial formalization or regulation. Usually this was scarcely or not at all the case in low-wage societies. In these poorer societies, deregulation of the 'free market' and the 'informalization' of labour relations and the labour market (Soto, 2000; Breman, 2001), resulting in the growth of *export processing zones, level playing fields*, and of a dark sector of 'sweat shops' and home industry, was not preceded by a substantial degree of formalization or regulation. And here we are confronted with a major similarity between the regimes of manners and emotions and labour regimes: without a critical degree of preceding formalization, both forms of informalization tend to brutalize relations, to re-establish the principle of 'might is right'.

In many Third World societies, the process of the formalization of labour relations had brought the unrestricted exploitation of labour under greater public control. This process has been stopped and reversed through the process of internationalization and informalization of labour relations and working conditions (Breman, 2004). The ensuing fragmentation of industrial and manual production as part of the rise of a new sector in the world economy, a sector that is controlled more by global corporations than by national states, has reduced both the protection and the possibilities for protection of the workers in this sector. Here, in regulating the process of internationalization or globalization of production, the interests of these workers in many poor countries are confronted with those of transnational corporations. In view of the highly uneven global balance of power between these corporations and the governments of poor countries, the cutting of its sharp predatory edges, as has happened in West-European welfare states, would most probably demand an international movement. From this perspective, the need for the 'Workers of the World [to] Unite!' is still as pressing as it was a century ago. In the early twentieth century, this movement shattered in the face of national and nationalistic interests. Early in the twenty-first century, there is a relatively weak International Labour Organisation, backed up by a weak international we-identification. National interests and national we-identifications still prevail and dominate, also in the European Union. In Europe and in its rich former colonies such as the USA, Canada, and Australia, international we-identification does cross territorial boundaries, but without much consequence. Moreover, next to national interests there are 'capital' interests which block the materialization of these we-identifications. There is no maxim for bankers of the world to unite because they *are* united, and via them, so are the owners of 'capital' and the captains of industry.

The late twentieth century saw the rise of an Anti-Globalization movement, critically following the actions of global organizations such as the IMF, the World Bank, and the WTO. At the time of writing, however, the main power resource of the Anti-Globalists is their nuisance value. In Europe and in its successful former colonies, moreover, only a tiny minority is interested in the movement, and only a fraction of them feels they are involved. Most people have become accustomed to the policy of buying off social conflicts. Thus, the rise in wealth (resulting from the process of economic interweaving at the global level) has rather stimulated a feeling of indolent contentment about material security and/or an 'equanimity of the welfare state' on which basis immaterial anxieties have risen: doubts about the quality of life, uncertainty about personal relations and insecurity about psychic well-being. At the same time, it has stimulated a quest for excitement and risks (see §7.2.3). After '9/11' 2001, when the USA started fighting a 'war against terrorism' and the fear of it, this contentment has diminished. It was further reduced by tensions stemming from governments and corporations having to adapt to international competitiveness by slimming down business organizations and making them more flexible, while keeping control over social conflict and a growing social divide in the population. Both in Europe and the USA, immigration and the contrast between 'old' and 'new' (or *nouveau*) Europeans and Americans seem to occupy not only the hearts and minds of increasing numbers of 'old' residents but also increasingly the political agenda. Of course, this does not particularly stimulate involvement in a movement for basic formalization of wage relations in Third World societies. In these less developed and relatively poor societies, global interweaving, and in its wake the informalization of labour regimes, seems to have stimulated the feeling of disenchantment and – for the time being – embittered resignation (possibly with the exception of 9/11).

In these poor countries, the informalization of the formal codes of the labour market has proceeded without a critical degree of preceding formalization. Without such a critical degree, the informalization of formal codes of manners and emotion regulation tends in the direction of re-establishing the principle of 'might is right' (which in Dutch is known as the 'law of the strongest'). For it is in processes of formalization that the level of mutually expected self-restraints rises, or, to put it differently, collective conscience formation builds up to a level allowing for increasing 'permissiveness', for a growing leniency in codes of manners, for increasing instead of diminishing behavioural and emotional alternatives. Only from a critical moment in the processes of social integration and formalization of the regimes of manners and emotions can an informalization of manners become a loosening and relaxation of these regimes, rather than a coarsening and brutalization. This critical moment demands that a relatively high level of self-restraint has come to be taken for granted, that is, mutually expected, and which in that sense functions as part of a collective conscience.

In other words, the relatively high level of social integration that allows for such an informalization of manners presupposes its psychic reflection: a corresponding level of psychic integration and an equalization and opening of psychic relations and functions. It presupposes an emancipation of emotions: the relatively open and flowing connections between the more direct emotions and impulses of 'first nature', the counter-impulses of conscience or 'second nature', and consciousness. In many respects, the processes of conscience formation can be perceived as processes of psychic formalization. From this perspective, psychic informalization is a process in which the rulings of conscience become less rigid, less automatic, allowing for more conscious, more flexible, and varied applications. In other words, it is a process towards the more reflexive and flexible self-regulation of a 'third nature'. Without the development of a critical level of psychic formalization, psychic informalization in the sense of a 'controlled decontrolling of emotional controls' will not be controlled enough and tend to run wild.

That is precisely the tenor of the story about a kindergarten in the early 1970s where children were allowed to take their 'weaponry' along. The arms race and fights did not reach the saturation point that the parents had hoped and waited for. The sociologist Paul Kapteyn concludes: 'The increased tolerance and flexibility of adults towards the children's violence, this violation of a taboo, could only be understood and followed by the children when they had first become quite familiar with the taboo – when they had first learned what they later to some extent could unlearn' (1980: 179). In this example, one may recognize a sequence that Piaget and Kohlberg incorporated in their models of intellectual and moral development, that is, the sequence in which children are at first preoccupied with their own emotions and cling to the social routines of what they perceive as 'the done thing'. From the age of 11 or 12 onwards, role-taking and the balancing of their own feelings and the feelings of others become more generally possible. From then on, they may learn to individualize and improvise, that is, to choose their *own* strategy or procedure for *this* situation and in relation to *that* person. Thus, in this respect, in individual 'civilizing' processes a similar structure can be discerned as in the 'civilizing' processes of societies, in which the long-term process of informalization was preceded by a long-term process of formalization.

The importance of formalization preceding informalization can also be illustrated from the difficulties faced by newcomers to such informalized societies, especially if they come from more hierarchical societies with a lower level of social integration and correspondingly lower levels of mutual identification and mutually expected self-restraint. In that case, the scope of their identification will tend to be more restricted, and they will not know or recognize these mutual expectations of self-restraint, which, therefore, will not apply to them, or only to a lesser extent. It is a form of social disorientation that may lead to the extremes of clamming up on the one hand, and to a more or less calculated running wild on the other. When they come to live in a society of people living in less hierarchical relations than they are used to, and have to orientate themselves to a code of manners they can hardly understand, if only because it is not backed up by the kind of external social controls they deem necessary, they come without the social and psychic instruments and functions deemed necessary in these societies. Thus, they are overburdened, just as the people in Third World societies are severely overburdened when struck by an informalization of economic (labour) relations before the formalizing of these relations has established a critical level of taken-for-granted protection.

Similarly, if informalization of psychic relations and functions takes place before their formalization (or conscience formation) has provided a level of taken-for-granted restraint, it tends to give free reign to 'the strongest', in this case to the 'might' of drives and emotions that can be dangerous for the people who give in to their 'inner might' as well as for others; they easily lead to humiliation and annihilation. Only persons who have developed a relatively strong 'third-nature' type of self-regulation – which gains strength as the level of social and psychic integration rises – are able to prevent this from happening. In confrontations between old established groups and groups of outsiders such as immigrants from countries where power balances are relatively unequal, the strength of the 'third-nature' type of personality is put to the test. In these clashes, members of the established groups are confronted with the 'weaknesses' that go hand in hand with strong forms of inequality. These weaknesses had been banned from their relations to the extent that they thought to have overcome them, and therefore they may fly into a rage that threatens existing levels of mutual identification, informalization, and 'civilization'.

These confrontations are social and psychic integration conflicts. On the social level, they entail the emancipation and integration of lower classes within nation-states and the integration of rich and poor countries and their inhabitants within global networks. On the psychic level, they involve emancipation and integration of 'lower' emotions and impulses within the personality structure. Together, the tensions on both levels may lead to an explosive mixture. As yet, however, integration conflicts have remained of limited size and duration.

Appendix 2: On Norbert Elias and Informalization Theory[26]

I

In the late 1960s, Norbert Elias began to come to Amsterdam regularly. I may have heard or seen him earlier, but our initial encounter took place in 1969 during a meeting of the study seminar on 'Sociology and Morality'. I remember the first question that I put to him. It was based on his reputation for wisdom, not just erudition. This reputation had been given momentum by Joop Goudsblom, the director of the seminar, but already in 1964 and 1965, I had heard similar comments about Elias from A. den Hollander at his American Studies seminars. Parsons, as I had come to understand from my teachers, had developed a sociological theory which was much more systematic than reality, while the theory of Elias, though less systematic, provided a workable model with greater explanatory power with respect to both social and psychic reality. That sounded marvellous, of course, and it made me wonder how someone could come to be so wise. Thus it came about that, having noted down such wise remarks as 'interdependence is inescapable, so power struggle is inescapable', towards the end of the session I asked Elias the naïve and blunt question whether he could explain the development of his wisdom. 'Difficult question, I don't know', he began his answer, and laughing mischievously he proceeded, 'Maybe it's because I have travelled a lot. You all seem so confined to your own country'. Much later, probably in 1987, when Elias told me that he wanted to call his work on Mozart *The Sociology of Genius* (1993), this moment of inquisitiveness about his reputation as a genius of wisdom came to my associative mind and we enjoyed recalling it.

It was through Elias himself that it dawned on me that this genius, although indeed world famous in Amsterdam, was largely unknown in the world of international sociology. On the first page of my first article, a paper for the Seventh World Congress of Sociology, held in 1970 at the Bulgarian sea resort of Varna, I had said something about the balance of detachment and involvement (1972). After having read that page, Elias told me that practically no reader or congress participant would understand these concepts. I had used them as if they had gained currency in the world at large, not just in my Amsterdam world.

In Varna I witnessed Elias volunteer to help organize a 'working group' for the following world congress four years later. I was then so young that this struck me as highly remarkable: 'so old', I thought, 'and yet counting on still going strong in four years' time'. Elias was then seventy-three. He would continue to be old for another twenty years, though increasingly older.

II

In those years when Norbert Elias came to Amsterdam from Leicester, where he lived, the Goudsbloms always hosted a *soirée* in his honour. There, to my mind, 'the established', 'the older ones' were invited. Somewhere in the early 1970s, my wife – now my ex – and I also gave a party, one specifically for 'the outsiders', 'the young people' (all of them now over fifty; never trust anyone under fifty!). It became a tradition; we did it every time Elias was in Amsterdam. Rummaging through my 'Eliasiania' I found a letter dated 11 June 1973 in which he thanks us for 'the party at your place'. So we must have started in that year.

In the early 1970s, I was a man who needed a job to earn a living, and furthermore, I had decided to be a 'family man', nothing more or less, leaving no more room for intellectual ambitions than doing some translation work. It was thus that the decision was reached to translate *The Established and the Outsiders* into Dutch. Through collaboration with Bram van Stolk this became a very pleasurable project. On our weekly meetings, we drank a glass or two, discussed the world and ourselves, and eventually also the bits of translation which we had done. In the summer of 1975 Bram and I had made enough progress to make us look forward to discussing the translation with Norbert, as we by then called him. We drove to Leicester where we lodged in his house. After that visit, Bram and I, by way of thanks for his hospitality, sent him a record of Bob Dylan's *Blood on the Tracks*. In his letter of thanks for the gift, Norbert wrote that he had difficulty in understanding the words. Thereupon I transcribed some texts from the record for him, among others the lyrics from *Shelter from the Storm*, and I told him what this song meant to me. In his letter of 2 January 1976 from Leicester he reacted in a way that is 'vintage Norbert'. Since he refers tacitly to Dylan's texts in this letter, before quoting from his letter, I must first quote these lines:

> Suddenly I turned around and she was standing there,
> with silver bracelets on her wrists and flowers in her hair,
> she walked up to me so gracefully and took my crown of thorns
> 'Come in', she said, 'I'll give you shelter from the storm'.

And:

> I've heard new-born babies wailing like a morning dove, and old men
> with broken teeth stranded without love.

Although I had drawn his attention to the strong ambivalence in the song – the 'she' of 'shelter' at a certain moment gives forth a lethal dose – in his reply Norbert completely ignored this double meaning, probably because I had added that to me the song as a whole tended to affirm one of its central questions, 'Is it hopeless and forlorn?'. For that is what he hits out at, however quiet and cordial the way in which he begins his letter:

Thank you very much for copying for me the text of Bob Dylan's song. It has very much helped me to understand what it is all about. I played your record on New Year's Eve, and understood it much better. Also, before, I did not play the record loud enough. Your comments have greatly helped me. They are excellent. I feel very much that you have your talents still half buried and not enough courage to bring them into the open. You must tell me more about your comments on Dylan. Why not write an article for *De Gids?* You can do it so well in a letter; you could do it just as well in an article; if it helps, imagine you are writing to someone – writing it as a letter. With regard to Bob Dylan this does not mean that I have given up my reservations. I certainly understand him better, you have given me the key; but both the text and the music grate on my sensibility. The mixture between serious and very genuine sentiments, stretches of genuine musical invention on the one hand and triviality plus sentimentality, self-pity, Weltschmerz coupled with stretches of monotonous, repetitive and (for me) somewhat boring musical accompaniment on the other hand still does not appeal to me. In former days men prayed to Mary mother of god, now to Heroine or the flower maiden with the silver bracelets on her wrists. That is not to say that I do not understand – I only say that moaning about the cold world and the lost shelter does not help. It is only a mother which can give (though not always does give) warmth and shelter without reciprocity, and it is only to an infant that she can give it. Dylan, in a very characteristic manner, does not say that the world is cold only for those who cannot give warmth and shelter to others and who only want to receive it from others. I may do him wrong because I have not heard or read his other things. I know as well as the next man that this can be a cold world and that everyone is in danger of becoming an old man with broken teeth stranded without love. But I also know, Cas my dear, I also know that it does not help, as Dylan seems to do, to poke around again and again in one's own wounds as if one enjoyed the pain. There is so much to do in this world, so much humans can do with and for each other, so much which to me at least appears intensely meaningful. I abhor preaching and what I say can easily appear as such. But I simply know that it is necessary for every grown up person – necessary for a person's own mental health, to find a balance between the pre-occupation with his or her own immediate needs for warmth and love and sexual gratification, for companionship and friendship on the one hand and, on the other hand, the devotion to a solid task of a less personal nature, a task for others without which no sense of personal fulfilment is possible.

You have given me great pleasure with your letter (and so has Bram with the pictures which are really very good). You can see it from the length of my answer – and, by way of countergift for your typing out of Dylan's poem

I have copied two of my poems. I am not sure you will like them. The German one comes from a cycle Totentänze. Both give some indication of a different mood. Is it perhaps a generation gap? I am quite aware of the cold and the storm. But I do not dream of someone, some mother goddess, to give me shelter from it. I not only know it is a futile dream, I also have no wish to return to the womb [Dylan sings: 'try imagining a place where it's always safe and warm / 'come in', she said, 'I'll give you shelter from the storm.' CW]. As you may know I have an ineradicable guilt feeling that I was unable to get my mother out of the concentration-camp before she died in a gas chamber. Everyone has his deep conflicts and irrationalities. But if I had not myself, with some help from an analyst, taken off my crown of thorns – if I had not made the effort myself, I would have been lost – a futile and miserable life.

The two poems that Norbert enclosed were to the point. One of the poems he had typed out for me was called 'Riding the Storm' and he had typed a final couplet which could be classed as courageous or 'daring':

born from the storm of such order
nomads of time without tiding
dare from border to border
riding the storm.

In the collection of poems, *Los der Menschen* [The Human Lot], published in 1987 (p. 81), the borders have completely disappeared and the 'storm of disorder' now belongs to the 'human condition':

born from the storm of disorder
nomads of time without tiding
in a void without border
riding the storm.

The poem from the *Totentänze* [Dances of Death] (which in *Los der Menschen* (p. 34) acquired the title *Verlassene* [Deserted]) ends with the lines:

und sinken schweigend tiefer ab ins Wunde	and descend silently deeper into the wound
vergebens grübelnd wie sie sich verpaßt	brooding in futility on how she is absent
und legen endlich mit gepreßtem Munde	and finally, with tight-pressed lips, lie down
gleich müden Tieren seidwärts sich am Grunde	like tired animals, sideways, on the ground
und lösen sich im Meer der großen Rast	and dissolve in the sea of great repose
und fort und fort strömt ungerührt die Stunde.	and on and on the untouched hour flows

Later, in 1978, at the time of my divorce, I received a poem from him, and there he again turns strongly away from self-pity:

Du bist	You are
zerfressen von Mitleid mit dir selbst	devoured by self-pity

kriechend mit wenig lieblichem
    Pathos.
	crawling with hardly lovable
	    pathos.

Wenn ich dich anfassen würde,
    dann könnte ich
	If I were to touch you,
	    I could

an meinen Fingern fett und feucht	feel the wormskins fat and moist
die Wurmhäute spüren.	at my fingers.

Bitte mich jetzt nicht um
    Wohltätigkeit:
	Please do not ask me for
	    charity now:

Geh fort bis die Knochen
    sauber sind
	Go away until the bones
	    are clean.

This poem, somewhat modified, is also included in the collection of poetry (p. 50).

III

The quotations from subsequent letters which now follow all relate to the direction of the civilizing process and what was later to be called informalization. Elias began to come regularly to Amsterdam when that city was still a self-declared magical centre where a springtide of informalization was battering against the old, traditional relations. He was highly interested in all of that and could discuss it eloquently. However, his answer to the question how these changes fitted into his theory was unsatisfactory. That is indicated, for example, in a report which I wrote up about a meeting, held in 1970 or 1971, of the seminar on 'Sociogenesis of crèches', to which I had invited Norbert Elias. That duplicated report contained a drawing which Elias had introduced as a 'didactic aid'.

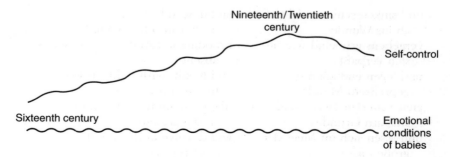

This representation was unsatisfactory to me, and not only to me, because the increasingly lenient and loose codes of behaviour and feeling seemed to place greater rather than fewer demands on self-control.[27] This whole problem area – the relation between recent changes and Elias's theory and, more specifically, the question of direction in civilizing processes – had been under discussion for years. Therefore, when Michel Korzec and Christien Brinkgreve gave it a new impulse in 1976, in their first report of changes in a Dutch agony column, *Margriet weet Raad*, I also touched upon this matter in a letter to Elias. At that time, I remembered that Elias had used the expression 'controlled decontrolling of emotional controls' in the early 1970s in a lecture on sport and pleasurable excitement. Whereas he had then restricted its use and meaning to indicate an important function of sports spectatorship and of leisure in general, I was on the point of taking this expression from the restricted level of leisure up to a societal level and to conceptualize it as informalization. The following quotation is taken from an undated letter, but given the fact that Elias wrote that we should see one another on 2 September, it must have been written in the summer of 1976. In my letter to him – I have no copy of it – I must have used this expression 'controlled decontrolling of emotional controls', since this was his reply:

...I cannot quite remember whether I used in my lecture the version 'controlled decontrolling of controls'. It seems to me that 'controlled decontrolling of affects or emotions' would be more appropriate and clearer. But whichever expressions one uses, Michael and Christien are certainly wrong if they suggest that this would impair the testability of my theory.

If I remember rightly I first used this expression in my studies of sport events. A football crowd can in fact loosen some emotional controls. The situation is, as it were, instituted in such a way that people – the spectators and to some extent also the players themselves are emotionally aroused. The spectators can shout and sing and also in other ways behave with less emotional control than is socially possible outside this particular setting and this pleasurable loosening of affect controls is one of the attractions as well as one of the social functions of this and other spectator sports. But it is a controlled decontrolling or loosening of emotional controls. Of course sometimes spectators as well as players go too far in decontrolling. They do not control the decontrolling of their impulses sufficiently. Players may push or otherwise bodily attack one of their opponents. Spectators may go wild because they believe that a linesman has done wrong to their own side, to the side with which they identify. If players cannot loosen their aggressive impulses sufficiently the game will be boring; if they decontrol too much they break the rules of the game which set very firm limits to their aggressiveness. The same goes for the spectators. Controlled decontrolling of emotions (or emotional controls) refers in this case to something clearly observable. As a theoretical concept it is perfectly testable. The same can be said with regard to the use of this term in relation to certain aspects of the present stage of the civilising process.

At the end of this letter Norbert wrote that he looks forward to reading my article '...when it is ready. If you tell me a little about it I shall not suffer so much from the language barrier'.

My article, 'Has the Civilising Process Changed Direction?', appeared in the December issue of the *Amsterdams Sociologisch Tijdschrift* and in it I referred to the above letter with the words: 'I have also benefited from correspondence with Norbert Elias.' After having submitted the article to the editors, I wrote to Norbert and apparently asked him, among other things, whether he would appreciate a translation of it as a contribution to the *Festschrift* for his eightieth birthday. His reply is dated 13 October 1976, and this is the opening of that letter:

I had written last night the note which I enclose and was just on the point to post it when I received your letter which has given me great pleasure. I am glad that you finished your paper. It is very reasonable to show it to your friends and to ask for their comments. It will also give me great pleasure to find it in the Festschrift.

My comments on the point which you raise with regard to my remark in Was ist Soziologie? are this. I have always regarded the idea that the principal characteristic of a civilising process is the increase in self-control as a very basic misunderstanding. One of the reasons is simply that you find in relatively simple societies often very strong demands for self-control. An example which, I believe, I have mentioned somewhere is the self-control demanded in some Amerindian societies of their young men during initiation rites where they were tortured but expected not to show by any movement or sound that they suffer pain. That was a preparation for their warrior existence. They should not shame their tribe if they were taken prisoner by another tribe and tortured by losing their pride and showing that they suffered. Or so one is led to believe. There are many other examples of social training for restraint in simpler societies. So if one simply says according to Elias a civilising process shows itself in increasing self-restraint that is simply wrong.

I have tried to make it clear that characteristic of a civilising process is firstly the allroundness of self-restraint (in the case of the Amerindians I have mentioned the social demand for self-restraint is confined to a highly specific situation and perfectly compatible with an equally extreme readiness to act in accordance with one's libidinal and affective impulses in other situations). Characteristic of such a process is secondly the evenness of restraints in all types of relationships with slight differences in degree (as you know) in the restraints which one is supposed to impose upon oneself in private and public life. But still one is no longer even supposed to beat one's wife or to be beaten by her which in trying situations, you will admit, requires a high degree of self-restraint and the level of that restraint even in private situations has, as you know, risen very considerably in all classes. It is not so long ago that one might have been regarded as a fool in the lower regions of society if one had suggested that a man is not allowed to beat his own wife (or perhaps the wife might have felt he does not love her any more if he had not beaten her from time to time). That is it: Greater evenness and allroundness in all, not only in some situations. But even that is not enough.

You can read it up: characteristic of a civilising process is thirdly allroundness and evenness of Selbstzwänge within a middle range, i.e. removed from extremes. Now my argument is and has always been that the self-restraints imposed upon biologically mature young people, say from 15, 16 years on and particularly on young girls (and to some extent on married women too) with regard to their sexual impulses were extreme and barbaric prior to the slow rise of what we call 'permissiveness' from about 1918 on. I have much more to say on this point but I hope you will see my point. What we call permissiveness is simply correcting a demand for extreme self-control and the stigmatisation of failure to do so. Michael and Christien have given a simplistic interpretation to my theory by implying that I regard the increase in self-control on its own as the main criterion of the level of civilisation while my theory is and has always been that it is the integration of temperate self-control (not too little, not too much) which is the criterion for the higher levels of a civilising process.

That does not vitiate your own argument. If I understand it rightly you are going to argue that what we call permissiveness involves not simply a loosening of built-in self-controls, but also the development of self-controls of a different kind. I fully agree with you. But I would still add that you seem to understand my theory in the same sense as Michael and Christien and, perhaps pay not enough attention to the fact that our attitude is, in my sense, more civilised, because it moderates some demand for an extreme self-control in sexual matters, particularly in the case of women, but also in that of teenagers generally which you might well compare with the demands made by the tribal Amerindians on their youngsters which I have mentioned before.

I hope I have given you as clear a comment to your query as I could. What you do with it I must leave to you. But it would be nice to hear from you whether what I say has any bearing on your paper. Please don't let me confuse you; I have not in the least said your argument is wrong. As far as I can grasp it sounds to me perfectly sound. But I wanted at least draw your attention to the fact that Michael and Christien are wrong in a much wider sense. (. . .)

If an English version of your paper exists already when I come to Amsterdam in November I can of course look through it should you want me to do that and we can correct together stylistic problems. . . .

By November I was able to provide Norbert with an English version of my paper. It was an awkward one because I had translated it myself. When he had read it, he immediately offered to help me with the translation. When we sat down together with that aim, however, he soon began to dictate to me, just like he used to do to his assistants. I had seen him thus with Gill, his assistant, whom I had met in Leicester. He warded off my protest of surprise with the words: 'Don't worry! Whenever you want to discuss anything, just interrupt me, and, of course, you must change whatever you like to change, it is and remains *your* paper.'

Anyone who compares my translation of the Dutch article with the version Norbert dictated (I still have both versions) will see that he certainly did not limit himself to translation. I introduced only a few changes and additions into the dictated version. I felt he had treated me in a generous way, which explains why I was surprised to read the opening lines of Norbert's letter dated 13 December 1976, written shortly after his return to Leicester:

My dear Cas,

When I left you at the airport I went away with the feeling that I had not given you as much help for your paper as you might have expected. But, then, though greatly stimulated intellectually by my stay in Amsterdam, I was also physically a little tired. So let me say first what I should have said to you personally how much it means for me that I can talk with you about the problems of my work as I can with few other people and generally that you give me your friendship. That is why I felt I had not helped you as much as I might have done if I had not been a little tired.

But there is also another reason. I simply had to think more about some of the problems you raised, especially the problem of informalisation. It is not as if I always know the answers. I hope you do not expect this. I had given a great deal of thought to the problem itself (without ever finding the appropriate concept) when I first came to England. The difference between the formality of the German standards of good behaviour and the seeming informality of the corresponding English standards is quite striking. There can be no doubt that the less formal standards of the English require a higher degree of built-in self-restraint. By tradition, the German code of highly formal behaviour – always shaking hands when coming and leaving, greeting in the street by raising one's hat and bending one's head in a graduated way according to rank etc. went hand in hand with a greater capacity of Germans to abandon all formal restraints, like a woman in former days might abandon at home the stays or 'corset' she has worn in public. I always remember how, on my first visit to Germany after the war the Frau Oberregierungsrätin, who had organised a course for higher civil servants where I was to give a lecture, got tipsy at the evening party in a manner no English woman of comparable standing would ever go tipsy in public, on a semi-official occasion. No one appeared to think worse of her because of it. In the Germany I knew (things may have changed a little) a high degree of formality, graded according to rank, went hand in hand with a high capacity for un-restraint, for loosening self-restraints on less formal occasions – a much higher swing of the pendulum from extreme formality to extreme – well there is the problem – to extreme forms of un-restraint (to use a slightly unusual word). But could one say to extreme 'informality'?

I know your problem is different. But the problem has still to be sorted out. It is more complex than it may appear and I have not yet thought it out fully. Still, perhaps what I say may help a little. There is a general trend of informalisation. The English have started their letters for a long time with Dear Mr X or Dear Professor. More Germans write to me now

'Lieber Herr Elias'. The student revolt in Germany has had the effect of loosening the use of the title 'Professor' (though it is coming back) and instead of 'Mit vorzüglicher Hochachtung bleibe ich Ihr sehr ergebner' etc. more people write now simply 'Mit freundlichen Grüssen Ihr'. Yet at the same time there remains a need for gradations and I have the feeling that this type of informalisation requires a higher degree of self-restraint. The 'stays' of formality, of the easy-to-be-learned formal phrases have gone and yet there is a need for shades, for 'nuances'. I think one has to distinguish this kind of informalisation (which seems to have gone less far in France than in either Germany or Holland) from – shall we call it 'formlessness'? – from behaviour dictated by a stronger dose of overt affects. To give you an example – I received a number of letters partly in connection with the short 15 minutes film shown in Germany. One letter from two Frankfurt 9th semester history students quite friendly though with overt Marxist criticism and a little facetious though by no means unfriendly. It ends with the phrase Mit 'barbarischen' Grüssen (Their '. . .' signs). I think one has to distinguish this half joking show of affects from what you mean by informalisation. Or one may have to distinguish different types of 'informality', one (as in the English case) requiring a high degree of deeply ingrained restraint (aristocratic informality is an example), one goes with a fair degree of unrestraint and might be called 'formlessness' if there is such a word. Dear Cas, as you can see I myself was not quite clear but perhaps this helps a little. Also I hope Rod Aya will help with the German quotations. I am very ready to have a glance at the semi-final version . . .

In 1977 and 1978 Elias delivered a number of lectures on informalization in Germany. Only in 1989, on the initiative of Michael Schröter, was the text which he wrote for this purpose edited and published; it is the opening article in *Studien Über die Deutschen* (published in English by Polity Press in 1996 as *The Germans*). At the time when Elias agreed to the proposal to produce this book, he told me that he was having great difficulty in getting used to the idea that he was about to be the author of a book on the Germans. Only a few months before the book came out, I read the edited opening article, entitled *Veränderungen europäischer Verhaltensstandards im 20. Jahrhundert* [*Changes in European Standards of Behaviour in the Twentieth Century*]. Michael Schröter had given me a copy. Reading it brought to mind one of Norbert's favourite stories: about Picasso, who would go out to see the work of a colleague, went home and did it better. In other words, I was struck by the great similarity between our two articles, even in many details, but also by the difference in quality: Norbert's version was indisputably better.

IV

In 1986, during one of our weekly Tuesday afternoon appointments for jogging,[28] something exceptional occurred. Norbert took me completely by surprise. It was shortly after the appearance of *Quest for Excitement* (1986), in which he had written a new introduction containing expressions like 'an enjoyable and controlled decontrolling of emotions' and 'the maintenance of a set of checks to keep the pleasantly de-controlled emotions under control' (Elias and Dunning, 1986: 44, 49). Since he had now published this expression, he told me without further ado that I was henceforth obliged to refer to him, and to his work, when I used this expression again. At that moment he had evidently forgotten that he had already published it before, and also, even more annoying to me, that I had given him full credit by always making reference to him. I was so bewildered – *what is this?* old age? – that it took me until the following Tuesday before I could bite back. Then I forced him to the point of realizing that it would really have been more appropriate to have provided a note to this expression in *Quest*, indicating that I had made fruitful use of it over many years. He promised to produce such a note at the next opportunity. And indeed, in 1988, while writing a paper for presentation in Marburg at the Seventeenth European Conference on Psychosomatic Research, he informed me that he had included the intended note in this paper. Shortly before the congress was due to take place (4–9 September 1988) Norbert felt too weak to go there and asked my friend and ex-colleague Herman ten Kroode to present his text at the meeting. Curious about the note in question, I asked him whether he had found it, but 'No', said Herman, 'there is no such note'. Before having the opportunity to ask Norbert what had happened, his assistant Rudolf Knijff told me he remembered that Norbert really had made reference to me when dictating the lecture. If it was not included in the selection to be read by Herman, Rudolf suggested, the note was proba- bly contained in another portion of the text. This is where I dropped the issue, partly also because Norbert at that time endeavoured with increasing frequency to avoid discussing controversies about his work. He certainly remained as amiable as ever, yet, to my knowledge, it was only with Michael Schröter, his editor and translator, that he still continued to discuss controversies about his work. In that last period of his life, he rather swiftly cut-off others who tried to initiate a polemic, with phrases such as 'no, no, you don't understand', and left it there. He gave the impression of defending himself against death by clinging on to his work, just as a papaya tree, shortly before dying directs its leaves high towards the sun, so that its fruits no longer hang, as they usually do, in their shadow.

Two years after his death, in 1992, my curiosity about the note again mounted to the extent that I asked Norbert's assistants Saskia Visser and Rudolf Knijff to make a search. At first I received a letter saying they had not been able to find such a note. So I concluded that Norbert had taken me for a ride. A few days later, however, the message came that what was sought had been found. The search had been for a note, whereas the reference was in fact placed in the running text. This story ends with that text:

Perhaps only those human groups survived who found ways and means to correct imbalances in the interplay between constraint of affective impulses and their unrestrained enactment. Perhaps the incidence of mimetic fights is so widespread among human groups because they make it possible for a group to correct imbalances in the interplay between constraint and the anarchy of violence. The controlled decontrolling (see Cas Wouters...) of fighting impulses in the form of mimetic struggles is one of the ways of doing this. At the present stage of knowledge it is difficult to decide whether such impulses have not only cultural, but also physiological components. Whatever future research may bring to light, the reference to fighting impulses and their possible control highlights once more the fact that references to a human property called aggressiveness associate the problem from the outset with a concept that has strongly evaluating undertones. To include mimetic fights such as games and other activities often conceptualised today as leisure activities in the evidence used in discussions on aggressiveness allows a restructuring of the problem. It opens the way to new questions.

Take the problem of happiness. ...

Notes

1 In this book, this concept of the balance of involvement and detachment is used mainly to refer to these qualities of social relationships. Conversely, in his *Involvement and Detachment* (1987), Elias has used this conceptual pair predominantly from the sociology of knowledge perspective: how knowledge (and command) of (non-human) nature and of societal processes has increased as humans gained greater detachment from their affective involvement of fearful and wishful fantasies.

2 Here lies a major difference between Foucault's views on 'expert knowledge' and 'discourse' and mine: changes in the regimes of manners and emotions include changes in discourse, not the other way around.

3 In comparison to Tarde, several accounts of the modelling function of good society are shallow and one-sided. The main form of one-sidedness is to think, and even take for granted, that the movement of manners is only from above downwards, not the other way around. This assumption remained rather implicit in Schlesinger's words. It was most explicit, however, in the work of the German ethnologist Hans Naumann in which he described a downward movement of all culture (*Kultur*). Down there, he wrote, among the people (*Volk*), in the *Unterschicht* (underclass), cultural creative power is lacking because there is no powerful expression of individuality: 'The people do not produce, they reproduce; the people are always backward; the remains that fall from the tables of the spiritual rich give them satisfaction' (Naumann, 1922: 5, quoted in Munters, 1977: 34). Today, Naumann's name is forgotten, but an expression he introduced is still very much alive, at least in the Netherlands: 'sinking cultural goods' or 'sunken cultural goods'. It is approximately as popular, I think, as the expression 'trickle effect' or 'trickle-down effect' in the English-speaking world. This 'trickle effect' is a well-known formulation of the modelling function of good society. It was introduced by Lloyd A. Fallers in 1954. The 'trickling' he meant, however, was restricted to goods and services, 'new styles and fashions in consumption goods to be introduced via the socio-economic elite and then to pass down through the status hierarchy, often in the form of inexpensive, mass produced copies' (1954: 314). His article contains no attempt to offer an explanation of the trickle effect nor does it consider the possibility of any trickling *up*. It is seen as a 'treadmill' mechanism, a 'mechanism for maintaining the motivation to strive for success, and hence for maintaining efficiency of performance in occupational roles' (1954: 315–16).

4 'Social stratification refers to social inequality, expressed in terms of high and low; it implies differentiation and vertical ranking', writes the sociologist Johan Goudsblom at the start of an interesting quest to understand why the image of verticality is accepted as if it were self-evident (1986: 3). Among the range of reasons and examples given to explain the power of the high and low

metaphor, this one would fit in well: The term 'foot folk' is a literal translation of the Dutch *voetvolk*, the folk on foot, and it is still a slightly condescending colloquial way of referring to the masses, the rank and file. Before this connotation became dominant, the term *voetvolk* referred to the foot soldiers in an army. This connotation probably goes back to military–agrarian societies.

5 However, in his study of English manners books, the historian Porter reports that it was only during World War I that 'it became possible for a hostess to introduce to one another two guests in the home. It was "impossible" in Edwardian days, for supposing she began an acquaintance-ship between two people who didn't want to know one another?' (Porter, 1972: 31). See §5.15.

6 Thanks to Sabine Latuska, Berlin, for this tip.

7 Although Kasson also writes in praise of the search for a 'real self', it was not in this context that he used the words quoted here, but in contrasting the demands of city life to that of smaller communities.

8 For an early and solid application of established–outsider theory to relations between black and white people in the USA, see Dunning (1972). See also Dunning (2004).

9 A similar opposition is observed or constructed by de Tocqueville in his comparison of middle-class American manners 'aristocracies', as he called them:

> In aristocracies the rules of propriety impose the same demeanor on everyone; they make all the members of the same class appear alike in spite of their private inclinations; they adorn and conceal the natural man. Among a democratic people manners are neither so tutored nor so uniform, but they are frequently more sincere. They form, as it were, a light and loosely woven veil through which the real feelings and private opinions of each individual are easily discernable. The form and substance of human actions, therefore, often stand there in closer relation. (Tocqueville, 1945 [1835]: 2:230)

10 I owe this idea to Michael Schröter.

11 Note the parallel with a 1950s young (American, Dutch, English)man being expected to say to his girlfriend, 'I think far too highly of you to want to have sexual intercourse with you yet'.

12 For an interesting comparison of English and Austrian habitus, see Kuzmics (1993) and Kuzmics and Axtmann (2000).

13 It is telling that rare exceptions in the English sources – sentences such as 'I have lunched in the house of a *nouveau riche* where they seemed to line the dining room with footmen and other servants, till it was positively oppressive' or 'One occasionally meets vulgar people who seek to impress those around them with their own (supposed) superiority' – were deleted from a later edition (Klickmann, 1902: 33, 48).

14 The English historian Dangerfield disagreed: 'The extravagant behaviour of the post-war decade, which most of us thought to be the effect of war, had really begun before the War. The War hastened everything – in politics, in economics, in behaviour – but it started nothing' (1970 [1935]: 14).

15 In a personal communication, Mrs Martin told me that Miss Manners was born in 1978, when she started to write about the decree of openness and instant intimacy often functioning as an excuse for many to be insulting. She called this 'bad manners', which to her surprise struck a chord with many people.

16 For a theoretical discussion of phases in processes and a proposal to integrate chronology and 'phaseology', see Goudsblom (1996). For a study that shows that not only in the social world outside the social sciences, but also in sociological theorizing some principal characteristics of the transformations in these phases can be observed, see Kilminster (1998: 145–72). In his analysis of developments in sociology since 1945, he has distinguished the 'monopoly phase: circa 1945–65', the 'conflict phase: circa 1965–80', and the 'concentration phase: circa 1980 to the present (?)'. These phases, the last two in particular, clearly correspond to the phases of emancipation and resistance, and accommodation and resignation as described here.

17 In *The Court Society*, Norbert Elias explains the French Revolution by reference to a growing divergence between power relations and rank, a divergence between the actual distribution of power among the different social cadres and the 'distribution of power anchored in the ossified institutional shell of the old regime' (Elias, 1983: 275).

18 The 'identification with the established' follows the same emotional logic as the 'identification with the aggressor' (Freud, 1966 [1936]).

19 Maffesoli's book *The Time of the Tribes* originally appeared in 1988. In contrast to my interpretation, he sees this rise of 'neo-tribes' as a decline of individualism in mass society: 'The autonomy (individualism) of the bourgeois model is being surpassed by the heteronomy of tribalism' (1996: 127).

20 For a critical review of postmodernism, see Wilterdink (2002).

21 Elias gave these lectures at the University of Amsterdam where I was a student. He and Eric Dunning had used similar expressions in their contribution to a conference in July 1969 in Magglingen (Switzerland), published as 'Leisure in the Spare Time Spectrum' in 1971. Their use was restricted to sport and leisure, and was an account – in terms of social and psychic processes, very Eliasian – of what others at the time usually called the 'safety-valve' function of sport and leisure: 'De-routinisation goes farthest in leisure activities but even there it is a question of balance. De-routisation and the de-controlling of restraints on emotions are closely related to each other. A decisive characteristic of leisure activities, not only in highly ordered industrial societies but, as far as one can see, in all other types of societies, too, is that the de-controlling of restraints on emotions is itself socially and personally controlled' (Elias and Dunning, 1971: 31). In my unpublished Masters thesis I took Elias's expression 'the controlled decontrolling of emotional controls' from its more limited context and used it to indicate the overall direction of social and psychic processes in the twentieth century. The first publication in which I used it in this sense was in a Dutch sociology journal (Wouters, 1976), and a year later in an English publication (Wouters, 1977). For more details, see Appendix 2 to this book.

22 Elias traced a spurt towards *homo clausus* as a mode of self-experience among the upper classes in the sixteenth century, but by the first half of the twentieth century it had become quite common among most classes.

23 Hans-Peter Duerr's criticism of Elias's theory of civilizing processes seems to have been fuelled by the attempt to save some simplicity and innocence in the world; see Wouters (1994 and 1999c); Hinz (2002); Goudsblom and Mennell (1997).

24 This seems to be a reversal of the direction of development from a shame-culture to a guilt-culture, as it has been represented in an extensive body of literature, especially the 'culture and personality' school of anthropology, of which Ruth Benedict's *The Chrysanthemum and the Sword* (1946) is a classic example. In the informalization process of the twentieth century, this development in the long-term formalizing phase seems to be reversed: from a guilt-culture to a shame-culture. It would be absurd, however, to equate the pattern of shame in what has been described as shame-cultures with the pattern of shame in informalized societies. The term reversal is accordingly misleading. In the informalization spurt of the 1960s and 1970s, many people discovered that self-constraints of all kinds were in fact constraints by others, or at least based upon such external constraints (Wouters, 1990c: 53). Obviously, a distinction between two types of shame mechanisms – or *shaming* mechanisms – corresponding to (at least) two types of external constraints (see Schröter, 1997: 102–4) is needed just as much as a distinction between two types of shame-cultures.

25 Since the unification of Germany, many artists from former East Germany have expressed the feeling that, under the new conditions, they are mostly met with indifference, whereas they were taken much more seriously under the old regime. A statement like 'Of course, a dictatorship is more colourful than a democracy' (Heiner Müller) expressed a similar nostalgia.

26 An earlier version of this text appeared in the Dutch book *Over Elias* [On Elias] (Wouters, 1993).

27 Today, the left part of the drawing would look the same, but to the right it would look more like this:

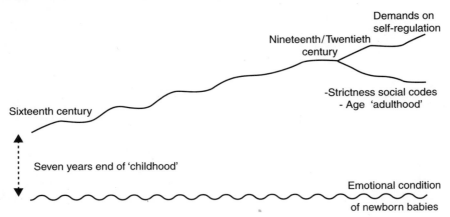

241

28 The word 'jogging' is of course idiotic, but 'walking' describes just as inadequately what we did. In fact it was a kind of dancing. Norbert did not want to be guided, but since in his later years he could no longer see, we had to link one another's arm. We did that very loosely, but sufficiently to enable his movements and mine to flow through our arms in such a way that there was no question of leading. I warned him when there was dogshit on the path, since to swerve without words for that purpose would require more guidance than our dance could accommodate.

References

Aerts, Remieg and Henk te Velde (eds) (1998) *De stijl van de burger*. Kampen: Kok.

Anderson, Digby (ed.) (1996) *Gentility Recalled. Mere Manners and the Making of Social Order*. The Social Affairs Unit and the Acton Institute.

Aresty, Esther B. (1970) *The Best Behavior*. New York: Simon and Schuster.

Ariès, Philippe (1965) (orig. 1960) *Centuries of Childhood*. New York: Vintage.

Ariès, Philippe (1974) *Western Attitudes toward Death*. Baltimore, MD: Johns Hopkins UP.

Bailey, Joe (1988) *Pessimism*. London: Routledge.

Baltzell, E. Digby (1964, 1987) *The Protestant Establishment: Aristocracy and Caste in America*. New Haven, CT: Yale UP.

Barnes, Emm (1995) *Fashioning a Natural Self-Guides to Self-Presentation in Victorian England*. Cambridge University, Dissertation Kings College.

Bauman, Zygmunt (1992) *Mortality, Immortality and Other Life Strategies*. Cambridge: Polity.

Bauman, Zygmunt (1999) 'On Postmodern Uses of Sex', in: Mike Featherstone (ed.) *Love & Eroticism*. London: Sage, pp. 19–34.

Bauwelt (1991) 'das Kombi-Büro' (editorial). *Heft*, 6: 224–34.

Benedict, Ruth (1946) *The Crysanthemum and the Sword*. Boston, MA: Houghton Mifflin.

Bennis, Warren G. and Philip E. Slater (1968) *The Temporary Society*. New York: Harper & Row.

Benthem van den Berg, Godfried (1986) 'The Improvement of Human Means of Orientation: Towards Synthesis in the Social Sciences', in: Raymond Apthorpe and Andreãs Krãhl (eds) *Development Studies: Critique and Renewal*. Leiden: Brill, pp. 109–36.

Blomert, Reinhard (1991) *Psyche und Zivilisation: Zur theoretischen Konstruktion bei Norbert Elias*. Münster/Hamburg: Lit.

Blumin, Stuart M. (1989) *The Emergence of the Middle Class. Social Experience in the American City, 1760–1900*. Cambridge UP.

Breman, Jan (2001) *A Question of Poverty*. The Hague: Institute of Social Studies.

Breman, Jan (2004) *The Labouring Poor*. Delhi: Oxford UP.

Brinkgreve, Christien and Michel Korzec (1976) ' "Margriet weet raad." Gevoel, gedrag, moraal 1954–1974'. *Amsterdams Sociologisch Tijdschrift*, 3/1: 17–32.

Bronfenbrenner, U. (1958) 'Socialisation and Social Class Through Time and Space', in: E.E. Maccoby, T.M. Newcomb, and E.L. Hartley (eds) *Readings in Social Psychology*. New York: Holt, Rhinehart and Winston.

Bruin, Kees (1989) *Kroon op het werk. Onderscheiden in het Koninkrijk der Nederlanden*. Meppel: Boom.

Caldwell, Mark (1999) *A Short History of Rudeness. Manners, Morals, and Misbehaviors in Modern America*. New York: Picador.

Cancian, F.M. (1987) *Love in America*. Cambridge UP.

Cancian, F.M. and S.L. Gordon (1988) 'Changing Emotion Norms in Marriage: Love and Anger in U.S. Women's Magazines Since 1900'. *Gender and Society*, 2: 308–42.

Carroll, Raymonde (1989) *Cultural Misunderstandings: The French-American Experience* (translated by Carol Volk). University of Chicago Press.

Carson, Gerald (1966) *The Polite Americans. A Wide-angle View of Our More or Less Good Manners Over 300 Years*. New York: William Morrow.

Cavan, Sherri (1970) 'The Etiquette of Youth', in: G.P. Stone and H.A. Farberman (eds) *Social Psychology Through Symbolic Interaction*. Waltham, MA: Ginn-Blaisdell, pp. 554–65.

Cmiel, Kenneth (1994) 'The Politics of Civility', in: David Farber (ed.) *The Sixties ... from Memory to History*. Chappel Hill: University of North Carolina Press, pp. 263–90.

Coleman, L. (1941) 'What is American? A Study of Alleged American Traits'. *Social Forces*, 19: 492–9.

Coopmans, J.P.A. (1983) 'Het Plakkaat van Verlatinge (1581) en de Declaration of Independence (1776)'. *BMGN*, 98: 540–67.

Coser, Lewis A. (1971) *Masters of Sociological Thought*. New York: Harcourt Brace Janovitch.

Curtin, Michael (1985) 'A Question of Manners: Status and Gender in Etiquette and Courtesy'. *Journal of Modern History*, 57: 395–423.

Curtin, Michael (1987) *Propriety and Position. A Study of Victorian Manners*. New York: Garland.

Daalen, Rineke van (1988) 'Public Complaints and Government Intervention: Letters to the Municipal Authorities of Amsterdam 1865–1920'. *Netherland's Journal of Sociology*, 24: 83–98.

Dahrendorf, R. (1969) *Society and Democracy in Germany*. Garden City, NY: Doubleday.

Dahrendorf, Ralf (1968) *Die angewandte Aufklärung*. Frankfurt am Main: Fischer.

Dangerfield, George (1970 [1935]) *The Strange Death of Liberal England*. London: Paladin.

Davidoff, Leonore (1973) *The Best Circles. Society, Etiquette and the Season*. London: Croom Helm.

Davis, K. (2003) *Dubious Equalities and Embodied Differences: Cultural Studies on Cosmetic Surgery*. Lanham, MD: Rowman & Littlefield.

Dunk, H.W. von der (1994) *Twee buren, twee culturen*. Amsterdam: Prometheus.

Dunning, Eric (1972) 'Dynamics of Racial Stratification: Some Preliminary Observations'. *Race*, XIII: 415–34.

Dunning, Eric (2004) 'Aspects of The Figurational Dynamics of Racial Stratification: A Conceptual Discussion and Developmental Analysis of Black–White Relations in the United States', in: Steven Loyal and Stephen Quilley (eds) *The Sociology of Norbert Elias*. Cambridge UP, pp. 75–94.

Durkheim, Émile (1964 [1893]) *The Division of Labour in Society*. London: Glencoe.

Elias, Norbert (1950) 'Studies in the Genesis of the Naval Profession. Part One'. *British Journal of Sociology*, 1: 291–309.

Elias, Norbert (1960) 'Die öffentliche Meinung in England', in *Vorträge gehalten anläßlich der Hessischen Hochschulwochen für staatswisschenschaftliche Fortbildung, 18. bis 25. April 1959 in Bad Wildungen*. Bad Homburg: Max Gehlen, pp. 118–31.

Elias, Norbert (1962) 'Nationale Eigentümlichkeiten der englischen öffentlichen Meinung', in *Vorträge gehalten anläßlich der Hessischen Hochschulwochen für staatswisschenschaftliche Fortbildung, 2. bis 18. Oktober 1960 in Bad Wildungen*. Bad Homburg: Max Gehlen, pp. 124–47.

Elias, Norbert (1983) *The Court Society*. Oxford: Blackwell.

Elias, Norbert (1987) *Los der Menschen. Gedichte/Nachdichtungen*. Frankfurt am Main: Suhrkamp.

Elias, Norbert (1991) *The Society of Individuals* (ed. Michael Schröter). Oxford: Blackwell.

Elias, Norbert (1993) *Mozart: Portret of a Genius*. Cambridge: Polity.

Elias, Norbert (1994) *Reflections on a Life*. Oxford: Polity.

Elias, Norbert (1996) *The Germans* (ed. Michael Schröter). Cambridge: Polity.

Elias, Norbert (1998 [1935]) 'The Kitsch Style and the Age of Kitsch', in: Johan Goudsblom and Stephen Mennell (eds) *The Norbert Elias Reader*. Oxford: Blackwell.

Elias, Norbert (2000) *The Civilizing Process. Sociogenetic and Psychogenetic Investigations*. Cambridge, MA: Blackwell.

Elias, Norbert and Eric Dunning (1971) 'Leisure in the Sparetime Spectrum', in: R. Albonico and K. Pfister-Binz (eds) *Sociology of Sport*. Basel: Birkhäuser, pp. 27–34.

Elias, Norbert and Eric Dunning (1986) *Quest for Excitement. Sport and Leisure in the Civilising Process*. Oxford: Blackwell.

Elias, Norbert and John L. Scotson (1994) *The Established and the Outsiders*. London: Sage.

Engler, Wolfgang (1991) 'Vom Deutschen. Reflexive contra selbstdestruktive Zivilisierung'. *Sinn und Form*, 43/2: 268–83.

Engler, Wolfgang (1992) *Die zivilisatorische Lücke. Versuche über den Staatssozialismus*. Frankfurt am Main: Suhrkamp.

Fallers, Lloyd A. (1954) 'A Note on the Trickle Effect'. *Public Opinion Quaterly*, 18: 314–21.

Finkelstein, Joanne (1989) *Dining Out. A Sociology of Modern Manners*. New York UP.

Finkelstein, Joanne (1991) *The Fashioned Self*. Cambridge: Polity Press.

Freud, Anna (1966 [1936]) *The Ego and the Mechanisms of Defense* (rev. ed.). New York: International Universities Press.

Fromm, Erich (1942) *The Fear of Freedom*. London: Routledge & Kegan Paul.

Frykman, Jonas and Orvar Löfgren (1987) *Culture Builders. A Historical Anthropology of Middle-Class Life*. New Brunswick and London: Rutgers UP.

Garland, David (1996) 'The Limits of the Sovereign State. Strategies of Crime Control in Contemporary Society'. *The British Journal of Criminology*, 36/4: 445–71.

Goffman, Erving (1959) *The Presentation of Self in Everyday Life*. Garden City, NY: Doubleday Anchor.

Goffman, Erving (1968) *Asylums*. Harmondsworth: Penguin Books (orig. 1961).

Gorer, Geoffrey (1948) *The American People. A Study in National Character*. New York: Norton & Co. (printed in 1959 as: *The Americans: A Study in National Character*. London: Arrow).

Goudsblom, Johan (1968) *Dutch Society*. New York: Random House.

Goudsblom, Johan (1977) *Sociology in the Balance. A Critical Essay*. Oxford: Blackwell.

Goudsblom, Johan (1986) 'On High and Low in Society and in Sociology. A Semantic Approach to Social Stratification'. *Sociologisch Tijdschrift*, 13: 3–17.

Goudsblom, Johan (1988) 'Het Algemeen Beschaafd Nederlands', in his book: *Taal en Sociale Werkelijkheid: Sociologische Stukken*. Amsterdam: Meulenhoff, pp. 11–29.

Goudsblom, Johan (1992) *Fire and Civilisation*. London: Penguin.

Goudsblom, Johan (1996) 'Human History and Long-Term Processes: Toward a Synthesis of *Chronology* and *Phaseology*', in: Johan Goudsblom, E.L. Jones, and

Stephen Mennell (eds) *The Course of Human History. Economic Growth, Social Process, and Civilisation.* Armonk, NY: Sharp, pp. 15–30.

Goudsblom, Johan (1998) *Reserves.* Amsterdam: Meulenhoff.

Goudsblom, Johan and Stephen Mennell (1997) 'Civilising Processes – Myth or Reality?' Review article on Hans-Peter Duerr, *Der Mythos vom Zivilisationsprozeße. Comparative Studies in Society and History*, 39/4: 727–31.

Gouldner, Alvin W. (1970) *The Coming Crisis of Western Sociology.* London: Heineman.

Graves, Robert and Alan Hodge (1941) *The Long Week-end. A Social History of Great Britain 1918–1939.* London: Readers Union Ltd. by arrangement of Faber and Faber.

Halttunen, Karen (1982) *Confidence Men and Painted Women.* New Heaven, CT: Yale UP.

Harrisson, Tom and Charles Madge (1986 [1939]) *Britain by Mass-Observation.* London: Cresset.

Hart, K. (1973) 'Informal Income Opportunities and Urban Employment in Ghana', in: R.E. Jolly, E. de Kadt, H. Singer, and F. Wilson (eds) *Third World Employment: Problems and Strategy.* Harmondsworth: Penguin, pp. 66–70.

Haskell, Thomas(1985) 'Capitalism and the Humanitarian Sensibility'. *American Historical Review*, 90: 339–61 and 547–66.

Haveman, Jan (1952) *De Ongeschoolde Arbeider, een sociologische analyse.* Assen: Van Gorcum.

Hemphill, C. Dallett (1996) 'Middle Class Rising in Revolutionary America: The Evidence from Manners'. *Journal of Social History*, 30: 317–44.

Hemphill, C. Dallett (1999) *Bowing to Necessities. A History of Manners in America 1620–1860.* New York: Oxford UP.

Hinz, Michael (2002) *Der Zivilisationsprozess: Mythos oder Realität? Wissenschaftssoziologische Untersuchungen zur Elias-Duerr-Kontroverse.* Opladen: Leske + Budrich.

Hochschild, Adam (1998) *King Leopold's Ghost.* Boston, MA: Houghton Mifflin.

Hochschild, Arlie Russel (1983) *The Managed Heart. Commercialisation of Human Feeling.* Berkeley, CA: University of California Press.

Hodges, Deborah Robertson (1989) *Etiquette. An Annotated Bibliography of Literature Published in English in the United States, 1900 through 1987.* Jefferson etc.: McFarland.

Human Development Report (2000 and 2004) *UN Development Program.* New York: Oxford UP.

Kalberg, Stephen (1987) 'West German and American Interaction Forms: One Level of Structured Misunderstanding'. *Theory, Culture & Society*, 4: 603–18.

Kapteyn, Paul (1980) *Taboe, macht en moraal in Nederland.* Amsterdam: Arbeiderspers.

Kasson, John F. (1990) *Rudeness and Civility. Manners in Nineteenth-Century Urban America.* New York: Hill and Wang.

Kelter, Jörg (1991) 'Büroplanung im Wandel. Ergebnisse repräsentativen Untersuchung'. *Office Design*, 1: 72–105.

Kennedy, James C. (1995) *Nieuw Babylon in Aanbouw: Nederland in de Jaren Zestig.* Amsterdam: Boom.

Kennedy, James C. (1997) 'New Babylon and the Politics of Modernity', *Sociologische Gids*, XLIV: 361–74.

Kesey, Ken (1999; orig. 1962) *One Flew Over the Cuckoo's Nest.* Harmondsworth: Penguin.

Kilminster, Richard (1998) *The Sociological Revolution. From the Enlightenment to the Global Age*. London: Routledge.

Klein, Josephine (1965) *Samples From English Cultures*. London: Routledge/ Kegan Paul.

Kohut, Heinz (1977) *The Restauration of the Self*. New York: International Universities Press.

Kool, Margo (1983) 'In de schoenen van het dialect'. *NRC Handelsblad*, November, 15: 2.

Krieken, Robert van (1990) 'The Organisation of the Soul: Elias and Foucault on Discipline and the Self'. *Archives of European Sociology*, XXXI: 353–71.

Krüger, Michael (1996) *Korperkultur und Nationsbildung: Die Geschichte des Turnens in der Reichsgründungsära*. Schondorf: Hofmann.

Krumrey, Horst-Volker (1984) *Entwicklungsstrukturen von Verhaltensstandarden*. Frankfurt am Main: Suhrkamp.

Kuzmics, Helmut (1993) 'Österreichischer und englisher Volkscharakter', in: H. Nowotny and K. Taschwer (eds) *Macht und Ohnmacht im neuen Europa*. Vienna: WUV.

Kuzmics, Helmut (2002) '(Europäische) Regionen zwischen (Des-)Integration und Identität', in: E. Busek (ed.) *Europa – Vision und Wirklichkeit*. Wien: Verlag Österreich, pp. 259–80.

Kuzmics, Helmut (2003) 'Neue Moral im neuen Eropa. Europäische Einigung, nationale Mentalitäten und nationales Gedächtnis am Beispiel der "Sanktionen" gegen Österreich', in: Karl Acham and Katharina Scherke (eds) *Kontinuitäten und Brüche in der Mitte Europas*. Vienna: Passagen.

Kuzmics, Helmut and Roland Axtmann (2000) *Autorität, Staat und Nationalcharakter. Der Zivilisationsprozeß in Österreich und England 1700–1900*. Opladen: Leske + Budrich.

Lasch, Christopher (1979) *The Culture of Narcissism*. New York: Warner.

Lewin, Kurt (1948) *Resolving Social Conflict*. New York: Harper and Row.

Lindqvist, Sven (1997) *Exterminate all the Brutes*. London: Granta.

Lipset, Seymour Martin (1967, orig. 1963) *The First New Nation: The United States in Historical and Comparative Perspective*. Garden City, NY: Anchor.

Lofland, Lyn H. (1973) *A World of Strangers*. New York: Basic Books.

Maffesoli, Michael (1996) *The Time of the Tribes*. London: Sage.

Martin, Judith (1985) *Common Courtesy. In Which Miss Manners Solves The Problem That Baffles Mr. Jefferson*. New York: Atheneum.

Martin, Judith (2003) *Star-Spangled Manners*. New York: Norton.

Martin, Judith and Gunther S. Stent (1990) 'I Think; Therefore I Thank. A Philosophy of Etiquette'. *The American Scholar*, 59/2: 237–54.

Mason, John (1935) *Gentlefolk in the Making: Studies in the History of English Courtesy Literature and Related Topics from 1531 to 1774*. Philadelphia, PA: University of Pennsylvania Press.

Mastenbroek, W.F.G. (1989) *Negotiate*. Oxford: Blackwell.

Mastenbroek, W.F.G. (2002) *Negotiating as Emotion Management*. Heemstede: Holland Business Publications.

Materman, Barry (1986) *Menno ter Braak en het dramaturgisch perspectief*. Amsterdam University: Publikatiereeks Sociologisch Instituut.

McCall, Jt., W. Morgan, and Michael M. Lombardo (1983) 'What Makes a Top Executive?' *Psychology Today*, 17/2: 26–31.

Meines, Rob (1989) 'De Grondigheidscultuur'. *NRC Handelsblad*, September 9.

Mennell, Stephen (1998) *Norbert Elias: An Introduction*. Dublin: University College Dublin Press. (Published first in 1989 at Oxford: Blackwell).

Montijn, Ileen (1998) *Leven op stand 1890–1940*. Amsterdam: Thomas Rap.

Mooij, Annet (1993) *Geslachtsziekten en besmettingsangst. Een historisch-sociologische studie 1850–1990*. Amsterdam: Boom.

Munters, Q.J. (1977) *Stijgende en dalende cultuurgoederen*. Alphen aan den Rijn: Samson.

Naumann, Hans (1922) *Gründzüge der deutschen Volkskunde*. Leipzig: Quelle & Meyer.

Newton, Sarah E. (1994) *Learning to Behave: A Guide to American Conduct Books Before 1900*. Westport, CT: Greenwood Press.

Nicolson, Harold (1955) *Good Behaviour, Being a Study of Certain Types of Civility*. London: Constable & Co.

Oosterbaan, Warna (1988) Article on Photography. *NRC Handelsblad*, 30–12–1988.

Openneer, Herman (1995) *Kid Dynamite*. Amsterdam: Mets.

Orwell, George (1954) *Nineteen Eighty-Four*. Harmondsworth: Penguin.

Orwell, George (1972 [1944]) 'Raffles and Miss Blandish', in: *Decline of the English Murder and Other Essays*. Harmondsworth: Penguin, pp. 63–79.

Orwell, George (1979 [1937]) *The Road to Wigan Pier*. Harmondsworth: Penguin.

Parry, Jonathan P., Jan Breman, and Karin Kapadia (1999) *The Worlds of Indian Industrial Labour*. London: Sage.

Parsons, Talcott (1978) *Action Theory and the Human Condition*. New York: Free Press.

Peabody, Dean (1985) *National Characteristics*. Cambridge UP.

Porter, Cecil (1972) *Not Without a Chaperone: Modes and Manners from 1897 to 1914*. London: New English Library.

Post, Arjan (2004) 'Has the Informalisation Process Changed Direction?: Manners and Emotions in a Dutch Advice Column 1978–98'. *Irish Journal of Sociology*, 13/2: 84–103.

Rapport der Regeerings-Commissie inzake het Dansvraagstuk (1931) 's-Gravenhage: Algemeene Landsdrukkerij.

Riesman, David with N. Glazer and R. Denney (1950) *The Lonely Crowd*. New Haven, CT: Yale UP.

Rothe, Hans-Joachim (ed.) (1991) *Karl Landauer. Theorie der Affekte und andere Studien der Ich-Organisation*, Frankfurt a/M: Fischer Taschenbuch.

Rothman, Ellen K. (1984) *Hands and Hearts: A History of Courtship in America*. New York: Basic.

Schlesinger, Arthur M. (1946) *Learning How to Behave: A Historical Study of American Etiquette Books*. New York: Macmillan.

Schlesinger Jr., Arthur M. (1992) *The Disuniting of America*. New York: Norton.

Schreiner, Gerth (1937) *'Wij Leven in Holland...'*. Amsterdam: Meulenhoff.

Schröter, Michael (1985) 'Wo *zwei zusammen kommen in rechter Ehe...*'. Frankfurt am Main: Suhrkamp.

Schröter, Michael (1997) *Erfahrungen mit Norbert Elias*. Frankfurt am Main: Suhrkamp.

Sennett, Richard (1998) *The Corrosion of Character*. New York: Norton.

Silver, Allan (1990) 'Friendship in Commercial Society: Eighteenth-Century Social Theory and Modern Sociology'. *American Journal of Sociology*, 95/6: 1474–504.

Smith, Dennis (2006) *Globalization: The Hidden Agenda*. Cambridge: Polity.

Sorokin, Pitirim A. (1964) *Social and Cultural Mobility*. New York: Free Press.

Soto, H. de (2000) *The Mystery of Capital*. London: Bantam.

Spiegel, Der (1993) 'Gesellschaft, Manieren'. Verbale Krawatten, 47/7: 243.

Spierenburg, Pieter (1981) *Elites and Etiquette: Mentality and Social Structure in the Early Modern Northern Netherlands.* Rotterdam: Centrum voor Maatschappijgeschiedenis.

St George, Andrew (1993) *The Descent of Manners. Etiquette, Rules & The Victorians.* London: Chatto & Windus.

Stearns, Peter N. (1994) *American Cool: Constructing a Twentieth-Century Emotional Style.* New York UP.

Stearns, Peter N. (1999) *Battle Ground of Desire. The Struggle for Self-control in Modern America.* New York UP.

Steele, Valerie (2001) *The Corset – A Cultural History.* New Haven: Yale UP.

Stolk, Bram van (1991) *Eigenwaarde als groepsbelang.* Houten: Bohn Stafleu Van Loghum.

Stolk, Bram van and Cas Wouters (1987) *Frauen im Zwiespalt.* Frankfurt am Main: Suhrkamp.

Swaan, Abram de (1979) 'Uitgaansbeperking en Uitgaansangst. Over de verschuiving van bevelshuishouding naar onderhandelingshuishouding'. *De Gids*, 142/8: 498–509.

Swaan, Abram de (1985) *Kwaliteit is klasse.* Amsterdam: Bakker.

Swaan, Abram de (1988) *In Care of the State: Health Care, Education and Welfare in Europe and the USA in the Modern Era.* Oxford: Polity.

Swaan, Abram de (1995) 'Widening Circles of Social Identification: Emotional Concerns in Sociogenetic Perspective'. *Theory, Culture & Society*, 12: 25–39.

Swaan, Abram de (1997) 'Widening Circles of Disidentification: On the Psycho- and Sociogenesis of the Hatred of Distant Strangers – Reflections on Rwanda'. *Theory, Culture & Society*, 14: 105–22.

Swaan, Abram de (2000) 'Dyscivilisation, Mass Extermination and the State'. *Theory, Culture & Society*, 18: 265–76.

Swildens, J.H. (1789) 'Over den tegenwoordigen toestand der samenleving in onze republiek', in: Knigge (ed.) *Over de verkeering met menschen.* Amsterdam: Allart

Tarde, Gabriel (1903 [1890]) *The Laws of Imitation.* New York: Holt and Co. Reprint 1962: Gloucester, MA: Peter Smith.

Tilburg, Marja van (1998) *Hoe hoorde het?* Amsterdam: Spinhuis.

Tocqueville, Alexis de (1945) *Democracy in America.* New York: Vintage, 2 volumes.

Tocqueville, Alexis de (1955 [1856]) *The Old Régime and the French Revolution.* Garden City, NY: Doubleday Anchor.

Turner, Ralph H. (1969) 'The Theme of Contemporary Social Movements'. *British Journal of Sociology*, 20/4: 390–405.

Veblen, Thorstein (1979 [1899]) *The Theory of the Leisure Class.* Harmondsworth: Penguin.

Visser, Margaret (1991) *The Rituals of Dinner. The Origins, Evolution, Eccentricities, and Meaning of Table Manners.* New York: Grove Weidenfelt.

Vree, Wilbert van (1999) *Meetings, Manners and Civilisation.* London/New York: Leicester UP.

Vuijsje, Herman (1986) *Vermoorde onschuld.* Amsterdam: Bakker.

Waldhoff, Hans-Peter (1995) *Fremde und Zivilisierung.* Frankfurt am Main: Suhrkamp.

Waller, Willard (1937) 'The Rating and Dating Complex'. *American Sociological Review*, 2: 727–34.

Wander, B. (1976) 'Engelse en continentale etiquette in de negentiende eeuw. Invloeden en ontwikkelingen; literatuurrapport'. *Volkskundig Bulletin*, 2/2: 1–17.

Wilkinson, Rupert (1984) *American Tough: The Tough-Guy Tradition and American Character*. Westport, CT: Greenwood.

Wilson, Edmund (1962) 'Books of Etiquette and Emily Post', in his: *Classics and Commercials. A Literary Chronicle of The Forties*. New York: Vintage, pp. 375–81.

Wilterdink, Nico (2002) 'The Sociogenesis of Postmodernism'. *European Journal of Sociology*, 43/2: 190–216.

Winter-Uedelhoven, Hedwig (1991) *Zur Bedeutung der Etikette*. Frankfurt am Main: Fischer.

Wolfe, Tom (1968) *The Electric Kool-Aid Acid Test*. New York: Farrar, Straus & Girouz.

Wolfe, Tom (1970) *Radical Chic & Mau-Mauing the Flak Catchers*. New York: Farrar, Straus & Giroux.

Wolfe, Tom (1976) *Move Gloves & Madmen, Clutter & Vine*. New York: Farrar, Straus & Girouz.

Wolfenstein, Martha (1955 [1951]) 'Fun Morality: An Analysis of Recent American Child Training Literature', in: Margaret Mead and Martha Wolfenstein (eds) *Childhood in Contemporary Cultures*. University of Chicago Press.

World Development Report (1995) *Workers in an Integrating World*. Washington: The World Bank.

Wouters, Cas (1972) 'On Youth and Student Protest', *Transactions of the Seventh World Congress of Sociology. Varna, 14–19 September 1970*. Vol. III, Sofia: International Sociological Association, pp. 197–205.

Wouters, Cas (1976) 'Is het civilisatieproces van richting veranderd?' *Amsterdams Sociologisch Tijdschrift*, 3/3: 336–60.

Wouters, Cas (1977) 'Informalisation and the Civilising Process', in: P. Gleichmann, J. Goudsblom, and H. Korte (eds) *Human Figuration. Essays for Norbert Elias*. Amsterdam: Amsterdams Sociologisch Tijdschrift, pp. 437–54.

Wouters, Cas (1986) 'Formalisation and Informalisation, Changing Tension Balances in Civilising Processes'. *Theory, Culture and Society*, 3: 1–19.

Wouters, Cas (1987) 'Developments in Behavioural Codes Between the Sexes; Formalisation of Informalisation, The Netherlands 1930–1985'. *Theory, Culture and Society*, 4: 405–29.

Wouters, Cas (1989) 'The Sociology of Emotions and Flight Attendants'. *Theory, Culture and Society*, 6: 95–123.

Wouters, Cas (1990a) 'Social Stratification and Informalisation in Global Perspective'. *Theory, Culture and Society*, 7: 69–90.

Wouters, Cas (1990b) 'Changing Regimes of Power and Emotions at the End of Life: The Netherlands 1930–1990'. *Netherlands' Journal of Social Sciences*, 26: 151–67.

Wouters, Cas (1990c) *Van minnen en sterven. Informalisering van de omgangsvormen rond seks en dood*. Amsterdam: Bakker.

Wouters, Cas (1992) 'On Status Competition and Emotion Management; The Study of Emotions as a New Field', in: Mike Featherstone (ed.) *Cultural Theory and Cultural Change*. London: Sage, pp. 229–52.

Wouters, Cas (1993) ' "Jaja, ik was nog niet zoo'n beroerde kerel, die zoo'n vrind had" ' (Nescio), in: Han Israëls, Mieke Komen, and Abram de Swaan (eds) *Over Elias. Herinneringen en anecdotes*. Amsterdam: Spinhuis, pp. 7–19.

Wouters, Cas (1994) 'Duerr und Elias. Scham und Gewalt in Zivilisationsprozessen'. *Zeitschrift für Sexualforschung*, 7: 203–16.

Wouters, Cas (1995a) 'Etiquette Books and Emotion Management in the 20th Century; Part One – The Integration of Social Classes'. *Journal of Social History*, 29: 107–24.

Wouters, Cas (1995b) 'Etiquette Books and Emotion Management in the 20th Century; Part Two – The Integration of the Sexes'. *Journal of Social History*, 29: 325–40.

Wouters, Cas (1998a) 'Etiquette Books and Emotion Management in the 20th Century: American Habitus in International Comparison', in: Peter N. Stearns and Jan Lewis (eds) *An Emotional History of the United States*. New York UP, pp. 283–304.

Wouters, Cas (1998b) 'How Strange to Ourselves are Our Feelings of Superiority and Inferiority'. *Theory, Culture and Society*, 15: 131–50.

Wouters, Cas (1999a) *Informalisierung. Norbert Elias' Zivilisationstheorie und Zivilisationsprozesse im 20. Jahrhundert*. Opladen/Wiesbaden: Westdeutscher Verlag.

Wouters, Cas (1999b) 'Changing Patterns of Social Controls and Self-Controls: On the Rise of Crime since the 1950s and the Sociogenesis of a "Third Nature."' *British Journal of Criminology*, 39: 416–32.

Wouters, Cas (1999c) 'Die verlegte "Rue d'Amour." Über Hans Peter Duerrs Kritik and der Zivilisationstheorie von Norbert Elias'. *Zeitschrift für Sexualforschung*, 12: 50–7.

Wouters, Cas (2001) 'Manners', in: Peter N. Stearns (ed.) *Encyclopedia of European Social History. From 1350 to 2000*. New York: Scribner's, Vol. 4, Section 17, pp. 371–82.

Wouters, Cas (2002) 'The Quest for New Rituals in Dying and Mourning: Changes in the We–I Balance'. *Body & Society*, 8: 1–27.

Wouters, Cas (2004a) *Sex and Manners. Female Emancipation in the West since 1890*. London: Sage.

Wouters, Cas (2004b) 'Changing Regimes of Manners and Emotions: From Disciplining to Informalizing', in: Stephen Loyal and Stephen Quilley (eds) *The Sociology of Norbert Elias*. Cambridge UP, pp. 193–211.

Young, Michael and Peter Willmott (1957) *Family and Kinship in East London*. Harmondsworth: Penguin.

Manners Books

A (1894) *Doodgewone Dingen*. Amsterdam: Centen.

Armstrong, Lucie Heaton (1908) *Etiquette Up-to-date*. London: Werner Laurie.

Bakker-Engelsman, Netty (1983) *Etiquette in de jaren '80*. Utrecht: Luitingh.

Baldridge, Laetitia (1990) *Laetitia Baldridge's Complete Guide to the New Manners of the 90's*. New York: Rawson.

Barrows, Sydney Biddle and Ellis Weiner (1990) *Mayflower Manners: Etiquette for Consenting Adults*. New York: Doubleday.

Bates, Karen Grigsby and Karen Elyse Hudson (1996) *Basic Black. Home Training for Modern Times*. New York: Doubleday.

Beyfus, Drusilla (1992) *Modern Manners. The Essential Guide to Living in the '90s*. London: Hamlyn.

Birch, Christiaan (1860) *De Mensch in de Zamenleving of de kunst van den omgang met menschen*. Tiel: Van Loon.

Bode, Janet (1989) *Different Worlds. Interracial and Cross-Cultural Dating*. New York: Franklin Watts.

Bolton, Mary (1955 and 1961) *The New Etiquette Book*. London: Foulsham.

Boswell, James (1986 [1791]) *The Life of Samuel Johnson*. Harmondsworth: Penguin.

Bradley, Julia M. (1889) *Modern Manners and Social Forms*. Chicago, IL: J.B. Smiley.

Breen-Engelen, R.A. (1959) *Etiquette. Een Boekje voor Moderne Mensen*. Bussum (4th ed.: 1969).

Bremner, Moyra (1989) *Enquire Within Upon Modern Etiquette and Succesful Behaviour for Today*. London: Century.

Brett, Simon (1986) *Bad Form. Or How Not to Get Invited Back*. London: Arrow (1st ed.: 1984, Elm Tree).

Bruck-Auffenberg, Natalie (1897) *De vrouw 'comme il faut'*. Leiden: Brill.

Bruyn, Klazien de (1957) *'Spiegel voor Eva' Goede manieren en het moderne meisje*. Maastricht: Schenk.

Burleigh (1925) *Etiquette Up To Date*. New York: Howard Watt.

Carnegie, Dale (1936) *How to Win Friends and Influence People*. New York: Simon and Schuster.

Cassell's (1921) *Cassell's Book of Etiquette, by 'A Woman of the World'*. London.

Censor (1884) *Don't: A Manual of Mistakes & Impropriaties more or less prevalent in Conduct and Speech*. London: Field & Tuer.

Chesterfield, Philip Dormer Stanhope Earl of (1826 [1775]) *Lord Chesterfield's Advice to his son, on men and manners: in which the principles of politeness, and the art of acquiring a knowledge of the world, are laid down, etc*. London: Chiswick.

Copeland, Lennie and Lewis Griggs (1986) *Going International. How to Make Friends and Deal Effectively in the Global Marketplace*. New York: Plume.

Courey, Anne de (1985) *A Guide to Modern Manners*. London: Thames and Hudson.

Crisp, Quentin (with John Hofsers) (1985) *Manners from Heaven*. London: Fonatana.

Crowninshield, Francis W. (1908) *Manners for the Metropolis. An Entrance Key to the Fantastic Life of the 400*. New York: Appleton.

Cunningham, Chet (1992) *How to Meet People and Make Friends*. Leucadia, CA: United Research Publishers.

Day, Beth (1972) *Sexual Life between Blacks and Whites. The Roots of Racism*. New York: World Publishing Co.

Debrett (1976) *Debrett's Correct Form*. Compiled and edited by Patrick Montague-Smith, Debrett's Peerage Limited in association with Futura, Macdonald & Co Ltd. (first published in 1970; first revised edition in 1976, reprinted 1979, 1984, 1989, 1991).

Debrett (1981) *Debrett's Etiquette and Modern Manners*. Edited by Elsie Burch Donald. London: Pan (2nd ed.: 1982).

Debrett (2002) *Debrett's Correct Form*. London: Hodder Headline.

Deinse, A.M.J. van (1962) *Levenskunst voor jonge mensen*. Amsterdam: Elsevier.

Devereux, G.R.M. (1927) *Etiquette for Men. A Handbook of Modern Manners and Customs*. London: Pearson.

Dietrich, Heinz (1934) *Menschen miteinander*. Berlin/Darmstadt: Deutsche Buch-Gemeinschaft.

Donleavy, J.P. (1976) *The Unexpurgated Code: A Complete Manual of Survival and Manners*. Penguin Books (New ed.: 1979, 1981, 1985; first in USA: 1975).

Dresser, Norine (1996) *Multicultural Manners*. New York: Wiley.

Duvall, Evelyn Millis, with Joy Duvall Johnson (1958 and 1968). *The Art of Dating*. New York: Association Press.

ECvdM (1911) *Het wetboek van Mevrouw Etiquette voor Heeren in zestien artikelen*. Utrecht: Honig.

ECvdM (1912) *Het wetboek van mevrouw Etiquette in 32 artikelen*. Utrecht: Honig (7th ed.).

Edwards, Anne and Drusilla Beyfus (1956 and 1969) *Lady Behave: A Guide to Modern Manners*. London: Boswell & Co.

Eichler, Lilian (1921) *The Book of Etiquette*. Gardan City, NY: Doubleday. Reprint 1923.

Eichler, Lilian Watson (1948) *The Standard Book of Etiquette*. New York: Garden City Pub.

Eijk, Inez van (1983) *Etiquette Vandaag*. Utrecht/Antwerpen: Spectrum.

Eijk, Inez van (1991) 'Titulatuur als omgangsvorm', in: G.H.A. Monod de Froideville, Sophie den Beer Poortugael, and Inez van Eijk (eds) *Titulatuurgids*. 's Gravenhage: SDU, pp. 13−44.

Eijk, Inez van (2000) *Etiquette. Over moderne omgansvormen*. Contact: Amsterdam.

Eldridge, Elisabeth (1936) *Co-Ediquette. Poise and Popularity for Every Girl*. New York: Dutton.

Eltz J. von (1908 [1902]) *Das goldene Anstandsbuch*. Essen: Fredebeul & Koenen.

Etiquette (1854) *Etiquette. Social Ethics and the Courtesies of Society*. London: Orr.

Etiquette for Everyone (1956) *Good Behaviour in Everyday Life*. London: Foulsham.

Etiquette for Gentlemen (1923/1950) *A Guide to the Observances of Good Society*. London: Ward, Lock & Co.

Etiquette for Ladies (1876) *A Complete Guide to Visiting, Entertaining and Travelling, with Hints on Courtship, Marriage and Dress*. London: Ward, Lock & Tylor.

Etiquette for Ladies (1900) *A Complete Guide to the Rules and Observances of Good Society*. London: Ward, Lock & Co.

Etiquette for Ladies (1923, 1950) *A Guide to the Observances of Good Society*. London: Ward, Lock & Co.

Eyk, Henriëtte van (1967) *De regels van het spel*. Amsterdam: Geïllustreerde Pers.

Ford, Charlotte (1980) *Charlotte Ford's Book of Modern Manners*. New York: Simon and Schuster.

Franken, Constanze von (1890) *Katechismus des guten Tones und der feinen Sitte*. Leipzig: Hesse.

Franken, Konstanze von (1937) *Handbuch des guten Tones*. Berlin: Hesse.

Franken, Konstanze von (1951/1957/1959) *Der Gute Ton. Ein Brevier für Takt und Benehmen in allen Lebenslagen*. Berlin: Hesse.

Gammond, Peter (1986) *Bluff Your Way in British Class*. Horsham: Ravette.

Gilgallon, Barbara and Sue Seddon (1988) *Modern Etiquette*. London: Ward Lock.

Graham, Laurie (1989) *Getting It Right. A Survival Guide to Modern Manners*. London: Chatto & Windus.

Graudenz, Karlheinz and Erica Pappritz (1967) *Etikette neu*. München: Südwest.

Grearson, Jessie Carroll and Lauren B. Smith (eds) (1995) *Swaying. Essays on Intercultural Love*. Iowa City, IA: University of Iowa Press.

Grosfeld, Frans (ed.) (1983) *Zo hoort het nu*. Amsterdam/Brussels: Elsevier (2nd, 3rd ed.: 1984).

Groskamp-ten Have, Amy (1939) *Hoe Hoort Het Eigenlijk?* Amsterdam: Becht. (1–3 ed.: 1939; 4, 5 ed: 1940; 6: 1941; 7: 1942; 8: 1947; 9: 1948; 10: 1953; 11: 1954; 12: 1957; 13: 1966, revised by Ina van den Beugel).

Groskamp-ten Have, Amy (1983) *Hoe hoort het eigenlijk?* Revised by Maja Krans and Wia Post. Amsterdam: Becht (2nd ed.: 1984).

Groskamp-ten Have, Amy (1999) *Hoe hoort het eigenlijk?* Revised by Reinildis van Ditshuyzen. Haarlem: Becht.

Gurlitt, Ludwig (1906) *Erziehung zur Mannhaftigkeit*. Berlin: Concordia.

Habits of Good Society (1859): *A Handbook of Etiquette*. London: James Hogg & Sons (Reissued unchanged: 1890).

Haeften, Olga van (1936) *Manieren. Wenken voor wie zich correct willen gedragen.* Amsterdam: Kosmos (2nd ed.: 1937, identical).

Haller, Joachim (1968) *Der gute Ton im Umgang mit Menschen.* München: Südwest Verlag. (7th ed.; orig. 1962).

Handbook (1868) *Handboek der wellevendheid of de kunst om zich...* Leiden: Noothoven Van Goor.

Hanson, John Wesley Jr (1896) *Etiquette of Today. The Customs and Usages Required by Polite Society.* Chicago: IL.

Hardy, E.J. (1909) *How To Be Happy Though Civil.* New York: Scribners.

Harland, Marion, and Virginia van de Water (1905/1907) *Everyday Etiquette.* Indianapolis: Bobbs-Merrill.

Höflinger, Christoph. (1885/1905) *Anstandsregeln.* Regensburg: Pustet.

Holt, Emily (1901; rev. ed.: 1904, 1920) *The Secret of Popularity: How to Achieve Social Success.* New York: McClure, Phillips.

Hopkins, Mary A. (1937) *Profits from Courtesy.* Garden City, NY: Doubleday.

Houghton, Walter R *et al.* (1882) *American Etiquette and Rules of Politeness.* Chicago, IL: Rand McNally (6th ed.).

Humphry, C.E. (1897) *Etiquette for Every Day.* London: Richards.

Jacobs, Bruce (1999) *Race Manners: Navigating the Minefield Between Black & White Americans.* New York: Arcade.

Kandaouroff, Princess Beris (1972) *The Art of Living. Etiquette for the Permissive Age.* London: Allan.

Killen, Mary (1990) *Best Behaviour. The Tatler Book of Alternative Etiquette.* London: Century.

Klanker, Dirk Johan, and Stefan de Vries (1999) *Het Blauwe Boekje.* Utrecht: Bluebeard Publications.

Kleinschmidt, Karl (1957) *Keine Angst für guten Sitten.* Berlin: Das Neue Berlin.

Klickmann, Flora (1902) *The Etiquette of To-day.* London: Girl's Own & Woman's Magazine (3rd ed.: 1915).

Kloos-Reyneke van Stuwe, Jeanne (1927) *Gevoelsbeschaving.* Rotterdam: Nijgh & Van Ditmar.

Knap, Henri (1961) *Zo zijn onze manieren.* Amsterdam: Bezige Bij.

Knigge, Adolph Freiherr Von (1977 [1788]) *Über den Umgang mit Menschen.* Frankfurt am Main: Insel.

Landers, Ann (1978) *The Ann Landers Encyclopedia, A to Z.* Garden City, NY: DoubleDay.

Lansbury, Angela (1985) *Etiquette for Every Occasion. A Guide to Good Manners.* London: Batsford.

Loon, H.F. van (1983) *Goede Manieren. Hoe Hoort Het Nu.* Amsterdam: Teleboek.

Löwenbourg, Sylvia Lichem von (1987) *Das neue Buch der Etikette.* München: Droemer Knaur.

Manners and Tone of Good Society (1879) [by] A Member of the Aristocracy. London: F. Warne. This book is published in 1910 as:

Manners and Rule of Good Society (1910) (32nd ed.: 1921) London/New York: Warne (42nd revised ed.: 1940; reprints 1946, 1947, 1950, 1955).

Marschner, Osw. (1901) *Takt und Ton.* Leipzig: Maier.

Martin, Judith (1979) *Miss Manners' Guide to Excruciatingly Correct Behavior.* New York: Warner/Atheneum (reprints: 1980/1981/1982/1983).

Martin, Judith (1983) *Miss Manners' Guide for the Turn-of-the-Millenium.* New York: Pharos /Fireside (reprints: 1984/1985/1986/1987/1988/1989/1990).

Martin, Judith (1985) *Common Courtesy. In Which Miss Manners Solves the Problem that Baffles Mr. Jefferson*. New York: Atheneum.

Martin, Judith (1996) *Miss Manners Rescues Civilisation*. New York: Crown.

McGinnis, Tom (1968) *A Girl's Guide to Dating and Going Steady*. Garden City NY: Doubleday.

Meissner, Hans-Otto (1951) *Man benimmt sich wieder*. Giessen: Brühlscher.

Meissner, Hans-Otto and Isabella Burkhard (1962) *Gute Manieren stets gefragt*. München.

Millar, James (1897) *How to be a Perfect Gentleman*. London: Rosters.

Miller, Llewellyn (1967) *The Encyclopedia of Etiquette. A Guide to Good Manners in Today's World*. New York: Crown.

Mitchell, Mary (1994) *Dear Ms. Demeanor... The Young Persons Etiquette Guide to Handling Any Social Situation with Confidence and Grace*. Chicago, IL: Contemporary Books.

Oheim, Gertrud (1955) *Einmaleins des guten Tons*. Gütersloh: Bertelsmann.

Oort, H.L. (1904) *Goede Raad aan de jonge mannen en jonge meisjes der XXste eeuw*. By a Business Man. Utrecht: Broese.

O'Rourke, P.J. (1983) *Modern Manners: Etiquette for Very Rude People*. London: Panther, and 1984, New York: Dell.

Pahlen, Christine Gräfin von der (1991) *Moderne Umgansformen von A-Z*. Köln: Naumann und Göbel.

Pauw van Wieldrecht, Agnies (1991) *Het dialect van de adel*. Amsterdam: Rap (5th ed.).

Penelope, Lady (1982) *Etiquette Today*. Kingswood, Surrey: Paperfronts (reprinted 1989).

Post, Elizabeth L. (1965) *Emily Post's Etiquette*. Revised by Elizabeth L. Post. New York: Funk & Wagnalls (Next ed.: 1968); 1975-edition: *The New Emily Post's Etiquette*. New editions in 1984 and 1992.

Post, Elizabeth L. (1992) *Emily Post's Etiquette*. New York: HarperCollins (15th ed.).

Post, Emily (1922) *Etiquette in Society, in Business, in Politics and at Home*. New York: Funk and Wagnalls (revised ed.: 1923; 1927; 1931; 1934; 1937; 1942; 1950; 1960; replica editon of first edition: 1969).

Rapport (1931) *Rapport der regeerings-commissie inzake het dansvraagstuk*. The Hague.

Regteren, Yvo van, Binnert de Beaufort, and Jort Kelder (2002) *Oud geld*. Amsterdam: Prometheus.

Rush, Sheila and Chris Clark (1970) *How to Get Along with Black People. A Handbook for White Folks (And Some Black Folks Too)*. New York: Third Press.

Schliff, Sebastian (1977) *Gutes Benehmen – Kein Problem!* München: Humboldt; repr. 1981.

Schmidt-Decker, Petra (1985, 1991, 1995) *Das große Buch des guten Benehmens*. Düsseldorf: Econ.

Schönfeldt, Sybil Gräfin (1987) *1 x 1 des guten Tons*. München: Mosaik; Hamburg, 1991.

Schramm, H. (1893) *Der Gute Ton oder das richtige Benehmen*. Berlin: Schulke (4th ed.).

Schrijver, Elka (1954) *Kleine gids voor goede manieren*. Assen: Born (reprints 1959, 1962).

Scott, H. (1930) *Good Manners and Bad*. London: Ernest Benn.

Seidler, H.J. (*circa* 1911–15) *Hoe men zich bij de heeren het best bemind kan maken*. Rotterdam: Bolle.

Sherwood, Mary E.W. (1907) *Manners and Social Usages*. New York: Harper.

Stewart, Marjabelle Y. (1987) *The New Etiquette. Real Manners for Real People in Real Situations – an A-to-Z Guide*. New York: St. Martin's.

Stratenus, Louise (1909) *Vormen*. Gouda: Van Goor.

Swartz, Oretha D. (1988) *Service Etiquette*. Annapolis, MD: Naval Institute Press (4th ed.).

Terry, Eileen (1925) *Etiquette for All, Man, Woman or Child*. London: Foulsham.

Troubridge, Lady L. (1926) *The Book of Etiquette*. Kingswood: Windmill (repr. 1927, 1928, 1931).

Troubridge, Lady L. (1939) *Etiquette and Entertaining*. London: Amalgamated Press.

Uffelmann, Inge (1994) *Gute Umgangsformen in jeder Situation*. Niedernhausen/ Ts: Bassermann.

Umgangsformen Heute (1970) *Die Empfehlungen des Fachausschusses für Umgangsformen*. Niedernhausen: Falken.

Umgangsformen Heute (1988/1990) Überarbeitete Neuauflage. Niedernhausen: Falken.

Vanderbilt, Amy (1952) *Amy Vanderbilt's Complete Book of Etiquette, A Guide to Gracious Living*. New York: Doubleday 1952 (reprints 1958, 1963, 1972).

Vanderbilt, Amy (1978) *The Amy Vanderbilt Complete Book of Etiquette*. Revised and Expanded by Letitia Baldrige. Garden City, NY: Doubleday.

Viroflay, Marguérite de (1916, 1919) *Plichten en Vormen voor Beschaafde Menschen*. Amsterdam: Cohen Zonen.

Viroflay-Montrecourt (*circa*1920) *Goede Manieren. Een Etikettenboek voor dames en heeren*. Amsterdam: Cohen.

Vogue (1948) *Vogue's Book of Etiquette. A Complete Guide to Traditional Forms and Modern Usuage*, By Millicent Fenwick. New York: Simon and Schuster.

Wachtel, Joachim (1973) *1 x 1 des guten Tons heute*. München: Bertelsmann.

Wade, Margaret (1924) *Social Usage in America*. New York: Crowell.

Weber, Annemarie (1956) *Hausbuch des guten Tons*. Berlin: Falken.

Weißenfeld, Kurt von (1927 and 1941) *Der moderne Knigge, Über den Umgang mit Menschen*. Berlin: Möller (1st ed.: 1919; many new editions until 1960).

Whyte, John (1943) *American Words and Ways Especially for German Americans*. New York: Viking.

Wickenburg, Erik Graf (1978) *Der gute Ton nach alter Schule*. Wien/München: Molden.

Wolff, Inge (1995) *ABC der Modernen Umgangsformen*. Niedernhausen/Ts.: Falken.

Wolter, Irmgard (1990) *Der Gute Ton in Gesellschaft und Beruf*. Niedernhausen/Ts.: Falken.

Woman's Life (1895) Published by George Neurnes Ltd. First issue 14 December.

Young Stewart, Marjabellle (1987) *The New Etiquette. Real Manners for Real People in Real Situations – An A-to-Z Guide*. New York: St. Martin's Press.

Zitzewitz, Rosemarie von (1986) *Wenn Sie mich SO fragen*. München: Mosaik.

Zutphen van Dedem, Mevr. van (1928) *Goede Manieren*. Amersfoort: Logon.

Name Index

A.   37, 44
Adelfels, Marie von   82, 115
Adlersfeld, Eufemia von   167, 168
Aerts, Remieg   143
Ali, Mohammed   86
Amsberg, Prince Claus von   146
Anderson, Digby   xi
Andreae, Illa   107, 123
Aresty, Esther B.   xi
Ariès, Philippe   35, 36, 211
Armstrong, Lucia Heaton   168
Axtmann, Roland   239
Aya, Rod   235

Baene, Duke of   142
Bakker-Engelsman, Netty   68,
    180, 181
Baldridge, Laetitia   x, 73
Baltzell, Edward Digby   102, 125,
    149, 150, 151
Barnes, Emm   137
Barrows, Sydney Biddle   179
Bates, Karen Grigsby   96
Bauman, Zygmunt   194
Bauwelt   69
Beatrix, Queen   18, 146
Benedict, Ruth   241
Bennis, Warren G.   212; see Slater
Benthem van den Bergh, Godfried
    van   215
Berger, Otto   129
Berlin, Irving   160
Beyfus, Drusilla   53, 56, 57, 74, 82, 83,
    87, 88, 99, 128, 136, 137, 175;
    see Edwards
Birch, Dr. Christiaan   39
Bismarck, Otto Eduard Leopold von
    111, 114
Bloch, Marc   1
Blomert, Reinhard   203
Blumin, Stuart M.   29
Bodanius, Walter   59
Bode, Janet   96
Bolton, Mary   54, 56, 63, 74, 127,
    128, 135
Boswell, James   37
Bradley, Julia M.   81, 82, 149

Breman, Jan   222; see Parry
Bremner, Moyra   106, 177
Brett, Simon   176
Brinkgreve, Christien   231, 233
Bronfenbrenner, Urie   198
Bruck-Auffenberg, Natalie   13, 70
Bruin, Kees   142
Bruyn, Klazien de   61, 62
Burkhard, Isabella   60
Burleigh   127, 170

Caldwell, Mark   xi
Camus, Albert   209
Cancian, Francesca M.   7, 173
Carnegie, Dale   162, 163, 209
Carson, Gerald   xi, 92, 150
Castiglione, Baldassar   35, 37, 38, 45
Cavan, Sherri   xi
Censor   151
Charles, Prince   88
Chesterfield, Philip Dormer Stanhope
    Earl of   81, 92, 149
Churchill, Winston Leonard
    Spencer   218
Ciccone, Madonna Louise   182
Clark, Chris   86, 188
Cmiel, Kenneth   174, 180
Coleman, L.   160
Coopmans, J.P.A.   102
Copeland, Lennie   162
Coser, Lewis A.   26
Courey, Anne de   75, 83, 88, 135, 137,
    177, 182, 183
Crisp, Quentin   176
Crowninshield, Francis W.   151
Cunningham, Chet   101, 162
Curtin, Michael   xi, 2, 17, 19, 24, 27,
    40, 51, 65, 66, 70, 92, 101, 109,
    131, 133, 135, 136

Daalen, Rineke van   47, 48
Dahrendorf, Ralf   105, 106
Dangerfield, George   239
Davidoff, Leonore   xi, 19, 27, 50,
    113, 131, 136, 137, 149, 151,
    167, 185
Davis, Kathy   182

Davis, Murray   82
Day, Beth   86
Debrett   46, 57, 66, 75, 88, 92, 99, 128, 176, 177
Della Casa, Giovanni   20
Den Hollander, Arie N.J.   226
Deutscher, Irwin   xi
Deutscher, Verda   xi
Devereux, G.R.M.   126, 170
Dietrich, Heinz   60, 93, 117, 121
Donleavy, James Patrick   134
Dresser, Norine   96, 165
Driver-Davidson, Lisa   xi
Duerr, Hans-Peter   241
Dunk, Herman W. von der   146
Dunning, Eric   xi, xii, 32, 104, 165, 214, 236, 239, 240
Durkheim, Emile David   26, 31
Duvall, Evelyn Millis   82, 162
Dylan, Bob   189, 190, 227, 228, 229

Easton Ellis, Bret   216
Ebhardt, Franz   106
ECvdM   46, 76, 135
Edwards, Anne   53, 56, 57, 74, 82, 87, 88, 137, 175
Eichler Watson, Lilian   53, 157, 170
Eijk, Inez van   77, 89, 99, 124, 181, 190
Eldridge, Elisabeth   172
Elias, Norbert   1, 3, 5, 6, 10, 13, 14, 16–22, 24, 25, 30, 32, 42, 43, 81, 86, 89, 91, 96, 100, 102, 104, 105, 111–16, 131, 134, 184, 191, 195, 196, 199, 200, 202–4, 208–11, 213, 214, 218, 226, 227, 230–2, 235, 236, 238, 240, 241
Eltz, Johann von   40, 114
Elwenspoek, Curt   107
Engler, Wolfgang   203
Erasmus, Desiderius   11, 20
Etiquette for All   70
Etiquette for Everyone   54, 74
Etiquette for Gentlemen   91, 126, 129
Etiquette for Ladies   27, 44, 51, 126, 128, 129, 130, 139
Evers, Barbara   xii
Eyk, Henriëtte van   176

Fallers, Lloyd A.   87, 238
Febvre, Lucien   1
Finkelstein, Joanne   xi, 182
Fletcher, Jonathan   xi
Ford, Charlotte   82
Foucault, Michel   194, 195, 238

Frakking, Oskar   xii
Franken, Constanze von   13, 78, 106, 123, 130, 153
Freud, Anna   98
Freud, Sigmund   31, 216, 240
Fromm, Erich   49
Frykman, Jonas   32

Gammond, Peter   55, 134
Garland, David   195
Gaultier, Jean Paul   182
Gilgallon, Barbara   75
Gladstone, William Ewert   111
Goffman, Erving   84, 111, 209
Gordon, S.L.   7, 173
Gorer, Geoffrey   59, 152, 154
Goudsblom, Johan   xi, 86, 88, 91, 102, 166, 188, 198, 218, 219, 226, 238, 240, 241
Gouldner, Alvin   209
Graham, Laurie   83
Graudenz, Karlheinz   71, 118, 119, 123
Graves, Robert   171
Grearson, Jessie Carroll   96
Griggs, Lewis   162
Grosfeld, Frans   61, 89, 93, 99, 124, 141, 180, 181
Groskamp-ten Have, Amy   68, 71, 76, 77, 81, 99, 130, 139, 140, 141, 180
Gurlitt, Ludwig   114

Habits of Good Society, The   37, 128
Haeften, Olga van   172
Haller, Joachim   78, 174
Halttunen, Karen   xi
Handboek der wellevendheid   39
Hanson, John Wesley Jr.   58, 59, 70, 149, 156, 158
Hardy, Edward John   163
Harland, Marion   72, 155, 157
Harrison, Tom   64
Hart, K.   221
Haskell, Thomas   25
Haveman, Jan   88
Hemphill, Dallett   xi, 19, 59, 101, 149, 154
Hinz, Michael   241
Hitler, Adolf   78, 99, 218
Hobbes, Thomas   26
Hochschild, Adam   218
Hochschild, Arlie Russell   91, 163, 209
Hodge, Alan   171
Höflinger, Christoph   11, 129
Holmes, Dr. Wendell   151
Holt, Emily   58, 155, 161

Hopkins, Mary A 162
Horkheimer, Max 144
Houghton, Walter R. 17
Howe Hall, Florence 168
Hudson, Karen Elyse 96
Huizinga, Johan 1
Humphrey, Hubert Horatio 94
Humphrey, Mrs. C.E. 129

Inglis, Tom xi

Jacobs, Bruce A. 97
Johnson, Samuel 37, 162
Juliana, Queen 18

Kalberg, Stephen 105
Kandaouroff, Princess Beris 134, 175
Kapteyn, Paul 224
Kasson, John xi, 19, 37, 50, 66, 92,
    209, 239
Kelly, Sir Gerald 87
Kelter, Jörg 69
Kennedy, James C. 147, 151
Kesey, Ken 189
Killen, Mary 83, 175
Kilminster, Richard xi, 240
Klanker, D.J. 148
Klein, Josephine 198
Kleinschmidt, Karl 117
Klickmann, Flora 125, 126, 131, 138,
    139, 239
Kloos-Reyneke van Stuwe, Jeanne 76,
    85, 169
Knap, Henri 76, 77, 143
Knigge, Adolph Freiherr von 15, 108,
    110, 112, 153
Knijff, Rudolf 236
Koelewijn, Jannetje 108
Kohlberg, Lawrence 217, 224
Kohut, Heinze 215
König, Wilhelm von 122
Kool, Margo 89
Korzec, Michel 231, 233
Krieken, Robert van 93
Kroode, Herman ten 236
Krüger, Michael 114
Krumrey, Horst-Volker xi, 19, 59, 60,
    71, 78, 82, 106, 107, 115, 118,
    121, 123, 129, 130, 167, 168, 174
Kuzmics, Helmut 89, 104, 196, 239

Landauer, Karl 144
Landers, Ann 82, 94
Lansbury, Angela 137
Lasch, Christopher 211, 212

Latuska, Sabine 239
Lenin, Vladimir 135
Leopold II, King 218
Lewin, Kurt 105, 106
Lindqvist, Sven 218
Lipset, Seymour, Martin 94, 102, 106
Locke, John 26
Löfgren, Orvar 32
Lofland, Lyn H. 47
Loon, H.F. van 81, 141
Löwenbourg, Sylvia Lichem von 99,
    122, 123, 153, 178

Machiavelli, Niccoló 216
Madame Etiquette 76, 176
Madge, Charles 64
Manners and Rule 40, 65, 136
Marion, J.H. 94
Marschner, Oswald 111, 138
Martin, Hans 60, 121
Martin, Judith xi, 83, 95, 96, 98,
    153, 160, 165, 179, 180, 189,
    193, 240
Marx, Karl 209
Mason, John xi
Mastenbroek, Willem 201
Mayo, Elton 159
McCall Jt., Morgan W. 201
McGinnis, Tom 160
Meines, Rob 109, 116
Meissner, Hans Otto 60, 103
Meister, Ilse 106
Mennell, Stephen xi, xii, 19, 241
Mill, John Stuart 135
Millar James 28, 70, 81, 124, 134, 151
Miller, Llewellyn 73, 82, 162, 168
Mitchell, Mary 95
Montijn, Ileen 144, 145
Mooij, Annet 145
Morgan, John Pierpont 125
Motley, John L. 102
Mozart, Wolfgang Amadeus 226
Müller, Heiner 241
Munters, Q.J. 238

Naumann, Hans 238
Nederkoorn, Erik Jan 108
Newton, Sarah 28, 29, 32
Nicolson, Harold xi, 67, 74,
    75, 163

Oheim, Gertrud 105, 118, 123
Oort, Dr. H.L. 33
Openneer, Herman 207
O'Rourke, Patrick Jake 176

Orwell, George   64, 117, 126, 189,
   215, 216
Özlü, Demir   209

Pahlen, Christien Gräfin von der   153
Pappritz, Erica   71, 118, 119, 123
Parry, Jonathan P.   221
Parsons, Tallcott   3, 226
Pauw van Wieldrecht, Agnies   190
Peabody, Dean   105, 131, 164
Penelope, Lady   54, 175
Piaget, Jean   217, 224
Picasso, Pablo   235
Porter, Cecil   xi, 19, 40, 132, 239
Post, Arjan   194
Post, Elizabeth L.   73, 74, 83, 95
Post, Emily   16, 52, 53, 58, 67, 72, 73,
   85, 86, 95, 97, 153, 156, 157, 158,
   159, 161, 162, 163, 170, 179, 193

Rapport 1931   207
Regteren, Yvo   148
Riesman, David   31, 106, 206, 213, 214
Ritter, Robert   205
Robertson Hodges, Deborah   xi, 94, 163
Rothman, Ellen   173
Rousseau, Jean-Jacques   26
Rush, Sheila   86, 188

Sartre, Jean Paul   209
Schelsky, Helmut   178
Schlesinger Jr., Arthur Meier   97
Schlesinger Sr., Arthur Meier   xi, 15,
   58, 152, 157, 168, 170
Schliff, Sebastian   78, 80, 120, 122
Schmidt-Decker, Peter   120
Schönfeldt, Sybil Gräfin   79, 119, 122,
   153, 178, 179, 191
Schramm, Hermine   109, 129
Schreiner, Gerth   145
Schrijver, Elka   61, 68, 77, 140
Schröter, Michael   xi, 181, 235, 236,
   239, 241
Scotson, John L.   14, 16, 42, 43, 96,
   191, 204, 218
Scott, H.   56, 190
Seddon, Sue   75
Seidler, Dr. H.J.   33
Sennett, Richard   194, 195, 196
Shaw, Bernard   87
Sherwood, Mary E.W.   155, 156
Silver, Allan   109, 110
Simmel, Georg   93
Slater, Philip E.   212
Smith, Adam   31

Smith, Dennis   221
Smith, Lauren B.   96
Sorokin, Pitrim   15
Soto, H.   222
Spencer, Herbert   26
Spierenburg, Pieter   15, 102, 161
St George, Andrew   xi, 135
Stalin, Iosif   135, 218
Stearns, Peter N.   92, 159, 163
Steele, Valerie   182
Stent, Gunther S.   xi
Stolk, Bram van   xii, 49, 97, 184,
   214, 227
Stratenus, Louise   41, 43, 47, 76
Swaan, Abram de   17, 98, 193,
   201, 209
Swartz, Oretha D.   180
Swildens, Johan Hendrik   15

Tarde, Gabriel   15, 18, 150, 238
Temple, Sir William   142
Terry, Eileen   56, 81, 126, 138, 170
Tilburg, Marja van   29
Tocqueville, Alexis de   15, 36,
   151, 239
Troubridge, Lady Laura   44, 52, 56, 74,
   127, 129, 130, 133, 139, 169, 172
Turner, Ralph   214

Uffelmann, Inge   80
Umgangsformen Heute   60, 79, 83, 84,
   100, 107, 119, 120, 121, 174, 178

Vanderbilt, Amy   73, 87, 94
Veblen, Thorstein   168
Velde, Hendrik te   143
Viroflay-Montrecourt, Marguérite de
   38, 61, 183
Visser, Margaret   xi
Visser, Saskia   236
Voerman, Julia   xii
Voerman, Sam   xii
Vogue's Book of Etiquette   53
Vree, Wilbert van   110, 142
Vries, Simon de   148

Wachtel, Joachim   78, 80, 87, 121,
   123, 174
Wade, Margaret   58, 150, 155,
   158, 171
Waldhoff, Hans-Peter   203, 204, 205,
   209, 219
Wander, B.   13
Water, Virginia van de   72, 155, 157
Weber, Annemarie   120, 121

Weißenfeld, Kurt von   108, 153, 169
Weiner, Ellis   179
Whyte, John   103, 106, 116, 164
Wickenburg, Erik Graf   153
Wilkinson, Rupert   164
Willmott, Peter   64
Wilson, Edmund   157
Wilterdink, Nico   240
Winter-Uedelhoven, Hedwig   xi
Wolfe, Tom   150, 189, 216, 219
Wolfenstein, Martha   171, 214
Wolff, Inge   79, 80
Wolter, Irmgard   83, 100, 178

Wouters, Cas   xi, 10, 27, 56, 62,
   92, 97, 98, 109, 144, 147, 159,
   160, 180, 184, 186, 201, 203,
   210, 211, 214, 221, 237,
   240, 241

Young, Michael   64, 74, 158, 214
Young Stewart, Marjabelle   95, 179

Zitzewitz, Rosemarie von   68, 78,
   107, 153
Zutphen van Dedem, Mevr. van   42,
   44, 45

Subject Index

accommodation processes   40, 48, 49,
    94, 100, 147, 166, 184, 187, 191
acquaintance, acquaintanceship   7, 14,
    24, 25, 26, 42, 43, 46, 51, 65, 70,
    75, 79, 80, 82, 109, 115, 117, 124,
    125, 126, 127, 129, 130, 138, 140,
    154, 155, 156
  for the nonce   117, 124
  undesirable   126, 129, 138
address, addressing   8, 14, 33, 41, 72,
    140, 151, 155
  forms of   61, 72, 73, 74, 75, 76, 77,
    78, 79, 85, 94, 99, 101, 106,
    107, 116, 117, 121, 145, 154,
    177
advice literature   7, 84
aggression, aggressiveness   1, 22, 23,
    51, 85, 219, 231, 237
alienation, alienated   31, 148, 207,
    209, 210
Al-Qaeda   208
ambivalence   48, 54, 78, 82, 83, 155,
    208, 210, 211, 212, 227
American Dream   16, 155
American studies   226
Americans   52, 55, 58, 67, 72, 92, 94,
    95, 97, 98, 103, 105, 106, 116,
    151, 152, 153, 154, 155, 157, 159,
    160, 161, 164, 165, 220, 223
  African   97, 100, 165, 188
  German   102, 106, 116
Amerindians   232, 233
Amnesty International   195
ancien régime   15
andragologie   141, 142
anger, angry   29, 37, 44, 45, 48, 133,
    134, 159, 163, 164, 165, 198,
    217, 219
animal, animals   23, 32, 126, 195, 207
animalic   21, 32, 134, 175, 199,
    205, 208
Annales school   1
Anti-Globalization movement/
    Anti-Globalists   223
anxiety, anxieties   31, 47, 71, 164,
    186, 203, 205, 209, 211, 214, 215,
    217, 223

apartheid   97
  social and psychic   98, 204
Arcadia   211
aristocracy   36, 52, 60, 101, 102, 105,
    111, 133, 136, 150, 153, 154, 190
aristocratic   17, 23, 92, 101, 102,
    104, 109, 110, 111, 112, 113, 133,
    137, 142, 153, 161, 168, 182,
    190, 235
  confidence   81
  ease   81, 161
  warrior code   102, 105, 111, 114
aristocratization of the bourgeoisie
    19, 102
arrogance   30, 51, 52, 99, 217
art, the art of   37, 38, 45, 91, 104,
    128, 136, 142, 168, 211
  avoiding and excluding   44, 45
  snubbing   129
ascendancy   24, 25
  physical   45, 46
  psychic   45, 46
at ease   3, 4, 23, 91, 92, 101
  see also ease of manner
At Home, visiting hours   3, 27, 129
authentic, authenticity   4, 10, 32, 90,
    92, 123, 174, 188, 208, 209, 210,
    211, 212
authoritarian personality   197,
    203, 204
authoritarian superego-dominated
    personality   204, 208, 215
authoritarian superego-dominated
    self-regulation   203
authority, authorities   x, 22, 36, 47,
    48, 53, 60, 65, 73, 78, 90, 107,
    116, 142, 144, 146, 147, 149, 151,
    173, 174, 178, 184, 192, 197,
    198, 200, 205, 206, 207, 208,
    212, 215
  psychic   205, 213, 214, 220
  social   214, 220
authorize, authorizing   65
aversion   38, 45, 69
avoidance behaviour   7, 35, 36, 38, 39,
    40, 42, 44, 45, 50, 54, 55, 57, 58,
    61, 65, 67, 135, 189, 217

balance, balances
  of controls   12, 48, 203
  between external and internal social
      controls   13, 199, 204
  of involvement and detachment   13,
      39, 48, 64, 69, 84, 97, 98, 115,
      195, 226
  of power   12, 13, 14, 19, 40, 77, 92,
      100, 110, 184, 187, 222, 225
  between Superego and Ego   203, 208
  of Superego and Ego   212
balancing-act   69
ball, balls   23, 33, 124, 136, 137
behavioural and emotional alternatives
      3, 8, 11, 57, 84, 203, 217, 223
best people   53, 54, 60
Best Society   52, 53, 67, 149, 171
bigotry   95, 96, 100
Bildung   112
Black, Blacks   2, 86, 94, 95, 96, 101,
      165, 188
  community   86, 96
Black Panthers   174
Body People   182
Body-Intellectuals   183
boundary, boundaries   13, 26, 43, 78,
      113, 129, 136, 139, 157, 214, 223
  maintenance   23, 65, 130, 133, 136
bourgeoisie   19, 24, 26, 27, 36, 60, 87,
      94, 102, 105, 165
  petit   205
bowing acquaintanceship   28, 65, 158
box, boxing   37, 38, 45
bra   181, 182
Bruderschaft   108, 115, 117, 119, 135
brutalization   224
bullshit degree   160

calculate, calculation   15, 110, 113,
      133, 213, 225
call, calls   129, 172
calm   37, 45, 47, 144
camaraderie   73, 170
camping   8, 121, 122, 123, 124
carrot-and-stick   39, 61, 64
  carrot   40, 41, 63
censorship, censor   215
  social and psychic   29, 215
charitable work, charity   145, 146,
      157, 161, 230
Christian names see first names
cinemas   41, 62
civil rights   147, 180
Civil Rights Movement   98, 188
civilities   70, 119, 163, 180

civilization   225
civilizing of emotions   205
civilizing process   19, 22, 111, 202,
      203, 207, 224, 230, 231, 232, 233
class   4, 6, 7, 8, 12, 17, 18, 58, 98,
      143, 149
  conflicts   104, 112, 164, 184
  conflicts, face-to-face   35, 38
  distinctions   3, 5, 6, 8, 15, 16, 55,
      56, 59, 60, 61, 67, 69, 129,
      131, 135, 141, 143, 145, 151,
      177, 192
  segregation   39, 40, 43, 60, 102,
      131, 165
  society   57, 59, 130, 133, 134, 136
classes   4, 8, 12, 13, 17, 18, 23, 27,
      35, 36, 54, 57, 58, 60, 81, 93,
      94, 96, 132, 152, 169, 180,
      186, 232
  lower   1, 2, 17, 18, 19, 32, 36, 37,
      38, 39, 40, 42, 43, 44, 46, 51,
      53, 55, 62, 63, 64, 66, 89, 94,
      100, 114, 133, 134, 135, 163,
      175, 188, 189, 198, 202, 204,
      205, 207, 208, 217, 225
  middle   23, 25, 27, 28, 29, 30, 31, 32,
      47, 53, 61, 64, 66, 87, 97, 102,
      103, 104, 105, 111, 112, 113,
      114, 119, 133, 137, 140, 142,
      143, 145, 153, 161, 163, 165, 175
  upper   12, 17, 19, 20, 22, 29, 31,
      40, 47, 59, 64, 85, 86, 94,
      104, 113, 114, 136, 148, 149,
      150, 168
classless society   8, 55, 56, 57, 58,
      59, 135
code, codes   xi, 1, 4, 6, 12, 17, 18, 20,
      47, 53, 67, 102, 111, 113, 141,
      144, 159, 176, 197, 215
  dominant   7, 14, 19, 84, 85, 89, 169
  formal   92, 221, 223
  of manners   3, 11, 12, 14, 18, 48,
      49, 50, 53, 57, 60, 64, 77, 84,
      102, 104, 131, 132, 149, 151,
      166, 167, 173, 181, 186, 221,
      223, 225, 234
  of manners and feeling   1, 3, 5, 6, 7,
      10, 12, 15, 63, 192, 230
  military   102, 103, 105, 110, 111,
      114
  national   7, 35, 57, 94, 104, 151
  social   11, 16, 19, 85, 199, 217
cohesion   97, 191, 193, 195
collective
  conscience   223, 224

collective *cont.*
  emancipation   86, 173, 184, 186,
    187, 220
  identification   16, 220
commercialization   38
  of human feeling   163, 209
communism   38, 160
communitarianism   196
compartmentalized,
    compartmentalization   98, 202,
    204, 217
competition   5, 22, 24, 26, 29, 32, 81,
    92, 105, 140, 150, 153, 164, 192,
    193, 221
  open   97, 98, 149, 150, 152,
    155, 159, 160, 161, 164, 165
  for status and a meaningful life   1, 5,
    11, 28, 36, 59, 67, 68, 91, 106,
    130, 143, 144, 148, 188, 201,
    216, 217
competition and cooperation   166,
    192, 200, 201, 210, 212, 213
composure   12, 28, 49, 204
compromise, compromising   4, 102,
    103, 104, 111, 142, 147, 159,
    201, 213
confident, confidential, confidentiality
    23, 66, 76, 78, 79, 91, 92, 104,
    117, 118, 121, 133
conflict, conflicts   x, 4, 19, 22, 29, 30,
    35, 37, 38, 62, 76, 89, 104, 112,
    133, 142, 147, 159, 164, 165, 184,
    186, 195, 196, 208, 213, 219, 220,
    223, 225
conflict model   186
conscience   4, 12, 18, 25, 71, 93, 147,
    198, 199, 202, 203, 204, 205, 208,
    213, 214, 215, 218, 224
  authoritarian   31, 33, 197, 198, 203,
    208, 212, 215, 219
  conscience formation   6, 7, 29, 30,
    219, 225
  collective   223
conscience-ridden personality   25, 215
consciousness   4, 21, 60, 71, 79, 98,
    134, 141, 143, 160, 161, 199, 202,
    203, 204, 205, 208, 212, 213, 215,
    217, 220, 224
consideration   4, 21, 25, 41, 42, 67,
    93, 123, 132, 136, 174
constraint, constraints   17, 21, 22, 57,
    80, 84, 91, 93, 108, 144, 159, 183,
    192, 194, 198, 203, 211, 213,
    215, 236
  to be unconstrained   4, 90, 91

contamination   7, 42, 44, 46
  psychic   42, 44, 45, 47, 61, 64
  social   42, 43, 45, 47, 49, 61, 64
contempt   39, 40, 41, 76,
    154, 189
contracts   25, 26, 31, 110, 111
  business   143
controlled decontrolling   222
  of emotional controls   9, 66, 93,
    148, 175, 182, 199, 212, 216,
    224, 231, 236, 237
  of superiority and inferiority feelings
    217, 220
convention, conventions   56, 57, 76,
    87, 92, 93, 126, 169, 170, 174, 179
cool   39, 47, 133, 134, 141
corset   182, 234
coterie, coteries   42, 43, 143, 148
counter-impulses   30, 31, 199, 200,
    205, 213, 224
court, courts, courtly regimes   13, 14,
    15, 18, 19, 20, 22, 23, 24, 27, 51,
    65, 81, 101, 102, 105, 112,
    113, 120, 122, 133, 136, 137,
    143, 211
courtesy   15, 17, 19, 23, 27, 65, 67,
    76, 92, 117, 139, 149, 163,
    169, 172
cruise ship   8, 137, 138, 139
cultural criticism   209, 210, 211
cut, cutting   8, 65, 128, 129, 130
  cut direct   129

dance, dancing   3, 35, 62, 64, 124,
    126, 136, 138, 139, 163, 171,
    183, 206
dance hall   41, 62, 63
dating system   162
Debrett's Peerage Limited   75
Declaration of Independence   102,
    153, 154
decolonization   2, 217, 218
defecate, defecating   1, 20, 175
deference   51, 91, 105, 116, 121, 130,
    149, 168, 169
  forms of   65
deftig, deftigheid   143, 144, 146,
    147, 148
democratization   18, 41, 50, 55, 60,
    63, 91, 146, 147, 217, 218
  functional   24, 113
deregulation
  of economic relations   222
  of labour relations   221, 222
  regulated deregulation   222

detachment 3, 13, 39, 48, 64, 69, 80, 97, 98, 115, 177, 195, 226
  level of 2, 54, 84
development 2, 5, 6, 8, 9, 12, 13, 16, 17, 21, 22, 25, 29, 30, 31, 32, 39, 51, 61, 69, 75, 84, 86, 89, 91, 93, 98, 101, 102, 104, 110, 111, 112, 131, 135, 139, 151, 160, 163, 164, 165, 173, 180, 181, 191, 198, 200, 213, 214, 215, 216, 217, 218, 219, 220, 224, 226, 233
  national 5, 8, 101
dialect, dialects 86, 88, 89
  of nobility 190
dichotomy, dichotomies 211
differentiation and integration 32, 38, 46, 196, 200, 212, 220
  of social functions 184, 185
dinners 23, 27
dirty, dirtiness 30, 39, 42, 46, 174, 204, 205
discipline, disciplining 6, 7, 25, 26, 29, 30, 31, 71, 86, 113, 141, 142, 144, 176, 179, 198, 204
discrimination 58, 65, 66, 94, 126, 135
disintegration 97, 193
distance 69, 75, 78, 79, 80, 93, 107, 118
  keeping a 28, 35, 39, 40, 57, 64, 67, 68, 69, 70, 71, 77, 112, 117, 120, 151, 155, 189
  psychic 2, 3, 4, 6, 7, 13, 36, 41, 55, 57, 71, 72, 77, 80, 81, 115, 119
  social 2, 3, 4, 6, 7, 12, 13, 28, 36, 38, 39, 40, 41, 55, 56, 57, 71, 72, 77, 80, 81, 105, 111, 115, 119, 135, 150
distinctions 21, 24, 38, 56, 61, 62, 65, 70, 79, 92, 105, 107, 109, 110, 120, 143, 144, 153, 184, 186, 203
distinguish x, 15, 21, 24, 48, 52, 59, 60, 61, 63, 65, 79, 91, 105, 109, 114, 117, 125, 129, 130, 149, 152, 156, 184, 188, 190, 203, 214, 218, 235
dividing lines 60, 216
  psychic 34, 202, 204, 213
  social 8, 12, 34, 35, 36, 43, 45, 46, 48, 49, 52, 59, 64, 121, 136, 156, 160, 202, 204, 213
  social, between formal and informal 165
  social, between public and private 165
division of functions 5
division of labour 5
domestics 36, 41, 44
dramaturgical perspective 209
drink, drinking, drunk, drunkard 1, 29, 79, 115, 119, 120, 171
drives 22, 32, 202, 203, 212, 225
Du, duzen 76, 77, 78, 79, 80, 99, 108, 109, 114, 115, 117, 118, 119, 120, 127, 230
Dutch Republic 142

ease of manner 81
  see also at ease
easygoing 98
egalitarian 51, 132
ego-dominated personality type 215
ego-dominated self-regulation 208
emancipate, emancipated 2, 19, 54, 64, 185
emancipation 4, 7, 9, 35, 40, 49, 63, 84, 89, 90, 91, 97, 98, 100, 141, 166, 181, 184, 185, 186, 187, 191, 214, 216, 217, 218, 240
  collective 40, 48, 49, 201
emancipation and integration 9, 90, 96, 97, 100, 158, 184
  of 'lower' impulses and emotions 202, 210, 212, 215, 225
  of 'lower' social groups 14, 97, 165, 167, 184, 185, 201, 202, 210, 212, 215, 225
emancipation and resistance 184
emancipation of emotions 4, 9, 71, 85, 135, 199, 202, 203, 206, 213, 214, 219, 220, 224
emancipation-via-segregation 97
embarrassment 1, 20, 21, 54, 91, 95, 201
embourgeoisement 19, 87
emotion regulation 1, 3, 4, 5, 6, 12, 18, 19, 84, 93, 97, 99, 102, 131, 132, 149, 151, 161, 166, 173, 175, 199, 201, 205, 206, 209, 210, 211, 221, 223
  domestic and foreign policy of 210
  signal function of 210
emotions 1, 3, 6, 8, 9, 12, 13, 18, 29, 30, 31, 37, 45, 55, 64, 71, 80, 85, 92, 99, 134, 197, 199, 201, 202, 203, 204, 210, 211, 212, 213, 214, 215, 216, 217, 218, 219, 222, 224, 225, 231, 236, 238, 240, 251
  'dangerous' emotions 30, 71, 159, 164, 201, 202

enmity 70, 84, 110
  anonymous 85
  instant 85, 90, 219
equality 28, 56, 57, 61, 70, 77, 82,
  90, 112, 115, 116, 126, 128, 131,
  135, 142, 143, 146, 154, 181,
  193, 200
equanimity of the welfare
  state 214, 223
escape 11, 32, 36, 50, 137, 180
  social 121
established, established groups 12, 14,
  16, 18, 39, 40, 42, 47, 61, 65, 69,
  81, 88, 90, 94, 96, 98, 100, 135,
  143, 147, 152, 153, 156, 157, 160,
  161, 166, 170, 173, 183, 184, 186,
  187, 188, 189, 190, 198, 200, 205,
  206, 208, 218, 220, 225, 227,
  239, 240
established–outsider relations 100, 206
ethnic
  groups 58, 94, 164, 165
  insults 95
  jokes 95
ethnicity 52, 98, 159
ethnocentrism 9, 217, 218, 220
etiquette x, xi, 2, 3, 13, 15, 16, 17,
  18, 23, 24, 27, 38, 52, 53, 55, 56,
  57, 58, 61, 65, 71, 74, 91, 95, 97,
  98, 109, 119, 126, 127, 131, 132,
  133, 135, 136, 142, 146, 149, 154,
  155, 156, 157, 161, 168, 171, 172,
  174, 176, 177, 179, 180
  business 159, 163
  interracial 94
European Americans 94, 100
European Union 90, 223
exclude, exclusion 12, 27, 36, 38, 76,
  93, 110, 131, 135, 136, 166
export processing zones 221, 222
Expressive Revolution 3, 9, 135, 167,
  174, 176, 200

familiarity 8, 67, 69, 70, 71, 72, 74,
  91, 118
fantasy 29, 45, 215, 216
fear, fears 2, 5, 17, 21, 22, 29, 30, 31,
  32, 36, 42, 43, 44, 45, 46, 49, 50,
  57, 61, 62, 71, 82, 90, 92, 98, 135,
  159, 161, 172, 186, 195, 198, 199,
  200, 203, 204, 205, 206, 207, 211,
  214, 215, 216, 218, 220, 223
  of falling 7, 48, 49, 50, 61, 62,
    63, 71
  of freedom 49

level of 160, 164, 187, 220
  of psychic contamination 7, 42,
    46, 47
  of rising 7, 48, 49, 50, 187
  of social contamination 7, 42, 43,
    44, 46, 47, 49
  of social depths 49
  of social heights 49
  of temptation, being tempted 28,
    118, 204, 205
feelings of powerlessness 186
Fin de Siècle 9, 167
first names 8, 69, 72, 73, 74, 75, 76,
  77, 78, 79, 80, 84, 85, 90, 145, 179
first nature 21, 31, 32, 182, 197, 213,
  218, 224
FKK 121, 122, 138
flexibility 96, 177, 193, 194, 195,
  201, 213, 224
flirting, flirtations 138
formality–informality span 121, 137
formalization 9, 11, 27, 31, 181, 184,
  187, 191, 204, 224
  of labour relations and the labour
    market 222, 223
  of manners 6
  psychic 224, 225
  of the regimes of manners and
    emotions 6, 167, 222, 224
  theory of 6
formalizing
  phase 9, 181, 202, 203, 207,
    218, 241
  processes 7, 30, 181, 200, 206
free trade zones 221
freedom 16, 49, 56, 59, 84, 94, 99,
  102, 123, 131, 138, 169, 170, 174,
  178, 187, 192, 194, 205, 214
friendship, friendships 8, 61, 63, 70,
  74, 75, 78, 108, 109, 110, 111,
  112, 113, 114, 115, 117, 118, 119,
  121, 126, 130, 162, 228, 234
fun 171, 214

gate keeping, gatekeepers 27, 125
gatecrashing 137, 139
gatekeeping regime 66, 173
gentleman 37, 38, 45, 46, 50, 54,
  114, 117, 120, 125, 128, 129,
  131, 132, 138, 139, 157, 163,
  215, 216
  crook 215
  English 113
  ideal of the 133
gentrification 111

ghetto   86, 97, 165, 188
  behaviour   188
  credentials   86, 188
Gilded Age   9, 168
global
  interweaving   2, 186, 223
globalization   190, 192, 222
Golden Rule   28, 201
good company   51, 109, 138, 150
good society, good societies   x, 7, 8,
    12, 13, 14, 15, 16, 17, 18, 19, 23,
    24, 25, 26, 27, 28, 35, 40, 50, 51,
    52, 53, 58, 59, 65, 66, 81, 104,
    109, 111, 112, 113, 114, 115,
    119, 121, 125, 128, 131, 132, 133,
    135, 137, 138, 143, 148, 149,
    150, 151, 152, 155, 156, 157,
    158, 160, 161, 163, 164, 165,
    166, 170, 180, 184, 185, 190, 201,
    202, 238
  gossip channels of   26
  gymnastic   114
  modelling function of   7, 14, 15, 16,
    18, 19, 25
Great Unwashed   205
Greenpeace   195
greet, greeting   80, 82, 83, 95, 101,
    128, 129, 130, 140, 234
  first   128, 129, 130
group charisma   12
guest worker, guest workers   78, 99
guilt   199, 214, 215, 229
  culture   241
  trip   214
gypsies   205, 208

habitus   1, 4, 6, 8, 12, 16, 55, 57, 70,
    102, 103, 105, 112, 116, 147,
    196, 239
  American   98, 159, 164
  counter-habitus   218
  Dutch   141, 142
  English   130, 133, 134, 177
  formation   5, 8, 101, 147, 166
  German   76, 104, 112, 119
  national   4, 8, 12, 18, 101, 102, 103,
    104, 166
harmony model   186
health   21, 108, 120, 122, 228
Hell's Angels   189
hierarchy   6, 14, 75, 77, 86, 88, 109,
    119, 146, 148, 176, 192, 238
high society   14, 67
Hollywood   13, 82, 150
homo clausus   203, 209, 212, 241

homosexuals   2, 97, 148, 181, 185
honour   33, 34, 40, 102, 108, 113,
    114, 137, 193, 227
host, hostess   58, 120, 125, 128, 140,
    151, 155, 180, 239
hotel   58, 76, 121, 123, 125, 127,
    138, 139
  abroad   125, 139
Human Relations school   159
human rights   186, 195
humiliation, humiliations   30, 42, 153,
    186, 193, 200, 204, 217, 218, 219,
    220, 225
humour   134, 188
  'send-up'   176
hygiene   21
hypocrisy   103, 147, 161, 162

ideal, ideals   5, 9, 12, 14, 18, 19, 23,
    51, 56, 59, 89, 107, 110, 113, 114,
    115, 119, 132, 133, 141, 144, 147,
    149, 150, 156, 157, 168, 182, 183,
    184, 185, 186, 187, 193, 194,
    198, 200, 203, 209, 211, 212,
    213, 217
  of equality   74, 147, 217
  of manliness   114
idealization   189, 211
  of street sense   189
identification   7, 13, 16, 18, 22, 55, 63,
    64, 84, 90, 93, 152, 156, 157, 188,
    189, 192, 193, 194, 210, 213, 220,
    225, 240
  circles of   2, 28, 64, 193, 195
  with the established   16, 153, 156,
    157, 186, 188, 190
  level of   49
  mutual   4, 8, 22, 23, 69, 84, 85,
    217, 224, 225
  with outsiders   188, 189
identification with the established   16,
    153, 156, 157, 186, 188, 190
identity   6, 12, 16, 43, 49, 89, 90, 92,
    98, 127, 153, 192, 212
ideology   x, 8, 16, 55, 58, 59, 135, 151
  market   186
I-feelings   193, 210
I-ideals   154, 191, 194, 195, 196
I-identity, I-identities   13, 16, 43, 44,
    153, 191, 192, 194
imagination   46, 154, 215, 216
  realm of   216, 217
IMF   195, 223
immigrants   2, 61, 98, 99, 106, 196,
    206, 220, 225

impression management 93, 160, 208
include, inclusion 4, 9, 12, 15, 27, 30,
    59, 70, 84, 85, 99, 136, 152, 166,
    181, 220, 237, 238
indignation 42, 43, 45
    moral 30, 77, 217
individualization 13, 67, 183,
    191, 192
industrialization 38
inequality 41, 90, 109, 147, 167, 186,
    201, 225, 238
    harmonious 183, 184, 185, 186
    power 167
inferiority 16, 30
    displays of 2, 3, 4, 9, 22, 28, 35
    expressions of 55, 92, 210, 217
    feelings of 2, 6, 9, 30, 38, 64, 116,
        216, 217, 219, 220
informal pronoun 69
informalization 3, 4, 8, 9, 10, 11, 19,
    50, 55, 57, 78, 84, 85, 87, 91, 141,
    146, 167, 168, 172, 173, 174, 175,
    176, 178, 181, 184, 185, 202, 206,
    215, 217, 221, 222, 224, 225, 230,
    231, 234, 235, 241, 248
    of economic relations 225
    of the economy 221
    laboratories of 138
    of the labour market 221, 222, 223
    of manners 4, 9, 221, 223, 224
    psychic 224, 225
    short term phases of 167, 181, 183
    theory of 6, 226
informalizing
    phase 9, 49, 60, 63, 68, 85, 86, 147,
        158, 169, 176, 177, 179, 181,
        188, 200, 207
    process, processes 3, 5, 6, 8, 9, 56,
        71, 85, 90, 91, 167, 168, 170,
        181, 183, 184, 185, 190, 191,
        196, 200, 202, 203, 208,
        220, 224
inner compass 31, 197
inner-directed, inner direction 31
inner-directed personality 206
integration, integration processes 2, 7,
    8, 14, 22, 38, 101, 163, 165, 171,
    184, 185, 186, 212, 213, 220
    conflict 196
    international 90, 195, 196
    into a larger unit 195
    level of national 142, 143
    level of psychic 225
    level of social 18, 132, 133, 151,
        199, 201, 225

national 4, 5, 14, 55, 90, 131, 154,
    187, 192
    phase of, phases of 9, 97, 181, 184,
        185, 191
    psychic 6, 9, 202, 210, 212, 214,
        215, 224, 225, 233
    social 6, 8, 9, 12, 13, 35, 46, 55,
        69, 85, 91, 96, 97, 104, 152, 158,
        166, 167, 198, 200, 202, 210,
        212, 214, 215, 220, 224, 225
    social and psychic conflict 225
    stalled social 164, 165
interdependence, interdependencies 4,
    16, 29, 36, 75, 130, 187, 201,
    217, 226
    networks of 5, 22, 30, 35, 38, 40,
        68, 94, 184, 185, 192, 195, 200,
        210, 221
international justice 195
internationalization 222
intimacy, intimacies 28, 32, 65,
    66, 71, 75, 81, 82, 83, 84, 88,
    109, 124, 126, 139, 197, 198
    instant 84, 85, 90, 219, 240
intimate xii, 13, 21, 70, 76, 79,
    82, 84, 109, 125, 134, 154,
    175, 211
introduction, introductions xi, 3, 7, 8,
    15, 23, 27, 28, 53, 58, 59, 63, 65,
    73, 96, 112, 113, 116, 117, 120,
    121, 124, 125, 126, 127, 128, 130,
    131, 135, 136, 137, 138, 139, 140,
    141, 149, 154, 155, 156, 157, 158,
    162, 164, 165, 176, 180, 236
    letters of 130
    unwelcome 126, 129
intrude, intruding 24, 65, 70, 156
Iron Curtain 62, 186, 195, 220
irritated nostalgia 209, 211
irritation 164, 208, 210, 211
Islam 99

Jekyll and Hyde 34
Jews 95, 150

keeping up 59
kindred spirits 119
kissing 81, 82, 83, 84
    see also social kissing
knecht 146, 148
knowledge
    self-knowledge 49, 92, 199
    social 49, 92
    sociology of 238
Kultur 112, 122, 238

labour 9, 146, 185, 190, 221, 222,
   223, 225
   conditions 221, 222
   market 9, 221, 222, 223
   regimes 222, 223
   relations 221, 222
labour-intensive production 221
Lambeth Walk 64
language, language usage
   Black 86
   formal 85
   Friesian 89, 97
   informal 8, 86, 90
   Kurdish 90, 97
law, laws 11, 30, 42, 60, 149, 172
liberation 3, 141, 167, 173, 182, 183,
   186, 191, 195, 211
logic of emotions 218
love-oriented discipline 198

manners
   aristocratic 17, 23
   bourgeois 23
   coarsening 169, 172
   code of 3, 7, 11, 12, 50, 64, 181
   egalitarian 133
   have-a-nice-day 164
   history of xi, 1, 2, 7, 12
   multicultural 96, 99, 165
   nineteenth century 13, 31
   trends in 12, 13, 18
manners books
   courtesy genre of 27
   East German 117
   etiquette genre of 27
market 25, 31, 104, 110, 111, 141,
   153, 186, 190, 221, 222
McCarthyism 98, 160
Médicins sans Frontières 195
mentality, mentalities 1, 2, 3, 4, 15,
   36, 73, 159, 162, 191
MES see mutually expected self-restraints
Middle Ages 1, 20
might is right 218, 222, 223
minority 14, 43, 90, 95, 99, 149,
   191, 223
   of the best 14, 43, 191
   of the worst 43, 191
moderates 49, 233
money
   new 35, 131, 185
   old 7, 35, 148, 185
monopolization 25, 26
morality 60, 144, 214, 226
   fun 171

Moroccans 99
multiculturalist, multiculturalism 97,
   165, 219
mutual consent 84, 201, 217, 219
mutually expected self-restraints
   25, 188
   level of 11, 57, 147, 159, 199, 201,
   223, 224

nation state 104, 196
national
   character 67, 245
   differences 7, 8, 55, 101, 151
   integration 4, 55, 90, 131, 154,
   187, 192
   similarities 8
nationality 8, 10, 152, 154,
   192, 213
natural 1, 4, 21, 32, 37, 41, 47, 53,
   64, 67, 72, 73, 83, 91, 92, 93, 108,
   122, 165, 167, 168, 169, 177, 207,
   208, 213, 239
nature 1, 7, 9, 29, 31, 32, 33, 99, 106,
   123, 129, 134, 147, 167, 182, 183,
   198, 199, 204, 205, 208, 213, 214,
   215, 216, 217, 218, 220, 224, 225,
   228, 238
nature's nobleman 53
Nazi Germany 205
Negroes 94, 206, 207, 208
   Negro music 206
newcomers 27, 40, 104, 131, 137,
   144, 166, 171, 185, 224
nine eleven, 9/11 223
nobility 19, 22, 43, 61, 105,
   109, 111, 112, 120, 142,
   148, 153
nostalgia 50, 56, 61, 171, 189, 210,
   211, 241
nostalgic irritation 209, 211
nostalgie de la boue 189
nouveau riches 2
nude sunbathing, nudism 122, 138

obtrusive, obtrusiveness 40, 51
office excursions, parties 79,
   109, 120
orderliness 26, 29
other-directed, other-directed person
   31, 214
outsiders, outsider groups 14, 40, 42,
   61, 69, 94, 96, 98, 100, 156,
   157, 158, 185, 186, 187, 190,
   192, 196, 201, 205, 206, 208, 225,
   227, 239

pacify, pacification   22, 25, 26, 102,
     159, 164, 192
party   24, 65, 74, 80, 119, 120, 125,
     129, 137, 140, 171, 176, 180, 181,
     227, 234
parvenu   28, 55, 130, 148, 151
patricians, patriciate   43, 102, 144, 161
     merchant   23, 101, 102, 142
permissive society   3, 80, 181
permissiveness   3, 10, 148, 181,
     223, 233
personality   4, 5, 6, 16, 25, 30, 31,
     49, 53, 71, 79, 81, 179, 187,
     197, 198, 199, 202, 203, 204,
     205, 210, 214, 215, 218, 220,
     225, 241
personality structure   5, 6, 9, 225
phase, phases
     of accomodation and resignation   184
     developmental   217, 218, 219
     disciplinary   204, 205, 218
     of emancipation and resistance   184
     of formalization   204, 207
     of informalization   9, 188
     of reformalization   9
Plakkaat van Verlatinge   102
pleasure   28, 29, 51, 62, 112, 125,
     130, 176, 210, 211, 214, 216,
     228, 232
political incorrectness, correctness   218
popularity   8, 16, 32, 122, 135, 137,
     139, 149, 159, 161, 162, 164, 183,
     196, 210, 216
pornoviolence   216
postmodernism   194, 240
power
     centres of   7, 8, 14, 18, 19, 23, 35,
          104, 105, 111, 152, 160, 164,
          166, 184, 185, 201, 202
     chance, chances   25, 167, 187,
          190, 200
     latent, manifest   187
     relations   12, 18
     resources   11, 110
     state   191
     structure   149
precedence   14, 28, 36, 46, 47, 48, 65,
     109, 128, 130
prejudice, prejudices   60, 95, 96
presence of mind   4, 92, 93
presentation of self   81, 181, 209,
     210, 211
prestige   17, 36, 189
pride   16, 52, 88, 89, 111, 112, 119,
     217, 232

privacy   8, 20, 24, 65, 66, 67, 68, 69,
     75, 109, 124
     right to   64, 65, 66, 67, 68, 69
private
     domain, sphere, sector   24, 68,
          87, 105
     life   18, 25, 77
Privatheit   69
privilege, privileges   5, 23, 40, 47, 60,
     67, 92, 104, 146
process-continuity   101, 105, 132, 160
processes
     of differentiation and integration
          85, 212
     social and psychic   2, 5, 6, 9, 49, 92,
          199, 203, 218, 219, 240
proletarianization of the bourgeoisie
     19, 87
promiscuity   144
     social   158, 162
pronouns
     formal   75, 77, 115
     informal   76, 78, 85, 117
     personal   3, 109
prostitution   144, 148
protocol   x, 136, 175
provocation, provocations   44, 45
proximity   13, 80, 125, 143
     psychic   13, 41, 56, 57, 69, 82,
          84, 90
     sexual   56
     social   13, 41, 56, 57, 69, 77, 82, 84,
          90, 135
prude, prudery   122
psychic emancipation and
     integration   202
psychic functions   66, 202, 205, 208,
     213, 225
psychic integration   6
     level of   214, 224, 225
psychic make-up   1, 30, 205
psychoanalysis   209, 219
psychogenesis   6, 213
public
     domain, sphere, sector   68, 85, 87,
          88, 105
     transport   48
punctuality   29, 93

quest for excitement
     and risks   214, 223

race issue   94
racism   9, 95, 96, 217, 218, 219
radicals   38, 49

rank, ranking   3, 4, 6, 11, 16, 21, 24, 28, 35, 39, 41, 42, 43, 47, 51, 52, 54, 58, 69, 75, 108, 112, 115, 121, 125, 128, 130, 131, 134, 137, 140, 143, 144, 145, 150, 158, 160, 161, 169, 187, 192, 196, 200, 201, 217, 234, 238, 239, 240
reflection, reflexive, reflexivity   4, 9, 62, 93, 198, 201, 208, 210, 212, 213, 220, 224
  level of   2, 92, 161
reformalization   5, 167, 172
  phase of   9, 167, 176, 177, 183, 188
  short-term phases of   9
regime, regimes
  of family, parental   9, 198, 199, 200
  of manners and emotions   5, 6, 7, 8, 11, 12, 19, 20, 22, 30, 35, 55, 136, 167, 173, 176, 186, 224
  pedagogical   197
  of personality   9, 198, 199
  of state   9, 198
regional accents   86, 89
regionalists   88, 89
regression-fears   206
regulated deregulation   222
regulation   1, 3, 4, 5, 6, 7, 10, 12, 18, 25, 26, 31, 46, 48, 49, 81, 131, 201, 213, 222
repugnance   20, 21, 30, 208
reserve   8, 24, 28, 36, 57, 62, 65, 66, 70, 71, 91, 104, 114, 131, 151, 189
respect   2, 5, 6, 19, 21, 22, 24, 26, 30, 39, 40, 41, 51, 52, 53, 57, 61, 68, 70, 71, 72, 73, 76, 77, 78, 88, 108, 114, 115, 127, 153, 161, 165, 176, 179, 189, 200, 207, 211, 212, 224, 226
right of recognition   28, 65, 119, 128, 129, 130
right to cut   8, 128
rigid, rigidity   8, 13, 29, 33, 34, 35, 36, 49, 56, 64, 92, 103, 106, 113, 125, 132, 137, 167, 176, 182, 183, 185, 186, 197, 199, 201, 202, 204, 208, 213, 224
risk of choosing   84
rite de passage   109, 118, 121, 135
ritual
  drinking   108
  mourning   92
Roaring Twenties   9, 85, 167, 169, 200
romance, romances   211
romanticize, romanticization   31, 32, 63, 64, 175, 189, 205, 209, 210, 211

royalty   18, 128, 136
rude, rudeness   12, 21, 44, 51, 75, 96, 99, 129, 157, 205

Salon sense   190
satisfaktionsfähig   113
seaside   32, 122, 137, 138, 139
Season   131, 136, 244
seclude, seclusion   26, 66, 69, 131, 132, 133, 138, 149, 151, 157
second nature   1, 17, 21, 30, 31, 203, 213, 217, 218, 224
  type of personality   7, 31, 32, 33, 197, 199
segregate, segregation   21, 47, 52, 64, 94, 97, 102, 131, 165, 167
self   3, 4, 5, 6, 7, 10, 11, 12, 17, 18, 23, 25, 26, 28, 29, 30, 31, 36, 39, 41, 43, 44, 45, 46, 48, 49, 53, 57, 62, 66, 69, 70, 71, 79, 81, 86, 92, 93, 96, 162, 195, 204, 205, 206, 208, 214, 217, 238
  experience   241
  false   92
  inner   71, 92
  real   92, 209, 239
  regulation
    forms of   30
  true   93, 203, 208, 209
self-aggrandizement   217
self-anxiety   71
self-control, self-controls   29, 31, 36, 37, 44, 46, 48, 136, 139, 156, 182, 183, 186, 192, 199, 203, 204, 205, 212, 213, 230, 232, 233
self-discipline   144
self-knowledge   49, 92, 199
self-mockery   133, 134
self-realization, actualization   141
self-regulation   6, 12, 22, 27, 81, 93, 159, 166, 192, 194, 199, 201, 202, 203, 208, 213, 214, 217, 220, 224, 225
  forms of   203
  patterns of   6, 92, 215
self-respect   200, 211, 212
self-restraints   4, 17, 21, 30, 91, 203, 205, 233, 234, 241
  mutually expected   25, 57, 147, 159, 188, 199, 201, 223, 224
sensibility, sensibilities   8, 11, 12, 14, 23, 25, 28, 43, 44, 49, 51, 67, 93, 144, 147, 186, 228
sensitive, sensitivity   1, 13, 21, 23, 28, 44, 48, 54, 56, 61, 64, 68, 69, 70,

sensitive, sensitivity *cont.*
88, 90, 92, 93, 94, 97, 98, 105,
109, 139, 146, 161, 165, 168, 169,
170, 200, 201, 211
servants   39, 40, 41, 55, 76, 88, 114,
119, 128, 140, 234, 239
service   52, 110, 114, 159, 163, 177,
179, 238, 272
shame   2, 19, 20, 21, 22, 30, 175, 198,
199, 201, 205, 214, 215, 217, 232
shame-culture   241
shame-fear   2, 198, 199, 201
shaming   30, 98, 146, 199, 217, 218,
219, 241
   mechanisms   241
   processes   98, 199
Sie, Siezen   76, 78, 79, 80, 108, 109,
115, 117, 118, 119, 120
signals, signs
   inward, outward   93, 209
slang   85
slave mentality   187
slippery slope   28, 32, 33, 126, 214
smoke bomb   146
snob   50, 163
snub, snubbing   48, 59, 83, 156
social classes   5, 6, 15, 36, 39, 49, 58,
85, 94, 127, 130, 166, 167, 198,
199, 204
social constraint towards self-restraints
4, 17, 21, 91, 159, 164
social controls   11, 21, 44, 66,
173, 201
   external   13, 71, 136, 139, 155, 156,
159, 160, 164, 199, 203, 212,
220, 225
   internal   13, 139, 199
social definitions   14, 16, 23
social degradation   200
social engineering   159, 162
social equalization   53, 56, 60, 77, 180
social inferiors   5, 7, 38, 39, 40, 41, 43,
47, 48, 49, 53, 119, 129, 130
social integration   4, 6, 7, 9, 57, 64, 94,
133, 185, 187
   level of   8, 94, 98, 112, 131, 132,
148, 201, 224
social interweaving   13, 57, 85,
200, 210
social kissing   3, 8, 69, 80, 81, 82, 83,
84, 85, 90
social manipulation   161, 162, 164
social mixing   7, 8, 18, 35, 36, 40, 41
42, 43, 46, 47, 48, 49, 50, 57, 58, 69
social stratification   35

social structure   5, 6, 9, 94
social superiors   2, 5, 21, 22, 37, 38,
39, 40, 43, 48, 49, 52, 54, 65, 74,
100, 119, 129, 130, 144, 166, 201
social water-tower   15, 17, 18, 158,
163, 165
sociogenesis   5, 109, 213
solidarity   49, 89, 114, 117, 123, 178,
186, 187, 193, 195, 196
sources of power and identity   5, 49
spiral
   movement   183, 191, 196
   process   6, 8, 9, 181, 184
spit, spitting   11, 19, 48, 151
spontaneity   78, 92, 208
sport, sports   32, 117, 119, 123, 136,
137, 179, 182, 215, 216, 217,
231, 240
Stadholder   142
stand   8, 60, 70, 80, 84, 116, 118, 125,
141, 143, 144, 145, 165, 197, 239
state   18, 22, 23, 24, 25, 26, 38, 41,
75, 97, 110, 142, 143, 164, 174,
190, 191, 192, 193, 195, 196, 197,
214, 215, 221, 222
States-General   142
status
   anxiety, anxieties   1, 7, 35, 36, 38,
39, 42, 43, 48, 61, 91, 93, 131
   aspiration   1, 200
   climbers   2, 14, 72, 149, 150, 161
   competition   1, 28, 36, 67, 68, 91,
130, 148, 216, 217
   difference   28, 93, 116
   fears   1, 2
   insecurity   149, 152, 161
   motives   2, 17
   ridden   61, 145
   secrets   219
   triumphs and defeats   2
stiff upper lip   31, 55, 134, 183, 206
stigma   86, 96
strangeness   204, 205, 206, 207,
219, 220
stranger, strangers   21, 28, 29, 40, 41,
51, 65, 67, 70, 79, 80, 85, 110,
112, 115, 124, 125, 127, 131, 132,
135, 138, 155, 162, 164, 204, 205,
207, 220
street sense   189
student fraternities   113
sublimate, sublimation   211, 216
submissiveness   50, 187, 198
subordinates   21, 36, 47, 71, 105,
192, 198

subordination 22, 49
success 17, 24, 26, 29, 55, 59, 62,
    81, 101, 102, 104, 114, 146,
    161, 162, 190, 201,
    209, 238
superego-dominated personality
    authoritarian 208
    we-less 208
superficialities 105, 118, 135, 174
superiorism 9, 220
superiority
    displays of 2, 3, 4, 9, 22, 28, 40, 46,
        49, 53, 205
    expressions of 22, 40, 50, 51, 52,
        55, 61, 210
    feelings 2, 6, 9, 22, 30, 38, 40, 42,
        46, 50, 51, 53, 54, 63, 96, 116,
        148, 160, 186, 216, 217,
        218, 220
superlatives 8, 159, 160, 164
superpower 13, 153, 154, 186,
    193, 195
survival signal function of
    emotions 210
suspicion, suspicions 57, 67, 97, 155,
    159, 165
    level of 160, 164, 187, 220
swear words 85, 88

taboo 2, 3, 9, 30, 54, 57, 87, 88, 134,
    165, 172, 173, 175, 201, 211, 216,
    218, 224
Taliban 208
tax, taxes, taxation 22, 142, 197
television 80, 81, 87, 88, 89, 90, 119,
    148, 174, 179
temper 37, 40, 44, 76, 129
tension-balance of attraction and
    repugnance 205, 208, 211
they-groups 204, 205, 208, 220
third nature type of personality 9,
    213, 214
Third World countries 221, 222,
    223, 225
    low-wage countries 221
tip, tipping 48, 187, 239
trade unions, trade unionists 185, 190
tram 44, 47
transnational corporations, global
    corporations 221, 222
trend, trends 1, 3, 4, 6, 8, 9, 10, 12,
    13, 17, 18, 20, 23, 31, 38, 46, 50,
    51, 52, 55, 73, 74, 76, 77, 78, 81,
    84, 87, 89, 90, 130, 134, 144, 159,
    167, 168, 172, 173, 179, 182, 183,

    185, 191, 195, 198, 200, 204, 207,
    216, 222, 234
    overall 5, 38, 173
trend-followers 49, 50
trial of strength 217
trickle effect 87, 238
    trickle down 87, 238
    trickle up 87
triumphs and defeats 216,
    217, 219
true self *see* self
trust 25, 26, 39, 57, 83, 121, 147,
    148, 155, 188, 190, 227
    mutual trust 57, 88, 97, 98, 134,
        148, 155, 159, 164, 165,
        198, 200
    see also mutually expected
        self-restraints
trustworthy 91
tucht 144, 146, 148
Turkey, Turks 90, 99, 100
Turnbewegung 114
tutoyeren 76, 77, 108
tyro-fears 206

unconscious, unconsciousness 31, 162,
    204, 205
undesirables 27, 131, 133, 135
urinate, urinating 20, 175
utopias 122, 211

vae victis 218
violence 22, 23, 25, 26, 29, 30, 85,
    110, 134, 154, 159, 164, 175,
    186, 192, 197, 215, 216, 219,
    224, 237
virtual reality 216
visiting cards 27, 29, 65, 74, 129,
    131, 132, 151, 152, 164, 172,
    182, 200
voetvolk, 'foot folk' 47, 239
vorstellungsfähig 113
vousvoyeren 76
vulgar 27, 48, 51, 52, 74, 85, 89, 130,
    134, 171, 239

waltz 183
War on Terrorism 160, 196, 220
WASP, WASPs 94, 95, 150,
    151, 152
watering places 137, 139
we-feelings 193, 194, 195, 203, 210
we-groups 13
We–I balance 13, 16, 191, 192, 193,
    194, 195, 196

we-ideal   153, 154, 191, 193, 194,
    195, 196, 206
we-identification, we-identity   13, 16,
    43, 153, 154, 186, 188, 190,
    191, 192, 193, 194, 195, 196,
    210, 223
  international   195, 196,
    222, 223
  national   13, 162
we-less I   203, 208, 210, 211, 212
we-less superego   203
we-less superego-dominated
    personality   208

white people   188, 239
Wilhelmine era, Wilhelmine Germany
    113, 114, 115
working classes   2, 36, 63, 64, 87, 104,
    143, 144, 181, 188
World Bank   195, 223
wrestling   35, 36, 37
WTO   195, 223

youth culture   13, 62, 189

zero-sum perspective   93
Zivilisation   112, 122